TAX TREATIES:
UNITED KINGDOM
LAW AND PRACTICE

AUSTRALIA
Law Book Co.
Sydney

CANADA and USA
Carswell
Toronto

HONG KONG
Sweet & Maxwell Asia

NEW ZEALAND
Brookers
Wellington

SINGAPORE and MALAYSIA
Sweet & Maxwell Asia
Singapore and Kuala Lumpur

TAX TREATIES: UNITED KINGDOM LAW AND PRACTICE

By Jonathan Schwarz

BA, LLB (Witwatersrand); LLM (University of California, Berkeley); FTII; Barrister; Advocate of the High Court of South Africa; Barrister and Solicitor, Alberta, Canada.

LONDON
SWEET & MAXWELL
2002

Published in 2002 by Sweet & Maxwell Ltd of
100 Avenue Road
London NW3 3PF
Typeset by Servis Filmsetting Ltd, Manchester, U.K.
Printed in England by Athenaeum Press Ltd, Gateshead, U.K.

No natural forests were destroyed to make this product; only
farmed timber was used and replanted.

A CIP catalogue record for this book is available from the British
Library

ISBN 0 421 72490 0

ISBN 0-421-72490-0

9 780421 724907

For Benjamin, Daniel and Adam

Preface

"You shall have one manner of law, as for the stranger, as for the home-born;"

Leviticus xxiv, 22.

The purpose of this book is to provide an examination of tax treaties from a United Kingdom perspective. Treaties by definition involve at least two countries. Consequently, there are sound arguments, which I support, for a common international approach to interpretation of treaties drawing on the views of courts around the world. This has become highly desirable, particularly as the OECD Model is now established as the backbone of a code of conduct for countries in allocating taxing jurisdiction and avoiding double taxation. Despite this ideal, each jurisdiction views treaties from its own unique perspective. Differences in not only tax rules, but administrative and constitutional rules, impose variations which reflect domestic values of each society. Thus, tax treaties need to be seen not only in the context of international tax problems, but also the wider legal systems of contracting states. This book is intended to assist practitioners and students concerned with the international aspects of taxation in the United Kingdom. Hopefully, it also reflects the considerable input that the United Kingdom has had in the development of tax treaties at an administrative level through its participation, not only in the work of the OECD Committee of Fiscal Affairs, but its antecedents in the Organisation for European Economic Cooperation and the League of Nations. The United Kingdom Courts, for reasons of both history and cogency, carry respect and authority worldwide. Countries of the Commonwealth share in many respects not only the legal traditions, but constitutional norms and approaches to questions of international law. In addition, English has emerged in recent times as the common language of tax treaties, with treaties between some countries not sharing a common language adopting English as the language of their treaties (for example, the Luxembourg–Korea Income Tax Treaty). The United Kingdom shares with its European Community partners problems in addressing the requirements of Community law.

The United Kingdom is a party to a variety of types of treaty – comprehensive income tax treaties, shipping and air transport tax treaties, estate and gift tax treaties, the multilateral transfer pricing arbitration convention and, at the time of writing, is on the verge of negotiating exchange of information treaties. The development of United Kingdom law and practice relating to these treaties has been unsystematic. There are many unanswered questions where guidance will inevitably be sought from foreign sources, as well as the Commentary to the OECD Model itself. In order to maintain a specific United Kingdom perspective, I have refrained from referring to foreign sources and made sparing reference to the Commentary and other works published by the OECD. I have also resisted the temptation to simply adopt the OECD Model as a framework, referring to the equivalent provisions in United Kingdom treaties. Instead, I have opted for a more conceptual approach, dealing with particular topics and areas of concern. Despite the presence of the OECD Model for nearly 40 years, United Kingdom treaties are by no means uniform. Each is based on negotiations relating to the state of the United Kingdom tax system at the time, the foreign tax system, the negotiating strength of the parties and the overall balance of each specific treaty. As in recent years, the pace of domestic change has become more rapid and the OECD Model itself is amended and updated more frequently. It does mean, however, that the norms established by it become less standard as a result of the rate of change. I have also dealt with a number of specific treaties. At the end of the day, however, there is no substitute for a close study of individual treaty provisions.

The book is grouped loosely into several parts, the first dealing with the legal framework both under United Kingdom and European law. The second deals with interpretation of treaties, followed by an examination of factors qualifying persons for treaty benefits. The fourth part looks at the distributive provisions of typical income tax treaties and the rules relating to credit for foreign tax. A further chapter examines treaty shopping and other avoidance, which draws significantly on my thesis submitted for the Chartered Institute of Taxation Fellowship. Finally, chapters deal with the practical administration of treaties, including claiming treaty benefits; dispute resolution, including the Transfer Pricing Arbitration Convention; and exchange of information. In writing on practical application of treaties, I have relied in part on my National Report submitted to the International Fiscal Association for the 1998 Congress on that subject. Self-assessment has developed considerably since that time and Inland Revenue treaty practice has become more accessible.

This book is generally up to date to the beginning of November 2001. The treaties commented on are generally in force at the time of writing. In the case of the United States, both the 1975 treaty and the new treaty signed on July 24, 2001 are considered, although the new treaty has not been ratified.

I would like to thank my secretary Odile Tilloy for her tireless work in typing and retyping the text, meticulous checking of references and proofs and deciphering my wholly illegible handwriting.

Peace and order, along with social and economic justice, form the cornerstones of a democratic society. These cornerstones do not come cheap. It is the responsibility of those able to pay to finance the cost of maintaining democracy. One consequence of the proliferation of treaties is that information may potentially be exchanged pursuant to them with countries which do not share these values. Caution should be exercised less the machinery of state in the maintenance of democratic objectives at home be used as an instrument of oppression elsewhere.

Jonathan Schwarz
Middle Temple
London
November 2001

Contents

Table of Cases

Table of Statutes

Table of Statutory Instruments

Table of Treaties—
Alphabetical

UNITED KINGDOM BILATERAL TREATIES

OTHER TREATIES AND MODEL CONVENTIONS

Table of Treaties— Chronological

CHAPTER 1
The Legal Framework: United Kingdom Law

1-01　Tax treaties are no different, juridically speaking, from any other treaty that may be entered into by the United Kingdom. Tax treaties do differ from their counterparts outside the tax area in that, with one exception, tax treaties are bilateral while the United Kingdom is a party to many other multilateral treaties. The distinction is of limited significance, although it arguably affects the way in which treaties are interpreted.

WHAT ARE TAX TREATIES?

1-02　A "treaty" is "an international agreement concluded between states in written form and governed by international law, whether embodied in a single instrument, or in two or more related instruments and whatever its particular designation".[1] Thus, although particular treaties may be labelled as "agreements", "conventions", "arrangements" or otherwise, they are in effect treaties under international law.[2] In modern treaty practice, the expression includes in particular agreements, conventions, declarations and protocols. Exchange of notes by way of letters between the contracting states have become increasingly important, particularly in treaty negotiations with certain developing countries. In some cases, notes are exchanged to clarify or expand the formal treaty document. This has been justified on the basis that certain items are more easily agreed in this way with the authorities of those contracting states than by their incorporation into the formal treaty. As a matter of international law, they are either part of the treaty or perhaps separate treaties in their own right. Exchanges of notes are also used to give flexibility in updating treaties. For example, the Malaysia Agreement[3] excludes from treaty benefits persons entitled to any special tax benefit under a law of either contracting states which has been identified in an exchange of notes. A note was exchanged contemporaneously with the signing of the treaty. In addition, it leaves the way open to relatively informal and speedy amendment in order to deal with subsequent developments in the domestic law of member states. To date, exchanges of notes have only appeared contemporaneously with the execution of treaties, but no doubt in the future, notes may be exchanged on other occasions.

The enabling legislation[4] refers to "arrangements". This is an unfortunate

---

[1]　Vienna Convention on the Law of Treaties 1969, Art. 2, para. 1(a).
[2]　See also Inland Revenue, *International Tax Handbook*, para. 501.
[3]　December 10, 1996, S.I. 1977 No. 2987, Art. 25(2).
[4]　Taxes Act 1988, s. 778.

expression given the fact that the word is used in other contexts to mean something totally different. It is presumably intended to denote a wide variety of agreements between the United Kingdom and other contracting states, although, in reality, it adds nothing to the term "treaty" as understood by the Vienna Convention. In this book, the word "treaty" is used throughout as a matter of consistency and to accord with the Vienna Convention.

TREATY-MAKING

1-03   The power to make treaties forms part of the conduct of foreign affairs and the power to make treaties is a function of the Crown. It is a residual power which exists as a matter of Royal prerogative.[5] Authority to negotiate and conclude treaties is given to agents of the Crown.[6]

The procedures involved in negotiating treaties have been well set out by R.T. Bartlett.[7] Only a few additional observations are appropriate. The negotiation and conclusion of treaties takes place behind closed doors. Although the Inland Revenue invites submissions from interested parties, when discussions are to take place with a view to concluding a treaty, the text of the treaty is not revealed until a draft Order is laid before the House of Commons. Thus, unlike domestic legislation including subsidiary legislation, there is no opportunity for interested parties to comment on the terms until the agreement has been concluded. The text of treaty provisions forms part of the work of the Solicitor of the Inland Revenue with formal constitutional and international law aspects addressed by Foreign Office lawyers.

Before any Order in Council proposed to be made is submitted to Her Majesty in Council, a draft of the Order must be laid before the House of Commons and the Order is not submitted unless an address is presented to Her Majesty by that House praying that the Order be made.[8] Thus, the opportunities for interested parties to comment on the acceptability of treaty provisions is extremely limited. Although the terms of the treaty may be the subject of debate in the House of Commons and in principle the House may decline to submit an address to the Crown for an Order to be made, requiring the treaty to be renegotiated, this has yet to happen.

TREATY IMPLEMENTATION

1-04   Although treaties validly concluded are binding on the state without parliamentary sanction, they do not have effect on the laws of the United Kingdom until appropriate legislative action has been taken. [9]

---

[5] See, *e.g.*, *Blackburn v. Attorney-General* [1971] All E.R. 1380 *per* Lord Denning M.R. at 1040: "The treaty making power rests . . . in the Crown; that is, Her Majesty acting on the advice of her Ministers. When her Ministers negotiate and sign a treaty . . . they act on behalf of the country as a whole. The exercise the prerogative of the Crown".

[6] See R.T. Bartlett, "The Making of Double Taxation Agreements" [1991] B.T.R. 76.

[7] *ibid.*

[8] Taxes Act 1988, s. 788(10).

[9] In *McLaine Watson v. Department of Trade* [1989] 3 All E.R. 523, HL, Lord Templeman said at 526: "A treaty to which Her Majesty's Government is a party does not alter the laws of the United Kingdom. Except to the extent that a treaty becomes incorporated into the laws of the

Income and Corporation Taxes Act 1988, section 788[10] contains enabling legislation to give effect to tax treaties. Section 788(1) specifies that:

> "If Her Majesty by Order in Council declares that arrangements specified in the Order have been made with the Government of any territory outside the United Kingdom with a view to affording relief from double taxation in relation to:
>
> (a) income tax;
> (b) corporation tax in respect of income or chargeable gains; and
> (c) any taxes of a similar character to those taxes imposed by the laws of that territory,
>
> and that it is expedient that those arrangements should have effect, then those arrangements shall have effect . . .".

The section does not provide for authority to conclude treaties, but simply refers to arrangements "that have been made", the authority to negotiate and conclude treaties being a matter of delegation of the Crown's treaty-making prerogative.

SCOPE OF TREATIES

1-05   There is no limit on what may be agreed in a treaty. The enabling legislation, however, does not give unlimited authority to give effect to treaties. In relation to income tax and corporation tax, section 788(3) of the Taxes Act 1988 prescribes that treaties shall have effect insofar as they provide for:

(1) relief from income tax or from corporation tax in respect of income or chargeable gains;

(2) charging the income arising from sources or chargeable gains accruing on the disposal of assets in the United Kingdom to persons not resident in the United Kingdom;

(3) determining the income or chargeable gains to be attributed:

   (a) to persons not resident in the United Kingdom and their agencies, branches or establishments in the United Kingdom; or
   (b) to persons not resident in the United Kingdom who have special relationships with persons not so resident;

(4) for conferring on persons not resident in the United Kingdom, the right to a tax credit under section 231 in respect of qualifying distributions made to them by companies which are so resident;

---

footnote 9—*contd.*
United Kingdom by statute, the courts of the United kingdom have no power to enforce treaty rights and obligations at the behest of a sovereign government or on behalf of a private individual".
[10] Hereinafter referred to as "Taxes Act 1988".

(5) relief from foreign tax by way of credit is not specifically authorised, although tax sparing as a sub-species of foreign tax credit relief is.[11]

Insofar as treaties apply to capital gains, authority is extended by reference to the income and corporation tax rules.[12] For capital gains purposes, references to income in Part XVIII of the Taxes Act 1988 are substituted by references to capital gains.

1-06 In the case of petroleum revenue tax, a similar device is used.[13] For the purpose of petroleum revenue tax, references in section 788 of the Taxes Act 1988 to income tax are treated as references to petroleum revenue tax and references to income are to include references to consideration brought into charge on receipts attributable to U.K. use of foreign field assets.[14] This only applies where the treaty includes petroleum revenue tax as a tax to which the treaty applies.[15] The petroleum revenue tax provisions are more precisely described in incorporating the references than is the case with capital gains. Thus, references to sections 788(3)(b), (c) and (d) are not incorporated by reference.

The scope of the enabling legislation was considered by the High Court in *Bricom Holdings v. IRC*.[16] The case involved the interaction between the Netherlands Treaty and the U.K. controlled foreign companies legislation. It was argued amongst other things by the Inland Revenue that the CFC charge[17] was not "corporation tax". It was argued that while the charge under section 747 of the Taxes Act 1988 is a tax, it is not corporation tax. The sum assessed under section 747(4)(a) is a sum "equal to" corporation tax; it is to be assessed on and recoverable from the resident company "as if" it were an amount of corporation tax chargeable on that company.[18] The Inland Revenue therefore argued that when the taxes that are referred to in Article 2(1) of the Treaty as forming the subject matter of the Treaty, the controlled foreign company charge is not included. Article 2(1) of the Treaty, however, referred not only to corporation tax, but also to taxes "substantially similar to corporation tax" as being included by Article 2(2). The Inland Revenue argued that corporation tax is tax charged on profits of companies. Profits means income and chargeable gains. The amount chargeable under the controlled foreign company rules is not a profit of the company assessed, but a sum equal to the corporation tax on a notional profit of the non-resident controlled foreign company. They argued that the controlled foreign company charge is a fiscal impost sui generis introduced to cover a specific form of tax avoidance. It has nothing to do with the profits of the company assessed.

1-07 The Special Commissioners concluded that the controlled foreign company charge is a tax, but that it is not a corporation tax. On the

[11] Taxes Act 1988, s. 788(5).
[12] Taxation of Chargeable Gains Act 1992, s. 277(1).
[13] Finance Act 1993, s. 174.
[14] Oil Taxation Act 1983, s. 12.
[15] Finance Act 1993, s. 194(2).
[16] [1996] S.T.C. 228, ScD and [1997] S.T.C. 1179, CA.
[17] Taxes Act 1988, s. 747.
[18] [1996] S.T.C. 228 at 234, ScD.

question whether the controlled foreign company charge is "substantially similar" to corporation tax, the Special Commissioners noted that the difference between that charge and corporation tax is principally that the CFC charge is levied only on U.K. resident companies having interests in controlled foreign companies. It is not charged on the profits of the U.K. company itself, but on profits (calculated essentially as for corporation tax) excluding capital gain and on certain assumptions. Only reliefs set out in Schedule 26 of the Taxes Act 1988 are available for setting against it. The Commissioners considered that the tax base is the most important factor in determining similarity: a tax computed on the same base as corporation tax, but charged on a specified class of company with some variations appropriate to that class of company, might well be substantially similar to corporation tax. There are differences not only in the class of company charged, but in the computation of profits, the person taxed on those profits and the reliefs available to be set against it. They regarded the matter as one of degree, but inclined to the view that the differences from corporation tax are not so great as to prevent the CFC charge from being substantially similar to corporation tax.

The Special Commissioners, however, recognised that before the taxpayer was entitled to relief, it still had to be the case that relief was available domestically under section 788 of the Taxes Act 1988. It was noted by the taxpayer that section 788(3)(a) refers only to relief "from corporation tax in respect of income or chargeable gains". It was argued for the taxpayer that the reference in this subsection should be read as including a reference to the controlled foreign company charge. This was on the basis that section 788(3) is a provision applying generally to corporation tax. It should therefore be read subject to the necessary modification that it should cover the controlled foreign company charge as if it were an amount of corporation tax as provided in section 747(4)(a). Section 754(1) requires the provisions of section 747(4)(a) to apply to "all enactments applying generally to corporation tax". The Special Commissioners, however, regarded section 754(1) as simply dealing with the machinery provisions as distinct from imposing a charge to tax. They concluded that section 754(1) did not have the effect of widening the scope of section 788(3) to cover the controlled foreign company charge.

1-08 The Special Commissioners noted, however, that the position is unsatisfactory because, if this conclusion is correct, the United Kingdom is in breach of the Treaty in not giving effect to it under domestic law. They did not regard this as affecting the result in the particular case.

The Court of Appeal recognised that the case raised fundamental questions on the relationship between the Treaty and the CFC charge. They found it surprising that the CFC rules had been on the statute book for more than 12 years and no dispute had previously arisen. The Inland Revenue argued that its understanding of the effect of the controlled foreign company provisions was so obviously correct that no one had considered it worthwhile to challenge the view previously.

1-09 In the Court of Appeal, it was observed[19] that treaties have no

---

[19] At 1190.

direct effect in English law. They are given effect by Part XVIII of the Taxes Act 1988. After certain formalities have been observed, "the arrangements contained in a double taxation agreement are given effect by section 788(3) of the 1988 Act". It was also noted that Part XVIII contains no reference to identical or substantially similar taxes. In framing the issues, the Court of Appeal noted that the final question for determination was whether the relief sought was granted by section 788, the questions relating to the application of the Treaty merely being preparatory to the asking of this question. Lord Justice Millett decided that the CFC charge was not within the relieving provisions of the Treaty anyway and that it was unnecessary to consider whether the issues related to substantially similar taxes. He did, however, regard the argument that the CFC charge is not a corporation tax as failing to give full effect to section 754(2) which provides "for the purposes of the Taxes Act any sum assessable and recoverable under section 747(4)(a) shall be regarded as corporation tax". Such a conclusion still avoids the issue as to whether section 788(3) extends to substantially similar taxes. In this context, substantially similar taxes are those taxes levied pursuant to the Corporation Tax Acts whether or not they are labelled as corporation tax in the narrow sense, as the Inland Revenue contended in *Bricom*.[20] In the context of foreign taxes, section 788(1)(c) refers to "any taxes of a similar character to those taxes imposed by the laws of that territory". The broad wording used to refer to foreign taxes analogous to the principal direct taxes of the United Kingdom and the purpose of the section as a whole would suggest an all-embracing interpretation of the term "corporation tax in respect of income and chargeable gains" rather than a restricted one.

1-10   The conclusion of the Special Commissioners in *Bricom* that U.K. law does not adequately implement the Treaty is, as they admitted themselves, an unfortunate conclusion. Is it correct? It is submitted that it is not. First, the treaty-making authority as a matter of Crown prerogative is generally unfettered. When Parliament wishes to fetter the Crown's treaty-making powers, it must do so in express terms.[21] Section 788(3) should not be viewed as imposing such a limitation.

In addition, the method by which Parliament gives effect to treaty obligations should not affect the way in which the courts resolve problems of interpretation that may arise where there is a discrepancy between the statutory wording and the wording of the treaty.[22] In *Garland v. British Rail*

---

[20] See above, n. 16.

[21] *R. v. Secretary of State for Foreign and Commonwealth Affairs, ex parte Rees-Mogg* [1994] Q.B. 552 at 567; [1994] 1 All E.R. 457 at 467 *per* Lloyd L.J.

[22] *Salomon v. Customs and Excise Commissioners* [1967] 2 Q.B. 116; [1966] 3 All E.R. 871, CA. In that case, the treaty in question was not incorporated into or referred to in the statute. Notwithstanding this, Lord Denning M.R. said at 874: "I think we are entitled to look at [the treaty] because it is an instrument which is binding in international law; we ought always to interpret our statutes so as to be in conformity with international law". Russell L.J. agreed with this where the statute is plainly intended to carry out the terms of the treaty.
In *Cheney v. Conn* [1968] All E.R. 799, Ch.D., a claim that the charge to income tax was invalidated by provisions of a Geneva Convention prohibiting nuclear weapons on the basis that a substantial part of the tax was to pay for such weapons, was denied on the basis that the relevant part of the Convention was not enacted into domestic law and the taxing statute was clear and unambiguous in its terms.

Engineering Ltd,[23] Lord Diplock said "it is a principle of construction of United Kingdom statutes now too well established to call for citation of authority, that the words of a statute passed after the treaty has been signed and dealing with the subject matter of the international obligations of the United Kingdom, are to be construed, if they are reasonably capable of bearing such a meaning, as intended to carry out the obligation and not to be inconsistent with it". It is the author's view that the same principle is equally applicable where a general provision such as section 788 is used to apply to treaties made both before and after its enactment. Since there are so many tax treaties, this approach, using general enabling legislation, has been adopted, rather than introducing legislation relating to each individual treaty. In some cases, tax treaties have been incorporated into domestic law by specific legislation and the same principle would apply there. Thus, although the implementation of tax treaties generally within specified limits is authorised by Parliament in advance, and the specific terms of the treaty become directly applicable through scheduling to an Order, the domestic legislation should be interpreted in a manner consistent with the treaty obligations.

1-11 Moreover, the argument raised by the Inland Revenue based on the non-enactment of the Treaty to the extent that it applies to similar taxes in the *Bricom* case, is itself contrary to international law and U.K. treaty obligations. Article 27 of the Vienna Convention on the Law of Treaties provides that a party may not invoke the provisions of its internal law as justification for its failure to perform a treaty. The only qualification to this is that a manifest violation of a provision of the internal law of a party regarding competence to conclude treaties may be invoked by that party in certain circumstances.[24] There is a presumption that Parliament intends to fulfil rather than break an international agreement.[25] Thus, where an Act is intended to give effect to a treaty, any doubt as to its meaning should, if possible, be resolved in favour of that which is consistent with the provisions of the treaty.[26]

This purposive approach in interpreting legislation which brings treaty obligations into domestic law has, however, not been applied in relation to tax matters in the same way as it has in other areas. In *R. v. Inland Revenue Commissioners, ex parte Commerzbank AG*,[27] the court refused to give effect to non-discrimination provisions of the German Treaty. In that case, the taxpayer, a German resident, claimed the repayment supplement pursuant to what is now section 825 of the Taxes Act 1988. This was denied on

---

[23] [1983] 2 A.C. 751 at 771; [1982] 2 W.L.R. 918 at 934 to 935, HL.
[24] Vienna Convention on the Law of Treaties, Art.46.
[25] See *Saloman v. Customs and Excise Commissioners*, above, n. 22, *per* Diplock L.J. at 875.
[26] *Quazi v. Quazi* [1980] A.C. 744 at 808; [1979] 3 All E.R. 897 at 903, HL *per* Lord Diplock: "Where Parliament passes an Act amending the domestic law of the United Kingdom in order to enable this country to ratify an international treaty and thereby assume towards other states that are parties to the treaty an obligation in international law to observe its terms, it is a legitimate aid to the construction of any provisions of the Act that are ambiguous or vague to have recourse to the terms of the treaty in order to see what was the obligation in international law that Parliament intended that this country should be enabled to assume".
See also more recently *R. v. Secretary of State for the Home Department, ex parte Brind* [1991] 1 A.C. 696.
[27] [1991] S.T.C. 271, QBD.

the basis that the section only permitted the repayment supplement on taxes overpaid if the taxpayer was resident in the United Kingdom. Article 20(1) of the German Treaty provided that "the nationals of one contracting state may not be subject in the other state to any taxation or any requirement connected therewith which is over or more burdensome than the taxation or connected requirements to which nationals of that other state in the same circumstances are or may not be subjected". The Inland Revenue attempted to argue that the words "requirement connected with" taxation could not cover entitlement to the repayment supplement. They argued that these words are primarily directed to the amount of tax payable, although not limited to this. The court rejected this argument and noted that if a German national is not entitled to the repayment supplement on the repayment of tax overpaid, it is subjected to a more burdensome requirement as regards the payment of tax than is a U.K. counterpart. The legislation was therefore clearly discriminatory within Article 20(1). The Inland Revenue, however, contended that the taxpayer could not rely on the Treaty in this respect. This was because treaties are to have effect in domestic law "insofar as they provide" for the matters set out in section 788(3)(a) to (d). It was held that the repayment supplement rules did not constitute either a charging or a relieving provision. They simply allowed in effect for interest on an overdue repayment of tax. Consequently, neither the non-discrimination nor any other provision of the Treaty could apply to the repayment supplement. In coming to this conclusion, the court rejected the argument that the repayment supplement fell within the terms of section 788(3)(b) which provides "for charging the income arising from sources or charging gains accruing on the disposal of assets in the United Kingdom to persons not resident in the United Kingdom".

1-12 It was noted in passing that the repayment supplement came into existence long after the provisions of section 788 were originally enacted and long after the German Treaty was made. Although the point was not argued, it is suggested that in the case of legislation such as section 788, the court should apply a construction which continually updates its wording to allow for changes since it was originally enacted. This is particularly appropriate, because the section acts as an umbrella which enables all treaties which are entered into by the United Kingdom to be enacted into domestic law without the necessity of specific legislation. It avoids the necessity of examining changes in treaty practice or the outcome of negotiations in relation to particular treaties in order to determine whether they will or will not be enacted into domestic law.

RETROSPECTIVE EFFECT

1-13 The enabling legislation authorises a degree of retrospectivity. Treaties may be given effect by virtue of section 788 if they provide relief for tax:

(1) for periods before the passing of the Taxes Act 1988; or

(2) before the making of the treaty in question.

Provision may also be made in such circumstances as to income or chargeable gains which is or are not subject to double taxation.

It would appear that such retrospectivity is therefore subject to limitations. Whatever the authorisation given by section 788(3) in relation to the ability of treaties to impose a charge not provided for under domestic law or to increase a charge imposed under domestic law, it is not clear that retrospective measures can only relieve or provide as to income or chargeable gains which is or are not subject to double taxation.

1-14 Such measures are typically contained in treaties where one is replaced by another, or in circumstances where the time delay between the negotiation of a treaty and its entry into force is lengthy as a result of protracted negotiations or delays in the ratification or exchange of instruments of ratification for domestic reasons in either contracting state.[28] Furthermore, an Order in Council which revokes an earlier Order may contain such transitional provisions as may be necessary or expedient as there is inevitably a delay between conclusion of a treaty and its final entry into force under domestic law. Current treaty practice is to provide for transitional measures in the terms of the treaty itself. Transitional measures implied unilaterally may well be in breach of a treaty obligation in certain circumstances.

TREATIES MADE UNDER OLD LAW

1-15 Section 789 of the Taxes Act 1988 also ensures continuity of enactment under domestic law of treaties made under the previous legislation relating to profits tax.[29] Thus, older treaties have effect in relation to corpo ration tax and income and gains chargeable to corporation tax in accordance with their terms where they are expressed to have effect in relation to profits tax and profits chargeable to profits tax. Accounting periods (the current term) are substituted for chargeable accounting periods.

Treaties made before March 30, 1971 which provide for exemption of income from surtax have effect as if they provided for that income to bear income tax at the basic rate or the lower rate, whichever is applicable and are to be regarded for the purposes of computing total income, other than as that expression is now understood by the Taxes Act 1988, section 835(5). Any reference in the Tax Acts to treaties under or by virtue of section 788 include a reference to treaties having effect by virtue of section 789.

EFFECT OF TREATIES

1-16 The precise effect of treaties in U.K. tax law and, in particular, whether treaties can impose or increase a tax liability beyond that provided as a matter of domestic law has been subject to some considerable debate.[30] Much of the controversy arises from the manner in which the enabling

---

[28] Article 28 of the Canada Treaty is a good example.
[29] Income Tax Act 1952, s. 347 or any earlier enactment corresponding to that section.
[30] See J.D.B. Oliver, "Double Tax Treaties in United Kingdom Tax Law" [1970] B.T.R. 388.

legislation has been drafted. Section 788(3) authorises that treaties shall "have effect" insofar as they provide:

> "(b) for charging the income arising from sources, or chargeable gains accruing on the disposal of assets, in the United Kingdom to persons not resident in the United Kingdom;".

Arguably, this would authorise a treaty to impose a tax on the income or gains of a non-resident which was not taxable under domestic law. These authorising provisions are, however, subject to the provisions of Part XVIII generally. Section 788(1) refers to arrangements made "with a view to affording relief from double taxation". Thus, it would appear that the purpose of the treaty must be to relieve double taxation and that if section 788(3)(b) creates a charge not existing under domestic law, then unless this was with a view to relieving double taxation, it would not be authorised.

1-17   The Inland Revenue approach to the issue is somewhat equivocal. On the one hand, the Inland Revenue *Inheritance Tax Treaty Manual* notes that treaties cannot create claims or increase the tax charge. It states[31] that: "it is important to remember that a Convention cannot create a tax claim that does not exist under U.K. law apart from the Convention, nor can it provide a greater tax charge than is available under our general law. So, for example, it is not possible for the U.K. to include in any of its Conventions one of the principles contained in the OECD Model Convention, about declining to deduct debts that would be allowable deductions under our general law". The *International Tax Handbook* simply notes[32] that where a treaty permits a liability to be imposed, this does not itself give rise to a charge if there is no general charge provided by domestic law. The Inland Revenue are, however, understood to have argued that in the context of transfer pricing, treaties may authorise an increase in liability. The argument in support of this is based on section 788(3)(c) which permits treaties to provide:

> "for determining the income or chargeable gains to be attributed—
>
> (i) to persons not resident in the United Kingdom and their agencies, branches or establishments in the United Kingdom; or
> (ii) to persons resident in the United Kingdom who have special relationships with persons not so resident;".

The exact extent of this wording is yet to be tested.

Section 788(3) also authorises treaties to provide for conferring on non-U.K. residents the right to a tax credit under section 231 in respect of qualifying distributions made to them by companies which are U.K. resident. The question as to whether treaties can impose a charge was argued in *Union Texas Petroleum Corporation v. Critchley (HM Inspector of Taxes).*[33]

---

[31] At para. 7.
[32] At para. 505.
[33] [1988] S.T.C. 691, Ch.D.; [1990] S.T.C. 305, CA.

1-18   Article 10(2)(a)(i) of the U.S. Treaty[34] provided that where a U.S. corporation was in receipt of a dividend from a U.K. resident company, the recipient is entitled to a payment from the United Kingdom of a tax credit equal to one half of the credit to which an individual resident in the United Kingdom would have been entitled had he received the dividend, subject to deductions withheld from such payment of an amount not exceeding 5 per cent of the amount or value of the dividend and of the amount of the tax credit paid to the U.S. corporation. The U.S. corporation argued that the payments to which it was entitled are amounts equal to one half of the tax credit to which an individual resident in the United Kingdom would have been entitled had he received the dividends. It was argued that the reference to "tax credits" in that subparagraph were not "tax credits under section 86 of the Finance Act 1972". Accordingly, no deduction may be made from them notwithstanding the concluding words of the treaty provision. The corporation was not assessable to U.K. income tax in respect of the dividends or the tax credit payment and the Treaty itself imposed no liability to U.K. tax in respect of those amounts. It was also argued that the Treaty itself did not impose a deduction requirement.

The Crown argued that a treaty has effect in English law and overrides anything to the contrary. Once the treaty extended the tax credit to a person, the credit is available for the purposes specified in section 86 of the Finance Act 1992. The U.S. corporation is chargeable to income tax under Schedule F and the Treaty had the effect of limiting that charge from the basic rate of tax to 5 per cent, which may be withheld from the payment in accordance with section 86(4) of the 1972 Act. It was argued that section 778(1)(d) could not apply because it did not incorporate any power to deduct taxes in circumstances such as existed under the U.S. Treaty.

1-19   Harman J. found the issue one of great difficulty to determine and noted in his judgment that his mind changed several times in the course of argument and of consideration. He upheld the Crown's argument on the incorporation of the Treaty into U.K. law and held that the references to tax credits in Article 10 were references to tax credits provided by section 86 of the Income and Corporation Taxes Act (ICTA) 1970. He accepted the Crown's submissions that the Treaty should be read with a reasonable desire to understand its purpose which was to fit the system of double tax relief into the system of tax credits on dividends introduced by the Finance Act 1972. In this regard, it was plain that Article 10(2) as a whole was specifically intended to fit provisions for double taxation of dividends to the U.K. imputation system. The Crown had argued that section 86(4) of ICTA 1970 provides for repayment of the tax credit which exceeds income tax chargeable on a taxpayer. Although the Treaty refers to a deduction from the payment due from the United Kingdom, interpreting the Treaty as limiting that amount as provided in the Treaty produces an economic result that was the same. The reasoning is therefore somewhat obscure, but the implication is that if the effect of the Treaty is to achieve an economic result similar to that under domestic law, then the Treaty presumably is capable of imposing a charge.

---

[34] Double Taxation Relief (Taxes on Income) (United States of America) Order 1980 (S.I. 1980 No. 568).

Although most treaties are implemented via section 788 of the Taxes Act 1988, occasionally a legislative "patch" is applied in order to deal with shortcomings. An example of this is Finance (No. 2) Act 1979, section 16. This extended the benefit of the United States Treaty to periods before the making of the Order in Council, notwithstanding that the Treaty withdrew relief from tax for those periods. This is extremely rare and indeed in the *Union Texas* case,[35] the Court appeared to accept the argument of the Crown that this provision did not have the effect of generally incorporating the Treaty into U.K. law.

PUTATIVE TREATIES

1-20   Where a treaty is negotiated and executed, and its terms are carried out by one of the parties, but formal ratification has not taken place, the precise legal position is unclear. This unusual possibility arose in the context of the 1977 Treaty with Ghana.[36] In the United Kingdom, the appropriate Order in Council was made and on June 6, 1978, the Inland Revenue announced that the Treaty had entered into force.[37] The United Kingdom applied the Treaty for some years, but in 1991, it emerged that the Treaty had never been properly ratified in Ghana.[38] Article 27 of the 1977 Treaty provided that the Treaty was to come into force on the date when "the last of all such things shall have been done in the United Kingdom and Ghana as are necessary to give the Convention the force of law in the United Kingdom and Ghana respectively". The conditions precedent were never fulfilled and as a result, the Treaty never entered into force and never had effect in either contracting state. Article 27 of the 1977 Treaty provided for termination of the earlier 1947 Treaty and since the entry into force was recognised to have potentially retrospective effect, permitted those provisions of the earlier Treaty to continue to have effect if they were more beneficial until entry into force of the 1977 Treaty. However, in effect the 1947 Treaty was never terminated and was still in force in both countries.

The Inland Revenue ceased to apply the 1977 Treaty once this was discovered and reapplied the 1947 Treaty. By concession and in recognition of the "wholly exceptional circumstances", the Inland Revenue offered the application of the most favourable terms of the two treaties during the period of mistake including permitting claims made out of time for a limited period.

The sensible approach adopted by the Inland Revenue obviated the need for detailed analysis of the strict legal position by taxpayers. Strictly, the 1947 Treaty was in effect and taxpayers were entitled to rely on it. However, since taxpayers had been led to believe that the 1977 Treaty was in effect, taxpayers had a legitimate expectation that they were entitled to rely on it, without having to look behind the steps taken at a diplomatic level between the contracting states.

---

[35] See above, n. 33.
[36] S.I. 1978 No. 785.
[37] Inland Revenue Press Release June 6, 1978.
[38] Inland Revenue Press Release January 31, 1991, [1991] *Simon's Tax Intelligence* 90.

STATE SUCCESSION

1-21 As a matter of international law, state succession describes a variety of changes in the sovereignty over a particular treaty. Political changes in Central and Eastern Europe have in recent times impacted on the U.K. tax treaty network. In recent history, most cases have involved the dissolution of sovereign entities. Given the variety of possible changes that may occur, there are no general rules of international law to the effect that upon a succession of states, the benefit or burden of treaties of a predecessor state are transferred to the successor by reason of the succession. On the contrary, if a state is extinguished, its rights and obligations under treaties are generally extinguished also.

The dissolution of the Union of Soviet Socialist Republics was perhaps the most significant. The 1985 USSR Treaty was in effect brought to an end by the dissolution. The position was clarified by the Inland Revenue in SP 3/92 issued on May 1, 1992. It indicated that the Treaty was regarded as being in force between the United Kingdom and the Russian Federation. Other remaining former Soviet Republics were, by that time, recognised by the United Kingdom as independent sovereign states. In addition, those Republics committed themselves to continue to respect all international obligations of the former Soviet Union. As a result, the provisions of the USSR Treaty continued to apply, with the exception of the Baltic States, Estonia, Lithuania and Latvia. The United Kingdom moved quickly to negotiate individual treaties with almost all of the successor states.

Similar issues arose in relation to the dissolution of Czechoslovakia. Both successor states committed themselves to honour all international obligations of the former Federal Republic and the Czechoslovakia Treaty is treated as remaining in force between the United Kingdom and respectively the Czech Republic and the Slovak Republic.[39]

1-22 A similar approach was taken in relation to the dissolution of Yugoslavia.[40] The Yugoslavia Convention is therefore treated as remaining in force between the United Kingdom and respectively Croatia and Slovenia. The legal basis of these appears to be a combination of recognition of the successor state by the United Kingdom and in effect a novation of the treaty by the successor state when it agrees to undertake the obligations.

Other changes in sovereignty have not so far raised problems in the tax treaty context. For example, the Treaty with Namibia is an extension of the Treaty with South Africa extended by Exchange of Notes on August 8, 1962 and amended by Exchange of Notes in 1967. Notwithstanding a finding by the International Court of Justice that South African occupation of Namibia (formerly South West Africa) was illegal, the agreement continued after the independence of Namibia in 1985.

1-23 The non-recognition of the homelands in South Africa similarly permitted treaty claims to be made by residents of those homelands pursuant to the South African Treaty. The reunification of the Federal Republic of Germany and the German Democratic Republic on October 3, 1990 brought

---

[39] SP 5/93.
[40] SP 6/93.

about an automatic extension of the Treaty with the Federal Republic to the territory of the former German Democratic Republic. The U.K. view was that treaties of the Federal Republic applied to the former territory of the German Democratic Republic. The German Ministry of Finance stated that they would apply those treaties from January 1, 1991.[41]

The return of Hong Kong to Chinese sovereignty has also produced unusual issues of state succession in the tax treaty context. Hong Kong maintains a tax system separate from China. The Chinese Treaty does not apply to Hong Kong. Unique to U.K. treaty practice, double tax measures relating to air transport are found in an air transportation agreement relating to Hong Kong and not in a separate tax treaty.[42]

RELATIONSHIP BETWEEN TREATIES AND SPECIFIC STATUTORY PROVISIONS

1-24   As a matter of international law, every treaty in force is binding upon the parties to it and must be performed by them in good faith.[43] This is simply a codification of the longstanding principle *pacta sunt servanda*. In the context of tax treaties, implementation of this principle calls for changes in domestic law to give effect to treaty provisions. Generally, the introductory wording to section 788(3), which requires treaties to take effect "notwithstanding anything in any enactment", establishes the primacy of treaties over domestic law. The effect of such wording is to ensure that in all cases, treaties take precedence over domestic law. While this is relatively straightforward, in relation to legislation in force when the treaty comes into effect, the issue is problematic in the context of subsequent legislation because of the constitutional principle that no Parliament can bind or restrict the legislative capacity of any future Parliament.

Treaty override

1-25   The doctrine of parliamentary sovereignty clearly means that should it wish to do so, as a matter of domestic law, Parliament may legislate to override a treaty. To do so would be a clear breach of international law. The remedies for such a breach, however, lie not at the hands of individual taxpayers but in the hands of the other contracting state. The question of the fundamental relationship between domestic law and treaties has come before the courts on several occasions. In *Ostime (HM Inspector of Taxes) v. Australian Mutual Provident*,[44] the simple point was made that the effect of the legislation is that, if and so far as there is any inconsistency between domestic law and the treaty, then the treaty having duly been given

---

[41] The definition in Article 2(1)(b) of the Treaty with the Federal Republic requires that "the Federal Republic" when used in a geographical sense, means the territory in which the Basic Law for the Federal Republic of Germany is in force". Thus the extension of the Constitution to eastern Germany extended the application of the Treaty automatically.

[42] See Chinese Treaty, Art.3(1)(a); Inland Revenue *Tax Bulletin* (IRInt 151, October 1996), p.397, and Hong Kong Air Transport Treaty of June 2, 1998 (S.I. 1998 No. 2566).

[43] Vienna Convention, Art.26.

[44] [1958] 28 T.C. 487.

statutory effect must prevail over domestic law. The case was relatively straightforward on this point in the sense that the legislation in question pre-dated the treaty.

In *IRC v. Collco Dealings Ltd*,[45] the question was whether legislation enacted in 1955 overrode provisions of the Treaty with Ireland dating back to 1926. The 1955 legislation was introduced to combat perceived abuse in relation to dividend stripping. The Treaty between the United Kingdom and Ireland was not enacted by virtue of the mechanism now found in section 788 of the Taxes Act 1988, but by way of specific legis-lation. It did not contain the wording making the Treaty prevail "notwith-standing any enactment". It was argued that to apply the later legislation would create a breach of the Treaty and would be inconsistent with the comity of nations and the established rules of international law. The potentially overriding domestic legislation had therefore to be construed so as to avoid this result. Viscount Simonds declined to accept the argu-ment and said at 526:

> "[B]ut it is said in the first place that it [the taxpayer] is not entitled under an enactment but under an agreement which the appellant company, to add weight to the argument, prefer to call a treaty. But this contention cannot be accepted. The company has no rights under any agreement. Its rights arise from the act of Parliament which confirm the agreement and give it the force of law".

He did not find the words in need of interpretation and adopted the view in *Maxwell on the Interpretation of Statutes*[46] which concludes: "but if the Statute is unambiguous, its provisions must be followed, even if they are con-trary to international law".[47]

1-26   His judgment on this was clearly influenced by the fact that the leg-islation in question was to counter perceived abuse. He continued:

> "I am not sure upon which of these high sounding phrases, the appel-lant company chiefly relies. But I would answer that neither comity nor rule of international law can be invoked to prevent a sovereign state from taking what steps it thinks fit to protect its own revenue laws from gross abuse or to save its own citizens from unjust discrimination in favour of foreigners. To demand that the plain words of the statute should be disregarded in order to do that very thing is an extravagance to which this House will not, I hope, give here".

Lord Morton of Henryton endorsed this view in somewhat less strident language, but nonetheless influenced by the anti-abuse nature of the provi-sions. He endorsed the views of Vaisey J. in the High Court[48] that:

---

[45] (1961) 39 T.C. 509.

[46] *Maxwell on the Interpretation of Statutes* (10th ed.), pp.148 and 149.

[47] In the High Court, this comment was also made with specific reference to " any international treaty or arrangements", at 517.

[48] See at 517.

"the plain object of section 4(2) was to prevent what is colloquially called 'dividend stripping', and if the decision of the Special Commissioners stands, residents in Ireland can do what their fellow taxpayers in this country are prohibited from doing. If that is the law, sobeit; but the consequence is not one which commands itself to me on general principles of justice or fairness".

1-27 Lord Reed agreed with the conclusion, but on somewhat different grounds. He noted that unless a limitation is implied, the later legislation enacted something inconsistent with the provisions of a treaty. He said that:

"there is by no means so strong a presumption against Parliament having done that. Although the infringement of a treaty may cause loss to individuals, the only person properly entitled to complain of such infringement is the other party to the treaty. No doubt if that other party is aggrieved, the infringement is a breach of the comity of nations and there is a presumption that Parliament did not intend to act contrary to the comity of nations, but I do not think that there is necessarily a presumption that every infringement of a treaty is a breach of the comity of nations. After a treaty has been made, circumstances may alter and it may be reasonable to take unilateral action in the expectation that the other party to the treaty will not object. Indeed, the other party may have been consulted and have raised no objection".

He continued:

"we do not know what happened in this case. But we do know that on a previous occasion, unilateral action was taken by section 52 of the Finance (No. 2) Act 1945 and this was followed by an alteration of the Treaty in 1947 which altered the scope of the original tax exemption to correspond with the provisions of the 1945 Act".

1-28 Lord Radcliffe recognised that statutory words apparently unlimited in scope may be given a restricted field of application if there is admissible ground for importing such a restriction and the consideration that if not construed in some limited sense, they would amount to a breach of international law, is well recognised as such a ground. However, he said that a supposed intention not to depart from the observance of the comity of nations is a much vaguer criterion by which to determine the range of a statute. When the departure consists in no more than a provision inconsistent with an inter-governmental agreement about taxation, which by its own terms is subordinated to the approval of the respective legislatures of the countries concerned and persists only so long as its terms are maintained in force as law by those legislatures, he argued that there is no useful aid at all to be obtained from this principle of interpretation. The arrangements between the United Kingdom and Ireland were unusual and modern tax treaty practice is to rely on section 788 of the Taxes Act 1988 to give effect to treaty obligations rather than specific legislation.

The Privy Council on an appeal from Ceylon upheld Ceylonese legislation inconsistent with the Ceylon Treaty in *Woodend (KV Ceylon) Rubber Antiques Co. Limited v. CIR.*[49] Although these cases are useful in considering general principles, they do not assist in interpreting section 788(3), because they do not contain the words "notwithstanding anything in any enactment". Thus, as a matter of general principle, Parliament is presumed to intend to fulfil rather than break a treaty. Where, however, on an informed construction, there is no real doubt about the real meaning of an enactment, effect must be given to it even if it is not in accordance with a treaty or contrary to international law. The effect of the wording in section 788(3), however, is that until Parliament exercises its power to override a treaty or treaties, it will not be presumed to do so and treaty provisions will prevail. In order successfully to override a treaty, clear express language to that effect must be used.

1-29   The most blatant and calculated instance of treaty override in the United Kingdom in the modern context is found in Taxes Act 1988, section 812. This aims at withdrawing the right to obtain repayment of tax credits for companies which are present in or have associated companies in a unitary state. The language of the section is unambiguous. It provides that "notwithstanding anything to the contrary in the arrangements" such companies are not entitled to repayment of tax credits which are provided for in a treaty. The section was enacted in order to retaliate against the introduction of unitary tax systems adopted by certain states in the United States, most notably California. The legislation is not in force until an order to that effect has been made which requires approval by a resolution of the House of Commons. Although the Government indicated in 1993 that they would defer retaliatory action against the State of California following the passage of legislation by that state to modify its unitary tax law, no move has been made to bring these provisions into force. They remain on the statute, however. Such provisions are clear treaty override as defined by the OECD Committee on Fiscal Affairs as "the enactment of domestic legislation intended by the legislature to have effects in clear contradiction to international treaty obligations".[50]

Similarly, legislation was enacted in relation to the treatment of U.K. resident members of partnerships controlled abroad in Finance (No. 2) Act 1987, section 62. This arose out of *Padmore v. IRC.*[51] The legislation here was clearly aimed at overriding the Treaty. The statute sought to disapply treaties in relation to the income and capital gains of U.K. resident partners. It requires that "the [treaties] . . . shall not affect any liability to tax in respect of the resident partners' share of any income or capital gains of the partnership".[52]

Override by interpretation

1-30   Another possible example of treaty override may be found in section 808A of the Taxes Act 1988. The section provides for rules of

---

[49] [1971] A.C. 321, PC.
[50] OECD Committee on Fiscal Affairs, *Tax Treaty Override* (1989).
[51] [1987] S.T.C. 36.
[52] This override has been perpetuated in Taxes Act 1988, s. 112(4) despite the fact that the entity approach to taxing partnerships is no longer applied (Taxes Act 1988, s. 111).

interpretation of interest provisions where a special relationship is present. Although arguably declaratory of the rules of interpretation in some respects anyway, the effect of section 808A is to require certain older treaties, in which the effect of the special relationship provision on interest is merely to regulate the rate of interest without reference to the amount of debt, to impose by way of interpretation that the special relationship provision should take into account the amount of debt in all such treaties. It was explained by the Financial Secretary to the Treasury that "we are now using this Bill to change the law to what we thought it was and to reflect the double taxation treaty".[53]

A similar device was adopted in relation to the formula for the repayment of tax credits on dividends. This arose out of the proceedings in *Union Texas Petroleum Co. v. Critchley*.[54] In this case, the legislation does not purport to override the treaty. Finance Act 1989, section 115 simply says that "the [Treaty] shall be construed as providing . . .". These provisions were made retrospective other than in relation to judgments given before the announcement or in proceedings which had already commenced.

In the case of the legislation arising out of the *Padmore* and *Union Texas* cases, the Inland Revenue were (or believed that they were about to be) on the losing side of cases before the courts. Since the Inland Revenue view of the interpretation of the treaty prevailed in *Union Texas*, the legislation did not in fact override the treaty. It may be described as attempted override. On the other hand, the suggestion that legislation overriding a judicial interpretation of a treaty where the Revenue has lost (as was apparently the case with Taxes Act 1988, section 808A) as a "correction", is a facile excuse for a simple exercise of Parliamentary supremacy.

1-31   No threat of losing a case appeared to have been at hand in the case of the introduction of Taxes Act 1988, section 808B by the Finance Act 2000. This section imposes an interpretation of the "special relationship" wording in treaties relating to royalties. The Inland Revenue stated in their document on double tax relief reform that in all cases, treaty benefits should be limited not only where the rate at which royalties are paid is excessive, but where in the absence of the special relationship, the arrangements under which the royalties are paid at all would not have been entered into. This in effect imposes a meaning on "special relationship" not supported by all treaties. The extensive anti-avoidance rules incorporated in section 808B can hardly be described as interpretation and are thus a clear treaty override.

Until recently, the only case in which treaty override in relation to U.K. tax law has been challenged in the courts is *Collco Dealings Ltd* (and that in relation to the Republic of Ireland where there were specific and unusual legislative arrangements).[55] Plainly, such challenges must fail in relation to express and unambiguous override. This was the case in *Padmore (No. 2) v. Commissioners of Inland Revenue*.[56] The taxpayer argued that Taxes Act 1988, section 788(3), which appeared in Part XVII of the Act, overrode

---

[53] House of Commons, June 30, 1992, at 452.
[54] [1988] S.T.C. 691.
[55] See above, n. 45.
[56] [2001] S.T.C. 280, Ch.D.

section 112(4), contained in Part IV of the Act. Tax treaties, it was claimed, had effect "notwithstanding anything in any enactment", but section 788 itself was "subject to the provisions of this Part". Thus, an effective treaty override had to be contained in Part XVII.

1-32   The court held that the treaty had been overridden. An alternative construction would deprive Taxes Act 1988, section 112 of all effect. Its purpose was to remove the exemption conferred on the taxpayer. The departure from the provisions of the Treaty was plainly and deliberately made and thus there was no scope for any presumption. Parliament did not intend that ambiguous or unclear domestic law should have to be tested for compliance with treaty obligations.

Restraint in exercising Parliamentary power in this way does indicate a compliant approach towards international law by the United Kingdom. Avoiding breaches of international law designed to demonstrate adherence to principles of international law will give other treaty parties confidence, which in turn will maintain the stability of the U.K. treaty network. There is no indication of contracting states rasing objections to these overrides and indeed there may be an emerging international custom of acceptance of such breaches in the context of tax treaties.

Limiting access to treaties

1-33   Legislative devices have become more ingenious in seeking to narrow the potential application of treaties. A further category of relationship between treaties and domestic law reflects other attempts to limit availability of treaty benefits. In the capital gains area, several measures have appeared over the years in order to prevent access to treaty benefits through changes in residence. Such measures include Taxation of Chargeable Gains Act (TCGA) 1992, section 83, which requires trustees becoming resident in a treaty country by virtue of tiebreaker provisions to be deemed to have disposed of assets which are treaty protected at the time that they become resident in the other contracting state. These rules cannot be regarded as treaty override, since the taxable events apply immediately before the taxpayer becomes resident in the other contracting state. Similarly, TCGA 1992, section 84 prohibits rollover relief on replacement of business assets under section 152 where new assets are acquired by trustees who are U.K. resident but are treated as non-resident for the purposes of a treaty and the assets in question are of a description "specified" in the treaty. Again, these measures preclude a specific class of persons from qualifying for treaty benefits. Further provisions deal with capital gains and dual resident settlements. Section 88 requires gains of trusts to be attributed to beneficiaries if the trustees are U.K. resident but are treated as non-resident for treaty purposes and if the assets are of a kind that would qualify for treaty relief in the hands of a resident of the other contracting state. In *Boote v. Banco do Brasil*,[57] the court upheld legislation designed to prevent branches of non-resident banks carrying forward or otherwise using losses resulting from income that was exempt by treaty notwithstanding a degree of retrospectivity.

---

[57] [1997] S.T.C. 327, CA.

Extension of treaty benefits

1-34   On the other hand, benefits are occasionally extended by domestic law beyond those given by treaty. Companies which are treated as resident in another contracting state by virtue of the application of a treaty are deemed to be non-resident for all purposes of the Taxes Act 1988 under Finance Act 1994, section 249.

CHAPTER 2

The Legal Framework: European Law

2-01 The European Community is established by treaty setting out its constitutional provisions.[1] Community law within its area of competence is supreme and renders ineffective any U.K. legislative, administrative, or judicial act which is contrary to it. The British Parliament cannot override European law in the way other treaty obligations may.[2] Community law impacts on tax treaties in two respects. First, treaties are subject to the same tests on legality as are the domestic laws of Member States. Secondly, certain areas of taxation traditionally occupied by treaties are now governed by European harmonisation measures.[3]

In the treaty context, the European Court of Justice ruled as early as 1986 in *EC Commission v. France*[4] that even in the absence of harmonisation of corporate tax, although a company's tax position depends on the national law applied to it, Article 43 (ex 52) of the EC Treaty unconditionally prohibits Member States from laying down in their laws conditions for the pursuit of activities by persons exercising their right of establishment which differ from those laid down for their own nationals.

The ECJ has consistently reaffirmed this opinion that although as Community law stands, direct taxation does not as such fall within the purview of the Community, the powers retained by the Member States must nevertheless be exercised consistently with Community law.[5]

Direct tax measures have been attacked under several articles of the EC Treaty:

---

[1] The constitution is now contained in the Treaty of Amsterdam, two treaties consolidating the previous treaties. Strictly, taxation is addressed by the Treaty establishing the European Community. The Treaty Establishing the European Union addresses political integration. References in this book to Articles are references to the Treaty establishing the European Community as contained in the Amsterdam Treaty. Articles have been renumbered in the Amsterdam Treaty. Cases before the renumbering have references to both old and new numbers. The term "European law" is used to describe the laws of the Community and the Union in their entirety.

[2] This is now trite law. See, *e.g.*, European Communities Act 1972, s. 2; Case 14/64 *Costa v. ENEL* [1964] E.C.R. 585, ECJ; *R. v. Secretary of State for Transport, ex parte Factortame Ltd* [1991] A.C. 603, HL.

[3] See below, Chapter 9.

[4] Case 270/83 [1986] E.C.R. 273.

[5] See, *e.g.*, recently Case C-279/93 *Finanzamt Köln-Altstadt v. Schumacker* [1995] S.T.C. 306; Case C-80/94 *Wielockx v. Inspecteur der Directe Belastingen* [1995] S.T.C. 876; Case C-104/94 *Asscher v. Staatssecretaris van Financiën* [1996] S.T.C. 1025; Case C-307/97 *Compagnie de Saint-Gobain, Zweigniederlassung Deutschland v. Finanzamt Aachen-Innenstadt* [2000] S.T.C. 854, ECJ.

(1)   Article 39 (ex 48): free movement of workers;

(2)   Article 43 (ex 52): freedom of establishment which includes the right to take up and pursue activities as self-employed persons and to set up and manage undertakings, in particular companies or firms;

(3)   Article 48 (ex 58): extends the freedom of establishment rules to companies formed in Member States and managed in a Member State;

(4)   Article 49 (ex 59): freedom to provide services;

(5)   Article 56 (ex 73b): free movement of capital.

DEFENCES TO DISCRIMINATION

2-02   Defences to discriminatory direct tax measures may be established on the basis of the following articles:

(1)   Article 46 (ex 56): public policy, public safety, public health;

(2)   Article 58 (ex 73d): distinction based on residence or place where capital is invested and to prevent infringement of national law, particularly taxation. This defence is restricted to Article 56 cases.

Since cases involving cross-border tax discrimination inevitably involve treaty issues, references to treaties appear in most cases that have come before the courts.

PERSONAL SCOPE

2-03   Article 12 (ex 6) of the EC Treaty prohibits discrimination on the grounds of nationality within the scope of application of the EC Treaty. The non-discrimination provisions are extended to companies or firms by Article 48 (ex 58) of the Treaty. Thus, a company or firm formed in accordance with the law of a Member State and having its registered office, central administration or principal place of business within the Community is to be treated in the same way as natural persons who are nationals of Member States for these purposes. The definition is therefore not dissimilar from the definition of "national" in Article 3 of the OECD Model read in conjunction with the definition of resident in Article 4(1) of the OECD Model.

The rules relating to discrimination based on nationality have also been extended to discrimination based on residence by the European Court of Justice.[6]

---

[6] The first occasion was in Case 152/73 *Sotgiu v. Deutsche Bundespost* [1974] E.C.R. 153. This has been followed in a series of tax cases concerning individuals such as, Case C-279/93 *Finanzamt Köln-Altstadt v. Schumacker* [1995] S.T.C. 306; Case C-80/94 *Wielockx v. Inspecteur der Directe Belastingen* [1995] S.T.C. 876, and Case C-104/94 *Asscher v. Staatssecretaris van Financiën* [1996] S.T.C. 1025, and in the case of companies in Case C-1/93 *Halliburton Services BV v. Staatssecretaris van Financiën* [1994] S.T.C. 655, and Case C-330/91 *R. v. IRC, ex parte Commerzbank AG* [1993] S.T.C. 605.

Citing *Sotgiu v. Deutsche Bundespost*, the ECJ held in *Biehl*[7] that: "the rules regarding equality of treatment forbid not only overt discrimination by reason of nationality but also all covert forms of discrimination which, by the application of other criteria of differentiation, lead to the same results". The ECJ recognised that a distinction based on residence, although applicable without distinction to nationals and non-nationals, should be viewed in the same way as a distinction based on nationality where the non-residents are in the main non-nationals. In *Schumacker*, Advocate General Leger noted[8] that "The criterion of residence is the main pillar of international tax law. Chosen by almost every state in the world, it is given precedence over nationality".

2-04   Unequal treatment between residents and non-residents does not automatically constitute discrimination. In *Schumacker*, it was recognised that the circumstances of residents and non-residents are not always comparable. The right to discriminate on the basis of residence in tax matters was given limited approval in certain circumstances by amendments introduced in the Maastricht Treaty.[9]

Member States are required to give treaty benefits to residents of other Member States in certain circumstances. In *Compagnie de Saint-Gobain v. Finanzamt Aachen Innenstadt*,[10] the ECJ considered *inter alia* the German Schachtelprivileg, a participation exemption granted by treaty with a non-EC member country to companies holding a specified percentage of shares in another company in respect of dividends therefrom and the underlying foreign tax credit for tax paid by a subsidiary in a non-member country to be credited against the corporation tax of the parent. It also considered a similar exemption in respect of capital tax.

Under German group tax rules, subject to certain conditions, a permanent establishment of a foreign company may be included in the Organschaft. The German subsidiaries were treated as a single entity along with the permanent establishment for German tax purposes. Under these rules, the parent company (in this case the permanent establishment) is liable for tax on the group's aggregate results. The profits and losses of the other companies are included in the profits and losses of the principal company. Saint-Gobain, a French resident and incorporated company, operated through a permanent establishment in Germany. It held as part of the assets of the permanent establishment 10.2 per cent of a U.S. corporation and effectively all of the shares of two German incorporated and resident subsidiaries. In this case, the permanent establishment was the principal company. The German companies had substantial holdings in companies established in Austria, Switzerland and Italy. Dividends were received from those companies and under the group profit transfer agreements were included in the income of the permanent establishment.

---

[7] Case C175/88 *Biehl v. Administration des Contributions du Grand-Duché de Luxembourg* [1990] E.C.R. I-1779.
[8] See above, n. 6, para. 35 at 312.
[9] Article 73d (now 58) of the EC Treaty.
[10] Case C-307/97 [2000] S.T.C. 854, ECJ.

2-05   Under German law, the dividends were attributed to the permanent establishment in Germany and liable to German tax. As a general rule, German resident companies are liable to unlimited (worldwide) liability to tax and permanent establishments to limited (German source) tax liability.

The German tax authorities refused to allow the benefit of treaties between Germany and the United States and Switzerland respectively. In each case, dividends paid by U.S. or Swiss companies were, subject to certain conditions, exempt from German tax on such dividends in the hands of German residents. These treaty exemptions were denied to the permanent establishment despite the fact that the dividends were included in the income of the permanent establishment.

The German tax authorities allowed credit (direct credit) in respect of tax withheld at source on dividends from the various countries. It, however, refused the underlying credit for corporate tax paid by the foreign subsidiaries. Under German domestic law, the underlying credit was granted only to German resident companies. There was no dispute that the concessions granted to domestic German groups resulted in a lighter tax burden.

2-06   The ECJ held all of the German provisions in question to be contrary to Article 43 (ex 52) and Article 48 (ex 58) of the EC Treaty because permanent establishments are less attractive than subsidiaries, since under German domestic law and bilateral treaties, the tax benefits are only granted to German subsidiaries. This restricts the freedom to choose the most appropriate legal form for the pursuit of activity in another Member State.

The German Government sought to justify the discrimination on the basis that the situations of resident and non-resident companies are not generally comparable. This is particularly because non-residents are only liable to limited tax liability whereas residents are subject to unlimited tax liability. The ECJ rejected this argument on the basis that the dividends were taxable in the hands of the permanent establishment, regardless of where the dividend paying companies were located, thus the restriction to local source income was theoretical. In fact, the only difference was that the permanent establishment was not entitled to credit or exemption from tax on dividends from foreign shareholdings. The German Government argued that the measures were justified by the need to prevent a reduction in tax revenue, given the impossibility for the German authorities to compensate for the reduction in revenue if equal treatment were given by taxing dividends distributed by non-resident companies.

The ECJ rejected this argument, simply on the basis that it is not one of the grounds listed in Article 46 (ex 56) of the EC Treaty and cannot be regarded as a matter of overriding general interest which may be relied upon in order to justify unequal treatment.

2-07   It was further argued that the discrimination was justified because there is no tax on the transfer of profits to the head office by a branch compared with the taxation of distributions by a subsidiary to a parent company. The ECJ did not accept that such advantages exist for permanent establishments and even if they did, they could not justify a breach of the equal treatment required by Article 43 (ex 52).

The effect of this decision on the personal scope of treaties is far-reaching. Thus, although the scope of treaties following Article 1 of the OECD Model is restricted to "persons who are residents of one or both of the contracting states", the decision in *Saint-Gobain* is to open up access to treaty benefits to nationals or residents of Member States who are not the contracting states of the treaty in question. This access is not unlimited. It applies where the national or resident of a Member State exercises a fundamental freedom such as the right of establishment and in the context of that exercise is put in the same position as a resident or national of the contracting state in question.

A distinction may be drawn between treaties concluded between Member States and those concluded with third countries.

TREATIES BETWEEN MEMBER STATES

2-08   Double taxation between Member States is specifically addressed in Article 293 (ex 220) of the EC Treaty. It provides that:

> "*Article 293 (ex 220)*
> Member States shall, so far as is necessary, enter into negotiations with each other with a view to securing for the benefit of their nationals: . . .
> —the abolition of double taxation within the Community;"

Thus, Member States are required to enter into negotiations with each other as necessary with a view to securing the abolition of double taxation within the Community for the benefit of their nationals. The scope and meaning of the article has been subject to much scholarly analysis[11] and debate but to limited consideration by the courts.

It has been argued that the expression "so far as is necessary" limits the obligation to the extent that European measures have not already done so. Thus, to the extent that European law already occupies the field, Member States individually would appear to have no obligation. It should be noted that the obligation is to enter into negotiations with a view to eliminating double taxation, rather than a legal duty to eliminate double taxation. The effect of this is therefore to preserve the right of Member States to enter into treaties with each other. In addition, the subsidiarity principle introduced in the Maastricht Treaty[12] requires that the Community must act within the powers conferred upon it by the EC Treaty. However, areas which do not fall within its exclusive jurisdiction are only amenable to Community action if and so far as the objectives of the proposed action cannot be sufficiently achieved by Member States.

2-09   The article itself does not prohibit double taxation. The application and scope of the article was considered by the ECJ in *Gilly v. Directeur des Services Fiscaux du Bas-Rhin*.[13] The question put to the court was whether the objective of abolishing double taxation must be regarded as having the status of a directly applicable rule under which double taxation

---

[11] See, *e.g.*, Wolfgang Gassner, Michael Lang and Eduard Lechner (eds), *Tax Treaties and EC Law* (Kluwer Law International, 1996).
[12] See Art.3b.
[13] Case C-336/96 [1998] S.T.C. 1014, ECJ.

may no longer take place, having regard for the time which Member States have had to implement it. The taxpayers in that case argued that the article created legally binding rules directly applicable on which they could rely. Several Member States appearing before the ECJ argued that the article does not have direct effect because it is not sufficiently clear and unconditional and does not confer on individuals a right to the abolition of all double taxation within the Community. The Commission argued that the article imposes on Member States an obligation to enter into negotiations, if necessary. It does not oblige them to achieve a specific result. In the view of the Commission, the Franco–German treaty did in meet the objective of Article 293 (ex 220). The Advocate General regarded these provisions as not laying down an absolute obligation but as leaving Member States with a wide discretion to decide whether to enter into negotiations. That discretion had been exercised by the contracting states when the treaty was signed in 1959 and when it was amended by successive protocols in 1969 and 1989. The taxpayer argued that the mere reduction of double taxation as opposed to its elimination did not meet the objective of Article 293 (ex 220).

2-10   The ECJ followed its earlier decision in *Ministère Public v. Mutsch*[14] on another aspect of Article 293 (ex 220), that the article is not intended to lay down a legal rule directly applicable as such. It merely defined a number of matters on which the Member States are to enter into negotiations with each other "so far as is necessary". The second indent of the article was held to indicate clearly that the abolition of double taxation within the Community is an objective of any such negotiations. Thus, although the abolition of double taxation within the Community is included among the objectives of the EC Treaty, it is clear from the wording of that provision that it cannot itself confer any rights on individuals which they might be able to rely on before their national courts.

Limits on the effect of treaties

2-11   In the absence of unifying or harmonising measures for the elimination of double taxation, Member States are competent to determine the criteria for taxing income and eliminating double taxation. The means of achieving this includes bilateral treaties.[15] Although Member States have retained their competence to enter into treaties with a view to eliminating double taxation, this competence must be exercised in a manner consistent with European law.

In *EC Commission v. France*, the ECJ considered whether France was in breach of its obligations under the EC Treaty, in particular Article 43 (ex 52), by not granting the benefit of shareholders' tax credits to branches and agencies in France of insurance companies established in other Member States. The court ruled that by virtue of Article 43 (ex 52) freedom of establishment for nationals of one Member State on the territory of another includes the right to take up and pursue activities and to set up and manage undertakings under the conditions laid down for its own nationals.

---

[14] Case 137/84 [1985] E.C.R. 2681 at 2694–2695, para. 11.
[15] *Gilly* above, n. 13, at 1038, para. 24. The Court referred particularly to treaties in accordance with the OECD Model.

2-12   The French Government argued that the difference in treatment arose by virtue of differences between the tax systems of Member States and the existence of tax treaties. Different measures are necessary in each case, it argued, in order to take account of the differences between taxation systems which ought to be justified under Article 43 (ex 52). The tax rules in question were governed by double tax treaties between the relevant Member States whose existence is expressly recognised in Article 293 (ex 220) of the Treaty. Furthermore, the rules which were contested were necessary, in particular to prevent tax avoidance.

On the role of tax treaties, the ECJ held that rights conferred by Article 43 (ex 52) are unconditional and a Member State cannot make them subject to the contents of an agreement concluded with another Member State. This clear statement has been reaffirmed in subsequent cases.[16] In particular Article 43 (ex 52) does not permit those rights to be made subject to a condition of reciprocity imposed for the purposes of obtaining corresponding advantages in other Member States. Consequently, provisions in treaties between Member States that do not comply with Community law are ineffective.

The court also rejected the risk of tax avoidance as justification in this context. It held that Article 43 (ex 52) does not permit any derogation from the fundamental principle of freedom of establishment on such a ground. The implication of the judgment is that equal treatment should have been given by domestic law or treaty.

Treaties authorising discrimination

2-13   Where the treaty is not itself discriminatory but authorises discriminatory taxation by a contracting state, the treaty itself may escape attack. In *Finanzamt-Koln-Altstadt v. Schumacker*[17] one of the questions put to the ECJ was whether it made any difference if the income in question was taxed in a Member State in accordance with the treaty between the Member States in question. The main point in issue was whether Article 39 (ex 48) of the EC Treaty allowed a Belgian resident who was otherwise in comparable circumstances with German residents to be denied equal tax treatment in Germany. In that case, there was no discussion of the treaty in question by the Advocate General or by the ECJ itself other than pointing out that the unequal treatment in question, namely, denying a married Belgian resident the benefits of taxation by reference to the treatment of married residents and taxing him as a single person instead, was permitted in the state of employment in accordance with the applicable treaty. The unstated underlying assumption seems to be that since Article 15(1) of the Belgian–German Treaty merely authorised the offending elements of German tax law, the provisions of the treaty were themselves not analysed or indeed strictly relevant and therefore discrimination lay in the German domestic law not in the Treaty. Unlike the French authorities in *Commission v. France*,[18] the German tax administration did not rely on the treaty to justify the discrimination in question.

---

[16] For example, Case C-330/91 *R. v. IRC, ex parte Commerzbank AG* [1993] S.T.C. 605, Advocate General's opinion.
[17] Case C-279/93 [1995] S.T.C. 306, ECJ.
[18] See above, n. 4.

Discriminatory treaties

2-14 Treaties may themselves give rise to discrimination. In *Saint-Gobain*, the German tax authorities included the shareholding in the American subsidiary in the domestic assets of the permanent establishment for the purpose of German capital tax. Germany did not allow an exemption for international groups, but did grant a concession, limited to domestic companies.

However, by virtue of Article 19 of the France-Germany Treaty, shareholdings of a German subsidiary in a foreign sub-subsidiary of a French company not resident in Germany were excluded from German capital tax. As a result, the exemption from capital tax in relation to international groups also produced a tax burden on a permanent establishment of a foreign company which is different from that on a subsidiary of a foreign company. The German government initially argued that the situation of a permanent establishment is different from a subsidiary, but conceded the discrimination at the hearing. Thus, treaties may give rise to illegal discrimination if, as a result of their terms, taxpayers in like circumstance are not taxed equally.

A treaty which grants concessions to subsidiaries of a contracting state but fails to extend the same concessions to permanent establishments of a contracting state is a source of discrimination. In *Saint-Gobain*,[19] the result was, however, not the ineffectiveness of the Treaty, but the domestic law of the contracting state whose rules have been made discriminatory by application of the Treaty. The fact that the resident or national of another Member State is treated more favourably in some respects, does not cure or offset discriminatory inequality where it exists.

2-15 A similar form of discrimination arose in *XAB & YAB v. Riksskatteverket*.[20] Swedish corporate income tax reliefs applied on the transfer of assets intra-group. They were applicable under Swedish law to companies in the same group, that is where the parent owned at least 90 per cent of the subsidiary. The reliefs applied on condition that the companies were all established in Sweden or in a single other state with which Sweden has a treaty containing a non-discrimination clause. This was attacked as discriminatory against companies in groups established in more than one Member State under Articles 43 (ex 52), 48 (ex 58), 56 (ex 73b) and 58 (ex 73d) of the EC Treaty.

In the case, 99.8 per cent of the shares of YAB were owned ultimately by XAB. About 58 per cent of those shares were owned directly by XAB. The balance were owned by other subsidiaries of XAB. A ruling was sought from the Swedish tax authorities on obtaining relief on intra-group transfers of assets in three circumstances:

(1) where XAB owned all of the shares in YAB itself or through Swedish subsidiaries;

(2) where 15 per cent of the shares in YAB were owned by ZBV, a Netherlands company wholly-owned by XAB;

---

[19] See above, n. 10.
[20] Case 200/98 [1999] E.C.R. I-8261.

(3) where ZBV and YGmbH, a Germany company wholly-owned by XAB, would each acquire 15 per cent of the shares in YAB.

2-16 Under Swedish domestic law, relief would be given in the first circumstance. Relief would also be given in the second circumstance on the basis it could be contrary to the non-discrimination clause of an applicable treaty, for example, that between Sweden and the Netherlands, for the relief to be denied. However, Swedish case law prohibited the cumulative application of two treaties, such as those between Sweden and Germany on the one hand, and Sweden and the Netherlands on the other. This was because the simultaneous application of two or more treaties was excluded on the basis that the provisions of each of those treaties applied only to undertakings of the contracting states and not to those of third states.

In upholding the claim of illegal discrimination, the ECJ noted that the freedom of establishment applies both to ensure that foreign nationals and companies are treated in the host Member State in the same way as nationals of that state, as well as prohibiting the Member State of origin from hindering the establishment in another Member State.

These rules were held to be discriminatory.[21] Although on the face of each of the Treaties in question, they were not discriminatory when placed in context of the domestic law, the presence of a treaty containing the requisite provisions established discrimination when a third country was involved.

Waiver of cohesion

2-17 The only justification for discriminatory taxation accepted by the ECJ is where the discrimination is necessary to maintain the cohesion of the tax system. In *Wielockx v. Inspecteur der Directe Belastingen*[22] the question of the effect of Article 18[23] of the OECD Model on discrimination was considered. The ECJ held that a non-resident taxpayer who received almost all of his income in the state where he worked as a physiotherapist and had a fixed base under Article 14(1),[24] but was not entitled to set up a pension reserve qualifying for deductions under the same tax conditions as a resident self-employed taxpayer, suffered discrimination. The Netherlands Government argued that the discrimination was justified on the basis that it was necessary to maintain the cohesion of the tax system.[25] The court, however, concluded that although a state may base the cohesion of its tax system on the principle of a correlation between the deductibility of contributions and taxation of pensions, it may also reject that principle. The court referred to Article 18 of the OECD Model, which reads as follows:

"Subject to the provisions of paragraph 2 of Article 19 [concerning *inter alia* civil servants' pensions], pensions and other similar remuneration

---

[21] The Swedish Government conceded that the rule in question was contrary to Art.43 (ex 52) and offered no justification, and the Court ruled on this basis. It accordingly refused to consider the further grounds.

[22] Case C-80/94 [1995] S.T.C. 876, ECJ.

[23] "Pensions and similar payments".

[24] "Independent personal services".

[25] Case C-204/90 *Bachman v. Belgium* [1994] S.T.C. 855, ECJ.

paid to a resident of a contracting state in consideration of past employment shall be taxable only in that state".

2-18   The Belgian-Netherlands Treaty was in identical terms to Article 18 of the OECD model. Advocate General Leger also referred in his opinion[26] to Article 22 of the Belgian-Netherlands Treaty[27] and noted that income of a resident of one contracting state not otherwise dealt with in the Treaty was taxable only in the state of residence. The effect of treaties which are an integral part of national tax law and override domestic tax rules is in that the cohesion applies at another level. Thus domestic cohesion is waived and cohesion is established at a treaty level. In that case he concluded that the result was that pension contributions are deductible in the country of payment even if the right to receive the pension is in the hands of a non-resident. Consequently there is no requirement of a rigorous correlation between deductibility of contributions and taxation of pensions in order to secure cohesion of the domestic tax system. Thus, where cohesion of the domestic tax rules is waived by treaty, it may not be relied upon as a justification for discrimination.

Most favoured nation treatment

2-19   Do the non-discrimination rules of Community law oblige a Member State to make available the benefits of a tax treaty negotiated with one Member State to residents of another? If the answer to this is yes, then residents of Member States will be free to choose the most beneficial treaty provisions entered into with other Member States. In *Metallgesellschaft Ltd and others v. CIR*,[28] it was argued that where a U.K. company was owned by a German parent company, the German parent was entitled to repayment of tax credits as permitted by Article 10 of the U.K.–Netherlands Treaty, where the U.K.–German Treaty did not provide for such credits. The ECJ decided that discrimination existed on other grounds and therefore regarded it as unnecessary to address this question. In similarly declining to address the question, the Advocate General noted that this raised "extremely complex issues".

The ECJ has already gone some way to recognising indirect access to treaties in *Saint-Gobain*,[29] in which it was held that the branch of a company established in one Member State could not be denied treaty benefits in relation to treaties between the Member State where the branch was established and a third country.

SPECIFIC TREATY PROVISIONS

Permanent establishment

2-20   In *Futura Participations SA and another v. Administrations des Contributions*,[30] the question arose as to whether the deduction of losses

---

[26] At para. 53, at 884.
[27] "Other income".
[28] Case C-397/98 [2001] S.T.C. 452.
[29] See above, n. 10.
[30] Case C-250/95 [1997] S.T.C. 1301, ECJ.

could be made conditional on maintaining accounting records within a Member State. The Luxembourg Government relied in part on the Luxembourg-French Treaty to justify requiring branch accounts to be kept there. They argued that under Article 4(2) of the Treaty, income may only be charged to tax which arises from economic activity conducted within the territory through the permanent establishment and that Article 4(4) provides that the competent authorities of both contracting states shall where necessary agree to lay down apportionment rules if there are no proper accounts showing clearly and precisely the profits attributable to the establishments in their respective territory. From this, the Luxembourg authorities argued that actual profits of the permanent establishment must be taxed and that the apportionment rules only apply where there are no proper accounts showing clearly and precisely the profits referable to the particular establishment. Article 21(2) of the Luxembourg-French Treaty provided that where a taxpayer resident in France has a permanent establishment in Luxembourg, the provisions relating to loss carry-forwards are to be applicable on the same conditions as they are to taxpayers resident in Luxembourg. This meant that the accounts had to be kept in Luxembourg. It was argued that there was no discrimination, because Luxembourg companies were required to keep accounts at their head office which was also in Luxembourg.

In supporting the Luxembourg Government, the United Kingdom referred to the OECD Model and the Commentary.[31] According to these authorities, it was argued that although contracting states are not obliged to require taxpayers to keep separate accounts, the Commentary suggests that this is the most accurate and reliable method of establishing losses. Since the signatory Member States have a margin of discretion in deciding the most appropriate way for establishing losses, a state cannot be prevented from choosing the best and most accurate method. According to their argument, effective fiscal control is only possible if losses are ascertained on the basis of proper accounts.

2-21 The Advocate General acknowledged[32] that the Model Convention does not expressly require separate accounts. However, in his opinion, the Commentary merely points out that precise figures relating to profits and losses could be obtained only on the basis of proper accounts and that this method is therefore to be used in normal cases. This does not mean that accounts must be kept at the branch. He also pointed out that the OECD Model cannot apply conclusively to Community law with respect to the question raised in this case.

The United Kingdom further argued[33] that with reference to the Commentary, it is quite normal for well-run businesses to produce separate branch accounts. This, the Advocate General reasoned, did not mean that the separate accounts had to be kept at the branch. The Advocate General noted that the permanent establishment rule contained in Article 4 and the provisions relating to elimination of double taxation in Article 24(2)(2)

---

[31] At para. 42, at 1309.
[32] At para. 47, at 1310.
[33] At para. 48, at 1310.

which maintain the principle of territoriality do not contravene Community law, even in relation to the carrying forward of losses. The relevant provision here was rather Article 21(2) which provides that where a French resident has a permanent establishment in Luxembourg, provisions dealing with losses there are subject to the same conditions as are applicable to Luxembourg residents. This simply refers to the tax law of Member States which requires taxpayers to keep proper accounts. Extension of this condition to branches of a non-resident company is, however, incompatible with Community law in the view of Advocate General Lenz. The Court agreed[34] that the territoriality principle did not itself entail any prohibited discrimination. In finding the rule discriminatory, the ECJ did not address specifically the argument raised by the United Kingdom about the interpretation of the Treaty.

Dependent personal services

2-22   The terms of a treaty itself were sought to be impugned in *Gilly v. Directeur des Services Fiscaux du Bas-Rhin*.[35] The case is significant in several respects. It is most important because it considered the impact of European law on important aspects of tax treaties. Mr and Mrs Gilly were resident in France near the German border. Mr Gilly, a French national, taught in a French state school. Mrs Gilly, a dual French-German national, taught in a state school in Germany in the frontier area.

Under French domestic law, income tax was payable on the aggregate income of the spouses regardless of where received. The French progressive rates were applied and the spouses could not opt to be taxed separately. In calculating allowances and deductions for family commitments, account is taken of taxable income in France. In their particular case, because income from French sources was less than one half of the total income (Mr Gilly's share of the income being 45 per cent), they were assessed to pay more income tax than if they were taxed separately.

In Germany, Mrs Gilly was not entitled to the preferential scale for married couples known as splitting. She was automatically deemed to be single, because her husband was not German resident. In her case, application of splitting would have resulted in reducing her tax liability in Germany. Thus, despite being deemed to be a single taxpayer without children, she was in fact married and had two dependent children. A credit was given in France for tax paid abroad which reduces the double taxation slightly, but does not eliminate it.

2-23   In its submission, the European Commission argued that the application of French law to the couple's total income and of German law to Mrs Gilly's income from Germany constitutes, by reason of the way in which her marital status is taken into account, an obstacle which is incompatible with the principles governing the freedom of movement of workers. The taxpayers argued that provisions of the Franco–German Treaty were discriminatory and illegal under European law.

---

[34] At para. 22, at 1317.
[35] See above, n. 13.

Articles 13, 14 and 16 of the Franco–German Treaty contained a variety of rules which determined whether employment income was taxable in the country of residence or the country of source.

Article 13(1) of the Treaty set out the principle as regards taxation of income from employment. It did not accord with the OECD Model in that it gave exclusive jurisdiction to tax to the place of performance. It read:

> "Subject to the provisions of the following paragraphs, income from dependent work shall be taxable only in the Contracting State in which the personal activity in respect of which it is received is carried out. In particular, salaries, wages, pay, gratuities or other emoluments shall be deemed to constitute income from dependent work, together with all similar benefits paid or awarded by persons other than those referred to in Article 14."

2-24 Article 13(5)(a) contained an exception to the general rule that income is to be taxed where the work is carried out, applicable to frontier workers. They were to be taxed in their state of residence. The article provided that:

> "By way of exception to paragraphs 1, 3 and 4, income from dependent work earned by persons who work in the frontier area of one Contracting State and who have their permanent home in the other Contracting State, to which they normally return each day, shall be taxable only in that other State".

The United Kingdom does not presently have provisions relating specifically to frontier workers in its treaties and the issue is not addressed in the OECD Model.

Article 14(1) of the Franco–German Treaty established a further special rule in respect of remuneration and pensions from the public sector. They were, in principle, taxable in the paying state. The article specifies that:

> "Salaries, wages and similar remuneration, and retirement pensions, paid by one of the Contracting States, by a Land or by a legal person of that state or Land governed by public law to natural persons resident in the other state in consideration for present or past administrative or military services shall be taxable only in the first State. However, that provision shall not be applicable where the remuneration is paid to persons having the nationality of the other State without being at the same time nationals of the first State; in such cases, the remuneration shall be taxable only in the State in which such persons are resident".

2-25 This accords in part with Article 19(1)(a) of the OECD Model. It differs materially from the OECD Model in that it distinguishes between nationals of one contracting state and dual nationals.

Article 16 of the Treaty laid down a special rule applicable to teachers who are temporarily resident in the contracting state other than the one in which they are normally resident. Under these rules taxation jurisdiction remained with the state of their normal residence. Thus the article required that:

> "Teachers resident in one of the Contracting States who, in the course of a period of temporary residence not exceeding two years, receive remuneration in respect of teaching in a university, college, school or other teaching establishment in the other state shall be taxable in respect of that remuneration only in the first State."

The OECD Model does not contain the specific provision for cross-border teachers although many treaties, including U.K. treaties, contain such provisions. The Commentary does not discourage such provisions.

2-26   The cumulative effect of these treaty clauses is to vary the tax consequences for employed individuals depending upon whether:

(1) they are teachers or not;

(2) they are frontier workers;

(3) they are in the public or private sector;

(4) they have the nationality of the state applying them;

(5) they are dual nationals;

(6) they are short-term visiting teachers.

The question for the ECJ was whether Article 39 (ex 48) of the EC Treaty, which guarantees free movement of workers, precludes the application of these treaty provisions. The court noted[36] that whilst abolition of double taxation within the Community is one of the objectives of the EC Treaty, no unifying or harmonising measure for the elimination of double taxation has been adopted at the Community level, nor have the Member States concluded any multilateral convention to that effect.[37] In the absence of such measures, Member States are competent to determine the criteria for taxation of income and wealth with a view to eliminate double taxation. In particular, it was not regarded as unreasonable for Member States to base their treaties on the OECD Model Convention.

2-27   There are a number of possibilities with special rules for frontier workers, state employees and teachers who are temporarily resident in a contracting state. Thus, different connecting factors allocate taxing jurisdictions in different circumstances. Nationality is one of the factors in relation to state employees. The ECJ did not regard the use of nationality as the criterion for allocating fiscal jurisdiction as discriminatory. This was because in the absence of unifying or harmonising measures adopted in the Community context, the contracting states are competent to define the criteria for allocating their powers of taxation as between themselves with the view to eliminating double taxation. The rule relating to public sector employees was

---

[36] At para. 23, at 1038.
[37] Except the Convention of July 23, 1990 on the elimination of double taxation in connection with the adjustment of profits of associated enterprises, [1990] OJ L225/10.

based on the OECD Model. The court accepted the Commentary on that article that the principle is justified by "the rules of international courtesy and mutual respect between sovereign states" and "is contained in so many of the existing conventions between OECD members that it can be said to be already internationally accepted".[38] The ECJ thus appears to be recognising a new defence specifically in the context of treaties: if a treaty is based on a provision of the OECD Model and if the OECD Model reflects internationally accepted practice, then its legitimacy may be supported. This observation was not strictly necessary for the decision based on the competence of the contracting states. The court noted that the second part of Article 14(1) of the Franco–German Treaty abandoned the paying state principle, where nationals of the other contracting state are involved. The court noted that throughout the OECD provisions on state employees, nationality is however a relevant criterion. In any event, even if the whole article were ineffective, Mrs Gilly would still have been taxable in Germany under other provisions. The court also found that the taxpayers had not established that they had been disadvantaged by the choice of the paying state as the state competent to tax income earned in the public sector. The disadvantages lay in the domestic rules of the two contracting states respectively and, in particular, in relation to their graduated rates of tax.

2-28   The ECJ also rejected the argument that Article 6 (ex 7) of the EC Treaty (the general prohibition on discrimination on grounds of nationality) prohibited nationality as the criterion for allocating taxing jurisdiction. In accordance with longstanding law, the general prohibition of discrimination on grounds of nationality only applies independently to situations governed by Community law in which the Treaty lays down no specific prohibition of discrimination. In this case, the issue was governed by Article 39 (ex 48).

In the view of the Advocate General, the criteria in the EC Treaty which have the purpose only of determining the power to tax certain income are neutral with regard to freedom of movement for workers because in the two states concerned, they do not in tax matters treat workers of other Member States less favourably than or differently from their own nationals who are in the same situation. He was further of the view that it cannot be discriminatory to provide that remuneration of an employed person is taxable in the state where he works or in the state where he resides, or by the state paying the remuneration. It is necessary in the final analysis to refer to the criterion of the recipient's nationality in order to decide which of the two states is to tax it. In his view, the consequences of the application of the treaty distributive provisions could not be regarded as capable of deterring a worker from exercising his or her freedom of movement between the two Member States in question. The allocation of taxing jurisdiction in these circumstances was not regarded as constituting prohibited discrimination.

Article 39 (ex 48) of the EC Treaty did not preclude the application of provisions such as those in Articles 13(5)(a), 14(1) and 16 of the Franco–German Treaty, under which the tax regime applicable to frontier workers differs

---

[38] At para. 32, at 1039.

depending on whether they work in the private sector or the public sector and, where they work in the public sector, on whether or not they have only the nationality of the state of the authority employing them; and the regime applicable to teachers differs depending on whether their residence in the state in which they are teaching is for a short period or not.

Elimination of double taxation: foreign tax credit

2-29   The *Gilly* case also considered whether the treaty rules for eliminating double taxation contained in the Franco–German Treaty were compatible with Article 39 (ex 48) of the EC Treaty. Article 20(2)(a)(cc) of the Franco–German Treaty, as amended by the protocol signed on September 28, 1989, read as follows:

> "2. Double taxation of persons resident in France shall be avoided in the following manner:
>
> (a) Profits and other positive income arising in the Federal Republic and taxable there under the provisions of this Treaty shall also be taxable in France where they accrue to a person resident in France. The German tax shall not be deductible for calculation of the taxable income in France. However, the recipient shall be entitled to a tax credit to be set against the French tax charged on the taxable amount which includes that income. That tax credit shall be equal: . . .
>
> (cc) for all other income, to the amount of the French tax on the relevant income. This provision shall apply in particular to the income referred to in Articles . . . 13(1) and (2) and 14".

These rules are based on Article 23B of the OECD Model in accordance with the "ordinary credit method". A similar approach is adopted in U.K. treaties.

2-30   The tax credit mechanism adopted by the Franco–German Treaty was not incompatible with European law. The ECJ recognised the distinction between the full credit method and the ordinary credit in that double taxation could be fully avoided only by a credit equal to the amount of tax charged in Germany. The court stressed that it is not the object of a treaty to ensure that tax in one state is no higher than that which the taxpayer would be subject to in the other. The object is simply to prevent the same income from being taxed in each of two states. The court accepted the arguments of several Member States that if the state of residence were required to accord a tax credit greater than the fraction of its national tax corresponding to the income from abroad, it would have to reduce its tax in respect of the remaining income. This would entail a loss of revenue for it and would thus encroach on its sovereignty in matters of direct taxation. The fact that the tax in the source country exceeded the tax in the residence country on the income from the source country, in conjunction with the distributive provisions of the treaty authorising taxation in the source state, therefore permitting excess foreign tax, is likewise not contrary to Article 39 (ex 48).

U.K. TREATIES WITH MEMBER STATES

2-31 The United Kingdom has comprehensive income tax treaties with all Member States and estate and gift tax treaties with five of them.[39] It is party to the multilateral EC Arbitration Convention along with all other Member States. The treaty network within the European Union is relatively old. Nine of the treaties were negotiated before either the United Kingdom or the other contracting states in question joined the Community.[40] All the estate and gift tax treaties, except that with the Netherlands, are in this category. Protocols have been signed in most cases subsequently. Many of these predate the 1986 decision of the ECJ in *Commission v. France*[41] and only a handful have been negotiated against the jurisprudence on tax discrimination which has only really started to develop in the mid to late 1990s. Although several of these treaties are under renegotiation, there is little evidence of the impact of European developments on the terms of the United Kingdom's intra-European treaties.

2-32 The legality of specific provisions of U.K. treaties with other Member States has not come before the European Court of Justice. Differences between the European concept of discrimination and that in U.K. treaties emerged, however, in the *Commerzbank* series of cases. Following its success in claiming benefits under the U.S. Treaty, Commerzbank, a German incorporated and resident bank, sought the repayment supplement on overpayments of tax made by it. In *R. v. Inland Revenue Commissioners ex parte Commerzbank AG*,[42] the High Court declined to order the repayment on the basis that the rules relating to the repayment supplement were in breach of the non-discrimination provisions of Article 20 of the German Treaty. Among the reasons for rejecting the claim was that the comparison required by the non-discrimination clause was between German and U.K. nationals in the same circumstances, rather than between German and U.K. residents. Nolan L.J., while accepting that this argument led to the unattractive conclusion that the non-discrimination provisions are as a result of no assistance to German companies, partnerships or associations, said that it was not uncommon, however, for treaty provisions to operate solely for the benefit of one party with no compensating advantage for the other. He cited Article 15 of the U.S. Treaty which gave rise to the underlying dispute as an example of such a provision where the United Kingdom was the loser. While accepting that this may not be the case under Community law, he held that judged by the standards of U.K. law, these arguments could not be faulted. Although the Community question was simply referred to the European Court of Justice, it was implicit that there were differences between non-discrimination under the applicable treaty and under Community law.

The ECJ did not consider the U.S. Treaty provisions, but concluded that U.K. domestic law in section 825 of the Taxes Act 1988 was discriminatory and contrary to Article 43 (ex 52) of the EC Treaty.

---

[39] France, Ireland, Italy, the Netherlands and Sweden.
[40] Austria, France, Finland, Germany, Greece, Luxembourg, Portugal, Spain and Sweden.
[41] See above, n. 4.
[42] Case C-330/91 [1993] S.T.C. 605.

Recent treaties with Member States

2-33   A Fifth Protocol to the 1969 Finnish Treaty signed in 1996, and a 1996 Protocol amending the Danish Treaty were, apart from very minor protocols signed with Austria and Spain, the first double taxation agreements which the United Kingdom concluded with another EU Member State that were negotiated against the background of decisions of the ECJ relating to discrimination in taxation which reveal any emerging approach taken to Community tax issues in treaty negotiations.

Non-discrimination

2-34   Article 26[43] of the Finnish Treaty is deleted by the 1996 Protocol. This is explained on the basis that personal allowances, reliefs and reductions of tax for residents of contracting states are available under Article 27(1) and under domestic law. The extension of such rights to residents of Member States is now clearly required by Community law. This might suggest that bilateral measures are redundant in some areas covered by Community law. The equivalent article in the Danish Treaty was left unaltered.

Interest and royalties

2-35   The look-through provisions introduced into the 1991 Protocol to the Danish Treaty relating to interest and royalties have been deleted. The effect of the look-through rules was to permit companies to claim treaty benefits only if they were listed on a stock exchange subject to certain criteria or controlled by residents of the contracting state in which the claimant was resident. These rules have been replaced by the standard anti-avoidance provision as set out above in relation to dividends.[44] The look-through rules were almost certainly contrary to Community law.

Pensions and similar payments

2-36   Significant changes have been made in relation to the taxation of pensions in the Danish Treaty. Although generally pensions, annuities and similar remuneration are only taxable in the hands of a resident of a contracting state where an individual moves from one contracting state to another, the first retains the right to tax that income. Pensions from government service and those paid under social security legislation continue to be taxable in the country of source.

These amended rules appear to be consistent with the decision of the ECJ in *Wielockx v. Inspecteur der Directe Belastingen.*[45] In that case, the ECJ held that a country may waive the fiscal cohesion of its tax system by treaty. The result of such a waiver is that a resident might obtain a tax deduction for pension contributions in one contracting state but the Member State would not be entitled to tax the pension income once the individual had ceased to be resident there.

2-37   The rules relating to the deductibility of contributions to pension

---

[43] "Non-discrimination".
[44] See below, Chapter 6.
[45] Case C-80/94 [1995] S.T.C. 876, ECJ.

schemes have also been amended. First, the references to the nationality of the contributor have been deleted. These again were susceptible to attack under European law on the basis that they may be discriminatory. In *Bachmann v. Belgium*,[46] the non-deductibility of pension payments to an insurer established in a Member State other than that where the contributor was resident was viewed as discriminatory.

The previous rules referred to nationals not resident in a contracting state. The new provisions allow individuals resident in a contracting state to make a contribution to a pension scheme established in the other contracting state. This again may avoid difficulties under European law. The conditions in which this can take place are, however, carefully prescribed. The conditions do not appear to raise European issues

The Protocol to the Finnish Treaty takes a much simpler approach. Pensions and annuities and social welfare payments are only to be taxed in the country of source. In European law terms the source states have therefore not waived the cohesion of their tax systems in this respect, although the residence states appear to have done so. The latter waiver has not come before the European Court of Justice.

Irish financial institutions

2-38 Generally, instances of discrimination are raised by taxpayers. An interesting example of the elimination of potential difficulties in this regard appeared in the context of interest payments made to Irish financial institutions.

The Inland Revenue *Double Taxation Relief Manual* referred to a practice to allow U.K. residents to pay interest gross to financial institutions in the Irish Republic without the institutions concerned making a claim pursuant to the Irish Treaty. This practice was discontinued from May 1, 1997.

An announcement in the *Tax Bulletin* indicated that interest must be deducted and accounted for under Taxes Act 1988, section 349(2), unless FICO International (now the Centre for Non-Residents) has given clearance pursuant to a treaty claim.

Transitional provisions were made for existing loans. The effect of this is to place Irish resident institutions in the same position as residents of other treaty countries. No explanation for this was given, but it must be expected that the Inland Revenue feared that by allowing this practice to continue, it would be viewed as discriminatory by institutions in other EU Member States, who might then seek to attack the U.K. system for administering treaty relief claims on that basis.

The current U.K. treaty negotiation programme includes renegotiation of important treaties with other Member States including Ireland, Germany and the Netherlands. It remains to be seen how far these principles appear in any revised treaties.

TREATIES WITH THIRD COUNTRIES

2-39 The position in relation to treaties between a Member State and a non EU country is more complex. Article 307 (ex 234) of the EC Treaty

---

[46] Case C-204/90 [1994] S.T.C. 855, ECJ.

provides that rights and obligations arising from agreements between Member States and third countries concluded before entry into force of the EC Treaty are not affected by the provisions of that Treaty. In the context of the United Kingdom, Article 5 of the 1972 Act of Accession[47] provides that Article 307 (ex 234) of the EC Treaty is to apply to new members (including the United Kingdom) to agreements or conventions concluded before accession. It has no application therefore to U.K. treaties concluded from accession on January 1, 1973. In *EC Commission v. Italy*,[48] the ECJ held that Article 307 (ex 234) is limited to guaranteeing rights of third countries arising out of pre-existing agreements. There are currently only 26 such treaties with countries which are not presently European Union members. The vast majority of these are with Commonwealth countries following the old colonial style.

In *R. v. Secretary of State for Transport, ex parte Factortame Ltd*,[49] Advocate General Mischo noted that as long as the rights of non member countries are not involved, a Member State cannot rely on the provisions of a pre-existing treaty with third states in relation to intra-Community matters.[50]

2-40   Thus, a discriminatory provision imposed by the third country in a treaty subject to Article 307 (ex 234) may not be liable to attack. However, Article 307 (ex 234) does require Member States to take all appropriate steps to remedy the inconsistency with Community law. This imposes a higher obligation than the duty of Member States to "so far as necessary, enter into negotiations . . . with a view to the abolition of double taxation" imposed in respect of intra-Community treaties. The United Kingdom has been subject to these rules for some 23 years and if there are incompatibilities with Community law in those old treaties, it is unlikely that the United Kingdom has discharged its obligation to take all appropriate steps as this would of necessity involve seeking renegotiation of the treaty in question.

Treaties entered into since accession will not benefit from the protection of Article 307 (ex 234). Therefore, even if the limitation provisions are solely for the benefit of a non EU member state, they fall to be tested in the same way as treaties between Member States.

2-41   Non EU nationals or residents will not be in a position to claim the benefits of Community law. Thus, third country nationals are unlikely to be able to attack limitation of benefits provisions. In *R. v. IRC, ex parte Commerzbank AG*,[51] the United Kingdom argued that the refusal to make the repayment supplement to a non-resident under the Taxes Act 1988, section 825 as it then stood was justified in part by the existence of the U.S. Treaty. The United Kingdom argued, *inter alia*, that the Treaty removed the possibility of discrimination against non-resident companies since they were exempt from the tax which only resident companies would pay. It was there-

---

[47] [1972] OJ Spec. ed., March 27, p.14.
[48] Case 10/61 [1962] E.C.R. 1.
[49] Case C-221/89 [1991] 3 All E.R. 769.
[50] See Case 286/86 *Ministère Public v. Deserbais* [1988] E.C.R. 4907 at 4926.
[51] See above, n. 42.

fore by virtue of the application of the Treaty that there is no discrimination with respect to the conditions concerning the recovery of overpaid tax.

However, in upholding the taxpayers' case that it had been discriminated against, the ECJ did not deal with the U.S.–U.K. Treaty issues. The decision did, however, establish clearly that discrimination on the basis of fiscal residence within a national territory falls to be treated in the same manner as overt discrimination by reason of nationality.

The facts of the case are unusual because a national and resident of a Member State (Germany) was able to claim the benefit of the U.S.–U.K. Treaty. In most treaty claims involving third countries the person claiming treaty benefits from a Member State will be a non EU national who will not be likely to have standing to enjoy the protection of Community law.

2-42 The first case to reach the ECJ on tax treaties with non member states was *Saint-Gobain*.[52] It was argued by the German Government that treaties with non member countries were not within the sphere of Community competence. This, they argued, is a matter for Member States who are at liberty to conclude bilateral treaties with non member countries. On the basis that bilateral treaties are based on the principle of reciprocity, the balance inherent in such treaties would be disturbed if the benefit of their provisions were extended to companies established in Member States which were not parties to them. The court, however, said that it was settled that taxing powers must be exercised consistently with Community law. The balance and reciprocity of treaties concluded with non member states in question would not be jeopardised by a unilateral extension of the category of recipients in Germany of the tax advantages provided for by those treaties. It would not in any way affect the rights of non member countries which are parties to the treaties and would not impose any new obligations on them. The court noted, in any event, that German domestic law had been amended in this respect, extending the credits and exemptions to permanent establishments of non-resident companies. It was argued by the Swedish Government that in extreme situations, extending the scope of bilateral treaties could lead to no tax being produced at all. This was rejected in the particular case since it had not been argued that there was a risk of non-taxation in any country.

Community law could be invoked in relation to a treaty with a third country where a company resident in a Member State acquires or establishes a company resident in another Member State. If the second company's entitlement to benefits under a treaty with a third country is denied, the second company would appear to have standing to impugn the treaty provision.[53] The claim would be against the country of residence rather than that of the third country which denied the treaty benefit.

2-43 A further possibility might exist where a EU national resident in a treaty country outside the EU is denied benefits. Unless a right under the EC Treaty is exercised, the equal treatment guaranteed by the EC Treaty may not be invoked.[54]

---

[52] See above, n. 10.
[53] Case C-1/93 *Halliburton Services BV v. Staatssecretaris van Financiën* [1994] S.T.C. 655.
[54] Case C-221/89 *R. v. Secretary of State for Transport, ex parte Factortame Ltd* [1991] All E.R. 769, at para. 19.

CHAPTER 3

Interpretation of Tax Treaties

3-01 The interpretation of tax treaties is a subject that has received considerable attention over the years. The starting point of most of the analysis has been whether treaties are to be characterised as essentially contractual in nature or whether they are a form of legislative enactment. Should they, therefore, be subject to the ordinary rules of statutory interpretation or should they be interpreted by rules of international law applicable to the interpretation of international agreements? Are they to be construed in the same way as any other fiscal legislation or are there specific rules?

The difficulty in coming to any conclusion is that treaties are in effect both. They are agreements between sovereign states, but under U.K. constitutional rules, in order to give effect to them under domestic law, they also acquire the status of legislative instruments. This duality of status has led some to conclude that treaties must be interpreted at both levels and that different rules might apply at each level. Tax treaties are interpreted by domestic courts and not supra-national tribunals (with the exception of the European Court of Justice which has thus far refrained from interpretation).

3-02 How do the rules of treaty interpretation differ from rules for interpretation of domestic statutes? In *Steele v. EVC International NV (formerly European Vinyls Corp (Holdings) BV)*,[1] Morritt L.J. commented[2] that it is debatable whether the principles expressed by Mummery J. differ from those now applied in the construction of domestic legislation. Since the *EVC* case involved the construction of domestic law provisions incorporated by reference into the treaty, the comments of Morritt L.J. do not illuminate the issue further.

Some writers have been quick to spot inconsistencies in the approach of the courts. The reality is that there is a specific body of law relating to the interpretation of treaties which does overlap to a greater or lesser extent with the rules applicable to the interpretation of tax statutes. Where they overlap, few difficulties arise—where they do not, a distinct body of rules applies.

The courts have traditionally articulated the view that treaties are agreements and required to be interpreted in accordance with particular rules. For example, in *Belgium Government v. Postlethwaite*,[3] Lord Bridge of Horwich said[4] that:

> "A treaty is 'a contract between two sovereign states and has to be construed as such a contract. It would be a mistake to think that it had been

---

[1] [1996] S.T.C. 785, CA.
[2] At 797g.
[3] [1987] 2 All E.R. 985, HL.
[4] At 991.

construed as though it were a domestic statute' [*CR v. Governor of Ashford Remand Centre, ex parte Beese* [1973] 3 All E.R. 250 at 254 *per* Lord Widgery C.J.] . . . It must be remembered that the reciprocal rights and obligations which the high contracting parties confer and accept are intended to serve . . . [a certain purpose]. To apply to . . . treaties, the strict cannons appropriate to the construction of domestic legislation would often tend to defeat rather than serve this purpose".

3-03 Similarly, in the tax treaty context, Harman J. said in *Union Texas Petroleum Corp. v. Critchley (Inspector of Taxes)*:[5]

"I consider that I should bear in mind that this double tax agreement is an agreement. It is not a taxing statute, although it is an agreement about how taxes should be imposed. On that basis, in my judgment, this agreement should be construed as *ut resident magis valet quam pereat*, as should all agreements. The fact that the parties are 'high contracting parties', to use an old description, does not change the way in which the Courts should approach the construction of any agreement".

Notwithstanding these comments, Harman J., only one paragraph later, relied on comments of Lord Dunedin in *Whitney v. IRC*,[6] a case that involved construing domestic legislation, for the proposition that "a statute is designed to be workable, and the interpretation thereof by a court should be to secure that object".

How helpful these statements are and what their precise import may be is far from clear. The courts have for some time adopted a liberal approach in interpreting international treaties. In *Re Arton (No. 2)*,[7] Lord Russell C.J. said:

"In my judgement, these treaties ought to receive a liberal interpretation . . ., which means no more than they should receive their true construction according to their language, object and intent".

3-04 Subsequently, in construing the Carriage of Goods by Sea Act 1924 which adopted the Hague Rules, in *Stag Lion Limited v. Foscolo, Mango and Co.*,[8] Lord MacMillan said that:

"It is important to remember that the Act of 1924 was the outcome of an international conference and that the rules in the Schedule have an international currency. As these rules must come under the consideration of foreign courts, it is desirable in the interest of uniformity that their interpretation should not be rigidly controlled by domestic precedents of antecedent date, but rather that the language of the rules should be construed on broad principles of general acceptance".

---

[5] [1988] S.T.C. 691, at 707, Ch.D.
[6] (1925) 10 T.C. 88.
[7] [1896] 1 Q.B. 509, at 517.
[8] [1932] A.C. 328, HL.

This approach was adopted by Lord Atkin who said[9] that:

"For the purpose of uniformity, it is, therefore, important that the Courts should apply themselves to the consideration only of the words used without any predilection for the former (English) law, always preserving the right to say that words used in the English language which have already in the particular context received judicial interpretation, may be presumed to be used in the sense already judicially imputed to them".

This approach has been followed in a number of cases involving non tax treaties.[10] In *James Buchanan and Co. v. Babco Ltd*,[11] Viscount Dilhorne said:

"In construing the terms of a convention, it is proper and indeed right, in my opinion, to have regard to the fact that conventions are apt to be more loosely worded than acts of Parliament. To construe a convention as strictly as an act may indeed lead to a wrong interpretation being given to it".

VIENNA CONVENTION ON THE LAW OF TREATIES

3-05   Whatever the precise approaches to treaty interpretations have been in the past, they have become of less significance since the conclusion of the Vienna Convention on the Law of Treaties. In *Fothergill v. Monarch Airlines Limited*,[12] Lord Diplock said that:

"In exercising its interpretative function . . ., in the case of Acts of Parliament giving effect to international conventions concluded after the coming into force of the Vienna Convention on the law of treaties, I think an English court might well be under a constitutional obligation to [have recourse to 'travaux préparatoires']. By ratifying that Convention, Her Majesty's Government has undertaken an international obligation on behalf of the U.K. to interpret future treaties in this manner and since under our constitution, the function of interpreting the written law is an exercise of judicial power and rests with the Courts of Justice, that obligation assumed by the U.K. falls to be performed by those Courts".

Article 4 of the Vienna Convention provides that it applies only to treaties concluded by states after its entry into force with regard to such states. It entered into force in accordance with Article 84 on January 27, 1980 (the 30th day following the date of deposit of the 35th Instrument of Ratification or Accession).

---

[9] At 343.
[10] *Riverstone Meat Co. Pty. Ltd v. Lancashire Shipping Co. Ltd* [1961] A.C. 807, HL; *Fothergill v. Monarch Airlines Ltd* [1981] A.C. 251, HL.
[11] [1973] 3 All E.R. 1048, HL.
[12] See above, n. 10.

3-06   The United Kingdom has some 30 treaties still in force that were concluded prior to that date. Most of the important cases, in which the rules of interpretation of tax treaties have been considered in detail, involve treaties which were concluded prior to that date. Secondly, strictly speaking on its terms, the Vienna Convention only applies to treaties that are concluded with contracting states who are parties to the Vienna Convention. Is the application of the Vienna Convention consequently restricted to post-1980 treaties with Vienna Convention contracting states? Lord Diplock, in the *Fothergill* case, noted that what is said in Articles 31 and 32 of the Vienna Convention does no more than codify already existing public international law.[13] On this basis, it would appear that in the U.K. courts, there ought to be little distinction on the basis that the Convention is merely a codification of existing customary international law. Lord Fraser of Tullybelton had reservations, however, on the extent of the authoritative value of the Vienna Convention. On the other hand, has the codification of customary law, at least among the parties to the Vienna Convention, arrested the development of customary international law which changes to meet developments?[14] Different rules of interpretation may apply as a result depending upon the contracting state in question.

Commerzbank principles

3-07   The most comprehensive recent statement of the courts' approach was set out in *I.R.C.V. Commerzbank AG*[15] by Mummery J. The treaty in question was not governed by the Vienna Convention. Nonetheless, the principles articulated drew on both traditional sources and the Vienna Convention as follows:

> "(1) It is necessary to look first for a clear meaning of the words used in the relevant article of the Convention, bearing in mind that 'consideration of the purpose of an enactment is always a legitimate part of the process of interpretation': per Lord Wilberforce [in *Fothergill*] at p.272 and Lord Scarman at p.294. A strictly literal approach to interpretation is not appropriate in construing legislation which gives effect to or incorporates an international treaty: per Lord Fraser at p.285 and Lord Scarman at p.290. A literal interpretation may be obviously inconsistent with the purposes of the particular article or of the treaty as a whole. If the provisions of a particular article are ambiguous, it may be possible to resolve that ambiguity by giving a purposive construction to the convention looking at it as a whole by reference to its language as set out in the relevant U.K. legislative instrument: per Lord Diplock at p.279.
>
> (2) The process of interpretation should take account of the fact that: 'The language of an international convention has not been chosen

---

[13] At 282.

[14] *Trendtex Trading Corp Ltd v. Central Bank of Nigeria* [1977] 1 Q.B. 529, CA, in which Lord Denning discusses the developing nature of customary international law and concludes that courts give effect to these changes without legislation.

[15] [1990] S.T.C. 285 ChD at 297–298.

by an English parliamentary draftsman. It is neither couched in the conventional English legislative idiom nor designed to be construed exclusively by English judges. It is addressed to a much wider and more varied judicial audience than is an Act of Parliament which deals with purely domestic law. It should be interpreted, as Lord Wilberforce put it in James Buchanan & Co. Ltd. v. Babco Forwarding & Shipping (U.K.) Ltd. [1978] A.C. 141, 152, "unconstrained by technical rules of English law, or by English legal precedent, but on broad principles of general acceptation" ': per Lord Diplock [in *Fothergill*] at pp.281–282 and Lord Scarman at p.293.

(3) Among those principles is the general principle of international law, now embodied in art. 31(1) of the Vienna Convention on the Law of Treaties, that 'a treaty should be interpreted in good faith and in accordance with the ordinary meaning to be given to the terms of the treaty in their context and in the light of its object and purpose'. A similar principle is expressed in slightly different terms in MacNair on the 'Law of Treaties' (1961) at p.365, where it is stated that the task of applying or construing or interpreting a treaty is 'the duty of giving effect to the expressed intention of the parties, that is, their intention as expressed in the words used by them in the light of the surrounding circumstances'. It is also stated at p.366 of that work that references to the primary necessity of giving effect to 'the plain terms' of a treaty or construing words according to their 'general and ordinary meaning' or their 'natural signification' are to be a starting point or prima facie guide and, 'cannot be allowed to obstruct the essential quest in the application of treaties, namely the search for the real intention of the contracting parties in using the language employed by them.'

(4) If the adoption of this approach to the article leaves the meaning of the relevant provision unclear or ambiguous or leads to a result which is manifestly absurd or unreasonable recourse may be had to 'supplementary means of interpretation' including 'travaux préparatoires': per Lord Diplock [in *Fothergill*] at p.282 referring to art. 32 of the Vienna Convention, which came into force after the conclusion of this double taxation Convention, but codified an already existing principle of public international law. See also Lord Fraser at p.287 and Lord Scarman at p.294.

(5) Subsequent commentaries on a convention or treaty have persuasive value only, depending on the cogency of their reasoning. Similarly, decisions of foreign courts on the interpretation of a convention or treaty text depend for their authority on the reputation and status of the Court in question: per Lord Diplock [in *Fothergill*] at pp.283–284 and per Lord Scarman at p.295.

(6) Aids to the interpretation of a treaty such as 'travaux préparatoires', international case law and the writings of jurists are not a substitute for study of the terms of the convention. Their use is discretionary, not mandatory, depending, for example, on the relevance of such material and the weight to be attached to it: per Lord Scarman at p.294".

3-08 In *Memec plc v. IRC*,[16] Robert Walker J. commended the whole of the above passage for careful study. He summarised the *Commerzbank* principles as follows:

"(1) the approach should be purposive;
(2) it should be international, not exclusively English;
(3) it should have regard to art. 31(1) of the Vienna Convention; [page 601];
(4) recourse may be had to supplementary means of interpretation such as 'travaux préparatoires';
(5) subsequent commentaries and decisions of foreign courts have persuasive value only;
(6) recourse to 'travaux préparatoires', international case law and the writings of jurists is discretionary, not mandatory. The Court of Appeal has recognised the official commentaries on successive versions of the OECD Model Convention as supplementary means of interpretation: see *Sunlife Assurance Co of Canada v. Pearson* (HMIT) (1986) 59 TC 250 at pp.330–331; [1986] BTC 282 at p.296".

In the Court of Appeal, Peter Gibson L.J. noted agreement between the taxpayer and the Inland Revenue on the correctness of the approach articulated by Mummery J. in *IRC v. Commerzbank*. Lord Justice Gibson noted the comment of Mummery J. that "interpretation should take account of the fact that a convention is not designed to be construed exclusively by English judges but is addressed to a wider judicial audience". He added that "in the case of a double taxation agreement, the judicial audience is, in addition to the judges found in the constituent parts of the U.K., only the judges to be found in the Courts of the other contracting party. It is not to be assumed that the convention is addressed to a wider international audience than that".[17]

3-09 While this may be true in one technical sense, because almost all U.K. tax treaties are bilateral, it is not true in the context of treaties generally. All treaties are based on successive model treaties which have been developed at a multilateral level. The use of more or less standard provisions throughout the global treaty network is increasing. Reference is made in countries around the world to treaty interpretation by foreign courts. It would certainly not be true in relation to the EC Arbitration Convention and even considering the U.K. treaty network alone, identical provisions are found in many instances in bilateral treaties between the United Kingdom and other contracting states. Both the *Commerzbank* case (concerning the U.S. Treaty) and the *Memec* case (concerning the German Treaty) were in respect of treaties that were not governed by the Vienna Convention. Any failure to explore the detailed application of the Vienna Convention to these cases is therefore to be expected.

---

[16] [1996] S.T.C. 1336 at p. 1349.
[17] [1998] S.T.C. 754, CA at p. 776.

GENERAL RULE OF INTERPRETATION

3-10   Given the lack of judicial analysis based specifically on the principles of the Vienna Convention, the Convention is used in this work principally as an outline to examine the way in which U.K. courts have addressed the issues expressed in it.

The general principles are set out in Article 31 as follows:

"1.   A treaty shall be interpreted in good faith in accordance with the ordinary meaning to be given to terms of the treaty in their context and in the light of its object and purpose.

2.   The context for the purpose of the interpretation of a treaty shall comprise, in addition to the text, including its preamble and annexes:

a)   any agreement relating to the treaty which was made between all the parties in connexion with the conclusion of the treaty;

b)   any instrument which was made by one or more parties in connection with the conclusion of the treaty and accepted by the other parties as an instrument related to the treaty.

3.   There shall be taken into account, together with the context:

a)   any subsequent agreement between the parties regarding the interpretation of the treaty or the application of its provisions;

b)   any subsequent practice in the application of the treaty which establishes the agreement of the parties regarding its interpretation;

c)   any relevant rules of international law applicable in the relations between the parties.

4.   A special meaning shall be given to a term if it is established that the parties so intended".

The ordinary meaning of terms

3-11   As is the case with statutory interpretation, the ordinary meaning of words is the first limb of the principle. The courts have relied on the ordinary meaning of words, rather than any alleged purpose of a treaty article. In *IRC v. Commerzbank*,[18] Article XV of the old (1945) U.S. Tax Treaty provided:

"Dividends and interest paid by a [U.S. corporation] shall be exempt from tax by [the U.K.] except where the recipient is a citizen, resident or corporation of the [U.K.]. This exemption shall not apply if the corporation paying such dividend or interest is a resident of the [U.K.]".

---

[18] See above, n. 15.

The Inland Revenue argued that the Treaty did not confer benefits on anyone other than residents or citizens of the United States. The Treaty was lacking by more modern comparison, because it had no general reference to its personal scope. It was held that the natural and ordinary meaning of the words of Article 15 was clear. Interest paid by U.S. corporations was exempt from U.K. tax, except where the recipient was a U.K. citizen resident or corporation.

3-12   Similarly, in *Strathalmond v. IRC*,[19] the same wording was considered in relation to dividends. The court decided that it exempted from U.K. tax, U.S. dividends and interest paid to a U.S. citizen resident in the United Kingdom who was not within the definition of "resident of the U.K.". This was because U.S. citizens were excluded from that definition.

In *Padmore v. IRC*,[20] the wording of the treaty was central to the conclusion that a Jersey resident partnership with no permanent establishment in the United Kingdom is not subject to tax here. In the High Court, Peter Gibson J. rejected an argument from the Crown that the general scheme of the Jersey Treaty was relevant in determining the meaning of the "profits of a Jersey enterprise" under paragraph 3(2) of the Treaty. He said:

> "the proper starting point is the language of para. 3(2). That to my mind is unequivocal in its meaning. All the industrial or commercial profits of a Jersey enterprise are not to be subject to United Kingdom tax, and that on its face plainly means those profits whether earned in Jersey or in the United Kingdom or elsewhere . . .".

3-13   He rejected the idea that any wider considerations would compel a different conclusion. Again, in the Court of Appeal, Fox L.J. said that:

> "Article 3(2) is expressed in language of very considerable width. It relieves from United Kingdom taxation all the profits of a Jersey enterprise (subject to an exemption which is not relevant). That enterprise in the present case is a partnership. The partnership is not an entity distinct from the partners. The profits belong to them. As a matter of construction of this wide language, I see no words which exclude the individual partner's share of the profits from the exemption. The exemption is in general terms and I see no reason why the greater does not include the less".

Despite noting the anomaly between the treatment of partnerships, sole traders and shareholders resident in the United Kingdom, he said:[21] "I do not think these are sufficient to displace what seems to me the natural meaning of Article 3(2)".

In *Sun Life Assurance Company of Canada v. Pearson*,[22] the intention of the drafters of the treaty was central. Vinelott J. said:

> "the problem is to identify those provisions of the law of the United Kingdom which the framers of the treaty intended to describe in Article

---

[19] [1972] 48 T.C. 537.
[20] [1989] S.T.C. 493, CA.
[21] At 379.
[22] [1984] S.T.C. 461.

6(7). Once it is accepted that section 430 (as amended by the 1956 and 1965 Acts) was a provision, and indeed the only provision which the framers of the treaty had in mind, the question whether or not it was accurately described as relating to the liability of an overseas life assurance company to tax in respect of income from investment of its life assurance fund becomes a barren one".

3-14 The second question was whether legislative amendments were provisions "relating to . . . liability to tax" within Article 6(7) of the Canadian Treaty, and if they were, whether the changes were or were not minor modifications not affecting the general character of the provisions in force on December 6, 1995, which the Treaty preserved. The Crown sought to argue that the domestic law provisions in question relating to the right of recovery of income tax deducted at source from a U.K. investment income were not provisions relating to the liability to tax of an overseas insurance company within Article 6(7). The court regarded that view as resting on too narrow a construction of the words "relating to the liability to tax". In the light of Article 6(2), Vinelott J. concluded that those words referred clearly to the overall liability of a Canadian enterprise carrying on business through a permanent establishment in the United Kingdom to U.K. tax including the tax on income from investments in the United Kingdom made for the purpose of the business carried on by that permanent establishment.

Similarly, the Court of Appeal in that case[23] rejected the argument that "profits" in Article 7 of the 1980 Canadian Treaty had a different meaning from "commercial and industrial profits" found in the earlier Canadian Treaty and in the Australian Treaty. It focused on the ordinary meaning of the words set in the context of the Treaty as a whole and supported by the OECD Model Commentary, an analysis of the changes in comparison to the previous Treaty and similar provisions in the Australian Treaty. This approach seems to suggest that more complex tools of interpretation are required for the most difficult questions, rather than suggesting that the ordinary meaning of words is inappropriate as the primary tool of interpretation.

3-15 A further case which considered Article 15 of the old U.S. Treaty and relied on other methods of interpretation was *IRC v. Exxon Corp.*[24] That case involved a dividend paid by a U.S. corporation resident in the United Kingdom to its parent company, a U.S. corporation resident for tax purposes in the United States. The question was whether the expression "a resident of the other contracting party" in the second sentence of Article 15 should be interpreted in accordance with the residence definitions set out in Article 2(1)(g) "resident of the United Kingdom" and (1)(h) "resident of the United States" or whether it should be treated as a "term not otherwise defined" for the purposes of Article 2(3) of the Treaty. The argument for the taxpayer that the plain meaning of the words was to be adopted, said Goulding J., was "to simply accept the consequence that the second sentence of the Article has either probably or certainly failed to achieve whatever

---

[23] [1986] S.T.C. 335.
[24] [1982] S.T.C. 356, Ch.D.

purpose its framers intended". The Crown argued that the broad policy behind the second sentence was clear, namely to deny exemption for dividends or interest paid to a U.S. company by a subsidiary trading and managed in the United Kingdom and merely incorporated in the United States. The learned judge agreed that the intended purpose of the second sentence of Article 15 could be discerned and that the plain meaning of the words used meant that the expression "resident of the other contracting party" does not import residence definitions. He said:

> "in coming to this conclusion, I bear in mind that the words of the Convention are not those of a regular Parliamentary draftsmen, but a text agreed upon by negotiation between two contracting governments. Although I am thus constrained to do violence to the language of the Convention, I see no reason to inflict a deeper wound than necessary. In other words, I prefer to depart from the plain meaning of the language only in the second sentence of Article 15 and I accept the consequence (strange though it is) that similar words mean different things in the two sentences".

3-16   The plain meaning of words was applied in *Steele v. EVC International NV*[25] in interpreting Article 10 of the Netherlands Treaty in relation to entitlement to repayment of the dividend tax credit. The repayment of the credit was denied where the company paying the dividend is controlled by a person or two or more associated or connected persons who would not have been entitled to the credit directly. The question of association or control was applicable if "under the laws of the United Kingdom relating to the taxes covered by this Convention, he or they could be treated as having control of it for any purpose" (Article 10(3)(d)(ii)). It was argued by the taxpayer that the mischief at which the article was aimed was treaty shopping and that this purpose is sufficiently achieved if the rules relating to connection only apply to persons who are genuinely connected, that is otherwise than through the mere coincidence of their exercising joint control of the company in question. Such an argument would require the exclusion of Taxes Act 1988, section 839(7) which connects together persons acting together to secure or exercise control of a company.

Lightman J. in the High Court dismissed this argument on the basis that the words in the treaty "for any purpose" clearly embrace connection under section 839(7). He said: "whether this is just may be a matter on which strong opinions may be held, but that is not enough to prevent the language used being given its full effect".[26]

3-17   On appeal, after summarising the *Commerzbank* principles of interpretation, Morritt L.J. said[27]: "the use of the word 'could' in conjunction with 'any purpose' seems to me to exclude any requirement that there is some substantive issue . . . other than the availability of the tax credit for the purpose of which the connection arises or is relevant". The wording was

---

[25] [1996] S.T.C. 785, CA.
[26] [1995] S.T.C. 31, at 51b, Ch.D.
[27] [1996] S.T.C. 785 at 797, CA.

to the effect that the persons in question could be treated as connected for any purpose, not for all purposes. He did not think that these conclusions arose from an unduly literal construction of the Convention. Although accepting the provision as an anti-avoidance measure designed to prevent the artificial creation of entitlement to tax credits, he said that it was fanciful to suppose that the draftsmen of the Convention intended to restrict the application of those provisions in cases in which they already applied or to limit those which did apply. Thus, the purposive construction which contended that the clause referred to a restricted definition of control was rejected.

Context

3-18   Article 31 of the Vienna Convention requires the ordinary meaning of terms to be given in their context. Context is explained, but not exhaustively defined in Article 31(2). The context for the purpose of interpretation of a treaty comprises primarily the text including its preamble and annexes.

It has become quite common, particularly in treaties with non OECD countries, to have exchanges of notes signed concurrently with the conclusion of treaties. These are typically written in order to modify, explain or clarify particular issues in a treaty. As already noted, such exchange of notes either constitute treaties themselves as a matter of international law, or form part of the formal treaty by reference and are included in the statutory instruments bringing the formal treaty into effect. The real implication of the introductory wording of Article 31(2) is that the context of a treaty is all of its constituent parts, rather than individual elements.

In accordance with the 1963 and the 1977 OECD Models, U.K. treaties invariably have the following title:

> "Agreement between the Government of the United Kingdom of Great Britain and Northern Ireland and the Government of [the Sultanate of Oman] for the avoidance of double taxation and the prevention of fiscal evasion with respect to taxes on income and capital gains".

3-19   A typical preamble reads:

> "The Government of the United Kingdom of Great Britain and Northern Ireland and the Government of the Sultanate of Oman
>   Desiring to conclude an agreement for the avoidance of double taxation and the prevention of fiscal evasion with respect to taxes on income and gains, have agreed as follows:".

This formulation is of longstanding use and shows up in every tax treaty. In *Imperial Chemical Industries Limited v. Caro*,[28] it was observed by Lord Evershed M.R.[29] that "it is proper to notice the avowed object" of the treaty as stated in its heading. In that case, it was regarded as important to demonstrate that the Treaty was intended to cover not only income tax, but other

---

[28] (1960) 39 T.C. 374.
[29] At 379.

taxes such as the national defence contribution subsequently known as profits tax. Donovan L.J. also said[30]:

> "does the direction in Article XII of the Agreement on its true construction allow credit to be given more than once? I think that question can be answered either way without doing violence to the express language of the agreement; and one must seek to answer, I think, from the general tenor of that document and its subject matter. The subject matter includes among other things profits tax and since it is levied upon the actual income of a period and not the conventional basis of the income of some other period, there could never be any question of allowing credit for Australian tax twice against profits tax".

3-20   In *Avery Jones (Rowley's Administrator) v. CIR*,[31] a claim was made on behalf of a deceased estate for exemption from U.K. income tax under Article 15 of the old U.S. Treaty. Dividends and interest paid by a corporation of one contracting state were exempt from tax by the other "except where the recipient is a citizen resident or corporation of that other contracting party". Although she was U.K. resident for domestic purposes, as a U.S. citizen she was not resident in the United Kingdom within Article 11 of the Treaty as a result of the *Strathalmond* decision.[32] The taxpayer argued that the expression "citizen" in Article 15 referred only to a citizen of the United States and not to a British subject, as the expression was not reciprocal so far as it concerned citizens, because the term "citizen" of the United Kingdom was unrecognised in U.K. law. This view was upheld by the High Court. The Special Commissioner rejected the idea that no meaning should be given to the phrase. Notwithstanding difficulties as a matter of construction, it seemed to them untenable to adopt such a view. They, therefore, accepted the arguments put forward by the Crown. In their view, it did less violence to the language of the agreement to hold that the deceased as a British subject and citizen of the United Kingdom and colonies was a citizen of the United Kingdom, than to hold that she was not. The court noted that if any sensible meaning is to be attributed to the term, it must include the taxpayer or else "the Court would have to decide that the provision was completely meaningless, a course which is never taken on the construction of any document, let alone a solemnly negotiated international treaty, save where there can be no other possible course available". The court observed that Article 15 was not the only place in which reference to citizenship occurs. It also occurred in Article 20A(1) and occurs there in a context which could not only be restricted to U.S. citizens. Similarly, protection given to teachers under Article XVIII applied on the basis of citizenship. The court rejected the idea that the draftsmen of the Treaty intended Article 15 to apply equally on the basis of reciprocity, as well as the notion that the citizenship concept only applied in relation to U.S. citizens.

3-21   Another case in which "paid" was held to mean just that and not

---

[30] At 390.
[31] [1976] S.T.C. 290.
[32] See above, n. 19.

to mean "payable" was *Union Texas Petroleum Corp. v. Critchley*.[33] Again, this conclusion was reached on the basis of the context in which it was used. The issue was whether a deduction from the amount of the dividend and associated tax credit was to be calculated before or after the deduction itself. In a related provision, reference was made to the dividend and tax credit "paid" without reduction for the deduction. The inference from this was that it was after deduction in all other cases, including the provision being interpreted. As a result, words were in effect ignored in order to prevent the provision having no effect. Context in this sense was the dividend article of the U.S. Treaty and not the treaty as a whole. Since the article was substituted by protocol, conceivably the "treaty" in this context was the protocol rather than the treaty as a whole amended by the protocol. This distinction was not made by the court, however.

In the Court of Appeal, the question was whether the absence of a definition of dividends in Article 18 (the tax credit) signifies that it is to be construed in that article as having the same meaning as in Article 6(4), or as having a meaning indicated by Article 2(3) which allows U.K. domestic law to determine its meaning. The overall context of the term "dividends" was taken into account noting that the draftsmen of the Treaty was careful to say whether a term defined only in a distributive article is to have the same meaning in another but not every article. In some articles of the Treaty, Articles 3(5) and 23(3)(b), references to dividends are construed as having the Article 4(4) meaning, but that was because both related to tax withheld on a dividend and so implicitly cross-referred to Article 4.

3-22 In *IRC v. Vas*,[34] the court considered the context of provisions relating to exemption for teachers, including the position of Article 21[35] and its relationship with other articles in the Hungarian Treaty, to consider the effect of the exemption not applying. Vinelott J. urged that caution should be exercised in searching for purpose from the context of a treaty, because treaties represent negotiated compromise for which policy reasons may not be discernable from the terms of the treaty other than where the OECD Model is followed.

In *Memec plc v. IRC*,[36] Peter Gibson L.J. analysed the whole scheme of the German Treaty and the relationship between the definition, the distributive articles and the rules for elimination of double taxation in considering whether a distribution from a German silent partnership which was treated as a dividend in Article VI(4) for withholding tax purposes was also a dividend for the purposes of qualification for underlying credit paid under Article XVIII, the tax credit provision.

3-23 Article 31(2) of the Vienna Convention includes, in the context of a treaty, any agreement relating to it which was made between the parties in connection with the conclusion of the treaty and any instrument made by a party in connection with the conclusion of the treaty and accepted by the

---

[33] See above, n. 5.
[34] [1990] S.T.C. 137, Ch.D.
[35] "Visiting teachers".
[36] [1998] S.T.C. 754, CA.

other parties as an instrument relating to the treaty. The extent of this is therefore precisely prescribed. First, both in relation to agreements and instruments, they must be made in connection with the conclusion of the treaty. Any agreement must be between the parties to the treaty and in relation to an instrument made by less than all parties to the treaty, it must be accepted by the others as an instrument related to the treaty.

3-24   In U.K. treaty practice, there are almost no examples of agreements relating to individual treaties other than notes exchanged. It has been suggested that the Commentary to the OECD Model may be viewed as such an agreement. In *IRC v. Commerzbank*,[37] it was said that subsequent commentaries on a treaty have persuasive value only. The Crown, in that case, sought support from a joint statement issued by the United States Internal Revenue Service and the Board of Inland Revenue in 1977.[38] The statement was made pursuant to Article 20A of the U.S. Treaty which authorises competent authorities to agree on the interpretation of provisions. Mummery J. regarded this statement as having no authority in English courts. It expresses the official view of the revenue authorities of the two countries. That view, he said,[39] may be right or wrong. Although Article 20A authorises the competent authorities to communicate with each other directly to implement the provisions of the Convention and to "assure its consistent interpretation and application", it does not confer any binding or authoritative effect on the views or statements of the competent authorities in the English courts. The Treaty in question, however, is not one governed by the Vienna Convention. This may be an instance where the rules might differ between a treaty where the Vienna Convention applies and where it does not. Article 31(3)(a) and (b) of the Vienna Convention requires that such mutual agreement, although not binding, must be taken into account when interpreting the treaty. There is no indication as to customary international law on this point.

3-25   In *Sun Life Assurance Company of Canada v. Pearson*,[40] when the use of the Commentary was first considered, it was noted that the articles in question were drawn in identical terms to the provisions of the 1977 OECD Model Treaty and that both the United Kingdom and Canada were member countries—therefore the point was not decided. In commenting on the allocation of income, the judge noted that any doubts he had about the position would be dispelled by the Commentary. This was despite the fact that the 1977 Commentary was not a commentary on the 1967 Canadian Treaty, which had a different origin. He noted, however, that "the views of the experts who sat on the Fiscal Committee on the Regulation of Double Taxation are entitled to very great weight". Indeed, the Commentary is referred to for support in relation to several aspects of the decision. The court also referred to the background of the 1967 Treaty, both in relation to the domestic law context and the OECD recommendation of July 30, 1963 adopting the 1963 draft Convention. The Court of Appeal[41] did not reiterate

---

[37] [1990] S.T.C. 285, Ch.D.
[38] Published in [1977] B.T.R. 494.
[39] [1990] S.T.C. 285 at 302c.
[40] [1984] S.T.C. 461, Ch.D.
[41] [1986] S.T.C. 335, CA.

the point that the Commentary related to the 1977 Model, but simply noted that it is common ground that the court is entitled to consider the Commentary on the authority of *Fothergill v. Monarch Airlines Ltd*.[42] In summarising the *Commerzbank* principles of interpretation in *Memec*, the judge referred to the Commentary as a supplementary means of interpretation.

Article 31(3) of the Vienna Convention seems to distinguish between those agreements and instruments which form part of the context under Article 31(2), and those which are to be taken into account together with the context. This does seem to suggest that even if it is correct that their consideration is mandatory, it ought to have a value which is lower than those agreements and instruments which form part of the context.

Object and Purpose

3-26   Article 31 of the Vienna Convention requires a treaty to be interpreted in the light of its object and purpose. In *Commerzbank*, for example, it was said that "a literal interpretation may be obviously inconsistent with the purposes of the particular article or of the treaty as a whole".[43] The earliest recognition of the object of the treaty was found in *Ostime v. Australian Mutual Provident Society*.[44] Upjohn J. said that[45]:

> "my approach to the relief order (which enacts the Australian Treaty) is that its whole object is to relieve from double taxation, and that therefore one is looking to those profits or surpluses which by the law of Australia or the U.K., as the case may be, are made the subject of taxation".

Full recognition of the object and purpose interpretation, and of Article 31(1), is found in *IRC v. Commerzbank*.[46] In that case, the court also referred[47] to the customary international rule as expressed by McNair in the *Law of Treaties*[48] where it was stated that the task of construing or interpreting a treaty is "the duty of giving effect to the expressed intention of the parties". In this respect, McNair says that the plain terms of a treaty or construing words according to their general and ordinary meaning or their natural signification are to be a starting point or a prima facie guide and "cannot be allowed to obstruct the essential quest in the application of treaties, namely the search for the real intention of the contracting parties using the language employed by them".

Mummery J. said[49]: "I can find no sufficient indication of the purposes of the Convention or in its surrounding circumstances, or in the provisions in articles other than Article 15 to qualify the clear words". The House of

---

[42] See above, n. 10 at 280.
[43] See above, n. 15, *per* Mummery J. at 297j.
[44] (1957) 38 T.C. 492.
[45] At 505.
[46] See above, n. 37.
[47] At 301.
[48] 1961 edition
[49] At 304d

Lords, in *Ostime v. Australian Mutual Provident Society*,[50] did not rely on this approach in coming to the same conclusion. In *ICI v. Caro*,[51] it was argued that the manifest intention of the two governments was to prevent double taxation. In that case, the Court of Appeal recognised that its conclusions on the meaning of the treaty gave rise to double taxation, but said that the only safe guide is to give effect to the plain meaning of the words.

3-27   A similar approach may be seen in relation to the *EVC* case. In that case, the court refused to accept that the purpose of the limitation of benefits was to prevent tax avoidance and that its application should be therefore restricted to circumstances which did entail such avoidance. Again, it preferred to rely on the plain meaning of words. In *Memec plc v. IRC*,[52] the Chancery Division held that a purposive approach should be adopted so as to construe the Treaty in as symmetrical a way as possible, unless the language is clearly against such a construction. Although the principle was not rejected by the Court of Appeal, it concluded that the symmetry which the judge sought required treating a special definition as a general definition and this did not do justice to the "coherent and careful drafting of the convention and the protocol". The symmetry contended for was not intended by the drafters of the Treaty.

The Special Commissioners decision in *A Sportsman v. IRC*[53] may be viewed as a purposive interpretation using the preamble as a statement of purpose in this regard. In that case, reference was made to the preamble in the French Treaty and the fact that it indicates a dual purpose of avoiding double taxation and preventing fiscal evasion with respect to taxes on income. It was noted that the statutory instrument bringing the Treaty into effect itself was designed to afford relief from double taxation. The issue arose as to whether credit should be given for tax payable under the treaty, as well as tax actually paid. The Special Commissioners ruled that the taxpayer had confused literal and ordinary meaning. They said[54]:

> "Double taxation conventions are not to create or allocate taxing rights, but to prevent double taxation. Taxing rights already exist. By entering into a double taxation convention, each government relinquishes all or part of its taxing rights according to domestic law in certain circumstances; one country gives up its claim in recognition of the fact that the other is going to take it. However, if there is no actual taxation by one country, there is nothing in the object and purpose of the convention to prevent taxation by the other".

3-28   The Special Commissioners noted that the second stated object of the Treaty is prevention of fiscal evasion. They ruled that if Article 24(a) (foreign tax credit) were to be construed in the manner in which the taxpayer contended, that object could be defeated. Sovereign states do not, as a matter of principle, enforce one another's revenue laws. To give credit in country A

---

[50] See above, n. 44.
[51] See above, n. 28.
[52] See above, n. 36.
[53] [1998] S.T.C. 289.
[54] At 295.

for tax payable but not paid in country B would encourage evasion of tax in country B by a taxpayer incurring a tax liability there and then returning to country A without meeting that liability. Since the taxpayer's interpretation makes evasion easy, thereby defeating a stated purpose of the Treaty, that tends to suggest that the interpretation should be rejected. While this line of reasoning is clearly flawed, it illustrates an attempt at a purposive approach to treaty interpretation.

SUPPLEMENTARY MEANS OF INTERPRETATION

3-29   Article 32 of the Vienna Convention provides for supplementary means of interpretation. It reads:

> "Recourse may be had to supplementary means of interpretation including the preparatory work of the treaty and the circumstances of its conclusion, in order to confirm the meaning resulting from the application of Article 31, or to determine the meaning when the interpretation according to Article 31:
>
> a)   leaves the meaning ambiguous or obscure; or
> b)   leads to a result which is manifestly absurd or unreasonable".

No explanation is provided as to what constitute supplementary means other than to say that it includes the preparatory work of the treaty and the circumstances of its conclusion. Supplementary means are clearly viewed as an aid to interpretation conducted in accordance with Article 31 of the Vienna Convention. The purpose of this recourse is either to confirm the meaning resulting from the application of Article 31, or to determine the meaning when Article 31 interpretation leads to ambiguous or obscure meaning or leads to a result which is manifestly absurd or unreasonable.

3-30   These rules are regarded as codifying customary international law. *Fothergill* preceded the decision in *Peper v. Hart*,[55] and the House of Lords was therefore keen to distinguish *Hansard*, which at that time could not be resorted to for the purpose of ascertaining what ambiguities or obscure provisions mean, from "travaux préparatoires". The distinction was explained by Lord Diplock in *Fothergill* thus[56]:

> "It is however otherwise with that growing body of written law in force in the United Kingdom which, although it owes its enforceability within the United Kingdom to its embodiment in or authorisation by an Act of Parliament, nevertheless owes its origin and its actual wording to some prior law-preparing process in which Parliament has not participated, such as the negotiation and preparation of a multilateral international convention . . . which Her Majesty's Government wants to ratify on behalf of the United Kingdom but can only do when the provisions of the convention have been incorporated into our domestic law.

---

[55] [1992] S.T.C. 898, HL.
[56] See above, n. 10, at 281.

Accordingly, in exercising its interpretive function of ascertaining what the delegates to an international conference agreed upon by their majority vote in favour of the text of an international convention, where that text itself is ambiguous or obscure, an English Court should have regard to any material which those delegates themselves had thought would be available to clear up any possible ambiguities or obscurities".

The conditions for the use of "travaux préparatoires" were set out by Lord Wilberforce in *Gatoil International Inc. v. Arkwright-Boston Manufacturers Mutual Insurance Company*[57]:

"First that the material is public and accessible; secondly, that it clearly and undisputedly points to a definite legislative intention".

3-31 In relation to preparatory works, the Special Commissioner said in *Commerzbank*,[58] following Lord Scarman in *Fothergill*, that "preparatory work are only aids in the interpretation of the relevant words of the treaty. If they appear to disclose an intention which cannot even with the best will in the world be read into the words of the treaty, then they are obviously not aids at all".

In the United Kingdom, the confidential nature of tax treaty negotiations means that in most cases, detailed preparatory work in the form of notes of meetings, exchanges of correspondence and the like are unavailable. The most important publicly available document is the Commentary to the OECD Model, which does form the basis of the U.K. negotiating position. Clearly, the text of the Commentaries prior to a treaty in question may only qualify as preparatory work. The Commentary does pose difficulties where the clause is not in the form of the OECD Model and where the treaty is not with an OECD member state. The OECD has started to collect comments from non member states on the Commentary and therefore this may be of some persuasive value in the context of treaties with states that participate in this process. Other multilateral statements such as the United Nations Model Double Taxation Convention between developed and developing countries, and the United Nations Manual for the Negotiation of Bilateral Tax Treaties between developed and developing countries may be helpful in some cases. The same might be said of those treaty partners that have their own model treaties, subject to the difficulty that unilateral statements of one of the contracting states will not normally be regarded as qualifying under this heading of the Vienna Convention.

OECD Model Commentary

3-32 The Commentary to the OECD Model has found a favoured position as an aid to interpretation by the courts. It has been recognised as "travaux préparatoires", but the courts have not refined the tests as to when it is required to be used and when it may be used, and its position in the

---

[57] [1985] A.C. 225 at 263.
[58] At 294h.

hierarchy of interpretive rules. Thus far, little attention has been paid to distinctions between treaties made after the various Model Conventions and their Commentaries have been published.

The effect of amendments to the Commentary is likely to become of increasing importance. The Commentary to the 1977 OECD Model Treaty was radically updated in 1992. From that time, however, it has been published in looseleaf form and regularly updated. As a result, only the version of the Commentary published at the time the Model Treaty was negotiated will normally qualify as "travaux préparatoires". Thus, under the Vienna Convention principles, is the Commentary an "agreement" made by the parties relating to a treaty between OECD members? If that is the case, it is required to be included in the context of a treaty. Subsequent agreements or practices between the parties are also required to be taken into account under Article 31(3), although they do not form part of the context. This might apply to later versions of the Commentary.

3-33   An important new development in this area has taken place in relation to the application of tax treaties to electronic commerce. The revision to the Commentary on Article 12[59] in 2000 purports by means of a change of interpretation to require contracting states to construe the meaning of royalties to exclude certain digitised products such as computer software in certain circumstances and to tax amounts received in connection therewith as business profits. Although it is clear that the effect of treaties can be changed as a matter of domestic law by legislation, it remains to be seen whether the courts will be prepared to give effect to this rather dubious attempt to change the provisions of tax treaties by interpretation through the Commentary without actually amending their terms.

There are no cases involving the Commentary to the United Nations Model Convention. This Commentary has not been updated and as a result some of the more difficult temporal issues will not arise. In the context of non OECD treaties, it is also arguable that given the influence of the OECD Model, the Commentary may also be useful in the context of treaties with non OECD member states.

Other treaties

3-34   Recourse has been made in several cases to parallel treaties. For example, in *Sun Life Assurance Company of Canada v. Pearson*,[60] the taxpayer placed reliance on the decision of the Court in *Ostime v. Australian Mutual Provident Society*,[61] which considered identical provisions in Article 3 of the Australian Treaty as supporting the interpretation of the same provisions in the Canadian Treaty. In *Padmore v. IRC*,[62] the Court compared the Swiss Treaty with the Jersey Treaty in order to conclude that additional wording appearing in the Swiss Treaty would have to have been included in the Jersey Treaty in order to reach the interpretation contended for by the Crown. Similarly, the fact that partnerships were referred to specifically in

[59] "Royalties".
[60] See above, n. 40.
[61] See above, n. 44.
[62] See above, n. 20.

the U.S. Treaty but not the Jersey Treaty was argued to mean that the Jersey Treaty did not deal with partnerships. The court noted that the provisions of other treaties are not of assistance in construing a particular treaty. Other countries may have negotiated different bargains. In *IRC v. Vas*,[63] the difference between the U.S. and Hungarian treaties dealing with visiting teachers was addressed by reference to the law in Hungary and a comparison between the expression in the earlier U.S. Treaty and the Hungarian Treaty in order to consider the provision in question.

Treaties between third countries may also be referred to on occasion. The Court of Appeal, however, in *Memec*[64] has questioned how much assistance can be obtained from treaties where the United Kingdom is not a party to them. In that case, Morritt L.J. noted differences in the wording between the German–Swiss Treaty and the U.K.–German Treaty in the context of determining the meaning of the term "dividends" under the U.K.–German Treaty. In placing reliance on such treaties, it is not only necessary to find similarly worded provisions in a similar context within the treaty, but also to identify a similar approach to the interpretation of treaties adopted by the courts responsible for construing the treaty in question.

Writings of jurists

3-35   The writings of jurists have had a somewhat uneven reception by the courts in the context of interpreting tax treaties. On the hand, writers such as Brownlie and McNair have been readily accepted by the courts in expressing principles of customary international law relating to interpretation of treaties. Commentary by jurists on specific provisions have been more equivocal. In *Commerzbank*,[65] Mummery J. said that reliance on commentaries was persuasive only and depended on the cogency of reasoning. In that case, the Inland Revenue relied heavily on the opinions of eminent jurists on international law, Sir Ian Brownlie and McNair, particularly in the absence of any preparatory work. The Special Commissioner relied on statements in Brownlie and McNair that the burden of proof was on the Crown to rebut the presumption that the words of Article 15 of the U.S. Treaty should bear their plain and ordinary meaning.

In *Memec*,[66] this view was echoed by Robert Walker J. The Crown sought to introduce extracts of *Vogel on Double Taxation Conventions*. Initially, the taxpayer objected to the extracts on the grounds that they constituted "surmise and guesswork". Ultimately in reply, the objection was modified and the taxpayer's counsel drew the Special Commissioners' attention to an extract not quoted by the Crown in support of their own case. The Special Commissioners admitted the relevant extracts but "found them to be of little assistance and much of Herr Vogel's commentary is verging on the incomprehensible".[67] The position changed somewhat in the High Court where Dr. Vogel was referred to as "an eminent German expert".[68] This time, the

---

[63] See above, n. 34.
[64] See above, n. 36.
[65] See above, n. 15.
[66] See above, n. 16.
[67] At 1343a.
[68] At 1356j.

Inland Revenue argued "that his view is tentative and reliance on it is not mandatory and depends on its cogency".

3-36 The views were ultimately expressed to be of some help, but not by themselves to be determinative. In the Court of Appeal, it was said that "the views of an acknowledged expert in this field, as Professor Vogel undoubtedly is, deserve respect".[69]

In *Trustees of Wensleydale's Settlement v. IRC*,[70] Dr. Vogel's work was again referred to on the meaning of "place of effective management" in the Irish Treaty. Although no views were expressed about the comment in the book, the Special Commissioners clearly placed reliance on it.

Foreign judgments

3-37 The courts have not taken an uncritical approach to foreign cases, although in *Fothergill v. Monarch Airlines Limited*,[71] Lord Scarman said "the decisions of a Superior Court or the opinion of a Court of Cassation will carry great weight". Thus, although the desirability of a common approach was fostered by the Vienna Convention, and indeed observations in the Introduction to the Commentary read "harmonisation of these conventions in accordance with uniform principles, definitions, rules and methods, and agreement on common interpretation, became increasingly desirable", the courts have proceeded cautiously. In *Commerzbank*,[72] the Crown relied on the decision of the United States Court of Claims in *Great West Life Assurance Company v. United States*.[73] That case was on the effect of Article 12 of the Treaty between the United States and Canada. It granted exemption in terms similar to Article 15 of the U.K.-U.S. Treaty. Mummery J. noted:[74]

> "that decision is of some interest as illustrating the basis on which the United States taxes foreign corporations trading in the United States, but it is of no real assistance in these cases because it is clear from the report that different principles were applied by the Court to the interpretation of that Convention than an English Court would have applied in accordance with the decision of the House of Lords in *Fothergill v. Monarch Airlines Limited*".

3-38 In particular, he referred to U.S. case law to the effect that the meaning given a treaty by an appropriate government and governmental agency is of great weight. The U.S. court, he said, was greatly influenced in its decision by the fact that the Departments of State and Treasury had interpreted Article 12 of the U.S.–Canadian Treaty as not conferring the exemption claimed and had negotiated other treaties on that basis. No such principle is applied by the English courts to the provision of a treaty and he therefore did not find that decision of much assistance in the present case.

---

[69] [1998] S.T.C. 754 at 768b, CA. See also the dissenting view of Sir Christopher Staughton at 770j.
[70] [1966] S.T.C. 241.
[71] See above, n. 10.
[72] See above, n. 15.
[73] 49 A.F.T.R. 2nd 82-1316.
[74] At 302f.

In *Memec*,[75] where the meaning of the term "dividends" was under examination in the German Treaty, reference was made to a decision of the German Bundesfinanzhof in construing the Treaty between Germany and Switzerland. In the Court of Appeal, Morritt L.J. noted that the German decision was on a differently worded article in a different context in a different treaty, and questioned how much assistance can be obtained from other treaties, particularly when the United Kingdom is not a party to them. A similar approach was adopted in *Padmore v. IRC*.[76] Although foreign decisions were not accepted in *Commerzbank* and *Memec*, nonetheless the courts have looked at them with great care.[77] In *Memec*, the court noted that it was not apparent in the German-Swiss Treaty whether the applicability of Article 10(6) was in issue, but in Article 28 of that Treaty it appeared to have been concerned to preserve the rights to apply withholding tax on dividends in the country of source and therefore a wide meaning of "dividends" was natural in that context. The court thus distinguished the Treaty without having to comment on the approach of the German court.[78]

3-39 In *QRS 1 Aps and others v. Frandsen*,[79] the court was called on to consider whether the enforcement of a judgment obtained by a liquidator on behalf of a foreign tax administration was a "Revenue matter" within the meaning of Article 1 of the Brussels Convention on Jurisdiction and the Enforcement of Judgments in Civil and Commercial Matters. In this regard, the court referred to a report of Professor Peter Schlosser on the 1978 Accession Convention by which the United Kingdom acceded to the Brussels Convention and to Dicey and Morris on the *Conflict of Laws*.[80] French decisions and writers on the subject were also considered. The court formulated the problem thus[81]:

> "There is no definition of 'Revenue matters' in the Convention and no decision of the Court of Justice of the European Communities bearing on the point. What then, one must ask, would the original member states themselves regard as Revenue matters for this purpose? Do they subscribe to the legal principle enshrined in Dicey's r3 and in particular that part of the rule barring the indirect enforcement of foreign revenue laws".

Simon Brown L.J. noted[82] that "there is no reason to doubt that the rule in France is just as fundamental and far reaching as in England and that it is rightly described in both jurisdictions as a rule international application. I should add that we were shown no contrary jurisprudence from any other member state".

---

[75] See above, n. 36.
[76] See above, n. 20.
[77] See above, discussion regarding *Commerzbank*.
[78] See also the dissenting opinion of Sir Christopher Staughton.
[79] [1999] S.T.C. 616.
[80] 12th Edition 1993, Vol. 1 p. 97.
[81] Simon Brown L.J. at 628j.
[82] At 629f.

STATUTORY RULES OF INTERPRETATION

3-40 As a rule, unless domestic law meanings are required to be applied to treaty provisions, the interpretation rules contained in domestic tax law are inapplicable. An important exception was enacted in 1992 in relation to the meaning of "special relationship" for the purpose of treaty provisions relating to interest. Section 808A of Taxes Act 1988 applies where a treaty makes provision for interest and contains the special relationship wording. That wording is defined in section 808A(a)(b) as, where owing to a special relationship, the amount of interest paid exceeds the amount which would have been paid in the absence of the relationship, the treaty provisions only apply to the last mentioned amount.

Special relationship

3-41 A series of specific interpretation rules are imposed. These require that the special relationship provision be construed as requiring account to be taken of all factors including:

- (a) whether the loan would have been made at all in the absence of the relationship;

- (b) the amount which the loan would have been in the absence of the relationship; and

- (c) the rate of interest and other terms which would have been agreed in the absence of the relationship.[83]

It further requires the provision to be construed as requiring the taxpayer to demonstrate that there is no special relationship or where there is one, to show what the amount of interest would have been in the absence of such a relationship.[84] Where a company makes a loan to another with which it has a special relationship, and the making of loans generally is not part of the lender's business, that fact is to be disregarded.[85]

The factors listed do not apply where the special relationship provision in the treaty expressly requires regard to be had to the debt on which the interest is paid in determining the excess interest and accordingly expressly limits the factors to be taken into account.[86]

The reason for the statutory interpretation provision is somewhat obscure. It arises out of the Special Commissioners' decision apparently in 1992, the details of which have not been published. One might surmise that the Commissioners concluded that the OECD Model wording permitted only an adjustment based on the rate of interest charged and not on the amount of debt overall. Since the decision was never appealed, it was presumably acquiesced in by the Revenue who sought the inclusion of the section in legislation. The interpretation rule itself is also in need of some

---

[83] Taxes Act 1988, s. 808A(2).
[84] *ibid.*, s. 808A(3).
[85] *ibid.*, s. 808A(4).
[86] *ibid.*, s. 808A(5).

interpretation. In particular, subsection (5) which excludes the application of the rule. It appears to disapply the provision where the treaty itself requires regard to be had to the debt on which the interest is paid. This notion is extended by the wording "and accordingly expressly limits the factors to be taken into account". It is unclear whether the presence of a provision requiring regard to be had to the debt on which the interest is paid is itself to be construed as an express limit or whether particular wording expressing a limitation must be found in the treaty. A reservation by the United Kingdom and changes in the OECD Model Treaty now reflect this position in any event.

3-42 A similar provision was enacted in relation to royalties in the Finance Act 2000. Article 12(4) of the OECD Model contains a provision denying the relief from source state tax to the extent that, by reason of a special relationship between the payer and the beneficial owner of the royalties, or between both of them and some other person, the amount of the royalties, having regard to the use, right or information for which they are paid, exceeds the amount which would have been agreed upon by the payer and the beneficial owner in the absence of such relationship. It has been U.K. treaty negotiating policy, to omit from that clause the words "having regard to the use, right or information for which they are paid". In most cases those words are replaced by the phrase "for whatever reason" but sometimes no alternative wording is included. In either event, the Inland Revenue have stated in their document on double tax relief reform (Inland Revenue, *Double Taxation Relief for Companies, A Discussion Paper* (1998)) that their view of the intention of this provision is that it should apply not only where the rate at which royalties are paid is excessive but where, in the absence of the special relationship, the arrangements under which the royalties are paid at all would not have been entered into.

3-43 Thus, paragraph 17 of Schedule 30 to the Finance Act 2000 introduces a new section 808B to the Taxes Act 1988. It provides that where a royalty clause refers to the special relationship rule, that it:

> "shall be construed as requiring account to be taken of all factors, including:
>
> (a) the question whether the agreement under which the royalties are paid would have been made at all in the absence of the relationship;
>
> (b) the rate or amounts of royalties and other terms which would have been agreed in the absence of the relationship".

OTHER REFERENCES TO DOMESTIC LAW

3-44 The most important general rule of interpretation applies to terms used in a treaty but not defined in it. Article 3(2) requires that:

> "As regard the application of the Convention by a contracting state, any term not defined therein shall, unless the context otherwise requires,

have the meaning which it has under the law of that state concerning the taxes to which the Convention applies".

This clause is found in all U.K. treaties. Although reference has been made to this article in a large number of cases, there are still several outstanding issues, which have not been addressed by the courts. In *Ostime v. Australian Mutual Provident Society*,[87] the court was called on to address whether the Australian Treaty prevented the attribution of investment income to the U.K. branch of a non-resident non-mutual insurance company. It was argued that the Treaty did not deal with purely notional or conventional profits and that "industrial or commercial profits" defined in Article 2(1)(i) of the Treaty must be given its natural and ordinary meaning. Article 2(3) (Article 3(2) of the OECD Model) had no application. On that basis, the Crown argued that industrial or commercial profits could not include purely notional or fictitious profits, but only refer to real or actual profit. Since there are none as a matter of domestic law, the Treaty has no application. The Court proceeded on the basis that the domestic law of the source state (*i.e.* the United Kingdom) was the relevant law. In *Imperial Chemical Industries Ltd v. Caro*,[88] the income in question was from Australian sources. However, in construing the operation of the tax credit granted under Article 12 of that Treaty in the context of the preceding year basis of assessment, it was provided that the reference to income referred to income as determined for U.K. purposes (*i.e.* the residence country). The case is perhaps an unusual one given the former preceding year basis, which resulted in a total mismatch. In addition, the court was moved by the general purpose of the Treaty in avoiding double taxation and was therefore inclined not to permit the same credit to be granted twice. It seems unlikely that it will establish any principle beyond the specifics of the now abolished preceding year basis in the context of deciding which contracting state laws should apply.

3-45   There are also numerous instances where a treaty makes specific reference to domestic law. For example, in the U.S. Treaty, Article 16(2)(b) refers to

> "a corporation (other than a United States corporation) which by reference to the provisions of section 283 of the United Kingdom Income and Corporation Taxes Act 1970 (as it may be amended from time to time without changing the general principle thereof) would not fall to be treated as a close company".

Clearly, in such cases, interpretation of the domestic statutory reference must be made in accordance with domestic rules interpreting the statutory provision in question. For other formulations of references to domestic law, see the Netherlands Treaty, Article 10. Similar references may be found to the law of the other contracting states. This commonly applies in relation to tax-sparing provisions which are described by reference to the legislation in

---

[87] See above, n. 44.
[88] See above, n. 28.

the other contracting state. Similarly, entities established in other contracting states are frequently described by reference to the domestic law of the other contracting state. The limitation of benefits provisions of Article 10(3)(d)(i) of the Netherlands Treaty refer to companies whose shares are officially quoted on a Netherlands stock exchange and which comply in certain respects with Council Directive 79/279/EEC.[89] In such a case, interpretation in accordance with Community law is required.

TREATIES IN MORE THAN ONE LANGUAGE

3-46   Although many U.K. treaties are concluded in English only, a large number are concluded in at least two languages. Where this is the case, the practice is to agree on the authoritative value of each text. Typical language in this regard is found, for example, in the execution provisions of the Canadian Treaty which reads: "Done in duplicate at London in the English and French languages, both texts being equally authoritative".

The interpretation of treaties authenticated in two or more languages is addressed in the Vienna Convention. Article 33 reads as follows:

"1. When a treaty has been authenticated in two or more languages, the text is equally authoritative in each language, unless the treaty provides or the parties agree that, in case of divergence, a particular text shall prevail.

2. A version of the treaty in a language other than one of those in which the text was authenticated shall be considered an authentic text only if the treaty so provides or the parties so agree.

3. The terms of the treaty are presumed to have the same meaning in each authentic text.

4. Except where a particular text prevails in accordance with paragraph 1, when a comparison of the authentic texts discloses a difference of meaning which the application of Articles 31 and 32 does not remove, the meaning which best reconciles the texts, having regard to the object and purpose of the treaty, shall be adopted."

3-47   The courts in the United Kingdom have not had to consider language versions of tax treaties other than in English. The opportunity to do so has arisen on occasion in relation to other non tax treaties and, in this context, Lord Wilberforce said in *Fothergill v. Monarch Airlines Ltd*[90]:

"My Lords, some of the problems which arise when the Courts of this country are faced with texts of treaties or conventions in different languages were discussed in *James Buchanan & Co. Ltd. v. Babco Forwarding & Shipping (U.K.) Ltd.*, [1978] A.C. 141. It is obvious that the present represents a special and indeed unique case.

Here it is not only permissible to look at a foreign language text, but

---

[89] Dated March 5, 1979.
[90] See above, n. 10, at 272.

obligatory. What is made part of English law is the text set out in Schedule 1, i.e. in both Part I and Part II, so both English and French texts must be looked at. Furthermore, it cannot be judged whether there is an inconsistency between two texts unless one looks at both. So, in the present case the process of interpretation seems to involve:

1. Interpretation of the English text, according to the principles upon which international conventions are to be interpreted (see *Buchanan*'s case and *Stag Line Ltd. v. Foscolo, Mango & Co. Ltd.*, [1932] A.C. 328, 350).
2. Interpretation of the French text according to the same principles but with additional linguistic problems.
3. Comparison of these meanings.

Moreover, if the process of interpretation leaves the matter in doubt, the question may have to be faced whether 'travaux préparatoires' may be looked at in order to resolve the difficulty".

This approach does not differ from the Vienna Convention Guidelines. In *Memec*, the court rejected an "over-subtle point" based on the wording of the French version of the 1963 draft Model Tax Convention on the meaning of "dividend" for underlying credit purposes. [91]

HUMAN RIGHTS AND THE EUROPEAN CONVENTION ON HUMAN RIGHTS

3-48 Although the United Kingdom was among the first signatories to the European Convention on Human Rights in 1951, it was only in 1998 as a result of the Human Rights Act 1998 that the key elements of the Convention were enacted into the law of the United Kingdom. Section 3 of the Human Rights Act 1998 creates a general requirement that all legislation, whether past or future, must be read and given effect in a way which is compatible with the legislation. It does this by providing that all legislation, primary and secondary, whenever enacted, must be read and given effect in a way which is compatible with Convention rights. It will no longer be necessary for there to be ambiguity in order to have resort to the Convention. This legislation creates a new hierarchy in the context of tax treaties. Thus, although section 788 of Taxes Act 1988 generally makes domestic law subject to tax treaties, section 3 of the Human Rights Act 1998 now makes even this provision subject to the application of the Convention. As a result, all tax treaties and their implementation must comply with the Human Rights Act and the Convention. This is likely to have an increasing impact, particularly in relation to issues such as exchange of information and the non-discrimination provision of tax treaties.

---

[91] See above, n. 36, at 767. See, however, the dissenting opinion of Sir Christopher Staughton at 770–771.

CHAPTER 4

Access to Treaty Benefits: Fiscal Domicile and Personality

WHO IS ENTITLED TO THE BENEFITS OF A TAX TREATY?

4-01 The starting point of any analysis is Article 1 of the OECD Model Convention. This specifies that the "Convention shall apply to persons who are residents of one or both of the contracting states". The Commentary to the OECD Model notes that, in principle, residents of a state should be entitled to treaty benefits.

This approach of the OECD is reflected in more recent U.K. treaties. The vast majority of treaties that the United Kingdom has entered into adopt the OECD Model Article 1. There are however some 27 treaties which do not include an article describing the scope of application of the treaty. Most of the treaties that do not have an article equivalent to Article 1 of the OECD Model are with Commonwealth countries. Other countries that do not have a general scope article include the treaties with the Faroe Islands, Israel, the Isle of Man, Jersey and Guernsey.[1]

Are treaty benefits for residents of contracting states only?

4-02 As a matter of U.K. law the absence of wording defining the scope of application of the treaty means that residents of third countries may be entitled to the benefit of treaties that their country of residence is not a party to. This point was clearly made by the High Court in *Inland Revenue Commissioners v. Commerzbank AG*; *Inland Revenue Commissioners v. Banco do Brasil SA*.[2] The 1945 U.S. treaty at that time contained no general scope provision. Article XV specified that:

> "Dividends and interest paid by a corporation of one contracting party shall be exempt from tax by the other contracting party except where the recipient is a citizen, resident or corporation of that other contracting party. This exemption shall not apply if the corporation paying such dividend or interest is a resident of the other contracting party".

---

[1] The U.S. treaty follows the OECD Model broadly. However it reads: *"except as specifically provided herein,* this convention is applicable to persons who are resident in one or both of the contracting states" (words in italics differ from OECD wording).

[2] [1990] S.T.C. 285, Ch.D.

The crucial issue in the case was whether the two banks incorporated in Germany and Brazil respectively were entitled to claim the benefit of an exemption from U.K. tax on interest paid to their U.K. branches by U.S. corporations under the U.S. Treaty. The Inland Revenue argued vigorously that treaty benefits ought not to be conferred on persons who were not residents or citizens of the United States. Before the Special Commissioners, the Inland Revenue Solicitor argued that benefits should not be so conferred unless they were explicitly included. It was argued that in bilateral treaties there is a presumption against an intention to benefit third parties. This was rejected by the Special Commissioners, and similarly by the High Court. In the *Banco do Brasil* case[3] the Commissioner noted that the State of Brazil was not involved and that all private persons, including those connected with the state entering into the agreement, are in this context third parties. In the *Commerzbank* decision, the Special Commissioner was of the view that the question of third party rights was only concerned with the acquisition of rights by third party states. He preferred the view of McNair's *Law of Treaties*[4] to the effect that, provided that the necessary implementation by municipal law has been carried out, there is nothing to prevent the nationals of single "third states" in the absence of any express or implied provision to the contrary from claiming the rights or becoming subject to the obligations created by a treaty.

4-03   It was also argued before the Commissioners that almost all of the articles of the Treaty were concerned with citizens, residents and corporations of contracting parties. The Commissioners found that this particular article was not. It was also argued by the Inland Revenue before the Commissioners that there was a general principle of treaties that the branches of non-resident corporations should be taxed in the country in which they were situated. No support for this was found other than a reference to the OECD Model Convention and the Commissioner noted that unusual provisions do find their way into treaties.

In the case of Brazil, there was no treaty. The Special Commissioner merely noted that this would mean that for example the Brazilian authorities could not participate in competent authority proceedings. The Inland Revenue tried to argue that in the context of *Commerzbank*, the German–U.S. Treaty operated to exempt from U.S. taxation the amounts of interest paid to the branch which were the subject of the appeal. The Special Commissioner regarded it as incongruous if the effect of an article of the U.K.–U.S. Treaty were to depend on the existence of otherwise of a treaty between one or other of those countries or one or more third countries.

4-04   On appeal to the High Court, Mummery J. was firmly of the view that the natural and ordinary meaning of the words of Article XV was clear. Interest paid by U.S. corporations was exempt from U.K. tax except where the recipient was a U.K. citizen, resident or corporation. This was so despite the fact that the claim for treaty benefits was made by a Brazilian and German resident respectively.

The submission by the Crown was that the Treaty read as a whole dealt almost exclusively with the right to tax or waive the right to tax citizens or

---

[3] At 293.
[4] 1961 Edition.

residents of and corporations of a contracting party. In the absence of express words to that effect, this ought to mean that the article in question should have been interpreted as not waiving the right to tax a corporation of a non contracting party. Mummery J. noted, however, that the Crown did accept, by the time the case reached the High Court, that there was no legal reason why a treaty cannot deal with rights and obligations of persons other than citizens, residents and corporations of the contracting parties. The court observed that at the time, the Treaty did not contain wording equivalent to Article 1 of the OECD Model Convention.

4-05   Mummery J. concluded that this construction did not give rise to any manifestly absurd or unreasonable consequences. There was no sufficient indication in the purpose of the Treaty or in its surrounding circumstances or in the provisions other than the article in question to qualify the clear words. There were articles in the Treaty which did not exclude persons from non contracting parties from tax exemptions conferred by the Treaty. There are also articles which expressly identify those who come within the benefit of the provisions and confine the scope of the provisions to those who are citizens or residents of one of the contracting parties. There was no such express restriction in Article XV. The exemption was therefore defined by reference to the character of the source of income and not to any characteristic of the recipient of the income from that source.

The decision has been criticised, particularly on the basis that McNair's statement does not support the proposition claimed by the court.[5] Nonetheless the decision was not appealed and treaties should be read against the background of this decision.

Most of the treaties that do not contain a personal scope article are with Commonwealth countries and are very old. The most recent example is that with Botswana which dates from 1978. In each of these treaties, the scope of application generally emerges from the text of individual provisions and there do not appear to be any major lacunae of the kind which gave rise to the *Commerzbank* case.

Non-discrimination

4-06   The United Kingdom has not included the final sentence of Article 24(1) of the OECD Model into any treaties. That sentence states specifically that nationals of a contracting state may not be discriminated against even if they are not resident in either of the contracting states in question. The wording is the only express recognition of the extension of treaty benefits to residents of third countries in the Model.

WHO IS A RESIDENT FOR TREATY PURPOSES?

4-07   The concept of "resident of a contracting state" fulfils a crucial role in determining the treaty's personal scope of application. In the majority of treaties which contain a personal scope article, qualification as a resident of

---

[5] [1990] B.T.R. 388 at 391. See also Klaus Vogel, *Double Taxation Conventions*, (2nd ed.), 1994 Supplement, p.5.

a contracting state is the *sine qua non* of a claim to treaty benefits. The approach to residence as adopted in U.K. treaties has an impact on the ability of persons in third countries to benefit from treaties, in addition to resolving dual residence problems.

OECD definition

4-08   The vast majority of treaties follow the OECD Models. A number follow the 1963 OECD Draft Convention which states that a "resident of a contracting State" means any person who under the law of that state is liable to tax therein by reason of his domicile, residence, place of management or any other criterion of a similar nature. The 1977 Model added the wording to exclude from this term any person who is liable to tax in that state in respect only of income from sources in that state or capital situated therein. The current version, as it appears in the Iceland Treaty, reads:

> *"Article 4: Fiscal domicile*
> 4(1) In this Convention, the term 'resident of a Contracting State' means any person who, under the laws of that State, is liable to tax therein by reason of his domicile, residence, place of management or any other criterion of a similar nature. But this term does not include any person who is liable to tax in that State in respect only of income or capital gains from sources in that State".

The Commentary notes that this is intended to apply to various forms of personal attachment to a state which form the basis of comprehensive taxation, that is, a worldwide basis. The second sentence of the definition, added in 1977, was intended to exclude a person subject only to taxation limited to income from sources within that state. The Commentary on this second sentence was amended in 1992 to take into account the Conduit Company Report. The Commentary now expresses the view that according to its wording and spirit, this sentence would exclude from the definition of a resident of a contracting state, foreign held companies exempted from tax on their foreign income by privileges tailored to attract conduit companies.

4-09   The Commentary does however recognise that this has inherent difficulties and limitations. It must therefore be interpreted restrictively because otherwise it might exclude from the scope of treaties all residents of countries adopting a territorial principle in their taxation a result which, the Commentary says, is clearly not intended.

In the context of treaty shopping, this amended text in the Commentary seems a clumsy and ineffective method of attempting to restrict treaty benefits. It is far from clear that the wording of the article has the effect contended for in the revised Commentary. Indeed, the natural wording might instead suggest that all taxpayers on a source basis only would be excluded from treaty benefits rather than those specifically foreign-owned companies designed to attract conduit operations. It seems unlikely that such an approach would be upheld by the courts simply on the strength of the Commentary, particularly, in the light of other anti-avoidance provisions available and, specifically, look-through and excluded entity rules. It is submitted that such specific provisions are the only realistic method of countering the issue raised in this paragraph of the Commentary. The negotiating position of the United Kingdom, revealed in treaties signed since the OECD Commentary was amended, would suggest that the Inland Revenue places little faith in this interpretation to prevent conduit operations.

Colonial definition

4-10   The older treaties, following the colonial pattern, adopt an entirely different approach to the question of residence. They generally state that a U.K. resident is any person resident in the United Kingdom for U.K. tax purposes and not resident in the other contracting state for the purpose of that state's tax and vice versa. In the case of companies, they are normally regarded as resident in the United Kingdom for treaty purposes if their business is managed and controlled in the United Kingdom and resident in the other contracting state if the business is managed and controlled in that contracting state. The treaty with Grenada for example reads:

> "2(g) The terms 'resident of the United Kingdom' and 'resident of Grenada' mean respectively any person who is resident in the United Kingdom for the purposes of United Kingdom tax and not resident in Grenada for the purposes of Grenada tax and any person who is resident in Grenada for the purposes of Grenada tax and not resident in the United Kingdom for the purposes of United Kingdom tax; and a company shall be regarded as resident in the United Kingdom if its business is managed and controlled in the United Kingdom and as resident in Grenada if its business is managed and controlled in Grenada".

4-11   The Inland Revenue view is that the management and control test for companies does not prevent the operation of the first test which refers to the domestic law of the contracting states.[6] It is on this basis they argue that exempt companies in the Channel Islands, for example, cannot claim treaty benefits. This conclusion is far from clear and may not be consistent with the specific exclusions of tax-favoured entities from entitlement to treaty benefits or their approach as showed by the Crown's arguments in *Forth Investments Ltd v. IRC.*[7]

The practical application of this form of residence clause came before the courts in the *Forth Investments* case. This involved a company incorporated in Barbados under the International Business Companies (Exemption from Income Tax) Act 1965. Essentially that Act allows Barbados companies who are foreign owned and who do not carry on business in Barbados to pay tax at a reduced rate of 2½ per cent. Unlike the current version, the 1949 Barbados Treaty did not exclude international business companies from claiming treaty benefits.

4-12   In the *Forth Investments* case, evidence indicated that the shares in the company were issued to a Bahamas company. It emerged that the

---

[6] Inland Revenue, *International Tax Handbook*, para. 520.
[7] [1976] S.T.C. 309, Ch.D.

structure formed part of a complicated arrangement to avoid U.K. tax and ultimately a U.K. resident individual accepted liability under section 478 of Income and Corporation Taxes Act 1970.[8] Although the arrangement did not form part of the subject matter of the case it likely induced a degree of scepticism about the facts presented.

The Inland Revenue refused to allow the claim on the basis that it was not satisfied that the company was resident in Barbados. The company had submitted a treaty claim form duly completed together with a certificate of authentication from the Barbados Deputy Commissioner of Inland Revenue. Only some of the additional information in support of the claim had been submitted, including the names and addresses of directors, a list of directors meetings and copies of some but not all minutes of those meetings.

The case ultimately turned on the admissibility of evidence that the business of the company was managed and controlled in Barbados and the certificate by the taxation authorities of Barbados that the company was a resident of Barbados. The court also rejected an argument that the company must be viewed as resident in Barbados if it was accepted that the company was subject to tax in Barbados because it would only be subject to tax if it was resident and that this had been accepted by the Inland Revenue. This argument was regarded by Brightman J. as circular and residence was not found to have been admitted by the Revenue.

4-13   The case was decided on the basis of evidentiary issues only. It is, however, implicit in the decision that the court considered that it was entitled to consider the treaty definition of residence quite separately from how it was treated for the tax laws of the other contracting state. The company was treated as a resident of Barbados by the Barbados tax administration. This was not determinative or even influential and evidence of the tax treatment in Barbados was dismissed as hearsay. There was no suggestion that this meant that the first test of residence in the treaty was satisfied. The exclusion of the evidence was on procedural grounds and not too much should be read into the decision. Despite this, the treaty definition of management and control only was applied to determine the residence of the company for treaty purposes.

Thus, unlike the OECD test, which refers simply to the domestic definition of the contracting states, the colonial style treaty adopts its own definition of corporate residence. While most Commonwealth countries adopt a form of management and control test of company residence, presumably a U.K. court would interpret the concept in accordance with U.K. law and there may be a divergence of approach between the U.K. and a foreign country resulting in a company being resident for treaty purposes although not necessarily for the purposes of the other contracting state's domestic law. These treaties refer to "management and control" rather than to "central management and control".

Dual residence: individuals

4-14   Domestic law on individual residence lends itself to dual residence problems. First, residence for part of a tax year means residence for the

---

[8] Now Taxes Act 1988, s. 739.

whole tax year. There are no statutory rules which apportion tax years of arrival and departure as a matter of law between periods of residence and non-residence. Secondly, the United Kingdom applies two separate tests of residence in this context, namely residence *simpliciter* and ordinary residence. Thirdly, the question of residence is essentially one of fact and a matter of degree. In particular, the circumstances of a taxpayer's visits to the United Kingdom may be of such a nature or may be either prolonged or repeated, so as to cause the taxpayer to become resident even though on average he spent only something over a quarter of the tax year in the United Kingdom,[9] and moreover, such visits may also make a taxpayer ordinarily resident.[10] This means that regular visitors to the United Kingdom for a significant minority of their time will become resident. Other anomalies may arise in relation to dual residence resulting from the unusual U.K. tax year ending on April 5. Conversely, total absence throughout a tax year is not necessarily conclusive of non-residence.[11] Under Taxes Act 1988, section 334, where a Commonwealth citizen or citizen of the Irish Republic whose ordinary residence has been in the United Kingdom leaves the United Kingdom for a purpose only of occasional residence abroad, then such individual will be regarded during that period of absence as actually residing in the United Kingdom. This applies where "a person who is not for a time actually residing in the United Kingdom, but who has constructively his residence there because his ordinary place of abode and his home is there, although he is absent for a time from it, however long continued that absence may be".[12]

4-15 Resolution of dual residence in U.K. treaties is far from uniform. In the case of dual resident individuals, this is addressed in treaties patterned on the OECD Model. A typical example is found in Article 3(2) of the French Treaty which reads as follows:

"Where by reason of the provisions of paragraph (1) an individual is a resident of both Contracting States, then this case shall be determined in accordance with the following rules:

(a) He shall be deemed to be a resident of the Contracting State in which he has a permanent home available to him. If he has a permanent home available to him in both Contracting States, he shall be deemed to be a resident of the Contracting State with which his personal and economic relations are closest (centre of vital interests).

(b) If the Contracting State in which he has his centre of vital interests cannot be determined, or if he has not a permanent home available to him in either Contracting State, he shall be deemed to be a resident of the Contracting State in which he has an habitual abode.

---

[9] *Lysaght v. IRC* [1928] A.C. 234.
[10] *Levene v. IRC* [1928] A.C. 217.
[11] See *Reed v. Clark* [1985] S.T.C. 325, Ch.D.
[12] *Lloyd v. Sulley* (1884) 2 T.C. 37, at 42.

(c) If he has an habitual abode in both Contracting States or in neither of them, he shall be deemed to be a resident of the Contracting State of which he is a national.

(d) If he is a national of both Contracting States or of neither of them, the competent authorities of the Contracting States shall settle the question by mutual agreement".

There have been no cases on the application of the tie-breaker.

Dual residence: companies

4-16 Although treaties patterned on the OECD Model contain tie-breaker provisions, a number of early treaties do not. Those following the colonial pattern (see Grenada above) define residence both positively and negatively. A resident of a contracting state is a resident of one contracting state who is not also resident in the other contracting state. The effect of these treaties is that dual residents are excluded from treaty benefits. The 1975 U.S. Treaty contains a tie-breaker in relation to individuals and trusts (Article 4(2) and (3)). There are no provisions for resolving dual residence of companies. Dual resident companies are specifically addressed in Article 1(2). They are not entitled to claim any relief or exemption from tax under the Treaty with limited specified exceptions. Similar definitions of residence were found in the 1946 U.S. Treaty with the additional criteria of citizenship. This gave rise to considerable difficulties of application.[13]

The impact of treaty residence on domestic law

4-17 Where a company is treated as resident in the United Kingdom for domestic tax purposes but is treated as resident outside the United Kingdom and not resident in the United Kingdom for the purposes of any treaty, then it is treated as not resident in the United Kingdom for all domestic tax purposes.[14] In such a case, the company is therefore non-resident for all purposes. This treatment is automatic and no claim for relief under the relevant treaty is required.[15] A company resident in the United Kingdom as a result of its place of incorporation or place of central management and control will clearly be a resident of the United Kingdom under this definition. If the central management and control is also in another jurisdiction, the company will still be a U.K. resident, at least for the purposes of Article 4(1) of the OECD Model.

Central management and control

4-18 From March 15, 1988, a company which is incorporated in the United Kingdom is regarded as resident there.[16] Certain limited exceptions apply to some U.K. incorporated companies which were prior to that date

---

[13] See *Strathalmond v. IRC* (1972) 48 T.C. 537, *Avery Jones v. IRC* [1976] S.T.C. 290, *IRC v. Exxon Corporation* [1982] S.T.C. 356.
[14] Finance Act 1994, s. 249(1).
[15] *ibid.*, s. 249(3).
[16] Finance Act 1988, s. 66.

resident outside the United Kingdom.[17] Companies incorporated outside the United Kingdom continue to be subject to the case law test, which applied to all companies prior to March 15, 1988. This test was enunciated at the beginning of the twentieth century in *De Beers Consolidated Mines v. Howe*,[18] in which Lord Loreburn said: "a company resides, for the purposes of income tax, where its real business is carried on . . . I regard that as the true rule; and the real business is carried on where the central management and control actually abides". Successive cases have consistently applied the central management and control test. The question where central management and control actually abides is one of fact. It is distinguished from the place where the company's trade or business is conducted. Under U.K. domestic law, a company may be resident in two jurisdictions.[19] Thus, central management and control can be divided on a geographical basis, so that a company can have a dual residence.

Management and control

4-19   Treaties following the colonial pattern referred to "management and control", rather than "central management and control". It may be argued that the two are distinct notions with "central management and control" under domestic law referring to the highest level of decision-making authority, "management and control" referring to a lower level of management of the company's business. The attraction of such an approach is that it may assist in resolving some dual residence conflicts. If the two expressions are synonymous, then only a more limited category of conflicts over residence are addressed.

Place of effective management

4-20   The tie-breaker in the case of dual corporate residence under the OECD Model is found in Article 4(3) of the Italian Treaty and reads as follows:

> "4(3)   Where by reason of the provisions of paragraph (1) of this Article a person other than an individual is a resident of both Contracting States, then it shall be deemed to be a resident of the Contracting State in which its place of effective management is situated".

There is little authority on the application of the tie-breaker in U.K. law. As a matter of administrative practice, the Inland Revenue have changed their view as between the 1997 and 1992 Model Conventions. At one time their view was that the U.K. concept of "central management and control" meant the same thing as "place of effective management" and there was a note to this effect in the Commentary on the 1977 OECD Model Double Taxation Convention. The Revenue now no longer believe that necessarily to be so and the note does not appear in the 1992 edition of the OECD Model. The place

---

[17] *ibid.*, Sched. 7.
[18] (1906) 5 T.C. 198.
[19] *Swedish Central Railway Co. Ltd v. Thompson* (1925) 9 T.C. 342.

of effective management, they say, is generally understood to be the place where the head office is—the head office in the sense of, not the registered office, but the central directing source, the place they believe where one would expect to find the finance director, for example, the sales director and, if there is one, the managing director. The company records would normally be found there together with the senior administrative staff.[20]

4-21   They are of the view that their revised idea of effective management is nearer to other European Union Member States' management tests than is central management and control. Nevertheless they believe it is not that easy to divorce effective management from central management and control and in the vast majority of cases they will be located in the same place.

Current administrative practice is contained in Statement of Practice SP1/90, paragraph 22 of which reads as follows:

> "The Commentary in paragraph 3 of Article 4 of the OECD Model records the U.K. view that, in agreements (such as those with some Commonwealth countries) which treat a company as resident in a state in which 'its business is managed and controlled', this expression means 'the effective management of the enterprise'. More detailed consideration of the question in the light of the approach of Continental legal systems and of Community law to the question of company residence has led the Revenue to revise this view. It is now considered that effective management may, in some cases, be found at a place different from the place of central management and control. This could happen, for example, where a company is run by executives based abroad, but the final directing power rests with non-executive directors who meet in the U.K.. In such circumstances the company's place of effective management might well be abroad but, depending on the precise powers of the non-executive directors, it might be centrally managed and controlled (and therefore resident) in the U.K.".

4-22   The only judicial decision that addresses the tie-breaker is *Trustees of Wensleydale's Settlement v. IRC.*[21] The case turned on whether the trustees of a settlement were to be deemed to be resident in the Republic of Ireland by virtue of the tie-breaker in the U.K.-Irish Treaty. In that case, reference was made to Klaus Vogel on *Double Taxation Conventions* in which it was said that the "place of management" in German treaty practice is very similar to the "place of effective management", since the former depends on factual conditions. This followed German case law which established that the place of management is the centre of top level management, that is where the management's important policies are actually made.

In the *Wensleydale* case, both the taxpayer and the Inland Revenue agreed that the "centre of top level management" was a good description of the place of effective management. Cases dealing with "central management and control" were referred to in this respect. On the facts, the Special

---

[20] Inland Revenue, *International Tax Manual* (INT 348).
[21] [1996] S.T.C. SCD 241 SpC 73.

Commissioner found that the Irish resident trustees acted as such in name rather than in reality. Although the trustee signed all the documents placed before her, the Special Commissioner believed that she would have fallen in with whatever the settlor requested. The distinction in this case was thus between management that was effective as opposed to management that was apparent or ineffective. The case offers little assistance in addressing the distinction between "central management and control" and effective management, particularly as both the taxpayer and the Inland Revenue offered as authority cases which deal with the domestic law concept of central management and control.

OECD discussion paper

4-23 In February 2001, the OECD published a paper on *The Impact of the Communications Revolution on the Application of "Place of Effective Management" as a Tie-Breaker Rule.* The paper notes that there is no definition of "place of effective management" and extremely limited guidance is given on its meaning in the Commentary. The paper comments on the central management and control concept, as adopted in English speaking countries, as well as the "place of management" concept adopted by some Continental countries. The paper does not draw a clear distinction between the notions of central management and control, place of management, and place of effective management, although it recognises that the analysis is based on the experience of a limited number of countries.

The underlying concern, however, is that as a result of the communications and technological revolution, the way in which people run their businesses is changing fundamentally. As a result of sophisticated telecommunication technology and fast efficient transportation, it is no longer necessary for a person or group of persons to be physically located or meet in any one place to run a business. This increased mobility and functional decentralisation may have a significant impact on the incidence of dual resident companies and the application of the place of effective management tie-breaker rules. The Inland Revenue position on this is understood to be that where directors use modern communication technologies such as video-conferencing, telephone or e-mail chat facilities to conduct board meetings, if part of the decision-making takes place in the United Kingdom, the company is U.K. resident. In their view, if one director is present in the United Kingdom when this takes place, this is sufficient. This, they say, can then be addressed by application of the tie-breaker in the context of dual residence involving treaty countries.

Triangular cases

4-24 Can a person otherwise resident in a third country locate the management and control of its business in a treaty country following the colonial pattern in order to benefit from a particular U.K. treaty adopting this formulation. In particular, it should be borne in mind that under U.K. domestic law,[22] a company may be resident in two places at the same time. It is therefore not

---

[22] *Swedish Central Railway Co. Ltd v. Thompson* [1925] A.C. 495, HL. See Inland Revenue, *International Tax Handbook*, para. 338.

inconceivable that a company may be entitled to treaty benefits under this model although also resident in a third country. In the *Commerzbank* case it was pointed out that treaties between two non-U.K. companies would have no bearing on the application of a treaty between the United Kingdom and a contracting state. Consequently the application of tie-breaker provisions in a treaty between two other countries would not have a bearing on the application of the U.K. treaty. The only possible exception might be in relation to a foreign provision analogous to Finance Act 1994, section 249.

The only non OECD Model treaty where this issue is expressly addressed is in the Australian Treaty, although there is no general scope article and the definition of resident is defined under domestic law.[23] An Australian company is defined in Article 3(1)(a) as:

(1) it is incorporated in Australia and has its centre of administrative or practical management in Australia whether or not any person outside Australia exercises or is capable of exercising any overriding control or direction of the company or its policy or affairs in any way whatsoever; or

(2) it is managed and controlled in Australia.

4-25 Under this definition, a company would qualify as an Australian company for the purpose of this Treaty even if it was also resident in another country which adopts a central management and control test similar to that of the United Kingdom in *De Beers Consolidated Mines Ltd v. Howe*.[24] The definition in Article 3(1)(a)(i) is somewhat similar to the "place of effective management" test in the OECD Model. However, the two tests are alternative and all other comments relative to the colonial pattern are equally applicable to the test in Article (3)(1)(a)(ii).

Another treaty which does not follow the OECD Model is that with the United States (1975). Separate definitions of residence are adopted for each contracting state. In the case of the United Kingdom, a resident includes a corporation managed and controlled in the United Kingdom under Article 4(1)(a)(ii). In Article 4(1)(b)(ii), a U.S. resident includes a U.S. corporation. This is defined in Article 3(1)(b)(i) as a corporation created or organised under the laws of a U.S. State or the District of Columbia. The absence of a management-based alternative test excludes access to the benefits of this Treaty as described above.

Dual residence: trusts

4-26 The domestic rules for determining the residence of trusts may easily give rise to questions of dual residence. For income tax purposes, where there is more than one trustee, the trustees will be treated as U.K. resident if one is U.K. resident and the settlor is or was resident, ordinarily resident or domiciled in the United Kingdom at the time of settlement.[25] A

---

[23] Article 2(j).
[24] (1906) 5 T.C. 198.
[25] Finance Act 1989, s. 110.

similar rule applies to the residence of deceased estates.[26] Thus, trustees may be U.K. resident even where a majority are outside the United Kingdom and the administration of the trusts takes place outside the United Kingdom. For capital gains tax purposes, however, the trustees are treated as a continuing body of persons resident and ordinarily resident in the United Kingdom unless the general administration of the trusts is carried on outside the United Kingdom and the trustees or a majority of them are not resident or not ordinarily resident in the United Kingdom.[27]

Dual residence: partnership

4-27 A partnership is not treated as an entity separate and distinct from its partners and tax liability is determined by reference to the partners.[28] As a result, the question of dual residence of a partnership does not arise.

PERSON

4-28 In most cases, it will be necessary to be both a "person" and a resident of one or both contracting states. The term "person" is defined in treaties following the OECD Model to include "an individual, a company and any other body of persons". Thus, any entity endowed with legal personality will be a person for treaty purposes. These expressions may be contrasted with the domestic definitions contained in section 832(1), Taxes Act 1988: "'Body of persons' means any body politic, corporate or collegiate, and any company, fraternity, fellowship and society of persons whether corporate or not corporate . . . 'Company' is defined to mean . . . any body corporate or unincorporated association, but does not include a partnership". The application of similar provisions was considered by the court in *Padmore v. IRC*.[29] The Jersey Treaty contained a definition similar but not identical to the OECD Model. Although "person" is deemed to include any "body of persons, corporate or not corporate", no definition of "body of persons" appears in the Treaty. Article 2(3) of the Treaty, however, provides that in the application of the Treaty by the United Kingdom or Jersey, any term not otherwise defined must have the meaning which it has under the laws of the United Kingdom, or as the case may be, Jersey relating to the taxes which are the subject of the Treaty, unless the context requires otherwise. Again, this is the OECD approach.

Partnerships do not have legal personality under Jersey or English law. Despite this, at that time, for U.K. income tax purposes, a partnership was assessed to trading profits on the partnership and was assessed separately from any other tax chargeable to the partners. Jersey income tax was similarly assessed. Residence for tax purposes was ascribed to partnerships by reference to management and control under both U.K. and Jersey law. The Court of Appeal decided that the definition of person was comprehensive

---

[26] *ibid.*, s. 111.
[27] Taxation of Chargeable Gains Act 1992, s. 69.
[28] Taxes Act 1988, s. 111(1).
[29] *Padmore v. IRC* [1987] S.T.C. 37, Ch.D.

and that a partnership is, as a matter of ordinary language, a body of persons. The court refused to apply the domestic meaning.

4-29   Following the *Padmore* decision, the United Kingdom sought to include provisions in its treaties designed to protect its right to tax U.K. resident partners on their share of income and gains of a foreign partnership, where the partnership qualifies for exemption from U.K. tax. An example is found in the Uzbekistan Treaty and reads:

> "24(1) Where, under any provision of this Convention, a partnership, joint venture or other entity is entitled, as a resident of Uzbekistan, to exemption from tax in the United Kingdom on any income or capital gains, that provision shall not be construed as restricting the right of the United Kingdom to tax any member of the partnership, joint venture or other entity who is a resident of the United Kingdom on his share of such income or capital gains; but any such income or gains shall be treated for the purposes of Article 22 of this Convention as income or gains from sources in Uzbekistan".

The main effect of this provision is to compel transparency from the perspective of U.K. taxation with respect to U.K. participants in partnerships, joint ventures or other entities. Since such entities may not be treated as transparent in the other contracting state and subject to local taxation, the income or gains of U.K. participants is treated as foreign source income for the purpose of applying credit for foreign tax paid. The precise scope of application of the rule may give rise to difficulties. This is only partly addressed by reference to the definitions in, for example, Article 3 of the Uzbekistan Treaty which treats a partnership or joint venture under Uzbekistan law as a taxable unit (Article 3(2)). The term "company" means any body corporate or any entity which is treated as a body corporate for tax purposes. As a result, entities not treated as a body corporate for tax purposes under Uzbekistan law (but which might be "taxable units") will be subject to transparent treatment in the United Kingdom with respect to U.K. resident participants.

Foreign entity characterisation

4-30   In *Padmore*, the characterisation of the entity was the same for both U.K. and foreign purposes. The characterisation of a foreign entity as a company is to be determined (in England) for domestic purposes under the rules of English conflict of laws by reference to the general law of the country of incorporation in the case of a corporate entity. English law will recognise the existence of a corporation duly created in a foreign country as a matter of common law.[30] Whether the entity in question is a corporation will depend on the law of the country where it is formed.

The only statutory recognition of this rule applies if a question arises whether a body which purports to have or, as the case may be, appears to have lost corporate status under the laws of a territory which is not a recog-

---

[30] *Lazzards Bros & Co. v. Midland Bank Ltd* [1933] A.C. 289, HL.

nised state should or should not be regarded as having legal personality as a body corporate under the law of any part of the United Kingdom. Under the Foreign Corporations Act 1991, if it appears that the laws of that country are at that time applied by a settled court system in that territory, the question and other material questions relating to the body must be determined and account must be taken of those laws as if the territory were a recognised state.

4-31 There are few cases either in tax or general law on this. An entity which according to its proper law possesses certain aspects of separate personality may not necessarily be regarded as a corporation. In *Von Hellfeld v. Rechnitzer & Mayer Frères & Co,*[31] it was held that a French partnership could not be sued in its own name in the absence of evidence that by French law, the partnership was a different legal entity from its partners. In *Dreyfus v. IRC,*[32] the Court referred to French law in determining whether an SNC (Société en nom collectif) constituted a company or not. U.K. resident members in the SNC successfully proved that under French law, an SNC was a legal person. Consequently, the members were not liable to U.K. super tax on the entity's profits as they arose. In that case, the question was whether the entity was a partnership or a company. (The Inland Revenue now view the SNC as transparent; see also *Ryall v. du Bois Co. Ltd,*[33] where a German GmbH was treated on analogy to an English private company.)

As a result of these rules, the possibility arises for entities to be treated as corporations for U.K. tax purposes even though in the country of their formation, they may be deemed to be fiscally transparent by the local tax law.

4-32 Administrative practice has adopted somewhat different terminology in dealing with entity classification. The Inland Revenue describes entities as fiscally "transparent" or "opaque". In the case of a "transparent" entity, the member is regarded as being entitled to a share in the underlying income of the entity as it arises. A member in an "opaque" entity is taxed only on the distributions made by the entity.[34] The Revenue have published a list of entities that they have examined and regard as being transparent or opaque (Tax Bulletin December 2000 page 809).[35] They do not regard the expressions "transparent" and "opaque" as being interchangeable with "partnership" or "body corporate". Thus, although a partnership is fiscally transparent for the purpose of U.K. tax on income, a fiscally transparent entity is not necessarily a partnership. The *Stamp Duty Manual* also contains a list of entities which have been considered as bodies corporate for the purpose of stamp duty.

The criteria they apply in deciding whether a U.K. resident has an interest in a foreign business entity which results in U.K. tax on the resident's share of profits of the entity as they arise or whether they are taxed on distribution only is determined according to matters such as:

    (a)   legal existence separate from that of its members;

---

[31] [1914] 1 Ch. 748, CA.
[32] [1956] A.C. 39.
[33] (1933) 18 T.C. 431.
[34] Tax Bulletin (December 2000), p.809.
[35] *ibid.*

(b) the existence of share capital or something else which serves the same function as share capital;

(c) whether the business is carried on by the entity itself or jointly by its members;

(d) are the members entitled to share in its profits as they arise or does the amount of profits to which they are entitled depend on a decision of the entity or its members after the period in which the profits have arisen to make a distribution of its profits;

(e) is the entity or are the members responsible for debts incurred as a result of carrying on the business;

(f) do the assets used for carrying on the business belong beneficially to the entity or the members.

Treaty classification

4-33   The precise manner in which an entity is classified for treaty purposes will depend upon the particular treaty in question. Article 3(1)(b) of the OECD Model defines a company as "any body corporate or other entity which is treated as a body corporate for tax purposes. Although the first part of the definition is similar to the U.K. domestic law definition, it requires the status of a body corporate to be determined by reference to tax rules rather than the general law. Apart from the statutory provisions, U.K. tax law determines corporate status by reference to the general law. This definition itself does not explain which contracting states tax purposes are relevant in this respect. The country of residence will apply its law in deciding whether a "person" is a resident of that contracting state. Where a foreign entity is treated as a corporation for U.K. purposes and qualifies for treaty benefits, the significance of this classification varies from treaty to treaty. Thereafter, it refers to the contracting state for the purposes of the tax of the contracting state where the convention is to apply. In other words, where U.K. tax is in question, U.K. classification is relevant. This would, as described above, point to the domestic general law of the other contracting state. Most U.K. treaties, and indeed the OECD Model, do not generally distinguish between benefits available to companies as opposed to other taxpayers. Classification as a company will principally determine entitlement to treaty benefits as a person resident in a member state.

U.S. entities and the U.S. Treaty

4-34   Not all U.K. treaties follow the OECD Model. The most significant of those that do not is the treaty with the United States. It is significant not only because it deviates considerably from the OECD Model, but also as a result of the new flexibility given under U.S. federal tax law, under the "check-the-box" regulations, to elect corporate or transparent status for a wide range of entities for U.S. federal taxpayers.

The U.S. Treaty (1975) does not follow the OECD Model and contains its own somewhat extended definition. A corporation means any one of the following:

(1) a U.S. corporation;

(2) a U.K. corporation; or

(3) any body corporate or other entity of a third state which is treated as a body corporate for tax purposes by both contracting states.[36]

A U.S. corporation is either:

(a) a corporation which is created or organised under the laws of the United States or any state thereof or the District of Columbia; or

(b) any unincorporated entity treated as a corporation for U.S. tax purposes. [37]

A U.K. corporation is any body corporate or unincorporated association created or organised under the laws of the United Kingdom excluding a partnership, local authority or a local authority association.[38]

4-35 Residence is defined in the new U.S. Treaty (2001) in a manner that is more consistent with the OECD Model. Several uncertainties in interpreting the OECD wording are addressed. This includes specific inclusion of pension schemes and other employee benefit schemes that are exempt from tax, as well as religious, charitable, scientific and other institutions that may similarly be exempt from tax under domestic law.[39]

The Inland Revenue take the view that for U.K. tax purposes, limited liability companies (LLCs) formed under the laws of various states of the United States should be regarded as taxable entities and not as fiscally transparent. They do not in principle recognise LLCs as qualifying for treaty benefits, but accept treaty claims from LLCs to the extent that the income in question is subject to U.S. tax in the hands of those members of the LLC who are residents of the United States (Tax Bulletin June 1997 page 440).[40] The logical extension of this treatment is to permit benefits under the Treaty for a member of a U.S. LLC resident in a third country, and not to deny it by virtue of participation in the LLC.

The new U.S. Treaty (2001) addresses fiscal transparency directly. Article 1(8) specifies that an item of income derived through a person that is fiscally transparent under the laws of either contracting state is regarded as derived by a resident of a contracting state to the extent that the item is treated for the purpose of the tax law of that contracting state as the income of the resident. This corresponds in general to the administrative practice adopted by the Inland Revenue under the 1975 Treaty.

Fiscal transparency

4-36 The fact that an entity does not qualify as a "person" will not automatically produce fiscal transparency. In *Memec plc v. Inland Revenue*

---

[36] Article 3(1)(a).
[37] Article 3(1)(b)(i).
[38] Article 3(1)(b)(ii).
[39] Article 4(3).
[40] *Tax Bulletin* (June 1997), p.440.

Commissioners,[41] a U.K. company (Plc) was the silent partner in a silent partnership under German law with a German resident and incorporated company (GmbH). It made a capital contribution to GmbH and obtained in return a contractual right to payment of 87.84 per cent of the annual profits of the partnership. Under German law GmbH remained the owner of the business assets and of the income from those assets. Plc as the silent partner had no proprietary interest in the assets. GmbH ran the business. A silent partnership has no separate legal personality under German law.

The dispute involved whether the income should be identified as dividends from a trading subsidiary of the silent partnership, divisible and distributable after expenses as prescribed by the partnership agreement or should be identified as Plc's contractual right under the partnership agreement to payment of the prescribed share of partnership profit.

4-37   After considering the categorisation of entities under both foreign and English law, Robert Walker J.[42] concluded that the arrangement embodied in the silent partnership was not transparent. Transparency, he said, is normally associated with a situation where the ultimate recipient of the underlying income in question has a beneficial interest in it from the start. If the income is not transmuted at some intermediate stage, for example by the need for trustees to exercise a discretion or by its being packaged so as to reach the ultimate recipient in the form of a fixed annuity or other form which is different from the underlying income, then the entity is transparent. This view was shared by the court of appeal.

In this case, the U.K. company did not receive or become entitled to dividends paid by the trading subsidiary. It was only entitled to an amount determined by reference to the dividends rather than the dividends themselves. Consequently, it could not qualify directly for treaty relief by way of credit for underlying tax paid by the trading subsidiary.

---

[41] [1998] S.T.C. 754, CA.
[42] In the Chancery Division [1996] S.T.C. 1136.

CHAPTER 5

Income from Business

DISTRIBUTIVE PROVISIONS OF INCOME TAX TREATIES

5-01 The distributive provisions of income tax treaties constitute the heart of the treaty system. These rules allocate taxing jurisdiction between the contracting states and determine the source of income and agreed maximum levels of taxation in source states. Any remaining double taxation after the application of these rules falls to be addressed by the double tax relief article (OECD Article 23) which in the United Kingdom generally allows credit for foreign tax paid against U.K. tax liability. In the context of non U.K. residents, the distributive articles determine the limits of the U.K. tax base. Collectively, the distributive provisions cover the whole of the U.K. tax system. As with domestic law, treaties have evolved significantly since the oldest of them was first negotiated. Furthermore, given the fact that each treaty is individually negotiated with its own trade-offs taking into account the interests of both contracting states, there is a wide variation in the detail. There is, as a result, no substitute for examining the precise wording of each treaty in considering its application.

The broad classification of sources of income for treaty purposes parallels the schedular system of U.K. taxation to a large extent. Although there are a number of areas of overlap, Table 5.1 is a general guide to classification under treaty and domestic law in relation to U.K. sources. It will be noted that within certain broad categories, various sectors are identified for special treatment. This is most notable in relation to business profits where shipping and air transportation, as well as artistes and sportsmen, have their own rules. Similarly, in the employment area, general rules are provided for dependent personal services with specific treatment applicable to directors' fees, artistes and sportsmen, pensions and government services.

5-02 Delimiting the boundaries between the categories does give rise to difficulties both under domestic law and treaties independently. It should be emphasised that these broad classifications will form a general guide only and that treaty classification and domestic law classification will not necessarily coincide in all cases. For example, in *Memec plc v. IRC*,[1] the treaty meaning of "dividend" under the German Treaty was not the same as the domestic meaning of the expression for the purpose of credit in relation to underlying tax under Taxes Act 1988, section 799. Changes in classification also occur such as the abolition of the charge under Schedule C by Finance Act 1996 in domestic law and the abandonment of Article 14 for independent personal services under the latest OECD Model (April 29, 2000) with

---

[1] [1998] S.T.C. 754, CA.

Table 5.1: Guide to classification under treaty and domestic law

Treaty	Article	Domestic Source
Art. 6	Income from immovable property	Schedule A
Art. 7	Business profits	Schedule D Case I & II
Art. 8	Shipping, inland waterways transport and air transport	Schedule D Case I
Art. 9	Associated enterprises	
Art. 10	Dividends	Schedule F
Art. 11	Interest	Schedule D Case III
Art. 12	Royalties	Schedule D Case III
Art. 13	Capital gains	Chargeable Gains
Art. 14	Independent personal services	Schedule D Case II
Art. 15	Dependent personal services	Schedule E
Art. 16	Directors' fees	Schedule E
Art. 17	Artistes and sportsmen	Schedule E/Schedule D Case II
Art. 18	Pensions	Schedule E
Art. 19	Government service	Schedule E
Art. 20	Students	
Art. 21	Other income	Various

those activities being subsumed in the notion of business profits under Articles 5 and 7. A further source of complexity in dealing with treaties arises from potential mismatches in classification between the United Kingdom and the other contracting state. This may arise because of different legal analysis of the underlying issues, differing approach to the determination of the source of income for tax purposes, or interpretation of the treaty.

PERMANENT ESTABLISHMENT

5-03   There are no reported cases in the United Kingdom on the meaning of permanent establishment. Notwithstanding this, the issue is identified by the Inland Revenue in their Internal Manuals as one of the more difficult aspects on which inspectors should seek advice from the International Division. Consequently, administrative practice and the extent to which domestic law coincides with treaty provisions is of particular importance.

The United Kingdom has a tradition of active participation in the OECD Committee on Fiscal Affairs and, in particular, its working parties responsible for both the OECD Model Tax Convention and the Commentary. In general, the Inland Revenue does not adopt an independent interpretation of permanent establishment, but relies heavily on the OECD Commentary. For some time, a single observation on the Commentary was entered by the United Kingdom in relation to dependent agents contracting in their own name.

More recently, the dissent by the United Kingdom on one of the key elements in the clarification of the application of permanent establishment definition to e-commerce agreed by the OECD Committee on Fiscal Affairs on December 22, 2000 will give rise to a second observation.

5-08   There is likewise very little administrative guidance on the meaning of "branch". The Inland Revenue state in the *International Tax Manual*[11] that they have been advised that the presence of a principal (in the case of a sole trader or partnership) or of employees on a more or less regular basis is likely to be an essential ingredient of a branch (although employees may also be agents). What is perhaps important in the context of the application of treaties is that, if this is indeed correct, then as a matter of domestic law, non-resident companies might be trading in the United Kingdom, but would not do so through a branch or agency where there is no human intervention.

While this view may pre-date recent discussions in relation to e-commerce, there is no suggestion that it has been viewed as inapplicable to other forms of activity where the trade is carried on mainly through automatic equipment. On this basis, it seems that even though in the treaty context a permanent establishment might be constituted by such automatic equipment, as a matter of domestic law, there may be no branch or agency in the United Kingdom and therefore a non-resident company would not be within the charge to U.K. corporation tax in any event and the question of treaty protection would not arise.

Permanent establishments in e-commerce

5-09   Changes to the Commentary on the OECD Model Tax Convention adopted by the Committee on Fiscal Affairs on December 22, 2000 in the context of e-commerce may also give indications as to how these issues might be viewed in the context of permanent establishments constituted by automated equipment in related technology. Modern examples include fixed automated telecommunications equipment such as backhaul ducts and cables, POP, transmission and switching equipment, backbone local loop, ducts and cables, leased lines, indefeasible rights of use and capacity deals.

Introductory comments on the amended Commentary indicate that human intervention is not a requirement for the existence of a permanent establishment. It notes that usually personnel conduct the business of the enterprise and that although that is still accurate in the context of e-commerce, it was not intended to rule out that a business may at least partly be carried out without personnel.

5-10   Specifically in the context of e-commerce, the changes to the Commentary make it clear that in many cases, the issue of whether computer equipment at a given location constitutes a permanent establishment will depend on whether the functions performed through that equipment exceed the preparatory or auxiliary threshold.

The United Kingdom has refused to participate in this consensus. Its view was first expressed in the Inland Revenue Press Release on April 11, 2000 to the effect that:

> "in the U.K., we take the view that a website of itself is not a permanent establishment. And we take the view that a server is insufficient itself to constitute a permanent establishment of a business that is conducting

---

[11] At para. 842.

e-commerce through a website on the server. We take that view regardless of whether the server is owned, rented or otherwise at the disposal
of the business".

It has been confirmed that in no circumstances do servers of themselves or
together with websites constitute a permanent establishment for e-tailers. An
e-tailer is essentially a content provider. New paragraph 42.9 of the
Commentary on Article 5 defines an e-tailer as an enterprise that carries on
the business of selling products through the Internet.

5-11 The United Kingdom intends to make an observation setting out
its views on this when changes to the Commentary are included in the OECD
Model Treaty. The result of these statements is that the presence of a server
will simply be one of the factors to take into account among others in determining whether or not a permanent establishment exists. By implication, it
is difficult to see the United Kingdom recognising a permanent establishment
that has no human participation. No indication is given of the extent to
which human intervention is required. In this regard, recourse may be had
to the more traditional view in relation to the maintenance and operation of
fixed automatic equipment explained in paragraphs 8 and 10 of the OECD
Commentary on Article 5. Thus, for example, the operation of equipment
by a non-resident company for its own account in the United Kingdom may
constitute a permanent establishment even if the activities of local personnel
are restricted to setting up, operating, controlling and maintaining such
equipment.

If the above analysis of whether a non-resident is trading in the United
Kingdom through a branch or agency simply via automated equipment
where there is no other presence is correct, then the question of treaty protection for non-residents operating in the United Kingdom in this way will
not arise as the statement about websites on servers simply reflects the
domestic law. On the other hand, if this notion is applied generally, then the
potential for double taxation will exist. If the United Kingdom does not recognise fully automated websites on servers as constituting foreign permanent
establishments, then the potential for double taxation will exist as a result
of any refusal to permit credits for tax paid in the foreign jurisdiction. It is
difficult to see how fully enabled trading websites on servers differ from
other automated equipment.

Agency establishments

5-12 A permanent establishment may exist despite the absence of a fixed
place of business. Agency permanent establishments are addressed in Article
5(5) and (6) of the OECD Model. The Swedish Treaty is an example which
reads as follows:

"5(5) Notwithstanding the provisions of paragraphs (1) and (2) of this
Article, where a person—other than an agent of an independent status
to whom paragraph (6) of this Article applies—is acting on behalf of an
enterprise and has, and habitually exercises, in a Contracting State an
authority to conclude contracts in the name of the enterprise, that enter-

prise shall be deemed to have a permanent establishment in that State in respect of any activities which that person undertakes for the enterprise, unless the activities of such person are limited to those mentioned in paragraph (4) of this Article which, if exercised through a fixed place of business, would not make this fixed place of business a permanent establishment under the provisions of that paragraph.

5(6) An enterprise shall not be deemed to have a permanent establishment in a Contracting State merely because it carries on business in that State through a broker, general commission agent or any other agent of an independent status, provided that such persons are acting in the ordinary course of their business".

5-13   These provisions track loosely the U.K. domestic machinery for assessing non-residents trading in the United Kingdom which are now contained in Finance Act 1995, sections 126 and 127. An early predecessor of this legislation (section 373(1) of Income Tax Act 1952) was considered by the courts in *Fleming v. London Produce Company*.[12] In that legislation, the reference to a "broker" included a general commission agent. The court determined that a general commission agent must have "broker-like qualities". Secondly, the exemption only applied to non-residents who merely employed brokers in the ordinary way, even if they regularly employ the same one. A general commission agent is one who holds himself out as being ready to work for clients generally and who does not in substance confine his activities to one principle or an insignificant number of principles. In *Willson v. Hooker*,[13] "regular agency" was distinguished from "casual or occasional agency". In that case, only a single trading transaction was entered into. However, he was the person through whom all the relevant steps were carried out and thus not a casual agent.

The current domestic legislation, that is Finance Act 1995, section 127(1), identifies the following categories of agent:

(a)   an agent of the non-resident who does not act in relation to the transactions in the course of carrying on a regular agency for the non-resident;

(b)   brokers who:

    (i)   carry on the business of a broker;

    (ii)   carry out the transaction on behalf of the non-resident in the ordinary course of that business;

    (iii)   where the remuneration received by the broker in respect of the transaction is not less than the rate than that which would have been customary for that class of business;

(c)   investment managers subject to the provisions of section 127(3); and

---

[12] (1968) 44 T.C. 582.
[13] [1995] S.T.C. 1142, Ch.D.

(d) Lloyds members' agents or managing agents of a syndicate where the non-resident is a member of Lloyds.

5-14   The expression "independent agent" is used only in the context of Finance Act 1995, Schedule 23. In this context, the only distinction between independent agents and others is that an independent agent is not liable to civil penalties or surcharge in respect of certain acts which he did not participate in or consent to, and is entitled to indemnities from his non-resident principal.[14] In this context, an independent agent means in relation to the non-resident any person "who is the non-resident's U.K. representative in respect of any agency from the non-resident in which he was acting on the non-resident's behalf in an independent capacity". For this purpose, a person:

> "shall not be regarded as acting in an independent capacity on behalf of the non-resident unless, having regard to its legal, financial and commercial characteristics, the relationship between them is a relationship between persons carrying on independent businesses that deal with each other at arm's length".

5-15   Domestic law does not distinguish between agents who contract in the names of their principals and those who contract in their own names as undisclosed agents for their principals. Treaties following the OECD pattern refer to agents who have authority "to conclude contracts in the name of the enterprise". The United Kingdom has entered an observation on the Commentary to the OECD Model. It considers that an agent is not an independent agent if he has the characteristics of a dependent agent and habitually exercises that authority, whether he does so in his own name or that of the enterprise.

The Inland Revenue has long taken the view that independent agent in Schedule 25 is intended to have the same meaning as in the OECD Model "except that it is not limited to agents ejusdem generis with broker or general commission agents".[15]

The Inland Revenue regard both points as reflecting civil law influence on the OECD Model. Paragraph 852 of the *International Tax Handbook* suggests that the making of contracts in the name of the principal would be regarded by civil law countries as a characteristic of a dependent agent, whereas contracts made in the agent's own name would be characteristic of independent status. It continues:

> "in our law, if contracts are made on behalf of and with the authority of the principal, the relationship of the agent to the principal is not affected by whether the contract is made in the name of the principal or the agent's own name. So agents, who in all other respects would be dependent agents according to the OECD Model, could in our law make contracts in their own name. We would not wish such agents to

---

[14] Finance Act 1995, Sched. 23, paras 5 and 6.
[15] Inland Revenue, *International Tax Handbook*, para. 963.

be regarded as agents of independent status under a treaty and therefore resist the literal meaning of 'in the name of' and argue that the word should be interpreted as 'on behalf of' which is an acceptable translation of the words 'au nom de' which appears in the French version of the Model Convention".

This approach has been included in the OECD Commentary since 1994.[16]

BUSINESS PROFITS

5-16 The permanent establishment article in conjunction with the business profits article forms the core of the treaty regime regulating the taxation of commercial activities. Article 7(1) of the OECD Model sets out the general rule. It is reflected in Article 7(1) of the Kazakhstan Treaty which reads as follows:

> "The profits of an enterprise of a Contracting State shall be taxable only in that State unless the enterprise carries on or has carried on business in the other Contracting State through a permanent establishment situated therein. If the enterprise carries on or has carried on business as aforesaid, the profits of the enterprise may be taxed in the other State but only so much of them as is attributable to that permanent establishment".

An "enterprise of a contracting state" is normally defined in Article 3(1)(c) to mean an enterprise carried on by a resident of a contracting state. Profits may be liable to tax in the other contracting state only if the enterprise carries on business there through a permanent establishment. In such circumstances, tax in the contracting state, where the permanent establishment is located, is limited to so much of the profits as is attributable to the permanent establishment. While articulating this principle is relatively straightforward, determining the profits attributable to a permanent establishment is one of the more difficult issues in the application of tax treaties. The principles to be applied in attributing profits are set out in the remaining paragraphs of Article 7.

Which profits are "business profits"?

5-17 Article 7(1) refers to profits of an enterprise that carries on business through a permanent establishment. The scope of the Article is restricted by Article 7(7) which specifies that where profits include items of income which are dealt with separately in other articles, then those articles are not affected by the business profits article. It is thus a general provision which may be excluded by more specific rules. Article 7(7) is absent, however, from a number of U.K. treaties. The notion of "carrying on business" has a wide meaning in U.K. tax law and does not generally express

---

[16] At para. 32.

taxing jurisdiction (other than in the context of Schedule A which is addressed under Article 6 (income from immovable property)). The expression clearly covers income taxed under Schedule D Case I in respect of trade. Its meaning must be understood in the context of particular circumstances. Thus, in *Sun Life Assurance Co. of Canada v. Pearson*,[17] it referred to investment income of a non-resident life insurance company. Treaties following the colonial pattern and some other early treaties refer to "commercial and industrial profits" in the context of permanent establishment provisions. This term may not be coextensive with "profits" in Article 7 of the OECD Model, as noted by Vinelott J. in the *Sun Life* case.[18] The scope of the expression varies from treaty to treaty, where different sources of income are included or excluded.

Attribution of profits to a branch

5-18   Allocation of profit to a permanent establishment is a controversial and awkward issue both in domestic and treaty practice. The U.K. approach to treaties is illustrated by Article 8(2) of the Thai Treaty which reads:

> "Where an enterprise of a Contracting State carries on business in the other Contracting State through a permanent establishment situated therein, there shall in each Contracting State be attributed to that permanent establishment the profits which it might be expected to make if it were a distinct and separate enterprise engaged in the same or similar activities under the same or similar conditions and dealing wholly independently with the enterprise of which it is a permanent establishment".

5-19   The legal basis for attributing profits to a U.K. branch of a non-resident company under domestic law is obscure. Section 11 of the Taxes Act 1988 brings a non-resident company within the charge to corporation tax in respect of its trade carried on in the United Kingdom through a branch or agency. Its chargeable profits are any trading income arising directly or indirectly through or from the branch or agency, and any income from property or rights used by or held for the branch or agency.[19]

There is little direct authority as to the method of determining income which arises "directly or indirectly" through or from the branch or agency. In an early case on the question of whether non-residents were trading in the United Kingdom is *Pommery and Greno v. Aptthorpe*.[20] Denman J. said[21]:

> "It may be that there may be some difficulty in some respects as to the manner of calculating the amount of expenditure to be put against profits, whether it would be a proper course to look at the goods sent

---

[17] See above, n. 8.
[18] [1984] S.T.C. 461, Ch.D.
[19] Taxes Act 1988, s. 11(2).
[20] (1886) 2 T.C. 182.
[21] At 189.

over to England and then to consider what profits they make, putting a fair valuation on them as they arrive, and as the money is transmitted, or whether it would be necessary in such a case to look more minutely at the profits and losses upon the whole trade carried on partly in France and partly in England . . . That is a matter of quantum, a matter for the consideration of persons skilled in dealing with such matters as assessing profits of trade".

5-20   This passage has been cited by the Inland Revenue as an early description of the arm's length principle. The problems of allocation in a non-treaty context are well illustrated in *Yates v. GCA International Ltd.*[22] In that case, an English company entered into a contract with a Venezuelan company to provide certain services. The remuneration was divided between work performed in the United Kingdom and work performed in Venezuela. Under the Venezuelan Tax Code, income was regarded as arising from a Venezuelan source *inter alia* if the originating cause of the income was within Venezuela or for services rendered to Venezuelan residents or technical services utilised in the country; however, for the purpose of determining the extent to which credit was available in the United Kingdom under what is now Taxes Act 1988, section 790(4), it was provided that the income in question must arise in the territory imposing the tax. Scott J. (as he then was) concluded that English law concepts as to identification of the place where income arises had to be applicable in determining to what extent the contractual remuneration was "income arising in" Venezuela. He held that apportionment of the source of profits was possible and that the Special Commissioners made the obvious apportionment, namely based on the contract itself, which he did not disturb.

In the *Sun Life* case, the court considered whether, in the context of the Canadian Treaty, insurance policies were made at or through a branch or agency in the United Kingdom in the following circumstances. A Canadian insurer divided its business into divisions. The British division comprised not only territories within the United Kingdom, but also the Republic of Ireland, Malta, Guernsey, Jersey and the Isle of Man. The Court of Appeal concluded that the branch or agency was constituted by the whole of the operation within the United Kingdom and that the offices outside the United Kingdom such as in the Republic of Ireland had no authority to conclude any insurance business. They were merely administrative channels whereby proposals reached London where they were effectively dealt with and where the policies were issued.

5-21   Little changed recently until the enactment of the Finance Act 1995, which introduced both substantive and procedural changes to the taxation of non-residents. The question of determining profits of non-residents was debated in Parliament as a result of perceived inadequacies of the proposed legislation.[23] In the course of the debate in the Standing Committee on the Finance Bill, the Government reaffirmed that "the arm's length principle applies generally to the measure of profits brought into charge on a

---

[22] [1991] S.T.C. 157, Ch.D.
[23] Hansard, HC Standing Committee D, March 2, 1995, p.547.

non-resident". The Government was unwilling to see amendments to the legislation, but thereafter the Inland Revenue issued a statement in *Tax Bulletin* (August 1995), p.237 with the agreement of the major tax professional bodies to the effect that the arm's length principle as set out in the OECD Model Treaty and as explained in OECD publications applies to the measure of profits chargeable on a non-resident in respect of trading in the United Kingdom as a matter of law irrespective of whether a treaty applies. In law, a branch is not a separate legal person from the company to which it belongs, but part of it. Finance Act 1995, section 126(4) states that for the purpose of that section (determining the liability of U.K. representatives of a non-resident (that is the branch or agency)), the representative is to be treated as if he were a separate and distinct person from the non-resident. This may give some statutory support for the separate entity hypothesis as a matter of domestic law.

The statutory transfer pricing provisions in Taxes Act 1988, Schedule 28AA do not themselves apply to the attribution of profits between a U.K. branch and other parts of a non-resident company. However, it should be borne in mind that if a non-resident company is within the U.K. tax charge, transactions between it and other companies where there is common management, control or capital as determined under Taxes Act 1988, Schedule 28AA, paragraph 4, will be within the U.K. transfer pricing rules. Thus, the determination of the transfer prices will be at two levels: first, between the company and the other parts of the group, and secondly, between the head office and the U.K. permanent establishment. Both levels are relevant to U.K. corporation tax.

5-22   General transfer pricing principles are, however, imported into the treaty rules contained in Article 7(2) of the OECD Model which require the profits attributed to a permanent establishment to be those which the establishment would have made if instead of dealing with its head office, it had been dealing with an entirely separate enterprise under conditions and at prices prevailing in the ordinary market. The application of the separate entity hypothesis has been examined by the courts in relation to treaties with Australia, Canada and the Netherlands. Two of these cases dealt with the attribution of profits of overseas life assurance companies to permanent establishments in the United Kingdom. The domestic legislation which provided for profit on a notional basis was itself designed to overcome difficulties of allocation. In *Ostime v. Australian Mutual Provident Society*,[24] Lord Radcliffe identified the problems of Article 7(2) thus[25]:

> "It is not left wholly to the will of the United Kingdom taxing authorities to decide the basis on which that attribution of commercial profits is to be made. Article [7(2)] provides by its terms for a basis which in effect requires the hypothesis that the branch is an independent enterprise dealing as an independent entity at arm's length with the head office. The profits which emerge from a calculation based on this

---

[24] (1958) 38 T.C. 492, HL.
[25] At 517.

hypothesis are to be deemed to be income derived from sources in the United Kingdom.

I do not think that it is open to us to decide what would be the consequences of taxing the Respondent's commercial profits according to this new formula. It is by no means easy to see what other hypotheses are required or excluded by the central hypothesis".

5-23 In his view, the formula of allocating notional profits could not be applied to the hypothetical independent enterprise "without violating the very hypothesis . . . designed to lay down the basis of taxability". In the same case, Lord Denning described the test in his dissenting judgment as:

> "The Agreement goes on to say how this amount is to be ascertained. It is by means of a given hypothesis. You are to treat the establishment here as if it were completely independent of the Australian head office and were dealing at arm's length with it, and you are to estimate the profits which such an independent enterprise might be expected to derive on its own, and then tax it on the amount so ascertained".

The importance of the way in which branch activity is actually conducted is highlighted in *General Reinsurance Company Ltd v. Tomlinson*.[26] A Dutch reinsurance company operated a branch in the United Kingdom. It maintained a portfolio of investment built up from the profits of its reinsurance business in London, made up of U.K. investments and certain dollar investments held in New York. Decision-making about the portfolio took place in the Netherlands. Investment income in this context was regarded as profits obtained in the carrying-on of the company's business. This applied to profit on U.S. investments, even though they were specifically earmarked for possible U.S. claims. Since the U.S. business was done by the company in London, the investment income was part of its profit as a matter of domestic law. In that case, it was considered that if the permanent establishment was to be treated as an independent enterprise, it must be considered to be necessary for it to have a portfolio of investments in order to carry on its business. Although the court recognised that there were difficulties in deciding what the appropriate size of the portfolio was, in that case, the court determined that because the London portfolio was built up from past profits of the business of the branch, there was nothing to suggest that the London portfolio was either too large or too small for the amount of the business carried on by the London branch.

5-24 The implications of the separate entity hypothesis has recently featured in the OECD discussion paper on the attribution of profits to permanent establishments.[27] The current U.K. administrative application of the separate entity hypothesis is that it is, however, only a tool for allocating

---

[26] (1970) 48 T.C. 81.
[27] OECD, *Draft Discussion on the Attribution of Profits to Permanent Establishments* (February 8, 2001).

such profits as exist with an enterprise and does not permit transactions between the permanent establishment and other parts of the enterprise to be hypothesised.[28]

In the Exchange of Notes of July 24, 2001 with respect to the U.S. Treaty (2001), explicit endorsement is given to the OECD Transfer Pricing Guidelines as the mechanism by analogy for determining the profits attributable to a permanent establishment. However, given the lack of agreement as to the extent to which the separate entity hypothesis is to apply, this statement is of limited value.

Deduction of expenditure

5-25 Deduction of expenditure of a permanent establishment is given express recognition in Article 7(3) of the OECD Model. It specifies that in determining the profits of a permanent establishment, deduction of expenses must be allowed where they are incurred for the permanent establishment. This includes executive and general administrative expenses incurred where they are in the state in which the permanent establishment is situated or otherwise. This clarifies the method of allocating expenses prescribed by Article 7(2).

Customary methods of allocation

5-26 Article 7(4) authorises the application of customary methods of attributing profits to permanent establishments. Its terms are reflected in Article 7(4) of the Romanian Treaty which reads as follows:

> "Insofar as it has been customary in a Contracting State to determine the profits to be attributed to a permanent establishment on the basis of an apportionment of the total profits of the enterprise to its various parts, nothing in paragraph (2) of this Article shall preclude that Contracting State from determining the profits to be taxed by such an apportionment as may be customary; the method of apportionment adopted shall, however, be such that the result shall be in accordance with the principles embodied in this Article".

5-27 The significance and application of these provisions has been highlighted in cases involving determining the U.K. profits of overseas life assurance companies. Under domestic law, overseas life insurance companies have been taxed on a conventional basis with the conventional profits for this purpose arrived at by reference to the proportion of investment income corresponding to the proportion of business done in the United Kingdom to the whole of the business done. In *Ostime v. Australian Mutual Provident Society*,[29] the court considered the 1947 Australian Treaty. "Industrial or commercial profits" was narrowly defined in the Treaty and specifically excluded income in the form of dividend, interest, rents, royalties, management charges or remuneration for personal services. The pro-

---

[28] Inland Revenue, *Banking Manual*, app. 9A.
[29] See above, n. 24.

visions attributing profits to a permanent establishment in Article III(2) did not contain wording preserving conventional methods of attributing income. The Treaty as a result overrode the application of the domestic rule.

In the *Sun Life* case, the Treaty provision relating to customary methods was considered by the Court of Appeal.[30] It concluded that there was no doubt as to the customary nature of the domestic statute law of attribution based on a fraction of worldwide income which had been in place since 1915. The court noted that Article 7(4) of the OECD Model does not require a close correspondence of the method permitted by that article and the separate enterprise principle in Article 7(2). Consequently, it held that Article 7(4) authorises some computation based on apportionment of total profits. Insofar as a conventional method is to give effect to the separate enterprise principle, it must to some degree be crude in its operation. The limits of Article 7(4) are imprecise and the court was not prepared to say that the domestic law was not in accordance with the principles of Article 7. Although apportioning total profits by reference to a formula is not an attribution of profits on a separate enterprise basis, the customary nature of the U.K. rules meant that the domestic law gave reasonable effect to the principles of Article 7.

INDEPENDENT PERSONAL SERVICES

5-28   Under domestic law, income tax is charged on the profits of any profession or vocation under Schedule D Case II. This is distinguished from the income of a trade taxed under Schedule D Case I. For many years, U.K. treaties, particularly those patterned on the OECD 1963 Draft and 1977 Model, have distinguished between business profits in Article 7 and "professional services and other activities of an independent character" referred to in Article 14. Article 14 was deleted from the OECD Model on April 29, 2000 on the basis of an OECD Report entitled *Issues Related to Article 14 of the OECD Model Tax Convention*.[31] The deletion was based on the fact that there were no intended differences between the concepts of permanent establishment as used in Article 7 and fixed base as used in Article 14, or between how profits were computed and tax was calculated according to whether Article 7 or 14 applied. The U.S. Treaty (2001) is the first U.K. treaty to adopt this approach. Article 15 does not appear and the term "business" is defined to include the performance of professional services and other activities of an independent character as recommended by the OECD to prevent a restrictive interpretation of "business" which might exclude such activities. This change in the U.S. Treaty alters the basis on which cross-border professional partnerships are taxable however.[32]

5-29   The OECD also recognised that it was not always clear which activities fell within business profits as opposed to independent personal services. There are similar problems of defining the boundaries under

---

[30] See above, n. 8.
[31] Adopted by the Committee on Fiscal Affairs on January 27, 2000.
[32] U.S. Treaty, Art.3(1)(d).

domestic law. A profession generally involves an occupation requiring purely intellectual skill or manual skill controlled by the intellectual skill of the operator such as painting.[33] The question is one of fact and degree. The essential question is the degree of intellectual skill involved.[34] Inland Revenue practice is generally to deal with independent personal services by analogy with business profits.[35] Their guidance notes that although the Article is mainly concerned with individuals who carry on a profession, it can also be relevant to an individual who carries on a trade. This addresses the lack of common boundary between "trade" under Schedule D Case I and "profession or vocation" under Schedule D Case II on the one hand, and the treaty concepts of "business profits" in Article 7 and "independent personal services" in Article 14 on the other. It also addresses distinctions between trade and professions in old cases that seem improbable in the modern context. Thus, a photographer is a trader[36] while a jockey carries on a vocation.[37]

TECHNICAL SERVICE FEES

5-30   Several treaties with developing countries make an important exception to the permanent establishment principle in the context of fees for technical services. An example is found in the Gambian Treaty. Article 14 reads in part:

> "14(1) Fees for technical services arising in one of the territories and paid to a resident of the other territory may be taxed in that other territory.
>
> 14(2) Notwithstanding the provisions of Article 7, such fees may also be taxed in the territory in which they arise and according to the law of that territory; but where such fees are paid to a resident of the other territory who is subject to tax there in respect thereof the tax so charged in the territory in which the fees arise shall not exceed 15 per cent of the gross amount of the fees arising there".

Thus, where technical services are provided, they may be taxed in the country of source, despite the absence of a permanent establishment. These articles are included at the instance of the other contracting states and are commonly aimed at protecting withholding taxes on gross fees paid to non-residents for consulting services. The rate of tax is usually linked to the rate set with respect to royalties.

5-31   These articles do cause significant problems in determining the boundary between cases involving technical services as opposed to independent personal services or business profits, as well as distinctions between

---

[33] *IRC v. Maxse* (1919) 12 T.C. 41.
[34] *Currie v. IRC* (1921) 12 T.C. 245.
[35] Inland Revenue, *Double Taxation Manual*, para. 1740.
[36] *Cecil v. IRC* (1919) 36 T.L.R. 164.
[37] *Wing v. O'Connell* [1927] I.R. 84.

technical service fees and royalties. Early versions of these articles contained fairly simple definitions. For example, Article 14(3) of the Gambian Treaty reads:

> "The term 'fees for technical services' as used in this Article means payments of any kind to any person, other than to an employee of the person making the payments, in consideration for any services of a technical or consultancy nature".

This definition does not assist greatly in identifying the boundaries between, for example, professional services which are "technical" on the one side, and payments for "know-how" which may fall within the royalty article. Later versions, such as Article 13 of the Indian Treaty (1993) contains lengthy descriptions of technical services with amounts deemed included and excluded. Technical service provisions may not apply where there is a permanent establishment, thus encouraging permanent establishments in the context of technical services, so as to avoid taxes on a gross basis. From a U.K. perspective, this will be important in the context of technical service contracts performed abroad, where tax on a gross basis may lead to effective taxation at rates in excess of U.K. rates. In some treaties, such as Gambia, a recipient of such fees can elect to have tax charged on a net basis. In addition, such treaties typically deem the source of payments to be the country in which the payer is resident. This will permit a U.K. resident to obtain credit for the tax paid, notwithstanding that the work is done in the United Kingdom.

SHIPPING AND AIR TRANSPORT

5-32 The allocation of taxing jurisdiction in respect of shipping and air transport is found in several kinds of treaties. It is always contained in comprehensive income tax treaties. It is also frequently found in treaties covering only shipping and air transportation, such as those with Algeria, Brazil, Cameroon, Ethiopia, Iran, Jordan, Lebanon, Saudi Arabia and Zaire. In the case of Hong Kong, relief from double taxation in relation to shipping and air transportation is included in a broader commercial treaty addressing those industries generally.

A number of treaties diverge from the OECD Model, although the general thrust of the article is to permit taxation in the resident state only in respect of international traffic. This is the case, even if there is a permanent establishment in the other contracting state. The OECD Model also restricts taxation to the resident state in respect of boats engaged in inland waterways transport. This provision is not found in many U.K. treaties. The United Kingdom has entered a reservation to Article 8 of the OECD Model to include in the Article profits from leasing of ships or aircraft on a bareboat basis and from the leasing of containers.[38]

---

[38] OECD Commentary on Article 8, para. 34.

ARTISTES AND SPORTSMEN

5-33 Entertainers and athletes constitute a further category of business identified for special treatment. Some treaties, following the old colonial pattern, simply exclude entertainers from the personal services articles (for example Belize and Germany). Others contain no specific provision leaving entertainers within the general rule for personal services (for example Gambia). The common thread in treaty provisions aimed at artistes and sportsmen is that they authorise taxation of the income of such individuals in the contracting state where their professional activities are exercised, despite the absence of a permanent establishment or fixed base. Thus, Article 17(1) of the Danish Treaty reads:

"Notwithstanding the provisions of Articles 14 and 15, income derived by a resident of a Contracting State as an entertainer, such as a theatre, motion picture, radio or television artiste, or a musician, or as an athlete, from his personal activities as such exercised in the other Contracting State, may be taxed in that other State".

5-34 A number of treaties make exceptions for certain kinds of performances. For example, state sponsored visits, non-profit organisations and official cultural exchanges are excluded in Article 17 of the Austrian Treaty. Others such as Article 19(1) of the Hungarian Treaty contain a *de minimis* provision for gross receipts not exceeding £8,000. In the 1975 U.S. Treaty, the level is US$15,000 (Article 17(1)). In some cases, the exclusion for state sponsored visits and non-profit organisations only applies to those organisations. Others such as the Canadian Treaty, Article 16, also exclude their employees.

In 1974, the Committee on Fiscal Affairs added wording to the 1963 OECD Draft Convention to deal with amounts accruing to persons other than the entertainer or athlete. An example of this is found in Article 18(2) of the New Zealand Treaty:

"Where income in respect of personal activities exercised by an entertainer or an athlete in his capacity as such accrues not to the entertainer or athlete himself but to another person, that income may, notwithstanding the provisions of Articles 8, 15 and 16, be taxed in the Contracting State in which the activities of the entertainer or athlete are exercised".

5-35 These rules do not apply under Article 17(2) of the 1975 U.S. Treaty if the entertainer or athlete and persons related to them do not participate directly or indirectly in the profits of the other person in any manner. Some treaties also include activities providing the services of public entertainers as constituting a permanent establishment (for example the Jamaican Treaty, Article 4(4)(a)).

The manner in which performers and sportsmen are taxed under domestic law varies considerably according to their circumstances. Commonly, such individuals may be employees subject to tax under Schedule E or exercising a trade or profession under Schedule D Cases I or II. Entertainers may also receive royalties typically in respect of copyright or similar rights. Where the source of income is employment or copyright royalties, withholding will apply under PAYE,[39] or in the case of copyright royalties.[40] While there is no general withholding mechanism in respect of income taxed under Schedule D Cases I or II, a withholding mechanism in respect of foreign entertainers applies pursuant to Taxes Act 1988, sections 555 to 558, and the Income Tax (Entertainers and Sportsmen) Regulations 1987 (S.I. 1987 No. 530).

Under domestic law, where a non-resident entertainer or sportsman performs a prescribed activity in the United Kingdom, an obligation to deduct tax on payments made in connection with that activity arises.[41] Where such a payment is made, the activity is deemed to be performed in the course of a trade, profession or vocation exercised by the entertainer or sportsman within the United Kingdom even if it would not otherwise be so.[42] The withholding mechanism provides for a reduction in withholding payments to take into account items such as expenses. However, treaty benefits are not normally taken into account in determining the level of withholding.[43] As a result, a claim for treaty benefits must be made separately, normally at the time of filing a tax return.

ASSOCIATED ENTERPRISES

5-36   All income tax treaties contain provisions equivalent to Article 9 of the OECD Model authorising the application of domestic transfer pricing rules. In the United Kingdom, the insertion of Schedule 28AA to the Taxes Act 1988, replacing section 770, had the stated objective of enacting Article 9(1) of the OECD Model into domestic law. The Canadian Treaty, patterned on the OECD Model, reads as follows:

"9.   Where:

(1)   an enterprise of one of the Contracting States participates directly or indirectly in the management, control or capital of an enterprise of the other Contracting State; or

(2)   the same persons participate directly or indirectly in the management, control or capital of an enterprise of one of the Contracting States and of an enterprise of the other Contracting State;

and in either case conditions are made or imposed between the two enterprises, in their commercial or financial relations, which differ from those which would be made between independent enterprises, then any profits which would but for those conditions have accrued to one of the

---

[39] Taxes Act 1988, s. 203 and related regulations.
[40] *ibid.*, s. 536.
[41] *ibid.*, s. 555.
[42] *ibid.*, s. 556(1).
[43] See FEU 50, para. A8.

enterprises, but by reason of those conditions have not so accrued, may be included in the profits of that enterprise and taxed accordingly".

5-37   Schedule 28AA was not, however, intended to enact Article 9(2) which reads:

"Where a Contracting State includes in the profits of an enterprise of that State—and taxes accordingly—profits on which an enterprise of the other Contracting State has been charged to tax in that other State and the profits so included are profits which would have accrued to the enterprise of the first-mentioned State if the conditions made between the two enterprises had been those which would have been made between independent enterprises, then that other State shall make an appropriate adjustment to the amount of the tax charged therein on those profits. In determining such adjustment, due regard shall be had to the other provisions of this Convention and the competent authorities of the Contracting States shall if necessary consult each other".

Article 9(2) confers entitlement to corresponding adjustments in a contracting state where there is an increase in tax liability in the other contracting state as a result of a transfer pricing adjustment. The Article does not appear generally in U.K. treaties (see for example the Kenyan Treaty). In those cases, the mutual agreement procedure under Article 24 is the only basis for the making of corresponding adjustments. There are, however, treaties that do contain this specific authority for corresponding adjustments.[44]

---

[44] See for example the Argentinian Treaty, Article 9(2), U.S. Treaty, Article 9(2).

CHAPTER 6

Income from Property

INCOME FROM IMMOVABLE PROPERTY

6-01 Article 6 of the OECD Model Treaty provides that income from immovable property may be taxed in the state in which the property is situated. Immovable property is given the meaning under the law of the contracting state in which the property is situated. The OECD Model was amended in 1977 to specify that income from immovable property includes income from agriculture or forestry. It also defined immovable property to include property accessory to immovable property, livestock and equipment used in agriculture and forestry, rights to which provisions of general law respecting landed property apply, usufruct of immovable property and rights to variable or fixed amounts as consideration for the working of or the right to work, mineral deposits, sources and other natural resources. Ships, boats and aircraft are not to be regarded as immovable property.

The situation of property is normally to be determined under the general conflict of law rules. Most importantly, land is situated in the country where it lies. However, in relation to choses in action, they are normally situated in the country where they are properly recoverable or can be enforced. Chattels are situated in the country where they are located at any given time. The classification of property between movables and immovables is adopted in civil law systems. However, in English law, the important distinction is between realty and personalty. Income from land subject to tax under Schedule A is perhaps the easiest source of income from immovable property to identify in this context. In this regard, both freehold and leasehold interests in land in England are regarded as immovable. A mortgagee's interest in land in England, including his right to payment of the debt, is regarded as an interest in an immovable. However, in the treaty context, mortgage interest is normally dealt with under Article 11 (Interest) on the basis that the more general provisions relating to immovable property are overridden by the specific reference in Article 11(3), so that "interest" includes income from "debt claims of every kind whether or not secured by a mortgage". In the U.S. Treaty (2001), the expression "real property" is used in Article 6, rather than "immovable property". Treaties following the colonial model do not contain an immovable income article. Since such treaties are not comprehensive, they do not generally limit the U.K. right to tax income from land.

6-02 Article 6(3) provides that the rights of the contracting state where the immovable is situated apply to "income derived from the direct use, letting or use in any other form of immovable property". This wording is not apt to cover deemed Case VI income arising in relation to the anti-avoidance provisions of Taxes Act 1988, section 776 on the disposal of interests in land.

Article 6(4) extends the application of this article to "the income from immovable property of an enterprise and to income from immovable property used for the performance of independent personal services".

Spain is a popular location for second homes owned by U.K. individuals. In order to address uncertainty as to the imposition of Spanish tax against U.K. holders of timeshares, Article 6(3) of the Spanish Treaty was amended by Protocol,[1] so that income from the use or letting of timeshare rights in respect of immovable property situated in a contracting state, which are owned by a resident of the other contracting state and which are for a period or periods which in the aggregate do not exceed four weeks in any calendar year, are excluded. In the computation of the period or periods, all timeshare rights owned by a resident of a contracting state in respect of immovable property situated in the other contracting state are to be taken into account.

DIVIDENDS

6-03 The text of dividend articles varies widely in U.K. treaties. The United Kingdom has undergone numerous changes in its domestic law relating to taxation since the oldest of the current existing treaties were negotiated over 50 years ago. At one end of the spectrum are those treaties that do not contain dividend articles at all, such as those with Guernsey, Jersey and the Isle of Man. A second group of treaties simply provide for exemption from tax on dividends paid by a company resident in one contracting state to a shareholder resident in the other, or limiting the rate of tax to be deducted to rates specified in the treaty. The third category of treaties at the other end of the spectrum provides for repayment of tax credits and follows the introduction of the imputation system of corporation tax into the United Kingdom in 1973. The treaty entitlement to repayment of tax credits has only been extended to selected treaty partners and a number of treaties negotiated since that time simply place limits on the tax that may be imposed by the source state. Current U.K. policy is not to grant repayment of tax credits to new treaty partners and to withdraw this benefit where it has previously been provided, as has been the case in Protocols with Denmark, Finland and the U.S. Treaty (2001).

Withholding tax

6-04 The United Kingdom does not impose a withholding tax on dividends under its domestic law. As a result, those treaties that simply limit the amount of tax that may be deducted at source have no application. The current domestic rules for the taxing of dividends paid by U.K. companies to non-resident shareholders is only affected by those treaties that permit repayment of the credit. Prior to April 6, 1999, U.K. resident companies were required to make a payment of advance corporation tax (ACT) on making a dividend payment.[2] Advance corporation tax was a pre-payment

---

[1] S.I. 1995 No. 765.
[2] Formerly Taxes Act 1988, ss. 14, 238.

of the company's corporation tax liability.[3] It was consequently able to be set off against the company's corporation tax liability for the accounting period in which it was paid. It could also be carried back six years or carried forward indefinitely.[4] Since ACT was levied on the company paying the dividend and not the shareholder, its application was not affected by the dividend article in treaties. Under the imputation system, U.K. resident individual shareholders were entitled to a tax credit on dividends paid by U.K. companies.[5] Apart from the timing of the payment, the key connection between ACT and the tax credit was that the rate of tax credit was normally set by reference to the rate of ACT. However, in recent years, following Finance Act 1993, section 48, the two were disconnected until ultimately the abolition of ACT by Finance Act 1998, section 31 in relation to distributions made from April 6, 1999 left a limited tax credit. In the year 1998–1999, the rate of ACT was 25 per cent of the dividend paid. The tax credit for U.K. taxpayers was 20 per cent on the dividend plus credit.

Repayment of tax credits

6-05   The first treaty providing for the repayment of tax credits was with the United States. Although the wording has varied from treaty to treaty, the approach in the U.S. Treaty (1975) is broadly representative and reads as follows:

"10(2) As long as an individual resident in the United Kingdom is entitled under United Kingdom law to a tax credit in respect of dividends paid by a corporation which is resident in the United Kingdom, paragraph (1) of this Article shall not apply. In these circumstances, dividends derived from a corporation which is a resident of a Contracting State by a resident of the other Contracting State may be taxed in the other Contracting State. However, such dividends may be taxed in the Contracting State of which the corporation paying the dividends is a resident, but if the beneficial owner is a resident of the other Contracting State, the tax so charged shall not exceed the tax provided in sub-paragraphs (a) and (b) below:

(a)   In the case of dividends paid by a corporation which is a resident of the United Kingdom:

(i)   to a United States corporation which either alone or together with one or more associated corporations controls, directly or indirectly, at least 10% of the voting stock of the corporation which is a resident of the United Kingdom paying the dividend, the United States corporation shall be entitled to a payment from the United Kingdom of a tax credit equal to one-half of the tax credit to which an individual resident in the United Kingdom would have been entitled had he received the dividend,

---

[3] *Metallgesellschaft Ltd and others v. CIR* [2001] S.T.C. 452, ECJ.
[4] Formerly Taxes Act 1988, s. 239.
[5] *ibid.*, ss. 231, 232.

subject to the deduction withheld from such payment and according to the laws of the United Kingdom of an amount not exceeding 5% of the aggregate of the amount or value of the dividend and the amount of the tax credit paid to such corporation;

(ii) in all other cases, the resident of the United States to whom such dividend is paid shall be entitled to a payment from the United Kingdom of the tax credit to which an individual resident in the United Kingdom would have been entitled had he received the dividend, subject to the deduction withheld from such payment and according to the laws of the United Kingdom of an amount not exceeding 15% of the aggregate of the amount or value of the dividend and the amount of the tax credit paid to such resident;

(iii) the aggregate of the amount or value of the dividend and the amount of the tax credit referred to in sub-paragraphs (a)(i) and (ii) of this paragraph paid by the United Kingdom to the United States corporation or other resident (without reduction for the 5 or 15% deduction, as the case may be, by the United Kingdom) shall be treated as a dividend for United States tax credit purposes. "

6-06 The manner in which the repayment of the tax credit was calculated was disputed in *Union Texas International Corporation v. Critchley*.[6] The U.S. Treaty wording differed slightly from other treaties granting the credit repayment. Although the court ultimately agreed with the Revenue's method of calculation, the law was changed retrospectively by Finance Act 1989, section 115.

Dividends on portfolio shareholdings, which are all dividends other than those paid to a company which alone or together with associated companies controls at least 10 per cent of the voting power in the company paying the dividends, are entitled to repayment of the tax credit after retention of 15 per cent of the aggregate of the dividend plus the tax credit. As the amount of tax credit declined from 25 per cent to 20 per cent in 1993, the value of treaty repayments of the credit declined. From April 6, 1999, the value of the tax credit was reduced to 10 per cent of the dividend plus tax credit. As a result, the amount retained by the United Kingdom under these treaty provisions will in practice cover the whole of the credit. The net result is that if a claim is made to repayment of the credit in respect of dividends paid after that date, there will be no balance of tax credits actually payable. Non-resident corporate shareholders with a substantial participation, namely those which directly or indirectly control 10 per cent or more of the voting power in the U.K. company paying the dividend, are entitled to repayment of one-half of the tax credit, less a retention of normally 5 per cent as provided in the U.S. Treaty. Similar treatment is found in the treaties with Belgium, Italy, Luxembourg, the Netherlands, Sweden and Switzerland. In the case of Canada and Norway, the retention is 10 per cent.

---

[6] [1998] S.T.C. 691, Ch.D.

6-07 In the *Union Texas* case, the 5 per cent retention was attacked by the taxpayer on the basis that it was not founded in a charging provision in the domestic law and that the treaty does not impose a charge to tax. This argument was rejected by the High Court on somewhat jurisprudentially unsatisfying grounds, the case was not appealed and it is understood that the Government were preparing retrospective legislation, should the result have been otherwise. The withholding under similar provisions of the Netherlands Treaty has also been attacked as contrary to European law in the *Océ Van Der Grinten* case.[7]

Taxes Act 1988, sections 812 to 815 contain measures to prevent the repayment of tax credits to shareholders resident in countries that apply unitary taxation. These provisions require a Treasury Order to come into force. They have never been activated, but were introduced in order to put pressure on the United States in relation to those states adopting unitary tax systems.

MEANING OF DIVIDENDS

6-08 U.K. domestic law does not generally refer to "dividends", but rather to distributions.[8] The OECD definition of dividends is reflected in Article 10(3) of the Norwegian Treaty which reads as follows:

> "The term 'dividends' as used in this Article means income from shares, or other rights, not being debt-claims, participating in profits, as well as income from other corporate rights which is subjected to the same taxation treatment as income from shares by the laws of the Contracting State of which the company making the distribution is a resident and also includes any other item which, under the laws of the State of which the company paying the dividend is a resident, is treated as a dividend or distribution of the company".

Treaties which permit tax credit repayments either include words to that effect or wording similar to that found in the U.S. Treaty, Article 10(4), which defines dividends for U.K. tax purposes to include any amount which under U.K. law is treated as a distribution. Thus, at present, the dividend articles have limited direct application to distributions. They do have an ancillary role in conjunction with the interest article in the context of thin capitalisation.

6-09 The meaning of the term "dividend" under the German Treaty was considered in *Memec plc v. IRC*.[9] Article 6(4) defined dividends in that article to include the income derived by a sleeping partner from his participation as such. The case arose out of distributions by a German silent partnership of dividends it received from German companies to a U.K. parent. The context in which the issue arose was whether the U.K. company was entitled to credit for underlying tax pursuant to Article 18(1) of the Treaty

---

[7] [2000] S.T.C. 951 ChD. see para 9-14 below.
[8] Taxes Act 1988, s. 209.
[9] [1998] S.T.C. 754, CA.

and section 792(1) of the Taxes Act 1988 in respect of underlying tax. This would be the case under the Treaty if the U.K. company receiving the dividend controls directly or indirectly at least 25 per cent of the voting power of the German company. The Court of Appeal determined that this wide definition of dividend applied only to the scope of the right to impose withholding tax on such distribution and to ensure that they do not come within the articles relating to business profits or interest. Dividend was undefined in Article 18 providing for U.K. credit against German tax paid and in this context the court applied the ordinary meaning of dividend, namely a payment of a part of the profits for a period in respect of a share of a company. This was not the view of Robert Walker J. in the High Court and in his dissenting judgment in the Court of Appeal, Sir Christopher Staughton agreed that the definition of dividend in Article 6 should apply throughout the Treaty, citing in particular a decision of the highest German tax court.

Dividend effectively connected with a permanent establishment

6-10   Most treaties following the OECD pattern disapply the rules relating to repayment of tax credits where the beneficial owner of the dividends has a permanent establishment with which the holding of shares in respect of which the dividends are paid is effectively connected. In such a case, the business profits rules apply. Under domestic law, a non-resident will be liable to tax under Case I or Case II of Schedule D as a result of a trade or profession carried on in the United Kingdom through a branch or agency. In most cases, this will be limited to share dealers. Taxes Act 1988, section 95 excludes distribution from Schedule F treatment in the hands of a dealer in shares and requires those amounts to be taken into account in computing profits of the dealer which are taxed under Case I or Case II of Schedule D. This treatment is thus authorised by treaties following Article 10(4). Similar authorisation is found where the dividends are effectively connected with a fixed base through which independent personal services are provided under Article 14. This latter element is present in some treaties (see for example the U.S. Treaty), but absent in others (see for example the Moroccan Treaty).

In the view of the Inland Revenue, a dividend would be "effectively connected" with a permanent establishment if, for example, a branch of a foreign company bought shares in a U.K. company out of surplus funds of the branch. If the branch merely invested funds supplied by its head office, any dividend would not be "effectively connected" with the permanent establishment.[10] More realistically, this rule is likely to apply to dealers trading through a branch in the United Kingdom in respect of whom distributions fall to be taxed under Schedule D Case I pursuant to Taxes Act 1988, section 95.

INTEREST

6-11   Under domestic law, income tax is to be withheld at source on yearly interest of money chargeable to tax under Case III of Schedule D *inter*

---

[10] Inland Revenue, *Double Taxation Manual*, para. DT214.

alia where it is paid by any person to another person whose "usual place of abode is outside the United Kingdom".[11]

The U.K. negotiating position on interest is to seek to eliminate withholding taxes entirely. As a result, some 24 treaties provide that interest arising in one contracting state may only be taxed in the country of residence of a beneficial ownership resident in the other state. The rate of tax in the source state in 44 other treaties is limited, insofar as it is below the current U.K. rate of tax deducted on interest at source of 20 per cent ranging from 5 per cent to 15 per cent. The remaining treaties specify higher rates, but as a result of the domestic law, these limitations do not have any practical impact on the rate of tax deducted in the United Kingdom. As a result of the reductions in U.K. tax on interest payments, treaties contain a number of detailed rules circumscribing the availability of treaty benefits.

It should be remembered that the treatment of interest paid to a non-resident as qualifying for benefits under Article 11 of the OECD Model will not simply go to the rate of tax, if any, to be deducted by the taxpayer under Taxes Act 1988, section 349(2). Although Article 11 does not extend directly to the rules relating to loan relationships generally or other rules relating to deduction of interest expense, where a treaty requires an amount to be treated as interest, this will override Taxes Act 1988, section 209(2). That section treats interest payments as distributions in certain circumstances. Where a treaty overrides these rules, the character of the payment as interest is preserved. The United Kingdom has entered into an observation to the Commentary on the OECD Model noting that certain interest payments can be re-characterised as dividends.[12]

Meaning of interest

6-12 The current meaning of interest under Article 11(3) of the OECD Model is set out in Article 10(5) of the Philippines Treaty as follows:

> "The term 'interest' as used in this Article means income from Government securities, bonds or debentures, including premiums and prizes attaching to such securities, whether or not secured by mortgage and whether or not carrying a right to participate in profits, and other debt-claims of every kind as well as all other income assimilated to income from money lent by the taxation law of the State in which the income arises. Penalty charges for late payment shall not be regarded as interest for the purpose of this Article".

It differs markedly from the definition found in the 1963 Draft Convention as found in Article 11(2) of the Austrian Treaty which reads as follows:

> "The term 'interest' as used in this Article means income from Government securities, bonds or debentures, whether or not secured by

---

[11] Taxes Act 1988, s. 349(2)(c).
[12] Commentary on Article 10, para. 68, and Commentary on Article 11, para. 37.

mortgage and whether or not carrying a right to participate in profits, and other debt-claims of every kind as well as all other income assimilated to income from money lent by the taxation law of the State in which the income arises".

A variety of forms is found in U.K. treaties. Some (for example Iceland) define interest entirely by reference to the domestic law of the contracting state concerned. It has become common to insert wording to the effect that interest does not include any item which is treated as a dividend under the dividend article. It may be noted that interest articles following the OECD Models will override Taxes Act 1988, section 209(2)(e)(iii), which treats interest on profit participation securities as a distribution.

6-13 Where an amount is not interest for treaty purposes, then treaty benefits of the relevant interest article will not apply. In *Bricom Holdings Limited v. IRC*,[13] the court concluded that profits of a Netherlands company which were comprised of interest payments were not interest for the purposes of Article 11 of the Netherlands Treaty in the context of a charge under the CFC rules. Article 11 of the Treaty provided that "interest arising in one of the states which is derived and beneficially owned by a resident of the other state shall be taxable only in that other state". A Netherlands subsidiary of a U.K. parent company with no other sources of income loaned its funds to the parent company. It was undisputed that the Netherlands company was a controlled foreign company and the Inland Revenue accepted that the effect of the treaty was to exempt the interest both from U.K. corporation tax and taxation of the interest by deduction at source in the hands of the Netherlands resident company who received it. However, the interest was not exempt from U.K. tax under the CFC charge. In determining the chargeable profits for CFC purposes, Taxes Act 1988, section 746(6)(a) referred to a purely notional sum equal to the chargeable profits, rather than the profits themselves.

Source of interest

6-14 The source of interest for treaty purposes is normally determined by Article 11(5) of the OECD Model. Interest is deemed to arise in a contracting state where the payer is a resident of that state, or the state itself, or a political subdivision, a local authority, or resident of that state. It also applies where the state itself, a political subdivision or local authority, is the payer. A special rule is provided in the case of permanent establishments. Where the payer of the interest has a permanent establishment in a contracting state in connection with which the indebtedness on which the interest is paid was incurred and the interest is borne by the permanent establishment, then the interest is deemed to arise in the state where the permanent establishment is situated. Treaties adopting this definition of source have a wider scope than may be the case under domestic law. The current Inland Revenue view on the location of the source for interest is based on *Westminster Bank Executor and Trust Company (Channel Islands) Limited v. National Bank*

---

[13] [1997] S.T.C. 1179, CA.

of Greece S.A.[14] In that case, the obligation in question, a guarantee payment, was made by a foreign corporation with no place of business in the United Kingdom. The principal debtor was also a foreign corporation and the obligation was secured on lands and public revenues outside the United Kingdom. In addition, funds for payment by the principal debtor would have been provided by a remittance from outside the United Kingdom. As a result, Inland Revenue practice is to regard the residence of the debtor as only one factor. The factors that they regard as important are:

(a) the residence of the debtor (being the place where the debt will be enforced);

(b) the source from which the interest is paid;

(c) where the interest is paid; and

(d) the nature and location of the security for the debt.[15]

Special relationship

6-15 Where there is a special relationship between the payer and the beneficial owner of the interest, or a special relationship between the both of them and some other person, treaty benefits may be limited. This crucial limitation of benefits is set out, for example, in Article 11(8) of the Canadian Treaty thus:

"Where, owing to a special relationship between the payer and the person deriving the interest or between both of them and some other person, the amount of the interest paid exceeds for whatever reason the amount which would have been paid in the absence of such relationship, the provisions of this Article shall apply only to the last-mentioned amount. In that case, the excess part of the payments shall remain taxable according to the law of each Contracting State, due regard being had to the other provisions of this Convention".

Where the amount of interest paid exceeds the amount which would have been agreed upon by the payer and the beneficial owner in relation to the principal of the debt in the absence of the relationship, the interest article only applies to the amount which would have been agreed upon in the absence of that relationship. Any excess must be treated in accordance with domestic law of the contracting states and the other provisions of the treaty.

Meaning of special relationship

6-16 Special relationship is undefined in treaty or domestic law. The Inland Revenue take a very broad view of this expression. The *Double Taxation Relief Manual* gives the lack of purpose or the borrowing forming part of an avoidance scheme as examples of borrowings which their view would not have taken place at all if the parties had been unconnected. It continues "a special relationship can extend beyond a common

---

[14] [1970] 1 Q.B. 251.
[15] Inland Revenue, *Tax Bulletin* (November 1993), p.100.

shareholding" and may apply to "some other sort of bond".[16] The OECD Commentary refers to circumstances of control, as well as relationships by blood or marriage and any "other community of interests".[17]

Taxpayers are required to show either that there is no special relationship or that the amount of interest is what would have been paid in the absence of the special relationship.[18] One concession is given in construing the special relationship: the fact that the lender is not in the business of making loans generally may be ignored.[19] Thus, in principle, comparisons made with banks or other money lending institutions may serve as valid indicators of the amount that would be paid in the absence of a special relationship even if only banks would make a loan on the terms made.

Effect of special relationship

6-17   The special relationship clauses place quantitative limits on the application of the benefits of the interest article. This applies to both the question of classification as interest for this purpose and the rate of tax that may be levied in the source state. A number of early treaties contained language which applied this rule only to the rate of interest, but not to the amount of debt. Article 9(6) of the Australian Treaty is an example:

> "Where, owing to a special relationship between the payer and the beneficial owner or between both of them and some other person, the amount of interest paid exceeds the amount which would have been agreed upon in the absence of such relationship, the provisions of this Article shall apply only to the last-mentioned amount".

Later treaties permit the examination of both the rate of interest and the amount of debt to which it relates. The wording in this regard sometimes follows that contained in Article 10(7) of the South African Treaty which reads as follows:

> "Where, owing to a special relationship between the payer and the recipient or between both of them and some other person, the amount of the interest paid, *having regard to the debt-claim for which it is paid*, exceeds the amount which would have been agreed upon by the payer and the recipient in the absence of such relationship, the provisions of this Article shall apply only to the last-mentioned amount".

6-18   Article 11(7) of the Latvian Treaty illustrates an alternative formulation:

> "Where by reason of a special relationship between the payer and the beneficial owner or between both of them and some other person, the amount of the interest paid exceeds, *for whatever reason*, the amount

---

[16] *Double Taxation Manual*, para. DT1919E.
[17] At paras 31, 32.
[18] Taxes Act 1988, s. 808A(3).
[19] Taxes Act 1988, s. 808A(4).

which would have been agreed upon by the payer and the beneficial owner in the absence of such relationship, the provisions of this Article shall apply only to the last-mentioned amount of interest. In such case, the excess part of the payments shall remain taxable according to the laws of each Contracting State, due regard being had to the other provisions of this Convention".

Finance (No. 2) Act 1992, section 42 inserted section 808A into Taxes Act 1988 in order to override the earlier treaties. The effect of this new section was to require all treaties which permitted the benefit of a reduction in or exemption from U.K. tax on interest where there was a special relationship clause to permit the special relationship to allow adjustment in respect of both the interest rate and the amount of debt, even in relation to those treaties that did not permit adjustment in relation to the level of debt. The amendment at that time was believed to be as a result of an unpublished Special Commissioners decision against the Inland Revenue on the point. In these cases, the special relationship provision must be construed as requiring all factors to be taken into account including specifically whether in the absence of the special relationship:

(a) the loan would have been made at all;

(b) the amount which the loan would have been; and

(c) the rate of interest and other terms which would have been agreed.[20]

6-19 The relationship between these rules and domestic law relating to interest and particularly its relationship to distributions is complex. Treaty developments to some extent have followed developments in domestic law. Section 209 of Taxes Act 1988 contains several measures which seek to recategorise interest payments as distributions.[21] The treaty definition of dividends will in many cases decide whether, and the extent to which, the distribution rules in Taxes Act 1988, section 209(2) are applicable. Those treaties that define dividends by reference to domestic tax law on distributions will in general allow section 209(2) to operate unimpeded. Treaties with self-contained definitions will typically narrow the application of these rules. The Inland Revenue accept that the South African Treaty, along with those with Austria, Fiji, Israel and Sudan, allow excessive interest to be characterised as a distribution, but prevent the paying company from being denied a deduction for the distributions (see Israeli Treaty, Article 7(5) for example). The treaty with Spain (Article 11(6)) prevents excessive intragroup interest being treated as a distribution.[22]

75 per cent group

6-20 Of particular importance are the rules relating to the thin capitalisation rules in Taxes Act 1988, section 209(2)(da) and equity notes in

---

[20] Taxes Act 1988, s. 808A(2).
[21] *ibid.*, s. 209(2)(d), (da) and (e).
[22] *Tax Bulletin* (June 1998), p.555.

section 209(2)(e)(vii). In both cases, interest payments are re-categorised as distributions. The domestic thin capitalisation rules apply in relation to interest payments where the U.K. resident corporate borrower is a 75 per cent subsidiary of the lender, or both lender and borrower are 75 per cent subsidiaries of a third company. Interest is treated as distribution to the extent that it would not have been paid if the companies had been "companies between whom there was (apart from the securities in question) no relationship, arrangements or other concession (whether formal or informal)". These rules apply both to the rate of interest and the quantum of debt.[23]

Equity notes may suffer the same treatment. Equity notes are generally debt securities with no redemption date or a term exceeding 50 years.[24] Interest on equity notes may be treated as a distribution if they are held by a company which is associated or is a "funded company".[25] Companies are associated if they are in a 75 per cent group.[26] A funded company is one where there are arrangements involving the company being put in funds directly or indirectly by the issuing company or a company associated with the issuing company.[27]

No 75 per cent group

6-21   Although the most common application of the special relationship provisions was originally thin capitalisation in the group context, Taxes Act 1988, section 209(2)(da), subject to applicable treaties, has addressed that issue since the Finance Act 1995, section 87. The provisions of Taxes Act 1988, section 808A(2) are, however, relevant where there is no 75 per cent group, or where the borrower is the ultimate group parent company. Section 209(2)(d) which treats interest on security in excess of a commercial rate of return, and section 209(2)(e)(i) to (vi) which treats interest on securities, in a variety of circumstances as distributions may be affected.

Interest attributed to a permanent establishment

6-22   Reduction or elimination of tax in the source country does not apply where the non-resident has a permanent establishment or fixed base in the source country and the debt claim in respect of which the interest is paid is effectively connected with that permanent establishment. In these cases, either the business profits article (Article 7) or the independent personal services article (Article 14) will apply. This rule will dovetail neatly on interest payments made to the U.K. branch of a foreign bank since Taxes Act 1988, section 349(3)(a) excludes interest on bank loans where the recipient of the interest is within the charge to corporation tax on the interest. In the exceptional case of *IRC v. Commerzbank AG; IRC v. Banco do Brazil SA*,[28] advantage was taken of the unusual wording in the 1945 U.S. Treaty to seek exemption from tax on interest paid by U.S. borrowers to U.K. branches of

---

[23] Taxes Act 1988, s. 209(8B).
[24] *ibid.*, s. 209(9).
[25] *ibid.*, s. 209(2)(e)(vii).
[26] *ibid.*, s. 209(10).
[27] *ibid.*, s. 209(11).
[28] [1990] S.T.C. 285.

a German and Brazilian bank. In that case, it was the branch that sought exemption. This would not apply to OECD patterned agreements and the effect of these articles in the United Kingdom would be to permit interest payments to be made gross where the lender has a permanent establishment in the United Kingdom, but is not a bank or is not within the charge to corporation tax.

Attribution of interest to a U.K. permanent establishment will also fall within the conditions which permit the payer to make payments gross under Taxes Act 1988, section 349A inserted by Finance Act 2001. Deduction of tax at source need not be made by a company if at the time the payment is made, it reasonably believes that one of the conditions in Taxes Act 1988, section 349(b)(2) are satisfied. This is where the person beneficially entitled to the income is a non-resident company carrying on a trade through a branch or agency in the United Kingdom and the payment falls to be brought into account in computing the chargeable profits of the non-resident company. Where these conditions are met, typically a permanent establishment will exist to which the interest is attributed. Section 349C authorises the board to give a direction requiring tax to be deducted where it is likely that the qualifying conditions will not be met and section 349D provides for assessment of tax not deductible as a consequence of reasonable but incorrect belief that the qualifying conditions were met.[29]

ROYALTIES

6-23   Royalties are only taxable in the country of residence of the beneficial owner in 24 treaties. A further 45 treaties authorise taxation in the source state, albeit at rates from 5 per cent to 20 per cent and thus below the basic U.K. rate of taxation (22 per cent in 2001).

Scope of the royalty article

6-24   The most common category of treaty restricts the royalty article to intellectual property, such as the Canadian Treaty, Article 12(4) which reads as follows:

"The term 'royalties' as used in this Article means payments of any kind received as a consideration for the use of, or the right to use, any copyright, patent, trade mark, design or model, plan, secret formula or process, or for the use of, or the right to use industrial, commercial or scientific equipment, or for information concerning industrial, commercial or scientific experience, and includes payments of any kind in respect of motion pictures and works on film, videotape or other means of production for use in connection with television broadcasting".

Some such as the Canadian Treaty specifically include reference to the right to use films or tapes for cinema, television or radio. Modern treaties do not refer to mineral extraction royalties, although some, such as the Antigua

---

[29]   See also Inland Revenue, *Tax Bulletin* (August 2001), p.867.

Treaty, which does not contain an article relating to immovable property, specifically exclude royalties or amounts paid in respect of the operation of a mine or quarry or other extraction of natural resources (Article 7(2)). A number of treaties particularly with developing countries include payments for the use of or the right to use any industrial, commercial or scientific equipment.

6-25   Under domestic law, deduction at source on royalties only applies in extremely limited circumstances:

(1) patent royalties or other sums paid in respect of the user of a patent[30];

(2) Copyright; this applies to payment on account of any royalties or sums paid periodically for or in respect of copyright.[31] In this respect, copyright does not include copyright in a cinematographic film or video recording or the soundtrack of such a film or recording so far as it is not separately exploited. Public lending rights have the same effect as copyright.[32]

(3) design royalties: royalties or sums paid periodically for or in respect of rights in a design are subject to deduction of tax where the owner is abroad[33];

(4) annual payments: where any annual payment is charged to tax under Schedule D Case III.[34] An annual payment is generally made pursuant to a legal obligation. It must have the quality of being recurrent or being capable of recurrence and must be pure income profit in the hands of the payee. This is potentially applicable to payments in respect of a variety of intellectual property rights such as trade marks and know-how.

Under proposals to reform the taxation of intellectual property, consideration is given to adopt a broad all-encompassing definition of intellectual property, possibly based on the OECD Model Article 12(2) definition and to impose deduction at source on all payments made to non-residents.

Source of royalty

6-26   Curiously, the OECD Model does not contain rules determining the source of royalties. The Inland Revenue *International Tax Handbook* (INT559) notes cryptically "there is, however, no definition of where royalties arise, so the domestic law of each partner determines this". The United Nations Model does however contain a clause addressing this issue and several U.K. treaties, including that with Argentina, include such a clause which reads:

---

[30] Taxes Act 1988, s. 349(1)(b).
[31] *ibid.*, s. 536(1).
[32] *ibid.*, s. 537.
[33] *ibid.*, s. 537B.
[34] *ibid.*, s. 349(1)(a).

"12(5) Royalties shall be deemed to arise in a Contracting State when the payer is that State itself; a political subdivision, a local authority or a resident of that State. Where, however, the person paying the royalties, whether he is a resident of a Contracting State or not, has in a Contracting State a permanent establishment or a fixed base in connection with which the obligation to pay the royalties was incurred, and such royalties are borne by such permanent establishment or fixed base, then such royalties shall be deemed to arise in the State in which the permanent establishment or fixed base is situated".

6-27 This approach adopts one similar to that taken by the OECD Model Article 11(5) in relation to interest, namely the location of the payer of the royalty. U.K. domestic law is unclear but probably takes a multiple factor approach. The residence of the payer is generally only one factor in relation to the location of source for the purpose of Schedule D Case III, others being the location of underlying intellectual property right and the place where payment is to be made and possibly the place where the contract is made. In this respect, a foreign copyright suggests a foreign source royalty, while a U.K. copyright or other intellectual property right suggests a U.K. source royalty. The Inland Revenue accept that unless a patent is a U.K. patent, the licence cannot be "for the user of a patent".[35] It may be noted that for capital gains purposes, patents, trade marks, service marks and registered designs are situated where they are registered, and if registered in more than one register, where each register is situated, and rights or licence to use such intellectual property are situated in the United Kingdom, if they or any right derived from them are exercisable in the United Kingdom.[36] Copyright, design right and franchises and rights or licences to use any copyright work or design in which design rights subsist are situated in the United Kingdom, if they or any right derived from them are exercisable in the United Kingdom.[37]

6-28 The Inland Revenue offer concessionary relief in circumstances where the payer is foreign, but the payment is for U.K. purposes treated as having a U.K. source. The concession reads as follows:

"ESC B8 Double Taxation Relief: Income Consisting of Royalties and 'Know-How' Payments
Payments made by a person resident in an overseas country to a person carrying on a trade in the United Kingdom as consideration for the use of, or for the privilege of using, in the overseas country any copyright, patent, design, secret process or formula, trade-mark or other like property may in law be payments the source of which is in the United Kingdom, but are nevertheless treated for the purpose of credit (whether under double taxation agreements or by way of unilateral relief) as income arising outside the United Kingdom except to the extent that they represent consideration for services (other than merely incidental services) rendered in this country by the recipient to the payer".

---

[35] *Double Tax Relief Manual*, para. DT1912.
[36] Taxation of Chargeable Gains Act 1992, s. 275(h).
[37] *ibid.*, s. 275(j).

Disposal of patents

6-29   The expression "royalty" refers payments as "consideration for the use of or the right to use". This does not in normal language include payment of the purchase price. Where a non-resident sells all or part of patent rights which are or include a U.K. patent, then he is chargeable to tax in respect of the net proceeds under Schedule D Case VI. The withholding procedures under section 349(1) apply to that sum as if it was an annual payment.[38] A payment of this kind is not within the scope of the normal royalty provision, but falls to be addressed under Article 13 of the OECD Model (capital gains). Article 12(3)(b) of the U.S. Treaty (1975 and 2001) includes in the definition of "royalties" gains from the alienation of intellectual property rights which are contingent on the productivity, use, or disposition thereof. The U.S. Treaty (1975) also includes the supply of assistance of an ancillary subsidiary nature furnished as a means of enabling the application or enjoyment of any intellectual right or property. This is excluded from the 2001 Treaty.

Royalties effectively connected with a permanent establishment

6-30   As is the case with dividends and interest, royalties effectively connected to a permanent establishment may be taxed in the state of the permanent establishment in accordance with the business profits rules (Article 12(3) of the OECD Model). The Inland Revenue *Double Taxation Relief Manual*, paragraph DT216, notes that a royalty may be effectively connected with a permanent establishment if the intellectual property right from which it is derived was acquired out of funds of the branch. A royalty, they say, may also be effectively connected if the branch played an active part in the creation or exploitation of the right in question, notwithstanding that it may not be regarded as an asset of the branch.

Special relationship

6-31   U.K. treaties patterned on Article 11 of the OECD Model deal with interest and Article 12 deal with royalties in somewhat similar terms. They envisage that these types of income will not be taxed in the source state or are taxed in the source state, albeit at a reduced rate. Both permit the treaty benefit to be restricted in the context of special relationships. Article 12(4) for example provides that to the extent that, by reason of a special relationship between the payer and the beneficial owner of the royalties, or between both of them and some other person, the amount of the royalties exceeds the amount which would have been agreed upon by the payer and the beneficial owner in the absence of such relationship, the treaty rate is limited to the latter amount.

The Namibian Treaty, Article 9(4) closely follows the OECD Model wording thus:

> "Where, owing to a special relationship between the payer and recipient of a royalty, the amount of the royalty, having regard to the use, right or

---

[38] Taxes Act 1988, s. 524(3).

property for which it is paid, exceeds the amount which would have been agreed upon by the payer and the recipient in the absence of such relationship, the provisions of this Article shall apply only to the last-mentioned amount. In that case, the excess part of the payments shall remain taxable according to the Contracting Parties' own laws, due regard being had to the other provisions of the present Convention".

6-32   It has been U.K. treaty negotiating policy to omit from that clause the words "having regard to the use, right or information for which they are paid". In most cases those words are replaced by the phrase "for whatever reason" such as in the Maltese Treaty, Article 12(6), but sometimes no alternative wording is included, such as in the Swiss Treaty, Article 12(4). In either event, the Revenue have stated that their view of the intention of the special relationship provision is that it should apply not only where the rate at which royalties are paid is excessive but where, in the absence of the special relationship, the arrangements under which the royalties are paid would not have been entered into at all. Consequently, paragraph 17 of Schedule 30 to the Finance Act 2000 introduced a new section 808B to the Taxes Act 1988, which overrides treaty provisions relating to royalties similar to the treaty override in relation to interest introduced in Taxes Act 1988, section 808A. Subsection (2) provides that where a royalty clause refers to the special relationship rule, that it:

"shall be construed as requiring account to be taken of all factors, including:

(a)   the question whether the agreement under which the royalties are paid would have been made at all in the absence of the relationship,

(b)   the rate or amounts of royalties and other terms which would have been agreed in the absence of the relationship.

Anti-avoidance

6-33   In relation to the above criteria, the override is much the same as Taxes Act 1988, section 808A is with respect to interest. However, section 808B goes further than that. A detailed anti-avoidance rule has also been tacked on by paragraph 808B(2)(c) in the guise of interpretation of special relationship. It applies where the asset in respect of which the royalties are paid, or any asset which that asset represents or from which it is derived, has previously been in the beneficial ownership of:

(a)   the person who is liable to pay the royalties;

(b)   a person who is, or has at any time been, an associate of the person who is liable to pay the royalties;

(c)   a person who has at any time carried on a business which, at the time when the liability to pay the royalties arises, is being carried on in whole or in part by the person liable to pay those royalties; or

(d) a person who is, or has at any time been, an associate of a person
who has at any time carried on such a business as is mentioned in
(c) above.[39]

6-34 Where these criteria are fulfilled, the special relationship provision
must be construed on the basis of the following factors:

(a) the amounts which were paid under the transaction, or under each
of the transactions in the series of transactions, as a result of which
the asset has come to be an asset of the beneficial owner for the time
being;

(b) the amounts which would have been so paid in the absence of a
special relationship; and

(c) the question whether the transaction or series of transactions
would have taken place in the absence of such a relationship.[40]

For these purposes, a person is an associate of another person at a given
time if:

(a) the first person participates directly or indirectly in the management, control or capital of the other, or

(b) the same person or same persons participate directly or indirectly
in the management, control or capital of the first person and the
other person within the meaning of Schedule 28AA to Taxes Act
1988.[41]

It should be noted that the "term" special relationship remains undefined.
Associates in this context are only relevant in relation to the anti-avoidance
provisions.

Burden of proof

6-35 The burden of proof is placed fully on the taxpayer. The special
relationship provision must now be construed as requiring the taxpayer to
show:

(a) the absence of any special relationship, or

(b) the rate or amount of royalties that would have been payable in the
absence of the relationship, as the case may be.[42]

Furthermore, the requirement on the taxpayer to show the absence of any
special relationship includes a requirement:

---

[39] *ibid.*, s. 808B(3).
[40] *ibid.*, s. 808B(4).
[41] *ibid.*, s. 808B(9).
[42] *ibid.*, s. 808B(5).

(a) to show that no person of any of the above descriptions has previously been the beneficial owner of the asset in respect of which the royalties are paid, or of any asset which that asset represents or from which it is derived, or

(b) to show:

   (i)   that the transaction or series of transactions mentioned above would have taken place in the absence of a special relationship, and

   (ii) the amounts which would have been paid under the transaction, or under each of the transactions in the series of transactions, in the absence of such a relationship.[43]

---

[43] *ibid.*, s. 808B(6).

CHAPTER 7

Employment and Pensions

INCOME FROM EMPLOYMENT

7-01   Employment income has traditionally been styled in treaties as "dependent personal services". This is now simply referred to as "Income from employment" in the OECD Model, to make the heading more consistent with the type of activities to which the article relates.

The general approach is that residents are normally liable to tax on employment income in their country of residence only, unless the employment is exercised in the other contracting state. The OECD rule is reflected in Article 15(1) of the Hungarian Treaty as follows:

> "[Subject to the provisions of Articles 16, 18, 19, 20 and 21,] salaries, wages and other similar remuneration derived by a resident of a Contracting State in respect of an employment shall be taxable only in that State unless the employment is exercised in the other Contracting State. If the employment is so exercised, such remuneration as is derived therefrom may be taxed in that other State".

U.K. domestic law insofar as it taxes non-residents on employment income is broadly consistent with this rule. Emoluments in respect of duties performed in the United Kingdom are liable to tax under Schedule E Case II for any year of assessment in which the person holding the office or employment is not resident in the United Kingdom.[1]

7-02   The treaty rule is made subject to other parts of the treaty which also deal with specialised aspects of employment income, namely Article 16 (directors' fees), Article 18 (pensions), and Article 19 (government services). In some cases, it is also subject to special rules provided for students and teachers, such as Articles 20 and 21 respectively in the Hungarian Treaty.

The source of income within the article is "an employment". Under domestic law, the charge under Schedule E applies to any "office" or "employment". An office has been described as "a position or post which goes on without regard to the identity of the holder of it from time to time" by Harman L.J. in *Mitchell and Edon v. Ross*.[2] The two notions are not mutually exclusive.[3] In general, the distinction between the two is not material and there is no suggestion that an office-holder is to be excluded from the provisions of Article 15. One exception may exist in relation to

---

[1] Taxes Act 1988, s. 19(1).
[2] (1961) 40 T.C. 11, HL.
[3] *Macmillan v. CIR* (1942) 24 T.C. 190.

126

company directors, who are dealt with under Article 16 of the OECD Model. A company director is regarded as holding an office rather than having an employment.[4] Article 15 refers to "salaries, wages, and other similar remuneration" in respect of the employment. In domestic law, tax under Schedule E is generally chargeable on "emoluments" which is defined in Taxes Act 1988, section 131(1) to include all "salaries, fees, wages, perquisites and profits whatsoever". The OECD Commentary suggests that this should cover all benefits in kind and there is no suggestion of a narrower construction in the United Kingdom.

Employment versus self-employment

7-03   The most important distinction in determining the application of the article will be between employment and self-employment. In addition to the difficulties that may arise in drawing this distinction under domestic law, the possibility of inconsistent categorisation or treatment between the United Kingdom and the other contracting state may arise. For example, it is not uncommon for professionals such as lawyers or accountants to hold an office in the course of their professional practice. Directors' fees are, strictly speaking, liable to tax under Schedule E. This would normally be assessable on the individual partners of a firm, but may be given Schedule D treatment pursuant to Extra-Statutory Concession A37, where the directorship is a normal incident of the profession and the particular practice concerned is only a small part of the profits and the fees are pooled for division amongst the partners by agreement.

ESC A37 also may have application in the context of cross-border corporate groups where, for example, a foreign parent company has the right to appoint the director to the board of a U.K. company and the director nominated is required to hand over any fees or other emoluments received in respect of his directorship to the company appointing him.

7-04   Where the fees are in fact so handed over, the concession will permit these amounts to be included in the nominating company's profits for corporation tax if it agrees to be so taxable. If the company is not within the charge to corporation tax, then it may agree to accept liability in respect of income tax deducted at the basic rate from the fees. This concession only applies to the U.K. tax treatment.

Further difficult issues arise in the application of treaties to so-called IR35 cases where services are provided through an intermediary pursuant to section 60 of and Schedule 12 to Finance Act 2000. Broadly, the IR35 provisions apply where:

(1)   an individual personally performs or is under an obligation to perform services for the purpose of a client; and

(2)   the services are provided not under a contract directly between the client and the worker, but under arrangements involving a third party; and

---

[4]   *Barry v. Farrow* [1914] 1 K.B. 632.

(3) the circumstances are such that if the services were provided under a contract directly between the client and the worker, the worker would be regarded for income tax purposes as an employee of the client.

7-05   The consequences of an engagement falling within these rules is that if the worker (or an associate of the worker) receives directly or indirectly from the intermediary a payment or other benefit that is not chargeable to tax under Schedule E, or has rights entitling him or which would entitle him to receive any such payment or other benefit from the intermediary, the intermediary is treated as making to the worker in that year and the worker is treated as receiving in that year a payment chargeable to income tax under Schedule E.[5] It is suggested that this deemed payment would not constitute "salaries, wages and other remuneration" within the treaty. Some old colonial style treaties adopt a single article for personal services, whether dependent or independent. In such cases, the distinction between them is irrelevant for treaty purposes. An example of this is found in Article 9(2) of the Antigua Treaty as follows:

"An individual who is a resident of Antigua shall be exempt from United Kingdom tax on profits or remuneration in respect of personal (including professional) services performed within the United Kingdom in any year of assessment if:

(a) he is present within the United Kingdom for a period or periods not exceeding in the aggregate 183 days during that year; and

(b) the services are performed for or on behalf of a person resident in Antigua; and

(c) the profits or remuneration are subject to Antigua tax".

Place of performance

7-06   The place where an employment is exercised for treaty purposes and the place where duties are performed under domestic law are likely to be co-extensive. Taxes Act 1988, section 132 only provides limited guidance. Section 132(1) simply associates periods of absence from the office or employment to the place of performance, unless the absence has been in respect of duties performed outside the United Kingdom. Similarly, section 132(2) associates duties performed in the United Kingdom which are merely incidental to the performance of other duties outside the United Kingdom with the foreign performance. It would appear that both under treaties and domestic law, the place of performance or exercise of employment is a question of fact. For example, in *Leonard v. Blanchard*,[6] a taxpayer sought to have apportioned to emoluments attributable to duties performed outside the United Kingdom a part of emoluments attributable to days when he had been absent from his duties. The Court of Appeal held that to show that if the tax-

---

[5] Finance Act 2000, Sch 12, para. 2(1)(b).
[6] [1993] S.T.C. 259.

payer on any day on which he was absent from employment, he would have performed duties outside the United Kingdom, if he had in reality been present, then evidence to this effect would have had to be presented.

Short stay employees

7-07 Employees spending short periods of time working outside their country of residence may be exempt from tax in the country of performance of their duties. The OECD approach is reflected in Article 15(2) of the Latvian Treaty as follows:

"Notwithstanding the provisions of paragraph (1) of this Article, remuneration derived by a resident of a Contracting State in respect of an employment exercised in the other Contracting State shall be taxable only in the first-mentioned State if:

    (a) the recipient is present in the other State for a period or periods not exceeding in the aggregate 183 days in any twelve-month period commencing or ending in the fiscal year concerned; and

    (b) the remuneration is paid by, or on behalf of, an employer who is not a resident of the other State; and

    (c) the remuneration is not borne by a permanent establishment or a fixed base which the employer has in the other State".

7-08 As a result, employees spending limited amounts of time in the United Kingdom for foreign employers will not be subject to U.K. tax. Earlier treaties referred to the 183-day test in any tax year, in line with the 1963 and 1967 Model Treaties. In determining whether a non-resident employee is present in the United Kingdom for the 183-day test, Inland Revenue practice is to count a part-day as a whole day.[7] This is in accordance with the OECD Commentary on Article 15, paragraph 5 which says "however brief the part of a day counts as a day of presence for this purpose". This differs from administrative practice in relation to determining residence, where the day of arrival and departure is ignored.[8] It may also be at variance with domestic law. In *Hoye v. Forsdyke*,[9] it was held that a "qualifying day" referred to a calendar day ending at midnight. In that case, the legislation specified that "a person shall not be regarded as absent from the United Kingdom on any day, unless he is so absent at the end of it". The taxpayer had argued that since the meaning of "day" was ambiguous, a "normal working day" was a more sensible interpretation than a calendar day ending at midnight. Consequently, in view of the different approaches in counting, presence means that an individual may well escape being resident in a year while exceeding 183 days' presence under this test. The test requires non-working days, such as weekends and holiday, to be included.

Remuneration must be paid by or on behalf of an employer who is not a resident of the source state. The Inland Revenue approach to this changed in

---

[7] *Double Taxation Relief Manual*, para. DT1921.
[8] Inland Revenue Booklet IR20, para. 1.2.
[9] [1981] S.T.C. 711, Ch.D.

1995 in relation to certain short stay employees. This applies where a formal contract of employment remains with an overseas employer, but the employee works in the business of a U.K. company, which attracts the risks and rewards of the work undertaken by the employee. The overseas employer often recharges the cost of the employee to the U.K. company in circumstances where the OECD has referred to the U.K. company as the "economic employer".

7-09   The OECD Commentary states that in applying the exemption, it is the economic employer, rather than the formal employer, who should be considered as the employer. This approach has been adopted in the United Kingdom in respect of employees commencing work after July 1, 1995.[10] A business visitor spending less than 60 days in the United Kingdom in a tax year, where that period does not form part of a lengthier presence in the United Kingdom, will be regarded by the Inland Revenue as insufficiently integrated into the U.K. business for that business to be regarded as the visitor's employer. In such circumstances, the visitor is viewed by the Inland Revenue as satisfying the conditions for the treaty exemption. The Inland Revenue will also seek to apply the "economic employer" approach in circumstances that they regard as constituting tax avoidance.[11] This may include cases where the overseas employer is based in a tax haven or the employee is nominally employed by a company which exists to provide his services to the U.K. user of those services. The Revenue will not allow a deduction for remuneration paid by a U.K. company on behalf of an overseas employer if the U.K. company has not been reimbursed for the expenditure on the basis of *Robinson v. Scott Bader & Co. Ltd.*[12]

7-10   The third requirement is that the remuneration is not borne by a permanent establishment or a fixed base which the employer has in the source state. The Inland Revenue accept that a permanent establishment cannot be said to "bear the remuneration" unless it is charged against its profits without a corresponding credit, for example by way of a management charge. However, they assume that in the absence of evidence to the contrary, that the cost of remuneration of an employee seconded to the permanent establishment is a deduction in computing the profits of the permanent establishment. This, they say, is the normal basis of allocating costs in accordance with international tax principles. The permanent establishment should therefore be regarded as bearing the cost of the individual's remuneration, unless there is evidence that the overseas head office continues to pay the employee and the cost is not allocated to the U.K. permanent establishment for U.K. tax purposes.[13] In the author's view, this is not a matter for presumption, but a matter for analysis in accordance with ordinary transfer pricing principles. Thus, an employee contributing to the profit-making activity, as a result of which income is allocated to the permanent establishment, will give rise to a deduction in respect of the employee's remuneration. On the other hand, an employee performing stewardship functions on behalf of the head office would not.

---

[10] Inland Revenue, *Tax Bulletin* (June 1995) p.220.
[11] *Double Taxation Relief Manual*, para. DT1922.
[12] (1984) 54 T.C. 757.
[13] *Double Taxation Relief Manual*, para. DT1923.

Share option gains

7-11 The Inland Revenue view the expression "salaries, wages and other similar remuneration" as being understood in the broadest sense and covering all income from employment including benefits and share option gains chargeable under Taxes Act 1988, section 135.[14] Their position is that share option gains should be regarded as accruing evenly between the grant and exercise dates. The highly controversial nature of this approach is revealed by their direction to inspectors to refer claims for treaty exemption to International Division where options are granted when an individual is U.K. resident, but exercised when resident in a treaty country and exemption from tax on the gain is claimed.[15] It may be noted that the charge to tax under section 135 only applies to options in respect of employment chargeable to tax under Case I of Schedule D. It has no application to options granted to employees who are non-resident or if resident not ordinarily resident. In relation to options that are within section 135, the gain does not accrue over time, but arises on exercise or other events referred to in section 135(1). Although that section requires the amount of the gain to be taxed under Schedule E, the gain is not "remuneration" as required by the article. The benefit of the option contract is a perquisite at the time of grant.[16]

U.S. Treaty (2001)

7-12 The Exchange of Notes of July 24, 2001 to the U.S. Treaty (2001) adopts an interpretation that requires "any benefits, income or gains enjoyed by employees" under share option plans to be regarded as "other similar remuneration" for the purposes of Article 14. The effect of this interpretation will commonly give rise to double taxation. The Exchange of Notes agrees an approach to alleviate this in certain circumstances, where an employee:

(a) has been granted a share option in the course of an employment in one of the contracting states;

(b) has exercised that employment in both states during the period between grant and exercise of the option;

(c) remains in that employment at the date of exercise; and

(d) under the domestic law of the contracting states would be taxable by both contracting states in respect of the option gain.

7-13 Pursuant to the Exchange of Notes, the contracting state of which the employee is not resident at the time of exercise will only tax that proportion of the option gain which relates to the period or periods between the grant and the exercise of the option during which the individual has exercised the employment in that contracting state. This approach accords with the policy set out in the Inland Revenue *Double Taxation Relief Manual*.

---

[14] *ibid.*, para. DT1920.
[15] *ibid.*, para. DT1925. See also Inland Revenue, *Tax Bulletin* (October 2001) p. 883.
[16] *Abbott v. Philbin* (1960) 39 T.C. 82, HL.

Recognising that this approach will likely give rise to difficulties, the Exchange of Notes states:

> "with the aim of ensuring that no unrelieved double taxation arises, the competent authorities of the contracting states will resolve by mutual agreement any difficulties or doubts arising as to the interpretation or application of Article 14 and Article 24 (relief from double taxation) in relation to employee share option plans".

SEAFARERS AND AIRCREW

7-14   An exception is made for seafarers and aircrew employed on-board a ship or aircraft operating in international traffic. The rule is designed to match the treatment of profits from shipping and aircraft operations themselves, so that under the OECD Model, these employees are only liable to tax in the contracting state where the enterprise has its place of effective management. An example is found in Article 13(2) of the Malaysian Treaty which reads as follows:

> "Notwithstanding the preceding provisions of this Article, remuneration in respect of an employment exercised aboard a ship or aircraft in international traffic may be taxed in the Contracting State in which the place of effective management of the enterprise is situated".

In some treaties, the reference to the place of effective management is replaced with the reference to the residence of the enterprise (Korean Treaty, Article 15(3)) or simply a reference to "an enterprise of a contracting state" (Latvian Treaty, Article 15(3)). These rules only apply to aircrew and seafarers and not to, for example, ground staff. Under U.K. domestic law, duties performed on a vessel not extending to a port outside the United Kingdom, or on a vessel or aircraft engaged on a voyage or journey beginning and ending in the United Kingdom, or on a part beginning or ending in the United Kingdom of any voyage or journey are deemed to be performed in the United Kingdom for the purposes of Schedule E Case I and II.[17]

DIRECTORS' FEES

7-15   Directors' fees are singled out for special treatment. The approach in the OECD Model is reflected in Article 16 of the Singapore Treaty which reads:

> "Directors' fees and other similar payments derived by a resident of a Contracting State in his capacity as a member of the board of directors of a company which is a resident of the other Contracting State may be taxed in that other State".

---

[17] Taxes Act 1988, s. 132(4)(a).

Thus, in principle, a contracting state may tax directors' fees in the country of residence of the company on whose board the director serves, even if duties are not performed there. Under domestic law, directors are taxed in the same way as other employees or officers, and consequently non-resident directors will only be taxable in respect of duties performed in the United Kingdom. Where this happens, the treaty will permit taxation notwithstanding that such duties are performed on short visits to the United Kingdom. Some treaties refer to other corporate officers consistent with the management structure under the corporate law of the other contracting state (see, for example, the Mexican Treaty, Article 16). Article 16 refers to "directors' fees and similar payments" unlike Article 15 which refers to "salaries, wages and other similar remuneration" in respect of employment. The extent to which there are any differences between these expressions is unclear. The OECD Commentary on Article 16, paragraph 1.1 indicates that the term is generally understood to include benefits in kind.

ACADEMICS

7-16 About one half of treaties contain specific provisions relating to visiting professors and teachers. More recent treaties have however tended to omit this. A simple form found in the Antigua Treaty, Article 11, reads as follows:

> "The remuneration derived by a professor or teacher who is ordinarily resident in one of the territories, for teaching, during a period of temporary residence not exceeding two years, at a university, college, school or other educational institution in the other territory, shall be exempt from tax in that other territory".

Implicit in this formulation is that the visiting academic remains ordinarily resident throughout the period in order to benefit from the exemption. This requirement does not appear in later formulations such as that found in Article 20(1) of the Belgian Treaty which reads as follows:

> "A professor or teacher who is or was formerly a resident of one of the territories, and who receives remuneration for teaching, during a period of temporary residence not exceeding two years, at a university, college, school or other educational institution in the other territory, shall be exempt from tax in that other territory in respect of that remuneration".

7-17 The second format contemplates that visiting academics may become non-resident and indeed not ordinarily resident during the period of their visit. This may hold out the prospect of tax-free income for those concerned. However, in some cases, the exemption only applies to an academic who is subject to tax in the home territory in respect of the remuneration in question (Australian Treaty, Article 16). The exemption is normally limited to remuneration derived from teaching. In the case of the U.S. Treaty (1975), it permits the exemption in relation to research. This is subject to the limitation in Article 20(3) that the research must be undertaken in the public interest and not "primarily for the benefit of some other private person or persons". The 2001 U.S. Treaty contains no article dealing with visiting academics.

Educational institution

7-18   Teaching must take place at a university, college, school or other educational institute. In *Barry v. Hughes*,[18] it was held in connection with domestic legislation that the words "other educational establishment" were not to be construed *ejusdem generis* with "university, college [or] school" because of the word "educational". In that context, education was considered to be devoted exclusively to training of the mind in contradistinction to training in manual skills. In that case, a unit at a hospital for training mentally subnormal individuals was not held to be an educational establishment. Such an interpretation, if applied in the treaty context, could lead to somewhat bizarre results where a visiting physical education teacher to a school might qualify for the exemption, whereas an English language teacher at an institution primarily providing manual training would not.

Two-year limit

7-19   The exemption applies in all cases to visits not exceeding two years. The application of this rule has given rise to dispute in two cases, both under the Hungarian Treaty. Article 21(1) of the Hungarian Treaty restricts the exemption to remuneration for teaching or research for a period "not exceeding two years from the date he first visits that state for such purpose". In *IRC v. Vaz*,[19] a Hungarian research associate had three visits to the United Kingdom. The first exceeded two years by two days. He accepted that this was not within the exemption, but argued that the two later visits which were each for less than two years qualified for exemption. The court concluded that the words "from the date he first visits" were designed to limit the exemption to the period of two years after the first visit to the United Kingdom for one of the purposes specified in the Treaty. It did not mean that any number of visits limited to two years throughout a taxpayer's working life would be exempt from U.K. tax provided he resumed foreign residence for a period between each of them.

7-20   In *Devai v. IRC*,[20] a Hungarian academic argued that he had made separate visits within the meaning of Article 21(1) when he came to the United Kingdom to take up an appointment at one university and left for a short period before taking up an appointment at another U.K. university. The Commissioner noted that the purpose of the visit must be to teach (or carry out research), but this is not expressed to tie to a particular establishment. In that case, he had spent a short period of time in Dublin between his appointment in Edinburgh and the second one in Belfast. Although he remained a resident of Hungary for tax purposes, it was found

---

[18] [1973] S.T.C. 103, Ch.D.
[19] [1990] S.T.C. 137, Ch.D.
[20] [1997] S.T.C. SCD 31 (SpC 105).

that throughout the period, his "home" was in Edinburgh where he and his family have lived since his initial appointment. The Special Commissioner also concluded that a trip to the home similarly does not interrupt the continuity of a visit provided that it is relatively short, social or recreational in character, and taken with the intention of resuming residence in the United Kingdom.

In most cases, visiting professors and teachers will be subject to U.K. taxation under Schedule E as employees. There may be cases where fees for individual lectures or projects may not be on this basis. Where the treaty does provide for specific treatment for academics, that specific treatment will apply. In other cases, the normal OECD Model Article 15 employment income provisions would apply or others in the case of non-employment income. The OECD Model does not contain a specific provision dealing with non-employment income of academics.

GOVERNMENT SERVICES

7-21   The application of the doctrine of sovereign immunity to the exercise of government functions is extended into the area of remuneration paid to government officials. Treaties addressing these issues usually distinguish between two categories of government employees. Members of diplomatic missions and consular posts are normally governed by OECD Model Article 27. An example of this is found in Article 28 of the Spanish Treaty which reads as follows:

> "Nothing in this Convention shall affect the fiscal privileges of diplomatic or consular officials under the general rules of international law or under the provisions of special agreements".

Customary international law is generally codified in this area under the Vienna Convention on Diplomatic and Consular Relations.

7-22   The modern approach to other individuals engaged in government service is set out in Article 19(1) of the Norwegian Treaty (2000) which reads:

> "(a) Salaries, wages and other similar remuneration, other than a pension, paid by a Contracting State or a political subdivision or a local authority thereof to an individual in respect of services rendered to that State or subdivision or authority shall be taxable only in that State.
>
> (b) Notwithstanding the provisions of sub-paragraph (a) of this paragraph, such salaries, wages and other similar remuneration shall be taxable only in the other Contracting State if the services are rendered in that State and the individual is a resident of that State who:
>
>   (i)   is a national of that State; or
>   (ii) did not become a resident of that State solely for the purpose of rendering the services".

7-23 Thus, in most cases, the contracting state or political subdivision thereof employing the individual will have the sole taxing right. Employment income may be taxed in the contracting state where the employment is performed where the individual is either both a resident and a national of that state, or is a resident but did not become so solely for the purpose of rendering the services in question. Thus, locally hired staff employed by foreign governments will normally be subject to U.K. taxation.

Since the role of the state functions vary from one country to another and have varied over time, employment in connection with commercial activities undertaken by a foreign government is taxed under the normal rules. This is illustrated by Article 19(3) of the Norwegian Treaty (2000) which reads:

"The provisions of Articles 15, 16, 17 and 18 of this Convention shall apply to salaries, wages and other similar remuneration, and to pensions, in respect of services rendered in connection with a business carried on by a Contracting State or a political subdivision or a local authority thereof".

PENSIONS

7-24 The funding of retirement is a complex issue in the international context because of radically different approaches taken by different countries. Pensions are addressed in the OECD Model in very simple terms. This is reflected in only a few U.K. treaties, one of which is with China. Article 19 reads:

"Subject to the provisions of paragraph (2) of Article 20 (Government Service), pensions and other similar remuneration paid to a resident of a Contracting State in consideration of past employment shall be taxable only in that State".

The scope of this article is extremely narrow, being limited to pensions in respect of past employment. As a result, a number of treaties deal with pensions and annuities together on a similar basis. Article 18, for example, of the Azerbaijan Treaty reads:

"18(1) Subject to the provisions of paragraph (2) of Article 19 of this Convention, pensions and other similar remuneration paid in consideration of past employment to a resident of a Contracting State and any annuity paid to such a resident shall be taxable only in that State where such pensions and other similar remuneration, and any such annuity, are subject to tax in that State.

18(2) The term 'annuity' means a stated sum payable to an individual periodically at stated times during his life or during a specified or ascertainable period of time under an obligation to make the payments in return for adequate and full consideration in money or money's worth".

7-25 Other treaties simply refer to pensions from a source within one contracting state (for example the Australian Treaty, Article 14(1); U.S. Treaty (2001), Article 17(1)). Exceptionally, Article 18(1) of the Swedish Treaty, although permitting taxation in the source state, requires a deduction of one-fifth of the amount to be allowed. On the other hand, Article 19 of the Zambian Treaty permits taxation in the source state only with exemption in the residence state. This applies where the employment in respect of which the pension is paid was exercised in the source state.

Social security pensions

7-26 Social security and old age pensions are not regarded as paid in consideration of past employment and are therefore not within the pensions article. The Inland Revenue treat them as within the other income article.[21] Social security pensions are addressed in a few treaties. Those with Denmark, Finland, Luxembourg and Sweden and the United States (2001) authorise taxation in the paying state. In the case of Germany, Article 9(2) provides that remuneration including pensions paid in respect of present or past services or work out of public funds is exempt from U.K. tax, unless the payment is made to a national of the United Kingdom who is not also a German national. In *Oppenheimer v. Cattermole*,[22] a German Jewish refugee fled to England in 1939 and became a British national in 1948. After the Second World War, he received pensions paid out of German public funds in respect of his work in Germany prior to immigration. The taxpayer argued that he was a German national. The House of Lords decided that the reference to nationality was to be determined by the state whose nationality is claimed. Under the basic law of the German Federal Republic enacted in 1949, former German citizens who had been deprived of their nationality for political, racial or religious reasons were entitled, although still residing abroad, to be renationalised on application. The taxpayer had not taken the appropriate steps to assert his rights under that law. In a related case heard at the same time, *Nothman v. Cooper*, the taxpayer also argued that the payments were in the nature of capital compensation. This was rejected. Annuities and pensions payable to victims of Nazi persecution by Germany or Austria are now not subject to income tax in the United Kingdom.[23]

Consideration for past employment

7-27 The requirement that pensions and similar remuneration be paid in consideration of past employment is related to but narrower than the definition of "relevant benefits" in Taxes Act 1988, section 612(1). This definition applies generally for employer provided retirement benefit schemes under Part XIV Chapter I. Relevant benefits extend to those:

> "given or to be given on retirement or on death, or by virtue of a pension sharing order or provision, or in anticipation of retirement, or, in

---

[21] Inland Revenue, *Double Taxation Relief Manual*, para. DT227.
[22] (1975) 50 T.C. 159.
[23] Taxes Act 1988, s. 330.

connection with past service, after retirement or death, or to be given on or anticipation of or in connection with any change in the nature of service of the employee in question, except that it does not include any benefit which is to be afforded solely by reason of the disablement by accident of a person occurring during his service or of his death by accident so occurring and for no other reason".

The expression "past employment" does not appear to extend to self-employment and thus retirement annuities under Part XIV Chapter III and personal pension schemes under Chapter IV in respect of self-employed individuals will not fall within pension articles following the OECD Model. Annuities paid to such individuals will likely fall within the annuity provisions. Income draw-down arrangements may not.

7-28   The scope of the article has not been considered by the courts. No comprehensive definition of pension is provided in the Taxes Act 1988. In the definition of relevant benefits in section 612(1), a pension (which includes an annuity) is however distinguished from a "lump sum, gratuity or other like benefit". In *Johnson v. Holleran*,[24] money received from trustees of a pension fund after the cessation of employment in recognition of previous employment and because of disability was a pension. The fact that payments were made on account of disability rather than for past services was immaterial. It was argued that to constitute a pension, the payments must be made (i) after retirement, (ii) to a former employee, (iii) for past services, and (iv) must continue for life. The taxpayer argued that he was not retired because if his disability ceased, the payments would cease and he would have to seek employment. It was held that it was sufficient that the particular employment must have ceased, but that this need not have been due to retirement rather than any other cause. The court, noting the absence of a judicial definition of pension, did not attempt one. In *Johnson v. Farquhar*,[25] the court confirmed that it was sufficient that the taxpayer became a member of the pension scheme because he was an employee and remained a member until he ceased to be an employee. It was not necessary for the payment to be for past services in the sense of being fully earned and a form of deferred salary. This approach suggests that, if past employment is one of the originating causes, this is sufficient. Other boundary issues arise in relation to lump sum payments paid to non-residents where they are not exempt under domestic law, or payments out of employee benefit trusts which do not constitute retirement benefit schemes, or other deferred compensation arrangements. "Past employment" would appear to refer to employment which has terminated and any reason for termination should suffice.

Source of pensions

7-29   The situs of the payer is the only rule for determining the source of pensions under domestic law. In particular, the underlying reason for the pension is irrelevant. Under domestic law, tax is payable under Schedule E

---

[24] [1989] S.T.C. 1, Ch.D.
[25] [1992] S.T.C. 11.

in respect of any pension which is paid otherwise than by or on behalf of a person outside the United Kingdom.[26] Foreign pensions are those paid by or on behalf of a person outside the United Kingdom and not charged under paragraph 4 of Schedule E. Foreign pensions are treated as foreign possessions liable to tax under Schedule D Case V.[27] This includes foreign statutory social security pensions.[28] U.K. residents receiving foreign pensions are entitled to a deduction of one-tenth of the amount.[29]

Contributions to pension schemes

7-30 Tax relief on contributions to fund pensions or other retirement benefits is generally only available for U.K. established occupational pension schemes meeting the requirements of Taxes Act 1988 section 596(1). Thus, only employees performing duties of employment in the United Kingdom, either as short stay employees liable to tax within Article 15 or those becoming resident and ordinarily resident but returning home after a period of employment, can participate in U.K.-based pension schemes in order to enjoy beneficial tax treatment.

7-31 A limited exception applies in relation to individuals earning foreign emoluments not liable to tax under Case I or II of Schedule E, if the foreign retirement benefit scheme in question corresponds to a U.K. approved scheme, a relevant statutory scheme or government scheme.[30] Restrictions on approval of personal pension schemes[31] in relation to retirement annuities[32] in effect limit such schemes to U.K. schemes. Notwithstanding the limitations placed on cross-border employment, treaty provisions addressing this issue are rare. Treaties with Denmark[33], the Irish Republic[34] and the United States (2001)[35] provide for relief in respect of contributions to a pension fund established in one contracting state in respect of employment exercised in the other. In each case, relief is subject to detailed conditions. The first of these, contained in the Irish Treaty, reads:

"17A(1) Subject to the conditions specified in paragraph (2) of this Article, where an employee ('the employee'), who is a member of a pension scheme which has been approved or is being considered for approval under the legislation of one of the Contracting States, exercises his employment in the other Contracting State:

(a) contributions paid by the employee to that scheme during the period that he exercises his employment in that other State shall be deductible in computing his taxable income in that State within the limits that would apply if the contributions

---

[26] Taxes Act 1988, s. 19(1), Sched. E, para. 3.
[27] *ibid.*, s. 58(1).
[28] *Albon v. IRC* [1998] S.T.C. 1181.
[29] Taxes Act 1988, s. 65(2).
[30] *ibid.*, s. 596(2).
[31] *ibid.*, s. 632.
[32] *ibid.*, s. 620.
[33] Article 28(3).
[34] Article 17A.
[35] Article 18.

were paid to a pension scheme which has been approved under the legislation of that State; and

(b) payments made to the scheme by or on behalf of his employer during that period:

(i) shall not be treated as part of the employee's taxable income, and

(ii) shall be allowed as a deduction in computing the profits of his employer,

in that other State".

7-32　As a result, both employer and employee contributions will qualify for relief in that employee contributions will be deductible in computing taxable income within the limits imposed by the state of employment as if they had been paid to a local pension scheme. Likewise, employer contributions are deductible by the employer and not treated as part of the taxable income of the employee. Only employees who are members of a pension scheme approved in one contracting state and exercising employment in the other contracting state qualify for this benefit. In addition, the Irish Treaty for example, imposes several conditions which must be met:

"17A(2) The conditions specified in this paragraph are that:

(a) the employee is employed in the other Contracting State by the person who was his employer immediately before he began to exercise his employment in that State or by an associated employer of that employer;

(b) the employee was not a resident of that State immediately before he began to exercise his employment there;

(c) at the time that the contributions referred to in paragraph (1)(a) of this Article are paid, or the payments referred to in paragraph (1)(b) of this Article are made, to the scheme the employee has exercised his employment in that State for:

(i) less than ten years where he was a resident of the first-mentioned Contracting State immediately before he began to exercise his employment in the other Contracting State, or

(ii) less than five years in other cases".

7-33　As a result, these benefits are only available to employees who move in the course of existing employment from one contracting state to the other in order to work in the second and were not resident there immediately before starting to work in the state of employment. The benefit is also subject to time limits. Contributions will only qualify if the employment was exercised for less than ten years in the state where the fund is not established, if he was resident in the state where the fund is established immediately before starting to work in the other. In other cases, it applies where the employee has exercised his employment in the state where the fund is not established for less than five years. Employment will qualify either with the same or an associated employer.

7-34   These provisions do not address the problems of cross-border pension arrangements comprehensively. The U.S. Treaty (2001) is the first to attempt a more rounded approach to the taxation of pensions and pension payments. Those treaties providing for relief for pension contributions only, address this issue in the context of occupational pensions. Pensions for self-employed individuals are not addressed. Apart from the absence of relief for contributions, the lack of specific measures also raises questions as to how pension fund investment returns are to be classified where the pension is financed by an individual's own contributions, if they are not specifically recognised under the pensions regime as such. Article 18(2) of the U.S. Treaty (2001) extends relief to participants in pension schemes in respect of self-employment along with employment. This applies in both cases only where the employment or self-employment began in the other contracting state. In addition, the pension scheme must "generally correspond" to a pension scheme established in that other state. General correspondence is a more liberal expression than required for corresponding schemes under domestic law and as required, for example, under Article 28 of the Danish Treaty. The Exchange of Notes of July 24, 2001 with respect to the U.S. Treaty lists pension schemes for the purpose of the Treaty and include U.K. employment related arrangements and personal pensions. Existing U.S. plans are also included, as well as any "identical or substantially similar schemes" which are established pursuant to legislation introduced after the date of signature of the Treaty. The Treaty further provides[36] that where an individual resident in one contracting state is a member or participant in a pension scheme established in the other contracting state, income earned by the pension scheme may only be taxed as the income of the individual, when it is paid to or for the benefit of that individual and, in particular, when it is not transferred to another scheme. Where the individual makes contributions in respect of income or profit which is taxed on the remittance basis, then relief may be reduced in proportion to the amount unremitted.[37] Furthermore, as a boost to the U.K. pension industry, contributions by U.S. citizens resident in the United Kingdom and employed by a U.K. resident or a permanent establishment in the United Kingdom may contribute to U.K. pension schemes for U.S. tax purposes and contributions are treated as deductible (or excludable) in computing taxable income in the United States.[38]

Government pensions

7-35   Government pensions are accorded separate treatment under treaties. They are typically excluded from the pensions article and addressed in the government services article. The OECD Model provisions are contained in Article 19(2) of the Vietnamese Treaty as follows:

> "(a) Any pension paid by, or out of funds created by, a Contracting State or a political subdivision or a local authority thereof to an individual in respect of services rendered to that State or subdivision or authority shall be taxable only in that State.

---

[36] See Art.18(1).
[37] See Art.18(4).
[38] See Art.5.

(b) Notwithstanding the provisions of sub-paragraph (a) of this paragraph, such pension shall be taxable only in the other Contracting State if the individual is a resident of and a national of that State".

As with employment income, a distinction is drawn between employees performing a state function and those who do not. The Inland Revenue *Double Taxation Relief Manual* notes that employment with a statutory body set up by a state is not usually regarded as involving payment by or the rendering of services to that state, even if the body is set up and funded by the state. Similarly, employees in nationalised industries are not regarded as coming within government services. They give the example of members of armed forces or teachers employed by a local authority as paid by the state for services rendered to that state. The widow or dependants of an individual who has rendered services to a state is regarded as being paid by the other state for services rendered to that state.[39]

7-36 As with government services, taxing jurisdiction is normally reserved to the paying state. Residents and nationals of the other contracting state are normally to be taxed in that state only, in order to facilitate the hiring of local staff.

---

[39] *Double Taxation Relief Manual*, para. DT908.

CHAPTER 8

Capital Gains and Miscellaneous Cases

CAPITAL GAINS

8-01   The approach adopted in treaties following the OECD Model to the taxation of capital gains is in broad terms similar to that adopted under U.K. domestic law, the underlying principle being that capital gains are generally only taxable in the contracting state of residence. A typical expression of this rule is found in Article 13(4) of the Bangladesh Treaty, which reads:

> "Capital gains from the alienation of any property other than those mentioned in paragraphs (1), (2) and (3) of this Article shall be taxable only in the Contracting State of which the alienator is a resident".

The balance of the articles constitute the exceptions to the general rule.

CAPITAL ASSETS OF A PERMANENT ESTABLISHMENT

Branch assets

8-02   Capital gains are subject to limited taxation in the hands of non-residents. The principal charging provision is Taxation of Chargeable Gains Act (TCGA) 1992, section 10. Persons who are not resident and not ordinarily resident in the United Kingdom are not generally liable to tax in respect of chargeable gains unless they are carrying on a trade in the United Kingdom through a branch or agency. Non-residents, who are within the charge, are only liable to tax on gains accruing on the disposal of assets situated in the United Kingdom:

(a)   and used in or for the purposes of the trade at or before the time when the capital gain accrued; or

(b)   used or held for the purposes of the branch or agency at or before that time or assets acquired for use by or for the purposes of the branch or agency.[1]

Only disposals made at the time when the person is carrying on the trade in the United Kingdom through a branch or agency are taxable.[2] This charge

---

[1] TCGA 1992, s. 10(1).
[2] *ibid.*, s. 10(2).

is ring-fenced by deemed disposals in the case of non-residents under section 25. Where an asset ceases to be a chargeable asset, because it is situated outside the United Kingdom, the non-resident owner is deemed to have disposed of it and immediately to have re-acquired it at market value.[3] Similarly, where a non-resident ceases to carry on a trade in the United Kingdom through a branch or agency, it is deemed to have disposed of the asset at that time and to immediately have re-acquired it at its market value.[4] These rules extend to a profession or vocation under Taxes Act 1988, Schedule D Case II.[5]

8-03   All treaties with capital gains articles authorise the contracting state where a permanent establishment is located to tax capital gains from the alienation of property forming part of the business property of a permanent establishment. Similar rules authorise taxation of capital assets forming part of a fixed base for the purpose of performing professional services. Article 8A(2) of the Israeli Treaty is a typical example:

> "Capital gains from the alienation of movable property forming part of the business property of a permanent establishment which an enterprise of one of the territories has in the other territory or of movable property pertaining to a fixed base available to a resident of one of the territories in the other territory for the purpose of performing professional services, including such gains from the alienation of such a permanent establishment (alone or together with the whole enterprise) or of such a fixed base, may be taxed in the other territory".

This will typically authorise taxation of gains on the disposal of branch assets in accordance with TCGA 1992, section 10.

Sale of U.K. patent rights

8-04   Where a non-resident sells all or part of any U.K. patent rights, the proceeds are generally chargeable to tax under Schedule D Case VI.[6] Such rights are not immovable property and disposals should not be liable to U.K. tax in the absence of a permanent establishment.

Immovable property

8-05   Under the OECD Model, gains from the alienation of immovable property may be taxed where they are situated. Article 13(1) of the Barbados Treaty contains the customary formulation:

> "Capital gains from the alienation of immovable property, as defined in paragraph (2) of Article 12, may be taxed in the Contracting State in which such property is situated".

---

[3] *ibid.*, s. 25(1).
[4] *ibid.*, s. 25(3).
[5] *ibid.*, s. 25(8).
[6] Taxes Act 1988, s. 524(3).

Development gains relating to land

8-06   Gains of a capital nature obtained from the disposal of land acquired with the sole or main object of realising a gain, or which is held as trading stock, or developed with the sole or main object of realising a gain from its disposal when developed, may give rise to a charge to tax under Schedule D Case VI by virtue of Taxes Act 1988, section 776. Treaties following the OECD Model will thus allow the charge under section 776.

The charge also applies in relation to a disposal of shares in a company within that section.[7] Since the alienation of immovable property does not normally include shares, a number of treaties authorise the taxation in the situs state of shares in companies whose value is based on immovable property. This ranges from a simple formulation found in Article 13(1) of the Egyptian Treaty to gains "from the alienation of shares in a company, the assets of which consist principally of such [immovable] property" to the complex provisions of Article 13 of the Canadian Treaty which creates separate rules depending upon whether the alienator and related or connected persons own less than 10 per cent of each class of the share capital of the company and whether the shares are quoted on an approved Stock Exchange.[8]

Exploration or exploitation shares

8-07   Gains accruing to a non-resident on the disposal of exploration or exploitation rights are treated as gains accruing on the disposal of assets used for the purposes of a trade carried on by that person in the United Kingdom through a branch or agency.[9] Exploration or exploitation rights in this context refer to assets used in the exploration or exploitation of the seabed and subsoil and their natural resources as are situated in the United Kingdom or a designated area. Shares deriving their value or the greater part of their value from exploration or exploitation assets are deemed to be such assets. Consequently, a disposal of shares in such a company where the assets are located in the United Kingdom may give rise to a charge to capital gains tax.

Several treaties also address rights to explore for or exploit oil and gas. These include treaties with Canada, Sweden, and Finland, which treat these rights in the same manner as immovable property. Similarly, shares in companies whose value is based on these rights are typically taxed. See for example the Canadian Treaty, Article 13(4)(b). The Canadian Treaty further authorises taxation in the situs state in relation to interests in partnerships or trusts, the assets of which consist principally of immovable property or oil and gas rights.[10] Treaties containing this article will typically permit taxation of non-residents under Taxes Act 1988, section 776. Treaties that have a capital gains article, but which do not authorise situs taxation of gains on immovable property are those with South Africa[11] and Zambia.[12]

---

[7] TCGA 1992, s. 776(10).
[8] See Art.13(5)(a), (6)(a).
[9] TCGA 1992, s. 276(7).
[10] Canadian Treaty, Art.13(5)(b).
[11] Article 12.
[12] Article 14.

Alienation of ships and aircraft

8-08   The normal rule is to give exclusive taxation on the alienation of ships or aircraft operated in international traffic to the country of residence. The rule is expressed in Article 14(4) of the Malaysian Treaty, thus:

> "Gains derived by a resident of a Contracting State from the alienation of ships or aircraft operated in international traffic by an enterprise of that Contracting State or movable property pertaining to the operation of such ships or aircraft, shall be taxable only in that Contracting State".

Exit charges

8-09   Where a company ceases to be resident in the United Kingdom, it is deemed to have disposed of all of its assets for capital gains purposes and to have immediately acquired them at market value immediately before it ceases to be resident.[13] The assets which remain within the charge to capital gains tax, because the company carries on a trade in the United Kingdom through a branch or agency, are excluded from this deemed disposal.[14] Since the disposal takes place before the company ceases to be non-resident, the charge will not be within the scope of treaties as the asset will not be owned by a resident of the other contracting state. However, where an election is made under section 187 to postpone the charge, the position is less obvious. The effect of the election is to deem the gain to accrue to the principal company.[15] The principal company is a 75 per cent shareholder which is resident in the United Kingdom.[16] It is submitted that since the actual disposal takes place in a company which is non-resident, gains, which in such circumstances would be protected by suitable treaty provisions, would be exempted by suitable treaty provisions.

A somewhat similar approach is taken in respect of trustees ceasing to be resident in the United Kingdom. If trustees of a settlement become neither resident nor ordinarily resident in the United Kingdom, they are likewise deemed to have disposed of their assets for capital gains purposes and to have immediately re-acquired them immediately before becoming non-resident.[17] Assets remaining within the charge to capital gains tax are excluded from this.[18] However, if the assets are such that after the trustees have ceased to be resident, gains on the assets concerned would be exempt under the treaty, then they are not excluded from the deemed disposal.[19] Similarly, trustees ceasing to be liable to U.K. tax while continuing to be resident because of the application of a treaty similarly suffer a deemed disposal.[20]

---

[13] TCGA 1992, s. 185(1), (2).
[14] *ibid.*, s. 185(4).
[15] *ibid.*, s. 187(3).
[16] *ibid.*, s. 187(1)(a).
[17] *ibid.*, s. 80(2).
[18] *ibid.*, s. 80(4).
[19] *ibid.*, s. 80(5).
[20] *ibid.*, s. 83.

Gains of former residents

8-10 A totally different approach is taken in relation to departing individuals. There is no deemed disposal for individuals ceasing to be resident in the United Kingdom. Temporary non-residents are, however, subject to the inclusion of gains accruing during their period of absence in the year they return.[21] This applies to individuals who leave the United Kingdom and return, where there are fewer than five tax years between the year of departure and return.[22] The interaction between these rules and tax treaties is not straightforward. The deemed timing of disposals during the intervening years occur during a year of U.K. residence when in principle exemption from U.K. tax under treaties is normally unavailable. Section 10A(10) says enigmatically: "this section is without prejudice to any right to claim relief in accordance with any double taxation relief arrangements". Actual disposals are those that take place during years of non-residence where the individual may in principle qualify for exemption under a particular treaty. The Inland Revenue interpret the legislation so that gains accruing during periods of non-residence will be subject to exemption in respect of any treaty with a country in which the taxpayer is resident at the time the actual gain is made.[23] The Manual states clearly that the charging provisions of section 10A are not intended to override any treaty. Consequently, any exemption specifically given under a treaty must be taken into account in arriving at any U.K. liability.[24] It is implicit in this analysis that in applying a treaty, the actual timing of the disposal is material rather than the deemed timing.

A significant number of treaties authorise contracting states to tax former residents on capital gains for a limited period of time. A current example is Article 13(6) of the Estonian Treaty, which reads:

> "The provisions of paragraph (5) of this Article shall not affect the right of a Contracting State to levy according to its law a tax on capital gains from the alienation of any property derived by an individual who is a resident of the other Contracting State and has been a resident of the first-mentioned Contracting State at any time during the five years immediately preceding the alienation of the property".

8-11 Although section 10A was inserted into TCGA 1992 by Finance Act 1998 and applies where 1997–98 is the year of departure and the taxpayer was ordinarily resident in the United Kingdom in that year on or after March 17, 1998, it is found in a number of older treaties such as that with South Africa (1969) and negotiated soon after the introduction of capital gains tax in the United Kingdom in 1965. Since the charge to capital gains tax is levied by reference to both residence and ordinary residence,[25] there may be circumstances in which a departing U.K. resident is non-resident of the United Kingdom both under domestic law and by virtue of a treaty, but

---

[21] *ibid.*, s. 10A(2).
[22] *ibid.*, s. 10A(1).
[23] Inland Revenue, *Capital Gains Manual*, para. CG26120.
[24] *ibid.*, para. CG26290.
[25] TCGA 1992, s. 21(1).

continues to be ordinarily resident in the United Kingdom. This form of wording will allow the United Kingdom to tax individuals not resident but ordinarily resident in the United Kingdom. The period of residence is less than five years in some treaties, for example two years in the Bolivian Treaty,[26] three years in the Oman Treaty,[27] and three years in the Austrian Treaty if the gain is not subject to tax in the country of residence at the time the disposal is made.[28]

Several older treaties do not contain a capital gains article. Most pre-date the introduction of capital gains tax and are patterned on the colonial model. Some more recent treaties similarly do not contain a capital gains article, notably those with Botswana and Cyprus. In neither treaty is capital gains tax a tax which is the subject of the treaty.

OTHER INCOME

8-12 Items of income which are not mentioned in a treaty fall to be taxed in accordance with the domestic laws of the contracting states. Treaties patterned on the OECD Model attempt to sweep up this residual category through the "other income" article. The simplest form of this article is found in the South African Treaty. Article 20 reads:

> "Any income not dealt with in the foregoing provisions of this Convention derived by a resident of a Contracting State who is subject to tax there in respect thereof shall be subjected to tax only in that State".

Consequently, income not expressly dealt with is taxable only in the state of residence. Treaties patterned on the OECD Model, however, contain an exception to this permitting income associated with the activity of a permanent establishment to be taxed in that state. This exception is found, for example, in Article 22(2) of the Spanish Treaty as follows:

> "The provisions of paragraph (1) of this Article shall not apply if the recipient of the income, being a resident of a Contracting State, carries on business in the other Contracting State through a permanent establishment situated therein, or performs in that other State professional services from a fixed base situated therein, and the right or property in respect of which the income is paid is effectively connected with such permanent establishment or fixed base. In such a case, the provisions of Article 7 or Article 14, as the case may be, shall apply".

8-13 The Inland Revenue view is that capital gains are not covered by the other income article.[29] Since this clause covers all items of income, it may have considerable significance. Normally, it covers income from all sources. In several treaties, however, other income may be taxed in the

---

[26] Article 13(6).
[27] Article 13(7).
[28] Article 13(5).
[29] Inland Revenue, *Double Taxation Relief Manual*, para. DT227.

country of source. This includes those with Argentina,[30] Singapore,[31] and Venezuela.[32]

It has also become customary for the other income article to be used to attach provisions relating to issues that do not fit neatly within the other parts of the treaty. Many deal with payments from trusts and estates in the course of administration. Article 20(1) of the Irish Treaty reads:

> "Items of income of a resident of a Contracting State, wherever arising, being income of a class or from sources not expressly mentioned in the foregoing Articles of this Convention, other than income paid out of trusts or the estates of deceased persons in the course of administration, shall be taxable only in that State".

A number of treaties do not pick up residual items of income, but simply use the article to refer to income from trusts or estates and, indeed in some cases, from trusts only.[33] In the case of France, a separate Article 7A was added by protocol to deal with taxation of the Channel Tunnel operations.

OFFSHORE EXPLORATION AND EXPLOITATION ACTIVITIES

8-14 Since the development of the offshore oil and gas industry in the United Kingdom from the early 1970s, treaties have contained provisions addressing the manner in which the activities of residents of treaty countries are to be taxed in that context. Jurisdiction to impose income tax, capital gains tax and corporation tax to exploration or exploitation activities in the North Sea under Finance Act 1973, section 38 applied to the exploration or exploitation of the seabed and subsoil and their natural resources situated both in the United Kingdom or a designated area of the Continental shelf. In the absence of such extension, the United Kingdom would normally be restricted to the areas of its territorial sea. The breadth of the territorial sea is 12 nautical miles from the coastline.[34] The definition of the United Kingdom is also extended in most treaties. For example, the United Kingdom is defined in the Canadian Treaty, Article 3(1)(a)(ii), to mean:

> "Great Britain and Northern Ireland, including any area outside the territorial sea of the United Kingdom which in accordance with international law has been or may be hereafter designated under the laws of the United Kingdom concerning the Continental shelf, as an area within which the rights of the United Kingdom with respect to the seabed and subsoil and their natural resources may be exercised".

8-15 This may be contrasted with early treaties, such as that with Greece. There, the United Kingdom means "Great Britain and Northern

---

[30] Article 21(5).
[31] Article 22(3).
[32] Article 21(3).
[33] For example, Falkland Islands, Article 24.
[34] Territorial Sea Act 1987, s. 1.

Ireland, excluding the Channel Islands and the Isle of Man" (Article 2(1)(a)). These provisions extend taxing jurisdiction to the U.K. areas of the Continental shelf and in a number of cases constitute exceptions to the taxing rules found in most treaties. Article 27A of the Canadian Treaty embraces the typical subject matter of these provisions. Pursuant to Article 27A(2) activities in connection with the exploration or exploitation of the seabed and subsoil and their natural resources situated in the other contracting state are generally deemed to be carrying on business in that other contracting state through a permanent establishment. This is not the case unless these activities are carried on for periods in excess of 30 days in the aggregate in any 12 months' period.[35]

Jurisdiction to tax employment income is similarly extended. Salaries and similar remuneration in respect of employment connected with the exploration or exploitation of the seabed may be taxed to the extent that duties are performed offshore in the other contracting state.[36] Thus, the normal exemptions for employment income do not apply in this context.

8-16   In Article 28A(4) of the Danish Treaty, profits from the operation in connection with offshore activities of ships or aircraft designed primarily for transporting supplies or personnel, or of tugboats or anchor handling vessels, are only taxable in the state in which effective management of the enterprise is situated. This does not apply to profits during any period in which such a ship or aircraft is contracted to be used mainly for purposes other than transporting supplies or personnel to or between places where offshore activities are being carried on.

Likewise, remuneration in respect of employment exercised on board a ship or aircraft, the profits of which are taxable in this way, are themselves taxable.[37] In several cases, independent personal services are also deemed to be carried on through a fixed base if they are exercised for periods exceeding 30 days in the aggregate in any 12 months' period.[38]

Further specific provisions are contained in the Norwegian Treaty dealing with trans-median line oil and gas fields[39] and several specific fields.[40]

STUDENTS

8-17   Payments received by students or business apprentices for the purpose of maintenance, education or training are commonly exempt from tax by treaty in the country of study. Article 20 of the current OECD Model is reflected in Article 19 of the Bulgarian Treaty as follows:

> "Payments which a student or business apprentice who is or was immediately before visiting a Contracting State a resident of the other

---

[35] See Art.27A(3).
[36] See Art.27A(4).
[37] See Art.28A(5)(b).
[38] For example, Netherlands Treaty, Article 22A(5).
[39] Article 24.
[40] Statfjord field reservoirs Article 25, Murchison field reservoir Article 26, and Frigg field Article 27).

Contracting State and who is present in the first-mentioned State solely for the purpose of his education or training receives for the purpose of his maintenance, education or training shall not be taxed in that State, provided that such payments arise from sources outside that State".

There are numerous variations on this theme. The treaty for Bolivia limits this to the first £3,500 in addition to personal allowances. No time limit is generally expressed although the words "who is or was immediately before visiting a contracting state" suggests that this is not open-ended. Others, such as the Belize Treaty, Article 12, simply require that the student be "from" a contracting state and those following the 1963 OECD Model apply to students who were "formerly" a resident of a contracting state. Some treaties, such as those with Bangladesh and China, contain extensive provisions dealing with this issue.

CHAPTER 9

Treaties and European Tax Directives

9-01   The supremacy of the EC Treaty over the bilateral treaties of Member States was considered in Chapter 2 above. This chapter examines the relationship between tax treaties and other Community legislative instruments. Given the close connection between taxation and sovereignty, the EC Treaty requires unanimous approval of all Member States for tax provisions to be enacted, amended or repealed. It is a crucial exception to the principle of majority voting. As a result progress in the field of harmonisation of company taxation has been extremely slow. The three direct tax measures enacted in 1991 had been in proposal form for over 20 years before becoming law. Those measures[1] have their legal authority based on Article 94 (ex 100) of the EC Treaty which provides broad authority for approximation of laws which directly affect the establishment or functioning of the common market. It is clear that subject to the fundamental freedoms granted by Community law, in the absence of harmonising measures, Member States are free to tax in accordance with their domestic law.[2] The manner in which this freedom may be limited is determined by the legal instrument chosen for harmonisation.

LEGISLATIVE INSTRUMENTS

9-02   Briefly, the legislative means available to the European Community are:

(a) Regulations: these are uniform rules and by definition binding in their entirety and directly applicable. They do not have to be adopted in the legislation of Member States. They confer rights on individuals which the courts of Member States must protect.[3]

(b) Directives: these are addressed to and binding upon Member States. The Member States are required to achieve the result

---

[1] Directive 90/434 on the common system of taxation applicable to mergers, divisions, transfer of assets, and exchanges of shares concerning companies of different Member States; Directive 90/435 on the common system of taxation applicable in the cases of parent companies and subsidiaries of different Member States, and the Convention on the Elimination of Double Taxation in connection with the Adjustment of Profits of Associated Enterprises (90/436).

[2] Case C-81/87 *R. v. H.M. Treasury and Inland Revenue Commissioners, ex parte Daily Mail and General Trust Plc* [1988] S.T.C. 787.

[3] Case C-83/78 *Pigs Marketing Board v. Redmond* [1978] E.C.R. 2347.

described in the Directive by legislation into national law. In certain circumstances, Directives may be of direct effect if national law is inadequate or if they have not been implemented into national law at all.

(c) Decisions: these are measures taken in an individual case. A Member State or persons may be required to perform or refraining from a particular action. These are seldom relevant to taxation.

(d) Opinions: these are issued by a single Community institution and constitute non-binding legal measures. It allows the institution to express a view on particular events to Member States or to persons generally.

DIRECT EFFECT

9-03 Regulations intrinsically have direct effect. In *Walder v. Bestuur der Sociale Verzerkeringsbank*,[4] the European Court of Justice considered the priority of a Regulation dealing with social security payments for migrant workers.[5] The ECJ held that the process by which rights and obligations are transferred by Member States from their domestic legal systems to the Community cannot be reversed by subsequent unilateral measures that are inconsistent with Community law. Similarly, the same result cannot be achieved by bilateral measures such as bilateral tax treaties. On this basis, bilateral treaties between Member States which are inconsistent with regulations effectively exceed remaining national jurisdiction and as a result have no effect.

The position is considerably more complex in relation to Directives because of their legal nature. Directives are addressed to Member States. The binding force according to Article 249 (ex 189) of the EC Treaty is limited to the result to be achieved upon each Member State to which it is addressed, whereas a Regulation is binding in its entirety. The result is described in the Directive and must be translated within the period specified in the Directive into binding provisions of domestic law of Member States. Member States remain free to determine the method and form. There is no reason in principle why effect might not be given to a Directive by means of a treaty. Thus, treaties might contravene the provisions of a Directive where it, along with the domestic law of a Member State, fails or fails properly to implement a Directive.

9-04 Directives may be of direct effect in whole or in part. The doctrine of direct effect was first considered in the tax context by the ECJ in the decision of *Becker v. Finanzamt Muenster-Innenstadt*.[6] The ECJ ruled that wherever the provisions of a Directive appear to be unconditional and sufficiently precise as far as the subject matter is concerned, those provisions may in the absence of implementing measures adopted be relied upon against any

---

[4] Case 82/72 [1973] E.C.R. 599.
[5] Regulation 1408/71, para. 3.
[6] Case 8/81 [1982] E.C.R. 53.

national provision which is incompatible with the Directive insofar as the provisions define rights which individuals are able to assert against that state. As a result, provisions of bilateral treaties between Member States which are inconsistent with a Directive will in this context have no effect.

TAX BY REGULATION: THE EEIG

9-05   References to taxation are found in certain EC non-tax legislation such as the European Economic Interest Grouping Regulation.[7] European Economic Interest Groupings (EEIGs) are a form of statutory joint venture. Article 40 of the Regulation requires flow-through tax treatment for EEIGs. It specifies that profits or losses resulting from the activities of a grouping shall be taxable only in the hands of its members. This does not provide a great deal of guidance about the precise treatment. An EEIG has full legal capacity. However, whether it has legal personality is dependent on the domestic law of its country of formation. Thus, whether the members would be liable to corporation tax or income tax is not determined by the Regulation. It would appear that even where an EEIG has legal personality that it is unable to qualify for treaty benefits. While it may be resident in a contracting state, it cannot be liable to tax in that contracting state by virtue of that residence, because profits or losses resulting from its activities are to be taxable only in the hands of its members. Whether one member of an EEIG constitutes a permanent establishment of another will depend on the terms of the EEIG contract and all relevant circumstances. The official address of an EEIG , under Article 12 of the EEIG Regulation, must be either where the EEIG has its central administration or where one of its members has its principal administration or principal activity. Will this constitute a permanent establishment for treaty purposes? Article 3(1) of the Regulation specifies that the purpose of a grouping is to facilitate or develop economic activities of its members, or to improve or increase the results of those activities. Its purpose is not to make profits for itself. The Article further specifies that activities must be related to the economic activities of its members and must "not be more than ancillary to those activities". Does this mean that the activities of an EEIG can never be more than "preparatory or auxiliary", as contemplated by Article 5 of the OECD Model Treaty and therefore never constitute a permanent establishment? Article 3(2) of the Regulation specifies activities which are prohibited as a consequence of these limitations imposed on EEIGs. Unfortunately, despite the fact that the Regulation is of direct effect, the EEIG Regulation does not provide sufficient detail to settle these issues.

DIRECTIVES AND TAX TREATIES: THE 1990 PACKAGE

9-06   The most important direct tax measures are the so-called package of three adopted in July 1990. The package comprised two Directives, namely the Parent-Subsidiary Directive 90/435 dealing with intra-group

---

[7] 2137/85; [1985] O.J. L189/31.

cross-border dividends and the Mergers Directive 90/434 dealing with cross-border mergers, divisions and corporate reorganisations. The third element of the package, the Arbitration Convention, relating to transfer pricing, started life initially as a draft Directive. It was finally adopted as a multilateral treaty. The two Directives entered into effect on January 1, 1992. Exchange of information has been covered by Directive since 1977 in relation to direct tax and in relation to VAT, customs duty and agricultural levies since 1976.

THE PARENT-SUBSIDIARY DIRECTIVE

9-07   The Parent-Subsidiary Directive is aimed at eliminating double taxation within the Community on the distribution of profits within corporate groups. It is of considerable importance in the treaty context since it occupies the same ground in many respects as Article 10 (Dividends) and Article 23 (Elimination of double taxation) of the OECD Model.

The main operative provisions of the Directive are:

(a) the exemption from withholding tax in respect of distributions paid on a 25 per cent or larger shareholding to a shareholder in another EC Member State[8]; and

(b) the exemption from or credit for underlying tax for the recipient company by the state of the parent company in respect of the distribution.[9]

The exemption from withholding tax has been held to be of direct effect in *Denkavit International BV and others v. Bundesampt für Finanzen*[10] on the basis that it is clear and unambiguous.

Qualification

9-08   There are a number of requirements that must be complied with in order to fall within the scope of the Directive:

(a) both parent and subsidiary must be forms of entity listed in an Appendix to the Directive;[11] it does not therefore apply to all entities characterised as corporations for the tax purposes of particular Member States;

(b) both parent and subsidiary must be resident for tax purposes in a different EC Member State[12] and must not be considered as resident outside the Community by virtue of any applicable treaty[13];

---

[8] Article 5(1).
[9] Article 4(1).
[10] Case 283/94 [1996] S.T.C. 1445.
[11] Article 2(a).
[12] Article 1(1).
[13] Article 2(b).

(c) both parent and subsidiary must be subject to one of the taxes listed in the Directive[14]; these are effectively corporate income taxes levied in the Community.

The 25 per cent equity stake may be replaced by a voting requirement by bilateral treaty.[15] Member States may also unilaterally impose a two-year holding period in order to qualify distributions under the Directive.[16] The Directive applies to distributions of profits only. Capital gains on the sale of shares of subsidiaries are not covered. It also does not apply to liquidation distributions.[17] The Directive permits both domestic or treaty based provisions to prevent fraud or abuse, but does not impose its own anti-avoidance provisions.[18] It is also not clear whether the Directive extends to second or lower tier subsidiaries, although the general view is that it does not. Article 7(2) is intended to preserve the position of treaties (and domestic law) to some extent. It states that the Directive does not lessen the effect of domestic or agreement based provisions designed to eliminate or lessen economic double taxation of dividends.

Implementation

Inward-bound distributions

9-09   Legislation to give effect to the Parent-Subsidiary Directive in the United Kingdom was introduced by Finance (No. 2) Act 1992, section 30 with effect from January 1, 1992. These measures eliminated the withholding on dividends received from a non-resident company where payment of the dividend is to U.K. residents through a U.K. paying agent or where the U.K. resident has a U.K. resident collecting agent.[19] The paying and collection agent regime was itself repealed in the Finance Act 2000. Inward-bound distributions of profits are relieved from double taxation by credit only available in the United Kingdom. In the author's view, it was only with the abolition of advance corporation tax on dividends from foreign sources in Finance Act 1994 and the final elimination of ACT by Finance (No. 2) Act 1997 that the U.K. system was fully in conformity with the Directive in this respect.

Although the Directive specifies a 25 per cent minimum holding in the capital of the subsidiary, the United Kingdom adopts a 10 per cent voting rights test for application of the underlying credit. Strictly however, Article 3 of the Directive only permits the substitution of voting rights for capital by means of bilateral agreement. Older treaties made no explicit reference to this. The Treaties with Greece and Portugal do not address this issue, although the effect of the domestic law may be as if the Directive had been complied with. There is no minimum holding period as a condition of the relief.

---

[14]   Article 2(c).
[15]   Article 3(2) first indent.
[16]   Article 3(2) second indent.
[17]   Article 4(1).
[18]   Article 1(2).
[19]   Formerly Taxes Act 1988, s. 123 Sched. 3 repealed by Finance Act 1996 and replaced with Taxes Act 1988, ss. 118A to 118K.

Outward-bound distributions

9-10   The United Kingdom does not, as a matter of domestic law, levy a withholding tax on outward-bound dividends and any residual argument about the status of advance corporation tax has become academic as a result of its abolition.[20]

Two decisions of the European Court of Justice provide important background to the U.K. position. In *Ministério Público and others v. Epson Europe BV,*[21] the ECJ considered the legality of a lump-sum tax on successions and donations levied annually on the income of certain securities (shares and bonds). Under Portuguese domestic law, dividends were subject to withholding tax under two separate laws. The first was under the corporate income tax law. The second was a 5 per cent withholding tax on dividends as a substitute for tax under the inheritance and gift tax legislation.

In defining qualifying companies for the purposes of the Parent-Subsidiary Directive in Article 2(c), reference is made to companies which are subject to specified taxes. In all cases, including Portugal, reference is made to the corporate income tax. No reference is made to the substitute withholding tax under Portugal's inheritance and gift tax legislation. The Portuguese Government took the position that the Directive did not change the application of this inheritance tax. As a result, dividends paid to parent companies in EU Member States were made subject to the 5 per cent substitute inheritance and gift withholding tax.

Substance over form

9-11   The Advocate General considered that the 5 per cent withholding tax was prohibited by Article 5(1) of the Directive. Article 5(1) did not specify any particular tax, and Community law did not operate on the basis of semantic distinctions and theoretical constructions relevant to national law. In any event, the 5 per cent withholding tax was within the Directive on a literal or any other method of interpretation.

He noted, in particular, that the substitute succession and donation tax was determined on the same basis as the withholding in respect of the corporate income tax. The withholding permitted under the Directive during the transitional period was therefore in effect cumulative in relation to both taxes. The distinction between the two taxes did not constitute a significant element in relation to its categorisation from a Community law perspective. Withholding at source cumulatively in relation to tax on companies under the Directive was prohibited.

9-12   The ECJ adopted a similar approach and ruled that the Portuguese withholding tax was a withholding tax within the Directive and was, therefore, within the rate limits during the transitional period for Portugal and prohibited thereafter. The ECJ held that the term "withholding tax" in Article 5(1) is not limited to specific types of national taxation. The substitute inheritance and gift tax, the court concluded, was a withholding tax for

---

[20] see Finance (No. 2) Act 1997.
[21] Case C-735/98 (Transcript) June 8, 2000.

which the chargeable event is the payment of a dividend and the taxable person is the holder of the shares. The substitute inheritance and gift tax has the same effect as a tax on income, and it is immaterial that the tax is called a "succession and donation tax" and that it is levied in parallel with the income tax.

The court noted that the objective of the Directive would be undermined if the Member States were permitted deliberately to deprive companies in other Member States of the benefit of the Directive by subjecting them to taxes having the same effect as a tax on income, even if the name given to the tax places it in the category of a tax on assets. Although the court used more restrained language than the Advocate General, the case represents a clear commitment to apply substance rather than form in judging the effect of the laws of the Member States.

ACT, not withholding tax

9-13 In *Metallgesellschaft Ltd and others v. Inland Revenue Commissioners and Attorney General*,[22] the ECJ noted that advance corporation tax was not a sum withheld on a dividend which was paid in full, but was rather corporation tax borne by the company distributing dividends paid in advance and set against the mainstream corporation tax payable in respect of each accounting period.[23] ACT could not be regarded as a tax on dividend.

Under the U.K. imputation system (which has largely been repealed), U.K. companies were required to account for advance corporation tax (ACT) at the time that dividends were paid.[24] No tax was or is withheld on the dividend. U.K. shareholders are required to include the dividend in their income, grossed up by an amount specified in the legislation. This was normally, but not always, connected to the rate of ACT. The same amount was applied as a credit to the grossed-up income. In the case of non-residents, there was no further U.K. tax. Some treaties with Member States (Belgium, Italy, Luxembourg, the Netherlands and Sweden), however, provide for a repayment of the tax credit to qualified treaty resident shareholders subject to a withholding tax on the dividend plus tax credit repayment which ranges from 5 per cent in the case of a substantial (10 per cent) participation to 15 per cent for portfolio investors.

Dividend tax credit repayment

9-14 The question of the status of tax credit repayments on dividends paid to parent companies in certain treaty countries has recently come before the U.K. courts in *Océ Van Der Grinten NV v. IRC*.[25] A Dutch parent company claimed against the imposition of the 5 per cent deduction on the repayment of the tax credit plus dividend, pursuant to Article 10(3)(a)(ii) of the Netherlands-U.K. Treaty, on the basis that the restriction of the tax credit

---

[22] Joined Cases C-397/98 and C-410/98 [2001] S.T.C. 452.
[23] At para. 6.
[24] See Chapter 6, para. 6-05.
[25] [2000] S.T.C. (SCD) 127.

repayment by the 5 per cent deduction was contrary to Articles 5(1) and 7 of the Parent-Subsidiary Directive.

Article 5(1) of the Directive provides:

> "Profits which a subsidiary distributes to its parent company shall, at least where the latter holds a minimum of 25% of the capital of the subsidiary, be exempt from withholding tax".

9-15   Article 7 reads as follows:

> "(1) The term 'withholding tax' as used in this directive shall not cover an advance payment or prepayment (*précompte*) of corporation tax to the member state of the subsidiary which is made in connection with a distribution of profits to its parent company.
>
> (2) This directive shall not affect the application of domestic or agreement-based provisions designed to eliminate or lessen economic double taxation of dividends, in particular provisions relating to the payment of tax credits to the recipients of dividends".

The elements of the dispute were:

(a)   first, whether the 5 per cent referred to in Article 10(3)(a)(ii) of the Netherlands Treaty was a "withholding tax" on "profits that a subsidiary distributes to its parent"?

(b)   secondly, if it was, is the Inland Revenue's right to require the deduction preserved by Article 7(2) of the Directive?

(c)   thirdly, assuming that Article 7(2) preserved the 5 per cent from the effect of Article 5(1), was Article 7(2) valid?

9-16   In the judgment of the Special Commissioner, the operation of Article 5(1) of the Directive depended on whether, as a matter of U.K. law, the 5 per cent retention was a tax and, if so, was it a tax on profits which a subsidiary distributed to its Netherlands parent? Furthermore, as a matter of Community law, if it was such a tax on profits, was the 5 per cent a withholding tax? He concluded that, in all the circumstances, the 5 per cent was a tax and a tax "on profits that a subsidiary distributes to its parent". The opening words of Article 5(1) of the Directive were capable of covering dividends such as those paid by the subsidiary to the taxpayer. Once it was recognized that the 5 per cent was a tax, it was chargeable under Schedule F in respect of all dividends and other distributions of a company resident in the United Kingdom. That was the case despite the fact that the 5 per cent might also be loosely described as a tax on the tax credit. The subsidiary's profits did not lose their character when distributed as dividends.

"Withholding tax", he concluded, is not a term of art in U.K. tax law. It usually means the tax which is deducted at source by the payer of income and accounted for to the Inland Revenue by some means or another. No tax was deducted from the dividend itself. The provision for payment of the tax credit in Article 10(3)(c) of the Treaty, however, required that the 5 per cent be deducted or withheld either by the Revenue on a claim made by the share-holder or by the paying company under the General Dividend Regulations.[26] Where an item of income was paid by a resident of one Member State to a recipient in another Member State, the term "withholding tax" was quite capable of referring to the tax on that income borne in the Member State of the payer. There was nothing in the Directive that appeared to distinguish between these two positions. The scope of the term "withholding tax" in the Directive was, however, too vague to enable him to decide with the requisite level of confidence whether the 5 per cent tax was a withholding tax within the context of Article 5(1) of the Directive. Therefore, the question should, in his view, be resolved by the European Court of Justice.

No double taxation

9-17   The taxpayer argued that Article 7(2) of the Directive did not pre-serve the United Kingdom's right to impose the 5 per cent tax. The provi-sions of the Treaty which authorise the imposition of the tax on the aggregate of the dividend and the tax credit did not "eliminate or lessen economic double taxation of dividends". Instead, they were calculated to impose or increase it. The Revenue argued that the treaty provisions were within Article 7(2). They were provisions "relating to" the payment of tax credits, and they were "agreement-based" provisions designed to eliminate or lessen the double taxation of dividends.

The Special Commissioner ruled that, had there been no treaty, there would have been no double taxation of the subsidiary's dividends because, under domestic law, section 233(1)(a) of Taxes Act 1988 precluded the div-idends from charge to income tax. The treaty had the effect of disapplying that section because the treaty gave the Netherlands recipient of the divi-dends a partial tax credit. The treaty left the U.K. Revenue with the 5 per cent tax charge on the aggregate of the amounts of the dividend and the tax credit. The treaty also compensated the recipient of the dividend by entitling it to payment of the balance.

9-18   This raised real doubt as to the operation of Article 7(2) in this context. In addition, the tax credits and their payment were, as far as U.K. tax law was concerned, an essential feature of the system of taxing dividends. They were not designed to eliminate or lessen the double taxation of divi-dends, nor were they examples of provisions that did. Consequently, the con-struction of Article 7(2), as advanced by the Revenue, would mean that it provided an exception to the exemption from withholding tax laid down by Article 5(1) of the Directive wherever the charge to such tax was associated with the payment of a tax credit. There was real doubt whether Article 7(2) could be read as providing that result, and there was nothing in the Directive that gave any indication of an intention to produce such an exception. As a result, this question was referred to the ECJ.

Validity of the Directive

9-19   The attack on the validity of Article 7(2) of the Directive is perhaps one of the more dramatic elements of this case. The taxpayer

---

[26] Double Taxation Relief (Taxes on Income) (General) (Dividend) Regulations S.I. 1973 No. 317.

argued that the article was never properly enacted. It claimed that Article 253 (ex 190) of the EC Treaty provides that directives must state the reasons on which they are based. This is argued to be one of the "essential procedural requirements" of the EC Treaty and is designed to allow those affected to understand the reasons for it and the ECJ to carry out its functions of legal review. The taxpayer has also attacked the validity of the article on the basis of the lack of consultation with the European Commission, the Economic and Social Committee and the European Parliament. Article 94 (ex 100) of the EC Treaty enables the Council to act unanimously upon a proposal from the Commission after consultation with the Parliament and the ESC.

Since the thrust of Article 7(2) is to preserve the domestic or treaty rules designed to eliminate or lessen the economic double taxation of dividends, the wider impact of the potential invalidity of the article is considerable. It will bring into sharp focus the application of Article 4 of the Directive, which requires the Member States either to refrain from taxing profits distributed within the scope of the Directive or to grant full credit for tax paid by the subsidiary. This may result in further challenges to either domestic or treaty rules providing for an exemption or credit for foreign tax.

Appeal to the High Court

9-20 The Inland Revenue attempted to block the reference to the ECJ by appeal to the High Court.[27] The Inland Revenue argued in the High Court that the 5 per cent withholding was not a tax as a matter of U.K. domestic law and that the reference to the ECJ was not necessary.

Jacob J. held that whether a particular national law was characterised as a "tax" as a matter of national law was immaterial to the question of whether it was a withholding tax as a matter of Community law. What mattered was how the law operated and not whether it could be called a "tax" under national law, following the reasoning of the ECJ in *Ministério Público Fazenda Publica v. Epson Europe BV* that the substance of the legislation rather than its form is determinative. He further concluded that the 5 per cent withholding was a tax under U.K. law in any event. It was a reduction in what the shareholder would have received if there had been no abatement. The deduction stemmed from the distribution, and this was supported by the language of the treaty.

Scope of Directive

9-21 The Parent-Subsidiary Directive is relatively narrow in its scope. As a result, it does not fully occupy the field relating to dividends or other profit distributions between Member States. Member States are therefore free to agree on the tax treatment of distributions outside the scope of the Directive. Examples as to how this interaction applies are set out in the Protocol to the Danish Treaty and the Fifth Protocol to the Finnish Treaty, which were the first agreements that the United Kingdom concluded with other Member

---

[27] *Océ Van Der Grinten NV v. IRC* [2000] S.T.C. 951, Ch.D.

States since the introduction of the Parent-Subsidiary Directive. The dividend article has been replaced in its entirety in both treaties.

Dividends

9-22   In the Danish Treaty, a general rate of withholding of 15 per cent on the gross amount of dividends is permitted. This is, however, made subject to the provisions of the Parent-Subsidiary Directive and dividends are exempt from tax if the beneficial owner of the dividend is a company which holds at least 25 per cent of the issued share capital of the company paying the dividends.[28] Entitlement to repayment of the tax credit in respect of the dividends paid by a U.K. company is no longer extended to Danish residents.

The definition of dividends has also been amended in that Treaty. Previously, a distribution under the law of either contracting state was treated as a dividend. Dividends now mean income from shares or other rights not being debt claims participating in profits as well as income from other corporate rights which is subjected to the same tax treatment as income from shares by the laws of the state of which the company making the distribution is a resident.[29] This means that even if the distribution is not treated as a dividend in the country of receipt under domestic law the categorisation in the paying country is to be adopted for treaty purposes.

9-23   The article also contains the standard U.K. limitation of benefits provision which excludes treaty claims if the main purpose or one of the main purposes of any person concerned with the creation or assignment of the shares or other rights in respect of the dividend is paid is to take advantage of the article by means of that creation or assignment.[30]

The Finnish Protocol also withdraws the repayment of tax credits on dividends paid to non-resident shareholders. Unlike the Danish Treaty, dividends may only be taxed in the country of residence of the shareholder.[31]

Elimination of double taxation

9-24   The rules relating to elimination of double taxation are significantly amended and updated in both treaties to take into account the Parent-Subsidiary Directive as well as recent developments in the contracting states.

In the Danish Treaty, double taxation continues to be relieved in the United Kingdom by the credit method.[32] Credit for underlying tax is given where the U.K. company controls directly or indirectly 10 per cent of the voting power of the Danish company paying the dividend.[33] Denmark however will only give credit for underlying tax where the Danish company owns 25 per cent of the issued share capital of the U.K. company.[34]

9-25   An Exchange of Notes between the contracting states confirms that by continuing to use the criterion of a holding of voting power in Article

---

[28] Danish Treaty, Art.10(2).
[29] Article 10(3).
[30] Article 10(6).
[31] Now Finnish Treaty, Art.11(1).
[32] Danish Treaty, Art.22(1).
[33] Article 10(1)(b).
[34] Article 22(2)(c).

22(1)(b) with respect to the operation of the foreign tax credit in the United Kingdom on dividends received by a U.K. parent from a Danish subsidiary the contracting states note that they are exercising the option provided in Article 3(2) of the Parent-Subsidiary Directive to derogate from Article 3(1) by replacing the criterion of a holding in the capital of a company of another Member State by that of a holding of voting rights.

The Protocol to the Finnish Treaty adopts a 10 per cent rule based on ownership of voting power for allowing credit for underlying tax paid by either contracting states on dividends received by a corporate shareholder in the other.[35] An Exchange of Notes between the contracting states confirms the exercise of the option under Article 3(2) of the Parent-Subsidiary Directive to adopt the voting rights criterion.

THE MERGERS DIRECTIVE

9-26 As with the Parent-Subsidiary Directive, the Mergers Directive came into effect on January 1, 1992. The purpose of the Directive is to facilitate mergers, divisions, transfers of assets and exchanges of shares between companies established in different Member States. The Directive is intended to remove tax barriers to such transactions in order to create conditions analogous to those of an internal market.

Qualifying transactions

9-27 There are six forms of qualifying transaction identified by the Mergers Directive. These are:

(1) merger by absorbtion: one or more companies transfers all of their assets and liabilities to an existing company in exchange for the issue of shares to the shareholders of the transferor company[36];

(2) merger by formation: two or more companies transfer all of their assets and liabilities to a company formed by them in exchange for the issue of shares in the new company to the shareholders of the transferor companies[37];

(3) merger of wholly-owned subsidiary: transfer of all of the assets and liabilities of a wholly-owned subsidiary to its parent company on dissolution[38];

(4) exchange of shares: the transfer of the majority of voting shares of a company to another company in exchange for the issue of shares by the transferee[39];

(5) transfer of assets: transfer of one or more branches of its activity to another company in exchange for the issue of shares to the transferor by the transferee[40];

---

[35] Finnish Treaty, Art.25(1)(b).
[36] Mergers Directive, Art.2(a) first indent.
[37] Article 2(a) second indent.
[38] Article 2(a) third indent.
[39] Article 2(d).
[40] Article 2(c).

(6) Division: the transfer by a company of all of the assets and liabilities to two or more new or existing companies in exchange for the pro rata issue to its shareholders of shares of the transferee companies.[41]

Tax consequences

9-28   The operational effects of the Mergers Directive are as follows.

Unrealised gains

No tax may be levied on the capital gain arising from a merger or division. In each case, the domestic law of the Member State is to be applied in determining the gain or loss in respect of the disposition of the assets.[42] In order to qualify, the assets and liabilities transferred must be effectively connected with a permanent establishment of the receiving company in a Member State where the transferring company is located following the transfer. The assets so transferred must also be used in generating income for tax purposes.

Subsequent gains and losses are computed as though the merger or division had not taken place and asset values for capital gains and depreciation purposes are carried over.[43] Where Member States operate an elective regime, which permits different base costs for depreciation and capital gains purposes, the roll-over will not apply to assets and liabilities for which such option is exercised.[44]

The roll-over does not apply to assets and liabilities that lie outside such permanent establishments. Special rules are set out for assets forming part of permanent establishments in third countries in the Community.[45]

Losses

9-29   The Mergers Directive permits transfer of loss compensation from the transferor company to the permanent establishment of a receiving company only if the Member State of the transferor allows the transfer of such losses for domestic reorganisations. The Directive does not contain restrictions relating to the carry-forward or carry-back of such losses against income from other sources of the receiving company.[46]

Shareholders' treatment

9-30   Shareholders will not be subject to income or capital gains tax on merger, division or exchange of shares provided that the shares received in the exchange carry over the base cost for tax purposes of the securities transferred.[47] Any subsequent transfer of securities so received may be subject to tax in full on any gain rolled over.

---

[41] Article 2(b).
[42] Article 4(1).
[43] Article 4(2).
[44] Article 4(3).
[45] Article 10.
[46] Article 6.
[47] Article 8.

Where a company receiving assets has shares in the transferring company, any gain accruing to the receiving company on the cancellation of its holding is not subject to taxation. Individual Member States may deviate from this rule where the receiving company's holding in the capital of the transferring company is under 25 per cent.[48]

Cash consideration

9-31   In each case, a cash payment not exceeding 10 per cent of the nominal value of the securities received may also be received without the tax free status of the transaction being jeopardised.[49] The cash portion may however continue to be taxable.

Permanent establishment

9-32   Under the transactions contemplated by the Directive, a company incorporated in a Member State may effectively be converted into a permanent establishment of a company in another Member State. Because in many cases, it will reduce the taxing jurisdiction from a worldwide basis to a local source basis, complex rules have been developed to deal with the problems that arise.

Where the assets transferred include a permanent establishment of the transferring company situated in another Member State, that latter state is required to renounce any right to tax, the permanent establishment. The state of the transferring company may re-instate losses of the permanent establishment that were previously set off against the taxable profits of the company in that state and which have not been recovered.[50]

In all other respects, the state of the permanent establishment must apply the roll-over rule as if it were the state of the transferring company.

Where the Member State of the transferring company taxes worldwide profits, it will be entitled to tax any profits or gains of the permanent establishment resulting from the merger on condition that it gives relief for tax that would have been charged on the permanent establishment in the same way and in the same amount as if that tax had actually been charged and paid.[51]

Anti-avoidance

9-33   Unlike the Parent-Subsidiary Directive, the Mergers Directive contains its own anti-avoidance provision. The benefits of the Directive may be refused if a transaction has as one of its principal objectives tax evasion or tax avoidance. If the operations are not carried out for valid commercial reasons such as the restructuring or rationalisation of the activities of the participating companies, this may be held to constitute a presumption of the existence of a tax avoidance purpose.[52]

---

[48] Article 7.
[49] Article 2.
[50] Article 10.
[51] Article 10(2).
[52] Article 11.

9-34 It will be immediately apparent that the nature of the relief granted under the Mergers Directive does not fit obviously within any neat category of treaties based on the OECD Model. Although both the Directive and Article 3 of the OECD Model deal with disposals of assets, the principal relief provided for in Article 4 of the Directive is deferral of tax on gains. By contrast, Article 13 of the OECD Model generally exempts residents of a contracting state from capital gains in the source state or authorises the source state to tax them. Treaty exemptions may be material to transactions involving cash consideration not exceeding 10 per cent which qualifies for deferral in relation to the non-cash consideration only. Deferral is not contemplated by U.K. treaties. Reliefs provided in Articles 5 and 6 of the Directive dealing with the carry-over of tax attributes in the form of provisions, reserves and losses are not addressed in bilateral treaties in the same coherent way. Treaty questions are squarely raised in the context of transactions contemplated by the Directive which involve permanent establishments. The United Kingdom does not use the expression in this context in its domestic law. Treaty definitions of permanent establishments are the only definitions available. Questions of discrimination may arise where differences in the scope of the permanent establishment clause in various treaties purport to exclude the operation of the Mergers Directive in relation to companies in some Member States.[53]

Although the Directive has entered into force, some of its provisions have not been given effect to in the United Kingdom to date. The fact that the proposed Tenth EC Company Law Directive which facilitates several of the transactions contemplated by the Mergers Directive has not been adopted, has been put forward by the Inland Revenue as a reason for not implementing the tax rules. Contributions of assets and share for share exchanges are, however, generally provided for.

PROPOSED INTEREST AND ROYALTY DIRECTIVE

9-35 In continuation of the process of harmonisation, the European Commission has released a further draft Directive on taxation of cross-border financial flows within corporate groups which proposes a common system of taxation applicable to interest and royalty payments made between parent companies and subsidiaries in different Member States.[54]

The draft Interest and Royalties Directive adopts a similar test to that in the Parent-Subsidiary Directive to determine which entity will be able to benefit under the new regime or where a third company owns at least 25 per cent of the capital of the payer and payee.[55] It is to apply to interest and royalty payments between parents and subsidiaries as defined for the Parent and Subsidiary Directive. Such payments are to be exempt from withhold-

---

[53] See Case C-43/00 Andersen og Jensen, Advocate General's Opinion (Transcript) September 11, 2001.

[54] Proposal for a Council Directive on a Common System of Taxation Applicable to Interest and Royalty Payments Made Between Associated Companies of Different Member States (COM (1998) 67 Final – 98/0087 (CNS) O.J. April 22, 1998 (C-123/9)).

[55] Draft Interest and Royalties Directive, Art.3.

ing tax (Article 1).[56] Greece and Portugal are to be permitted to levy a with-holding tax for seven years after entry into force of the Directive. Any such tax may not exceed 10 per cent during the first five years and 5 per cent during the last two years of the seven-year transitional period.[57] These rates are subject to existing bilateral treaty rates. Greece and Portugal have the poorest treaty networks amongst Community Members. In accordance with OECD practice, only beneficial owners qualify for the benefits of the Directive which contains its own definition of "beneficial owner".[58]

9-36   Where interest and royalty payments are made to a permanent establishment of a recipient located in the same Member State as the payer, the withholding tax exemption will apply only if the Member State does not impose a withholding tax on payments of that kind between resident parent companies and their subsidiaries.[59]

The definition of interest for the purpose of the draft Directive follows Article 11 of the OECD Model Convention. It means income from "debt claims of every kind whether or not carrying the right to participate in the debtor's profit including premiums and prizes attaching to bonds or debentures".[60] Member States are permitted to re-characterise interest as distributions in certain circumstances[61] and the benefits of the Directive are restricted to what would have been agreed in the absence of a special relationship by analogy to the OECD Model.[62] The proposal does not deal with the deductibility of interest and royalty payments, or their inclusion in income by the recipient.

Royalties similarly follow Article 12 of the OECD Model. They include payment of any kind received as consideration for the use of or the right to use any copyright of literary, artistic or scientific work including cinematographic films; any patent, trade mark, design or model, secret formula or process; or for the use of or the right to use industrial, commercial or scientific equipment; or for information concerning industrial, commercial or scientific experience.[63] The definition does not, however, reflect current OECD thinking which effectively excludes lease payments on industrial, commercial or scientific equipment.

9-37   A Commission commentary on an earlier version of the Draft Directive, however, distinguishes between royalties paid for the use of equipment and payment constituting consideration for the sale of equipment. The latter are not royalties. Where the principal purpose of a leasing contract is that of hire, even the hirer has the right to purchase the equipment outright, lease rentals paid by the hirer will qualify for the exemption. A distinction is therefore drawn between financial and operating leases.

The proposals made no mention of the deductibility of interest and royalty payments or their inclusion in income by the recipient. However, Member

---

[56] Draft Art.1.
[57] Draft Art.8.
[58] Draft Art. 3(1)(c).
[59] Draft Art.1(2).
[60] Draft Art.2(1)(a).
[61] Draft Art. 4.
[62] Draft Art. 5.
[63] Draft Art.2(1)(b).

States may refuse to apply the benefits of the Directive where the recipient is subject to a lower rate of tax than normal, or benefits from a reduction in the tax base which would not otherwise normally be available.[64]

As is the case with the Parent-Subsidiary Directive, the proposed Interest and Royalty Directive will not replace Articles 11 and 12 of the OECD Model. It will occupy the field in certain group and joint venture relationships, but beyond that treaty rules will continue to apply.

NON-DISCRIMINATION

9-38   The 1996 Protocol to the Finnish Treaty deleted Article 26, which extended personal allowances to residents of the other treaty state from the treaty. European law on non-discrimination is developing and arguably even the broader non-discrimination provisions of bilateral tax treaties are redundant as between Member States.

ASSOCIATED ENTERPRISES

9-39   The conclusion of the Convention on the Elimination of Double Taxation in connection with the Adjustment of Profits of Associated Enterprises in effect applies a uniform application of the arm's length principle following Article 9(1) of the OECD Model in relation to transactions between associated enterprises, as well as Article 7(2) in relation to the allocation of profits between a permanent establishment and head office. While this may make similar provisions in bilateral treaties redundant to some extent, it does not enjoy the status of a directive or other legislative instrument under European law. It is simply a treaty entered into among Member States and which may be amended by agreement between the parties.[65]

EXCHANGE OF INFORMATION

9-40   Detailed rules on mutual assistance by the competent authorities of Member States in the field of direct and indirect taxation has been dealt with among Member States by directive since December 1977. Council Directive 77/799/EEC is considerably more detailed and extensive than those found in Article 26 of the OECD Model. Again, arguably exchange of information provisions in bilateral treaties between Member States are redundant.[66]

---

[64] Draft Art.7.
[65] See Chapter 13.
[66] See Chapter 15.

CHAPTER 10

Elimination of Double Taxation: Credit for Foreign Tax

10-01 The principal mechanism adopted by the United Kingdom for avoiding or minimising double taxation on income is the credit method. It is implicit in this approach that income profits or gains are subject to tax twice, once in the country of source and then again in the country of residence. In this respect, the treaty provisions dealing with credit for foreign tax paid should be viewed as a residual clause. The other distributive provisions of the treaty will determine to what extent the source country is entitled to tax the item concerned. If, as a result, the item is subject to tax in a foreign country of source, then in general terms, U.K. treaties grant credit for foreign tax paid against U.K. liability in respect of the same item in the country of residence. Although this approach is generally in line with the policy underlying the OECD Model Treaty, Article 23B, the wording adopted in U.K. treaties does not follow the OECD Model. The form of wording, which has changed little over the years, usually adopted is typified by the Ugandan Treaty which reads:

"23(1) Subject to the provisions of the law of the United Kingdom regarding the allowance as a credit against United Kingdom tax of tax payable in a territory outside the United Kingdom (which shall not affect the general principle hereof):

(a) Ugandan tax payable under the laws of Uganda and in accordance with this Convention, whether directly or by deduction, on profits, income or chargeable gains from sources within Uganda (excluding in the case of a dividend, tax payable in respect of the profits out of which the dividend is paid) shall be allowed as a credit against any United Kingdom tax computed by reference to the same profits, income or chargeable gains by reference to which the Ugandan tax is computed".

10-02 There are several important differences between the U.K. approach and that of the OECD Model. U.K. practice is to set out the U.K. rules relating to the credit for foreign tax in clauses separate from the equivalent relieving mechanism adopted by the other contracting state, rather than using the bilateral language of the OECD. This facilitates different approaches to the elimination of double taxation by treaty partners, particularly in relation to those countries adopting the exemption method. As will be seen, the key principles adopted in the OECD Model, while not appearing in the text of the article, are generally given effect to in the domestic law.

Credit is given "subject to the provisions of the law of the United Kingdom". This means, in accordance with the provisions of the "Credit Code"[1] by virtue of Taxes Act 1988, section 788(4) and in the case of capital gains, the Credit Code is incorporated by reference.[2] A detailed examination of the rules of the Credit Code is beyond the scope of this work. The interrelationship between treaties and the domestic law is examined in this chapter. Although the credit is expressed to be "subject to the provisions of the law of the United Kingdom", the wording inevitably indicates that this "shall not affect the general principle hereof". Following Finance Act 2000, the road to obtaining credit for foreign tax paid has become considerably more tortuous. The extent to which the domestic law may be amended to reduce the availability of the credit thereby affecting the general principle is as yet undetermined.

TREATY VERSUS UNILATERAL RELIEF

10-03   Credit for foreign tax is available unilaterally where there is no treaty providing for the relief, in circumstances similar to those provided by treaty.[3] The credit mechanism referred to in the treaty is expressed in domestic law in section 793(1). It makes explicit that foreign tax in this context means only the credit allowed under the treaty in respect of tax chargeable under the law of the other contracting state.[4] Furthermore, no credit may be allowed beyond that authorised by the treaty in question.[5]

Finance Act 2000 inserted section 793A into the Taxes Act 1988. Credit may not be given where relief in respect of an amount of tax, that would otherwise be payable under the law of a territory outside the United Kingdom, may be allowed by treaty or under the law of the other contracting state as a result of the treaty. This applies regardless of whether the relief has been used or not.[6] Secondly, credit by way of unilateral relief may not be allowed in respect of tax where credit may be allowed under a treaty in respect of the same amount of tax. This makes clear that credit cannot be claimed both under treaty and unilateral relief. As a result, U.K. taxpayers, seeking to claim credit for foreign tax paid, must in the first instance obtain relief available in the other contracting state or under the treaty. These requirements are in addition to the duty to minimise foreign tax by virtue of section 795A(1).[7] Furthermore, recourse must be had to the tax credit provisions of an applicable treaty, since unilateral relief will not be permitted where credit may be allowed in respect of an amount of tax.[8] These rules have an element

---

[1] Taxes Act 1988, Pt XVIII, Chap.II, "Rules governing relief by way of credit".
[2] Taxation of Chargeable Gains Act (TCGA) 1992, s. 277(3).
[3] Taxes Act 1988, s. 790(1), (3).
[4] *ibid.*, s. 792(3).
[5] *ibid.*, s. 793(2).
[6] *ibid.*, s. 793A(1).
[7] See Chapter 12, para. 12-36 to 12-38.
[8] *ibid.*, s. 593A(2).

of retrospectivity in that they have in effect in relation to claims for credit made on or after March 21, 2000. The legislation also contemplates that treaties may contain express provisions to the effect that relief by way of credit is not to be given in specified cases or circumstances. This will apply in relation to treaties made on or after March 21, 2000. See below, Chapter 12 on time limits for claiming foreign tax credit relief.

10-04 There are important differences between credit for foreign tax by treaty and unilateral tax credit relief. Credit for foreign tax under treaties is limited to the taxes which form the subject of the treaty. The single biggest source of difficulties in relation to credit in respect of treaty countries is in federal systems, such as the United States and Canada, where treaties are negotiated with the federal government, but no constitutional mechanism exists whereby states or provinces are bound by the treaty. Additionally, states or provinces may not have the constitutional right to conclude treaties, leaving unilateral relief as the only option.

SAME INCOME, DIFFERENT PERSON

10-05 The OECD Model applies specifically to juridical double taxation, that is double taxation where the same person is liable to tax irrespective of the same item in both contracting states. The U.K. treaty approach is wider, covering in principle economic double taxation where the same income or gain is subject to tax in both jurisdictions. This allows for the possibility that the item may be taxed in the hands of one person in one jurisdiction, but in the hands of another in the second, and still qualify for credit.[9] The Inland Revenue *International Tax Handbook* gives examples of the application of this principle. Thus, taxation of income in the hands of a settlor in one jurisdiction and tax in the hands of a beneficiary, say in the United Kingdom, will permit the beneficiary to obtain credit for tax paid by the settlor. Similarly, where directors' fees are treated as income of a partnership or a company under Extra-Statutory Concession A37, tax credit relief is available to the partnership or company despite the fact that the foreign tax may be imposed on the director.[10] The scope of the principle and the relationship between the income or gain to the person claiming credit has not been examined by the courts. In the Inland Revenue view, where the U.K. charge is made on deemed income or gains, such income or gains are not the same income or gains as charged abroad and, on this basis, they do not accept that income taxable in the hands of a U.K. resident under Taxes Act 1988, sections 739 and 740 would come within the credit rule, because the resident cannot be identified with any particular part of the income which the non-resident has received or because the resident is charged by reference to a benefit received out of the assets rather than the income itself.[11] These comments, at least in relation to section 739(2), are inconsistent with their other views on attributed income and in the author's view incorrect.

---

[9] Inland Revenue, *Double Taxation Relief Manual*, para. 507; *International Tax Handbook*, para. 618.
[10] *Double Taxation Relief Manual*, para. 507.
[11] *International Tax Handbook*, para. 620.

10-06   This issue is addressed specifically in the Exchange of Notes of July 24, 2001 to the U.S. Treaty (2001) in the context of fiscally transparent entities and trusts. In that exchange (with respect to Article 24), the contracting parties recognised that in the case of an entity which is fiscally transparent under the laws of either contracting state, there may be a mismatch between the persons taxed in the two countries. In such cases, income is generally treated as accruing to resident of a contracting state for tax credit purposes, even if another person is taxable in the other contracting state. Similar rules are adopted in relation to trusts, where there may be mismatches between contracting states with tax being imposed possibly on the settlor, the trustees or beneficiaries.

MATCHING FOREIGN INCOME AND TAX WITH U.K. LIABILITY

10-07   The wording found in almost all U.K. treaties refers to credit against U.K. tax computed by reference to "the same profits or income by reference to which the [foreign tax] is computed". This wording was adopted following the decision in *Duckering v. Gollan*,[12] which involved the 1947 New Zealand Treaty. In that Treaty, credit was given "in respect of income from sources within New Zealand" and credit allowed "against any United Kingdom tax payable in respect of that income". The case arose out of a change in New Zealand from taxation on the preceding year basis to the current year basis. The United Kingdom applied the preceding year basis throughout the years in question. The taxpayer paid New Zealand tax on his income in each year, although in the transitional year it was measured in a different way. This wording referred to as the "statutory basis" for credit is now only found in very few old treaties.[13] Under the current language credit is applied on the "root income basis" meaning that it is allowed on foreign tax against any U.K. tax computed by reference to the same income by reference to which the foreign tax is computed.[14] The Inland Revenue permit the root basis to be used even for those treaties where the statutory basis applies.[15]

Some of the more difficult problems arising out of the statutory basis have been resolved by the abolition of the preceding year basis of taxation. Where foreign tax is levied by way of deduction, there is usually little difficulty in matching the foreign tax paid with the U.K. tax liability. Where tax is assessed on profits on an annual basis, problems may arise because of differing tax years calling for apportionment. In *Imperial Chemical Industries Ltd v. Caro*,[16] the application of U.K. rules for new sources of income resulted in Australian source income being relevant to U.K. tax liability in more than one year. Notwithstanding this, it was held that the credit could only be claimed once. Problems relating to relief in respect of income arising in years of commencement is now addressed by Taxes Act 1988, section 804.

---

[12] (1965) 42 T.C. 333, HL.
[13] See for example, Myanmar Treaty Article 14(1).
[14] *Double Taxation Relief Manual*, para. 600.
[15] *ibid.*, para. 603.
[16] (1959) 35 T.C. 374, CA.

SOURCE RULES

10-08   Source rules may be different under a treaty and domestic law. This may be both as to what the appropriate connecting factors are, as well as the location of the source. Subject to permitted exceptions[17] and Inland Revenue concessions,[18] credit will not be given for foreign tax in respect of U.K. source income. Apart from individual source rules in the distributive provisions of treaties, most U.K. treaties adopt the OECD approach in treating income which may be taxed outside the residence state as arising in the other. For example, the Yugoslavian Treaty reads:

> "22(5) For the purposes of the preceding paragraphs of this Article, profits, income and capital gains owned by a resident of a Contracting State which may be taxed in the other Contracting State in accordance with this Convention shall be deemed to arise from sources in that other Contracting State".

This is of particular importance in relation to trading or professional profits taxed under Schedule D Case I or II in respect of foreign branches or where, as is the case in some countries involving technical or management fees, tax is deducted in the paying country.[19] Inland Revenue *Double Taxation Relief Manual* at paragraph 581 sets out concessionary relaxations of the strict rules.

RESIDENCE

10-09   Unlike the OECD Model, the general credit language of the article does not refer to U.K. residence as a requirement. Taxes Act 1988, section 794(1) limits credits for foreign tax allowed by treaty to U.K. residents only. By contrast, unilateral relief is made available in limited circumstances to non-residents under section 794(2). It is available for residents of the Isle of Man or of the Channel Islands in respect of tax paid in the Isle of Man or Channel Islands, in addition to U.K. residents.[20] It is also available for foreign tax computed by reference to employment income where duties are performed wholly or mainly in the same foreign country against income tax charged under Schedule E and computed by reference to that income, if the person is resident either in the United Kingdom or in that other territory.[21] Finance Act 2000 inserted section 794(2)(bb) in the Taxes Act 1988 to grant unilateral relief to a branch or agency in the United Kingdom in certain circumstances. These provisions were enacted to give effect to the decision of the ECJ in *Compagnie de Saint-Gobain, Zweigniederlassung Deutschland v. Finanzamt Aachen-Innenstadt*.[22] However, to the extent that

---

[17] Taxes Act 1988, s. 790(5).
[18] Extra-statutory Concession B8.
[19] See *Yates v. G.C.A. International Ltd* [1911] S.T.C. 157, Ch.D.
[20] Taxes Act 1988, s. 794(2)(a).
[21] *ibid.*, s. 794(2)(b).
[22] Case C-307/97 [2000] S.T.C. 854.

treaties provide more generous treatment than unilateral relief, the United Kingdom may still not comply fully with that decision.

FOREIGN TAX PAYABLE

10-10   Treaty language typically talks about credit of "tax payable" in a territory outside the United Kingdom. In *Sportsman v. IRC*,[23] the taxpayer attempted to argue that he was entitled to credit for French tax in relation to a tax year where no assessment was raised in France, no income tax was paid by him, and no other party made any payment such as by way of withholding on his behalf. He argued that the credit was not confined solely to tax which has been paid, but that it applied to tax that may or should be paid. The Inland Revenue attempted to argue that paid and payable were interchangeable in this context, but ultimately the Commissioners appeared to decide that there was no French liability to tax. The Commissioners accepted evidence that, in the circumstances, he could not be assessed to tax, nor was there an obligation on his French employer to withhold tax. The Commissioners formed the view that not only had tax not been paid, but there was no basis on which it might be paid, and therefore no credit was allowed.

TREATY RESTRICTIONS ON CREDIT

10-11   Legislation permitting restrictions on foreign tax credits by way of treaty was introduced into the Taxes Act 1988 by Finance Act 2000. Section 793A(3) provides that if a treaty contains express provision to the effect that credit for foreign tax is not to be given under the treaty in specified cases or circumstances, then credit may not be given either by treaty or unilateral relief in those circumstances. This rule has effect in relation to treaties made on or after March 21, 2000. The first treaty made after that was with Norway signed on October 12, 2000, and the U.S. Treaty, signed on July 24, 2001.

This rule will have particular impact on U.K. companies claiming credit for tax paid in the United Kingdom. Article 24 of the U.S. Treaty contains several limitations on creditability of U.S. tax against U.K. taxation. Article 24(4)(c) denies the benefit of credit for underlying tax on dividends paid by a U.S. resident company, where the United Kingdom treats the dividend as beneficially owned by a U.K. resident, the United States treats the dividend as beneficially owned by a resident of the United States and the United States has allowed a deduction to a U.S. resident in respect of an amount determined by reference to that dividend. This is aimed at certain hybrid financing arrangements, whereby payments may be treated as interest in the United States and as dividends in the United Kingdom. A second limitation on tax credits is imposed by Article 24(6) in relation to U.S. citizens or former citizens, or long-term residents who are resident of the United Kingdom. In such a case, the United Kingdom is not "bound" to give credit to such residents for U.S. tax on profits, income or gains

---

[23] [1998] S.T.C. SCD 289.

from sources outside the United States as determined under U.K. law. In the case of such items from U.S. sources, the United Kingdom will take into account in determining the credit to be allowed only the tax that the United States may impose under the treaty on a U.K. resident who is not a U.S. citizen. The ability to limit tax credits pursuant to section 793A(3) of the Taxes Act 1988 is bolstered by Article 24(4)(d) of the U.S. Treaty which excludes Article 1(2) of the Treaty from Article 24(4).

LIMIT ON CREDIT

10-12   Under the OECD Model, credit is to be limited to the tax in the country of residence attributable to the income which is taxed in the other state. This does not appear in U.K. treaties, but is applied pursuant to the domestic law under section 796 in respect of income tax and section 797 in respect of corporation tax.

CREDIT FOR UNDERLYING TAX

10-13   It is generally U.K. policy, both under domestic law and treaty, to grant credit for underlying tax paid, where the U.K. company controls directly or indirectly at least 10 per cent of the voting power in the company paying the dividend. The Ugandan Treaty is, again, a typical example:

> "(b)   In the case of a dividend paid by a company which is a resident of Uganda to a company which is a resident of the United Kingdom and which controls directly or indirectly at least ten per cent of the voting power in the company paying the dividend, the credit shall take into account (in addition to any Ugandan tax for which credit may be allowed under the provisions of subparagraph (a) of this paragraph) the Ugandan tax payable by the company in respect of the profits out of which such dividend is paid".

10-14   The treaty rules allowing credit for underlying tax are more specific. The credit is only available for U.K. resident companies and the source is only dividends from companies resident in the other contracting state, where the requisite shareholding is present. The vast majority of treaties adopt a 10 per cent voting test in order to qualify for underlying source. Some (see the German Treaty, Article 18(1)(b)) require 25 per cent of the voting power. The domestic law relating to the credit for underlying taxes generally is set out in Taxes Act 1988, sections 799 to 803A. Underlying tax is excluded from the general tax credit provisions, but provided for specifically. The normal form of wording was considered in *Memec plc v. IRC*.[24] Credit for underlying tax was denied on the basis that distributions derived by a U.K. silent partner from its participation in a German silent partnership

---

[24] [1998] S.T.C. 754, CA.

were not "dividends" either for the purposes of the tax credit provision of the German Treaty (Article 18), nor for the purposes of the Credit Code. This was despite the fact that in the dividend article of the Treaty, the term "dividends" included income of a silent partner from its participation as such. Peter Gibson L.J. for the majority was of the view that in the Treaty the ordinary meaning of dividend should be applied, namely that it is a payment of a part of the profits for a period in respect of a share in a company.[25] It is implicit in the decision that a dividend under the tax credit article of the Treaty is also a dividend under the Credit Code.

TAX SPARING

10-15   Many countries grant different kinds of tax concessions to attract investment, including in particular tax exemptions or tax holidays when no tax is paid during a specified period. The benefits of these concessions may be eliminated in relation to U.K. businesses investing in such countries, because the profits in respect of branch operations in those countries will nonetheless continue to be subject to U.K. tax. Similarly, dividends from subsidiaries will be taxed in the United Kingdom in full, since there will be no underlying tax in respect of which credit could be claimed. Consequently, the United Kingdom has agreed with a number of developing countries to treat tax spared (that is not actually paid) as deemed paid for the purposes of enabling U.K. companies to obtain credit, thus maintaining the efficacy of the foreign incentive. Section 788(5) provides specific authority for tax sparing provisions to be included in treaties. The Indonesian Treaty sets out a modern version of such articles:

> "21(3) For the purposes of paragraph (1) of this Article, the term 'Indonesian tax payable' shall be deemed to include any amount which would have been payable as Indonesian tax for any year but for an exemption or reduction of tax granted for the year or any part thereof under Article 15(5) and Article 16(1) and (2) of Law No 1 of 1967 of Indonesia to the extent that these provisions continue in force by virtue of Article 33(2)(a) of Act No 7 of 1983 of Indonesia.
>
> Provided that relief from United Kingdom tax shall not be given by virtue of this paragraph in respect of income from any source if the income arises in a period starting more than 10 years after the exemption from, or reduction of, Indonesian tax was first granted in respect of that source".

10-16   In line with a change of policy in the OECD generally,[26] U.K. policy is to seek to eliminate tax sparing from treaties, other than on a selective closely targeted basis and within specific time limits. Taxes Act 1988, section 785 was amended by Finance Act 2000, so that tax sparing credit will not generally flow in relation to dividends between related companies but in different jurisdictions under section 801, unless the treaty in question makes express provision for this relief.

---

[25] At 768.
[26] See OECD, *Tax Sparing: A Reconsideration* (1998).

CHAPTER 11

Treaty Shopping and Other Avoidance

11-01 Tax treaty provisions like their counterparts in domestic tax legislation are undergoing a fundamental change in perspective. Historically, treaties were entered into in order to avoid double taxation. A second objective was the prevention of evasion by means of exchange of information between tax authorities. In recent times, however, particularly as treaty networks have grown, attention in relation to tax avoidance has spread from the domestic to the treaty area. Several major U.K. departures from the OECD Model in terms of its negotiating position are addressed almost entirely to avoidance issues. These include the purpose-based test for benefits relating to investment income and the provisions relating to partnership taxation.

WHAT IS AVOIDANCE?

11-02 Tax avoidance as a juridical concept is difficult to define and even more difficult to apply. A convenient starting point in the treaty context is the Inland Revenue *International Tax Handbook*, which addresses avoidance in the international context. Their comments on the meaning of the expression are revealing.

Paragraph 101 reads as follows:

> "As our tax code becomes more complex, Inspectors are increasingly called upon to form a judgement whether, on the facts of a particular case, there has been 'tax avoidance'. The distinction that is drawn is between tax mitigation which may well be considered acceptable and tax avoidance which will not. At one end of the scale, no-one would suggest that moving savings from a bank account into National Savings certificates was objectionable even though the tax payable has been reduced.[1] At the other extreme, when liability is reduced in a wholly artificial way without the taxpayer incurring a loss or expenditure, then that will plainly be avoidance.
>
> Many judges have tried to explain the distinction between mitigation and avoidance—see for example the judgments of Lords Goff and Templeman in *Craven v. White* and of Lord Templeman in *Ensign*

---

[1] Despite this, the Inland Revenue argued (unsuccessfully) in *Beneficiary v. IRC* [1999] S.T.C. (SCD) 134 that the transfer of funds from a U.K. bank account to a non-U.K. account by a non-resident, non-domiciled individual was tax avoidance.

Tankers, but these attempts have not been entirely successful. Perhaps the dividing line is impossible to define. In any event, distinctions between the mitigation and tax avoidance are of less concern to the Government than the effect on the yield to the Exchequer".

11-03 This statement is a fair assessment of the issues relating to avoidance in several respects. First, the term "tax avoidance" is placed in quotation marks suggesting that as a concept with a defined content, it may well not exist in general terms. Secondly, it recognises that at least some activity is unobjectionable. Thirdly, it appears to acknowledge that while the extremes may be easy, the dividing line may be impossible to identify. Fourthly, it concedes that this is less an issue of principle, than one of revenue raising.

The *International Tax Handbook* then outlines the *Ramsay*[2] approach in general terms and turns to the subject of avoidance in the international context. In this regard, it says:

> "Within the Revenue we do not categorise avoidance in quite the narrow way that the Courts have done. Of course we make a distinction between mitigation and avoidance. However, if a taxpayer takes advantage of the law to get a tax advantage which is not, in our understanding, within the spirit of the legislation, we tend to look on that as avoidance. But unless the prerequisites of the new [*Ramsay*] approach are present, such avoidance can only be countered by legislation brought in for this purpose".[3]

It is troubling that tax avoidance is used here in a policy sense to describe inadequacies in the tax base in the same breath as the reference to transactions which may be rendered ineffective by application of the *Ramsay* doctrine.

11-04 The most helpful recent formulation of the statutory meaning of avoidance is that made by Lord Nolan in the House of Lords in *IRC v. Willoughby*.[4] In that case, he accepted the argument advanced by the Inland Revenue as to what was meant by "tax avoidance" for the purposes of Taxes Act 1988, section 741. He said[5]:

> "Tax avoidance was to be distinguished from tax mitigation. The hallmark of tax avoidance is that the taxpayer reduces his liability to tax without incurring the economic consequences that Parliament intended to be suffered by any taxpayer qualifying for such a reduction in his tax liability. The hallmark of tax mitigation on the other hand is that the taxpayer takes advantage of a fiscally attractive option afforded to him by the tax legislation, and genuinely suffers the economic consequences that Parliament intended to be suffered by those taking advantage of the option".

---

[2] *Ramsay v. IRC* [1982] A.C. 300, HL.
[3] At para. 103.
[4] [1997] S.T.C. 995, HL.
[5] At 1003.

In referring to investment in personal portfolio bonds, he continued:

"In a broad colloquial sense, tax avoidance might be said to have been one of the main purposes of those who took out such policies, because plainly freedom from tax was one of the main attractions. But it would be absurd in the context of section 741 to describe as tax avoidance the acceptance of an offer of freedom from tax which Parliament has deliberately made. Tax avoidance within the meaning of section 741 is a course of action designed to conflict with or defeat the evident intention of Parliament".

TREATY INTERACTION WITH DOMESTIC ANTI-AVOIDANCE RULES

11-05 In an era when domestic legislation is increasingly laced with anti-avoidance provisions, the relationship between treaties and domestic anti-avoidance rules requires examination. As a general rule, treaties override domestic legislation. As a result, legislative provisions of any kind, including anti-avoidance rules, are normally overridden by treaties. Although treaties may override them, this is not to say that anti-avoidance measures may be ignored in the treaty context. Provisions labelled as anti-avoidance do not enjoy special status in relation to treaties and the way they interact with treaties must be treated in the same way as other legislation.

Statutory anti-avoidance rules may broadly be classified as follows.

Non-arm's length rules

11-06 Transfer pricing and thin capitalisation are examples of this. They may be consistent with treaty provisions or they may be overridden by treaty provisions.

Re-characterisation rules

11-07 These are rules that re-characterise income or gains from a transaction or the nature of a transaction. These might include Taxes Act 1988, section 703 anti-avoidance transactions in relation to securities, or the accrued income scheme in sections 710 to 728, or section 776 transactions in land and sales and leasebacks. In many cases, whether the re-characterisation is effective in the treaty context will depend on whether the term or issue is exclusively dealt with in the treaty in question and the manner in which undefined terms are dealt with. In treaties that follow Article 3(2) of the OECD Model, undefined terms follow the definitions in the tax law the treaty is sought to be applied to. Difficult issues of characterisation were illustrated in *Memec plc v. IRC*,[6] which involved characterisation of a German silent partnership and dividends both under treaty and domestic provisions.

---

[6] [1998] S.T.C. 754, CA.

Imputation rules

11-08   These are rules that treat the income of one person as belonging to another. Included in this are Taxes Act 1988, section 747, the controlled foreign company rules; section 739, transfers of assets abroad; possibly section 553, the personal portfolio bond rules; and section 13 of Taxation of Chargeable Gains Act (TCGA) 1992, attribution of gains to members of non-resident companies, for example. These are typically not specifically dealt with in treaties and can give rise to finely balanced judgments as was the case in *Bricom Holdings Ltd v. IRC*,[7] a case on CFCs and interest.

Interpretation rules

11-09   Statutory rules of interpretation may be used to limit the application of a rule. The most important of these in recent times is to be found in Taxes Act 1988, section 808B. The broad import of the section is to impose an interpretation of the "special relationship" provisions of double tax treaties relating to royalties as contained in Article 12 of the OECD Model. In principle, treaty benefits are only available where there is a special relationship to the extent that the royalty is on arm's length basis. Subsection 808B(3), however, imposes a complex set of rules where the asset giving rise to the royalty payment has previously been in the ownership of the payer or persons associated with the payer, among others. In order to satisfy the arm's length requirements of this section, it is necessary to demonstrate not only that the royalty which is the subject matter of the treaty in question, but amounts in respect of any transactions as a result of which the asset is in its current ownership, are on an arm's length basis. These rules aim at limiting treaty benefits, for example where intellectual property is moved around in groups or where there are back-to-back licensing arrangements.

Pure tax avoidance rules

11-10   These rules seek to deny the application of particular rules if they are used to avoid tax. Examples include section 137 of TCGA 1992 which denies roll-over relief for tax avoidance in the context of share for share exchanges and reconstructions or amalgamations under sections 135 and 136 respectively, and Finance Act 1996, Schedule 9, paragraph 13, loan relationships for unallowable purposes.

TREATY SHOPPING

11-11   The subject of treaty shopping is perhaps one of the key underlying policy issues surrounding the development of treaties. The exact meaning of the term is unclear and is often taken to have a pejorative meaning. It is the major topic identified for analysis under the heading "Improper use of the Convention" in the Commentary to the OECD Model Convention. A variety of other terms have been used such as treaty abuse and limitation of

---

[7] [1997] S.T.C. 1179, CA.

benefits in the context of the same issue although these concepts would appear to be wider in scope than treaty shopping.

Problems relating to improper use of treaties were examined in detail by the Committee on Fiscal Affairs of the OECD. In 1987, they published the Conduit Companies Report and the Base Companies Report. The key conclusions of those reports are now included in the Official Commentary to the OECD Model. The Conduit Companies Report considered improper use of treaties to exist where there is "a person (whether or not a resident of a Contracting State) acting through a legal entity created in a State with the main or sole purpose of obtaining treaty benefits which would not be available directly to such person". This chapter will consider opportunities for treaty shopping following this definition in circumstances where the person is neither resident in the same country as the legal entity interposed nor in the country of source.

At a more practical level, all forms of treaty shopping involve a taxpayer selecting from various tax treaties that may be available to him through the use of intermediate entities in order to produce the least amount of tax. The element in treaty shopping identified by the Conduit Company Report as improper, is that treaty shopping involves a claim to the benefit of tax treaties by persons who are viewed as not having the requisite connections with a country whose treaty they seek to benefit from.

11-12 A crucial practical element is the interplay between the treaties selected and the domestic tax law of contracting states involved to produce significant overall reductions in tax. In some cases contracting states deliberately offer such facilities as a matter of policy. In others it arises as a result of domestic tax laws which permit this without deliberately setting out to do so. This chapter focuses on the treaty aspects. The impact of treaty shopping is principally on the state of source. It may involve tax benefits in the residence country, for example where tax sparing credits are sought.

There are generally considerable incentives for taxpayers to engage in treaty shopping in international transactions. The United Kingdom has about 100 treaties covering the whole of the OECD, the majority of Eastern European countries and a large number of developing and lesser developed countries. A handful of treaties follow the old colonial style but the vast majority are patterned on various OECD Models. More recent treaties with developing countries show some influence of the UN Model. To some extent the fact that there are now so many countries that have relatively standardised treaty provisions with the United Kingdom removes some of the incentive for treaty shopping at a fairly rudimentary level. Thus in many cases for example, the use of conduit countries to secure reduced rates of withholding tax, permanent establishment benefits or other treaty benefits in straightforward situations is reduced simply because treaties exist with so many countries where investors are located. However, the United Kingdom has important trade and investment links with countries where there are no treaties in place and indeed where there are fundamental differences in tax policy between the country where investors or traders are located and the United Kingdom. Accordingly, even where treaties exist, there are sufficient variations between them to encourage taxpayers to attempt to chose those that provide the most beneficial treatment.

TREATY BASED ANTI-ABUSE MEASURES

11-13   This part focuses on treaty provisions aimed at preventing treaty shopping as adopted in U.K. treaties. It also considers anti-avoidance measures which may be aimed more broadly than at treaty shopping only but which may also limit treaty shopping. Treaty benefits are normally only available to residents of a contracting state in modern treaties. This issue is examined more fully in Chapter 4 above.

Beneficial ownership

11-14   Articles 10, 11 and 12 of the OECD Model authorise the reduction or elimination of tax in the source state only in respect of the "beneficial owner". The OECD Model Commentary[8] suggests that the concept of beneficial ownership does deal with at least some situations of improper use of treaties. The Commentary provides little guidance on the meaning of the term beneficial owner. The only comment in the Commentary is the suggestion that treaty benefits are not available when an intermediary such as an agent or nominee is interposed between the beneficiary and the payer.[9]

This incorporates the Conduit Company Report suggestion that treaty benefits would not be available in cases where a person enters into contracts or takes obligations under which he has a similar function to those of a nominee or agent.

11-15   This would suggest that a conduit company can normally not be regarded as the beneficial owner if, although the formal owner of certain assets, it has very narrow powers which render it a mere fiduciary or an administrator acting on account of the interested parties. The Conduit Company Report regards such parties as most likely to be the shareholders of the conduit company. In recognising the difficulties in dealing with this both the Commentary and the Conduit Company Report suggest that contracting states clarify this issue further if they so desire in the course of their negotiations. Although the beneficial ownership concept is widespread in the dividend, interest and royalty articles of U.K. treaties no special definition or elaboration of the concept is to be found in any of them as advocated by the Conduit Company Report.

The majority of the 19 treaties that have dividend, interest or royalty articles with no reference to beneficial ownership are those dating back to the late 1940s and early 1950s involving former colonies. Most of those treaties do not have interest articles, nor do they deal with the repayment of tax credits under the current imputation system. Consequently it is only the royalty articles that may have any practical significance in this context.

11-16   Another group of treaties which do not include the beneficial ownership concept are those with Germany (1964), Malaysia (1973), Namibia (1962), Portugal (1969), Singapore (1966) and South Africa (1969). In each case the relevant interest and royalty articles provide that the withholding tax reductions in the country of source are only applicable if

---

[8] Commentary on Art.1, para. 10.

[9] Commentary on Art.10, para. 12, on Art.11, para. 8 and Art.12, para. 4.

those items of income are subject to tax in the country of residence of the recipient. Consequently, as a practical matter, if the beneficial owner of the shares were to be a person not resident in any of those contracting states and not subject to tax in those contracting states then U.K. tax benefits would not be available. Thus every item of income in question must be received by a resident of that contracting state who is subject to tax on that income in the country of residence in question.

11-17   The concept of beneficial ownership is not one that has been exhaustively considered in domestic tax law and there are no cases considering the treaty term. The closest parallel is to be found in Taxes Act 1988, section 838(3) which prescribes that, in the context of share ownership for a group and consortium purposes, ownership means beneficial ownership. However, section 838 refers generally to ownership of shares whereas Articles 10 to 12 of the OECD Model refer respectively to beneficial ownership of the dividend, interest or royalty in question. Section 838 does not in any event explain what beneficial ownership is. Domestic law provisions that deal with interest or royalties paid to non-residents do not explicitly refer to beneficial ownership. Where the United Kingdom is the source state the rights in respect of which the income arises will normally be created by U.K. law. Thus, the underlying rights under the applicable domestic general law must be considered. The cases dealing with beneficial ownership for domestic tax purposes have all involved English law.

11-18   A number of cases have considered the question of beneficial ownership in the context of shares. In *Parway Estates Ltd v. IRC*,[10] the taxpayer of the company agreed to sell the shares in a subsidiary but before completion of that sale to purchase the assets of the subsidiary. For stamp duty purposes (relief under section 42 of Finance Act 1930) beneficial ownership of the corporate group is required. The court concluded that where an unconditional sale is executed (of shares in that case) the subject matter of the contract becomes in equity the property of the purchaser. Jenkins L. J. equated equitable and beneficial interest in the shares. He agreed with the views of Upjon J. in the Chancery Division to the effect that the words "beneficial owner" in section 42 of Finance Act 1930 must be construed in "its ordinary or popular sense". However Jenkins L. J. found it difficult to understand what an ordinary person would understand from the words "beneficial owner" in their ordinary sense. He did not think that this had any difference from the legal meaning and effectively equated beneficial with equitable ownership.

11-19   In *English Sewing Cotton Company Ltd v. IRC*,[11] the taxpayer was the owner of shares in a U.S. company. On July 21, 1941 on the occasion of a loan by the U.S. Government to the U.K. Government an agreement was entered into between the American Reconstruction Finance Corporation as representative of the U.S. Government and the U.K. Government, under which securities owned by persons or companies in Great Britain including the common shares of the taxpayers U.S. subsidiary were mortgaged to the corporation as security for the loan. The U.K. company argued that for the purposes of excess profits tax that it was not

---

[10] (1958) 45 T.C. 135.
[11] [1947] 1 All E.R. 679.

the beneficial owner of the U.S. company. Lord Greene M.R. noted that there was no special meaning to be extracted from the specific legislation which would result in the words "beneficial owner" having some meaning other than their ordinary meaning. The court found that the terms of the mortgage were those found in quite ordinary mortgages. It was clear that if the mortgage had been voluntarily given, beneficial ownership in the shares would have unquestionably have remained in the owners. They simply created a relationship of mortgagor and mortgagee. This did not deprive the mortgagor of beneficial ownership. The same was true in relation to an involuntary hypothecation. The impact of the law governing the rights in question was not raised in this case. The shares were in a U.S. company and there was no indication of the law governing the various arrangements.

11-20   In *Wood Preservation Ltd v. Prior*,[12] it was held that where a parent company had contracted to sell shares in a subsidiary subject to a condition precedent solely for the benefit of the purchaser that beneficial ownership of the shares had passed to the purchaser even while the contract had remained conditional on the basis that the purchaser could waive the conditions. The case is more important, however, as an illustration of circumstances where beneficial ownership passes rather than to explain the meaning of the term. The conclusions are however based on the application of equitable remedies and is thus by implication supportive of the view that beneficial ownership equates to equitable ownership.

11-21   The meaning of beneficial ownership of shares has been most extensively examined in *J Sainsbury plc v. O'Connor*.[13] Again, despite lengthy analysis of numerous previous cases, the case is rather more important in describing the circumstances in which beneficial ownership exists rather than attempting any all embracing definition of the term. Clearly as a result of that case, beneficial ownership will not exist without equitable ownership. As Millett J. said[14] "beneficial ownership involves more than equitable ownership. It requires more than the ownership of an empty shell bereft of those rights of beneficial enjoyment which normally attach to equitable ownership".

In the treaty shopping context it may be worth noting his comments[15] to the effect that beneficial enjoyment of dividends is an important feature of beneficial ownership of shares. He also noted that the right to beneficial receipt of dividends which are declared must be distinguished from the right to cause them to be declared. Consequently beneficial ownership has nothing to do with control. He noted that in the *Wood Preservation* case, what prevented the taxpayer from being beneficial owner of the shares pending fulfilment of the conditions was not its inability to cause dividends to be declared but its inability to do so for its own benefit. In the context of OECD Model wording, the question is likely to be for whose benefit may dividends be declared.

He also considered that it would be improper to substitute an economic

---

[12] [1968] 2 All E.R. 849.
[13] [1990] S.T.C. 516, Ch.D. and [1991] S.T.C. 318, CA.
[14] [1990] S.T.C. 516, at 530.
[15] At 531.

test for a legal one and to confuse the existence of legal rights with their value. He stated that "beneficial ownership has nothing to do with the value or economic attributes of ownership". He argued that this was demonstrated by the need for the enactment of what is now Taxes Act 1988, section 413(7) and (8).

This particular approach was not commented on by the Court of Appeal. While it is clear that value in the sense of a quantitative view of ownership would not determine beneficial ownership, entitlement to economic attributes is clearly relevant. The reasoning expressed in the Court of Appeal does not put an end to the relationship between beneficial and equitable owners. The Crown argued in that case that they were not the same thing. Although it is still unclear as to how they differ Lloyd L. J. declined to accept the argument of the Crown to form "a balanced judgment" as to whether the ownership of shares by Sainsbury's was or was not beneficial. He was only prepared to say that where legal ownership was a mere shell, it is relatively easy to draw the inference as a matter of construction that Parliament could not have intended to confer the advantages of group relief. A similar conclusion is likely to result in relation to treaty provisions, although precisely where the dividing line is, remains unclear.

Nourse L. J. was of the view that beneficial ownership simply means ownership for one's own benefit as opposed to ownership as trustee for another. In his view it ought not to be difficult to ascertain beneficial ownership albeit that it may arise in a variety of ways.

11-22 The question of beneficial ownership in the context of a loan was considered by the Court of Appeal in *Swiss Bank Corporation v. Lloyds Bank Limited*.[16] An exchange control notice required Bank of England consent to be obtained to a transfer involving a change of beneficial ownership. In that case an equitable charge and the proprietary equitable interest thereby conferred did not constitute the person with whom the title documents in securities had been deposited as the "beneficial owner" for that purpose.

In the context of treaty shopping it may be possible to distinguish several different circumstances where beneficial ownership may be in issue. The first is in relation to dividends where a person other than the legal (registered) owner of the shares is not the beneficial owner by virtue of some contractual arrangement, declaration of trust or other arrangement considered in the cases above. Similarly, ownership may be split between capital beneficiaries (entitled to the proceeds of sale of a share) and income beneficiaries (entitled to the dividends). These cases all involve ownership of the underlying asset which gives rise to the income in question.

11-23 A more difficult question is raised in relation to those treaties that do not refer to beneficial ownership. If it was found necessary to insert a reference to beneficial ownership in later treaties presumably this was intended to distinguish between beneficial and legal owners. For example, Article 7 of the Antigua Treaty does not refer to beneficial ownership. Would this permit trustees resident there to claim treaty benefits on royalties even where some or possibly all beneficiaries are resident elsewhere?

---

[16] [1990] 2 All E.R. 419.

The concept of beneficial ownership did not appear in the 1963 OECD draft convention. It appeared in the 1977 OECD Model and has been retained in all other model treaties such as the United Nations Model Double Taxation Convention between developed and developing countries as well as the U.S. Model Treaty. The purpose of the introduction of the beneficial ownership concept was to prevent treaty shopping. The OECD Committee on Fiscal Affairs had apparently originally considered making treaty benefits dependent on payments being liable to tax in the state of residence but opted for the beneficial ownership concept in its place. The "subject to tax" approach would have involved various allocation questions and resultant problems and the "beneficial ownership" wording was therefore ultimately agreed upon.[17] This earlier view of the OECD has clearly manifested itself in the treaties still in place from the mid-1960s to early 1970s[18] which do not have the beneficial ownership requirement but which impose a "subject to tax" test.

11-24   However, on the basis that the move to the beneficial ownership concept in the 1977 OECD Model reflected a change in the meaning, it does leave open the question as to whether the very early colonial treaties entitled "legal owners" to treaty benefits. Vogel suggests further that on the basis of a "substance over form" approach the new wording does not in fact introduce a new concept, but simply clarifies the existing position. This conclusion seems inconsistent with the notion that the OECD Committee of Fiscal Affairs considered beneficial ownership as an alternative to the "subject to tax" approach in dealing with a perceived problem of avoidance arising out of the earlier wording.

It may be noted that the Double Taxation Relief (Taxes on Income) (General) Regulations 1970 which provide for authorisation of deduction of tax at source at treaty rates only deal with "a person . . . who is beneficially entitled to the income".[19] While this does not assist in interpreting treaties without a beneficial ownership wording, it may indicate that the regulations were drafted on the assumption that such wording is unnecessary.

Specific countermeasures

11-25   It was recognised by the Fiscal Affairs Committee that the fiscal domicile and beneficial ownership provisions may not be adequate. The Conduit Company Report sets out a number of possible approaches that might be adopted in particular bilateral treaties. It also suggested that in the absence of specific safeguards, treaty benefits would have to be given even if they were considered to be improper.[20] Although the OECD has noted the growing tendency for the use of conduit companies to obtain treaty benefits not intended by contracting states, it has refrained from drafting definitive texts of counter-measures. It has also specifically avoided making any strict recommendations as to the circumstances in which such counter-measures should be applied. The OECD is of the view that in dealing with such

---

[17] See Klaus Vogel, *Double Taxation Conventions* (2nd ed.), p.456.
[18] Treaties with Germany, Malaysia, Singapore, South Africa and Portugal.
[19] S.I. 1970 No. 488, reg.2(2).
[20] At para. 43.

counter-measures, the treaty negotiators should consider the degree to which tax advantages may actually be obtained by conduit companies, the legal context in both contracting states and the extent to which bona fide economic activities might be unintentionally covered by such provisions.

The United Kingdom appears to follow the OECD thinking on this issue in the sense that it has not formulated a general anti-abuse clause in relation to its treaties, an approach that is consistent with current thinking on avoidance in the domestic context. A variety of anti-treaty shopping techniques are applied to specific items in particular treaties where abuse has been identified or feared.

"Subject to tax" approach

11-26   The OECD suggests that treaty benefits may be restricted to circumstances only where the income in question is subject to tax in the state of residence. This is explained on the basis that the aim of treaties is to avoid double taxation. However, for a number of reasons, the OECD Model Convention does not recommend such a general provision. It should be restricted to typical conduit situations, rather than normal international tax relationships.

The principal context in which U.K. treaties apply the "subject to tax" approach is in relation to income and gains taxable on the remittance basis.[21] The vast majority of treaties contain such a provision. In general these rules are aimed at individuals who are resident but not domiciled in the United Kingdom. The question arises as to their application in the context of companies using treaty shopping structures. Some jurisdictions tax foreign source income in the hands of individuals and companies on a remittance basis. The impact therefore of such provisions is to limit benefits in relation to U.K. source income to the extent that it is remitted to the other state.

11-27   Recent treaties have adopted a much tougher formulation of this principle, which goes beyond the "subject to tax" approach. For example, Article 24(1) of the Singapore Treaty in common with all recent treaties provides that relief in the source state for remittance basis taxpayers is only "to so much of the income as is taxed in the other contracting state".

The distinction between taxed and subject to tax is made clear by the Inland Revenue,[22] a person is subject to tax if for example:

(a)   he does not pay U.K. tax because his income is covered by personal allowances or reliefs;

(b)   income is wholly covered by capital allowances.

The effect of this can work extremely harshly in some circumstances. The test is a strict one and no tax avoidance motive is required. It does not take into account normal commercial circumstances such as losses in the country of residence, nor does it take into account personal circumstances such as persons who do not pay tax because they have low income or other reliefs.

---

[21]   Other than as described above.
[22]   Inland Revenue, *Double Taxation Relief*, para. 802.

The Singapore Treaty does provide some prospect for relief. Article 24(2) provides that the limitation would not apply to any person as may be agreed between the competent authorities of the contracting states. No guidelines are provided as to when such agreement would be appropriate, nor is there any obligation on the competent authorities to actually agree. None of the other treaties even contemplate exclusions by way of agreement.

11-28   The rule is somewhat anomalous when compared with countries that tax on a territorial basis only without taxing foreign income or gains remitted to the territory. Companies resident in contracting states such as Venezuela would qualify for treaty benefits notwithstanding that the income in question would not be subject to tax. The application of the remittance rule in this way to treaty benefits in the United Kingdom appears to be more a consequence of certain foreign tax systems then a deliberate policy on the part of the Inland Revenue to apply a subject to tax approach.

Another example of the subject to tax approach was found in Article 10(3)(d) of the Danish Treaty which disapplied the tax credit repayment rule if the beneficial owner of the dividend is exempt from tax in Denmark. See also the Italian Treaty, Article 10(3)(d) to the same effect.

Exclusion of tax favoured entities

11-29   Another commonly used device is to exclude specific types of companies that enjoy tax privileges in their state of residence. The oldest of these is the Luxembourg holding company. Over 15 treaties contain provisions excluding certain entities from claiming treaty benefits. They focus on entities intended to be foreign held and exempt from tax either generally or on foreign income. There are four basic forms of clause designed to exclude tax favoured entities:

The Caribbean formula

11-30   Article 23 of the Barbados Treaty is a typical example. It excludes from all treaty benefits "companies entitled to any special tax benefit under the Barbados International Companies (Exemption from Tax) Act 1965–50 as in effect on July 26, 1965 or any substantially similar law enacted by Barbados after that date". Similar clauses are found in the treaties with Antigua and Barbuda, Jamaica and Luxembourg. All refer to specific incentive legislation which permits foreign owned companies to either be exempt or enjoy minimal local tax.

The Cypriot formula

11-31   Article 24A of the Cypriot Treaty contains a unique limitation rule. Although it refers to tax favoured entities in Cyprus the limitations only apply in relation to dividends, interest and royalties. In addition, individuals resident in Cyprus who are not Cypriot citizens and enjoy a beneficial tax treatment in Cyprus are also excluded while the rate of tax charged on them is less than normal Cyprus income tax rates. A *de minimis* exception permits treaty benefits for such individuals on the first £1,500 sterling of U.K. source income in a year of assessment.

The Channel Islands formula

11-32   More recently amendments were made to the arrangements with each of Guernsey, Jersey and the Isle of Man to take into account new tax favoured entities in each of those jurisdictions. In each case all treaty benefits are excluded in the case of persons assessed in accordance with or who are exempt from assessment by virtue of the incentive legislation unless the person is assessed on the whole of the income or profits at less than the standard rate imposed in that jurisdiction generally.

Article 23 of the Maltese Treaty is somewhat similar. Treaty benefits are not available to companies entitled to benefits under the Malta International Business Activities Act 1988 except those who elect to be subject to the normal provisions of income tax. This option is not available, however, to shipping companies claiming special benefits under the Maltese Merchant Shipping Act 1973.

The CIS formula

11-33   More recently, the United Kingdom has introduced a new form of limitation of benefits clause in its treaties with the former members of the Soviet Union. For example, Article 23(2) of the Azerbaijan Treaty reads:

> "A resident of a contracting state who as a consequence of domestic law concerning incentives to promote foreign investment is not subject to tax or is subject to tax at a reduced rate in the contracting state on income or capital gains shall not receive the benefit of any reduction in or exemption from tax provided for in this convention by the other contracting state if the main purpose or one of the main purposes of such resident or a person connected with such resident was to obtain the benefits of this convention".

Identical provisions are found in the treaties with Belarus, Estonia, Kazakhstan, Latvia, Mongolia, Russia, Ukraine and Uzbekistan. The purpose test is not included in the Russian and Ukrainian treaties.

11-34   The precise intent or effect of this clause is not entirely clear. In the case of Estonia and Latvia, exchanges of notes indicate that incentives to promote foreign investment should not be interpreted as including incentives promoting only domestic investment. It is not clear from this clause whether it applies to outward bound investment from either of the contracting states or whether it is intended to cover inward bound investment from outside the contracting states or both. In addition (apart from Russia and Ukraine), the limitation only applies where one of the main purposes of the resident or a connected person is to obtain the treaty benefits. The motivation in seeking to introduce such a clause is perhaps prophylactic. The tax systems of these countries are very undeveloped and such a clause might assist in limiting benefits if some form of entity which facilitates treaty shopping were to be established under the domestic laws of any of these countries. There was no similar provision in the 1985 Treaty with the Soviet Union and similar clauses have not appeared in other recent developing country treaties such as those with Bolivia and Vietnam.

In a number of cases the exclusion of tax favoured entities has been included by protocol negotiated specifically to deal with that issue. Domestic law in contracting states can clearly be changed more quickly than a treaty renegotiated. Thus, there may be a period during which tax favoured entities do qualify for treaty benefits. It is perhaps for this reason that the Inland Revenue has sought to include the CIS clause even though it may not be entirely effective at eliminating the mischief that the Inland Revenue is apparently seeking to prevent. A slightly different approach is seen in relation to Malaysia. For example, companies established in the Labuan tax haven of Malaysia were excluded from treaty benefits under the 1973 Treaty. They continue to be excluded under the new treaty. The mechanism has changed, however. The Treaty now provides in Article 25(2) for treaty benefits to be denied to persons entitled to any special tax benefit under the law of either contracting state which is identified by exchange of notes. This change in legislative strategy will no doubt enable the tax authorities easily to add to or amend the list of disqualified persons. How far they may be able to go in using such a technique to prevent treaty shopping is unclear.

11-35   The revised OECD Commentary relating to residence suggests the use of exchange of information in order to determine the eligibility of entities for treaty benefits. The provisions which include ineligible entities from treaty benefits do not exclude the authorization of exchanges of information or recourse to mutual agreement procedure. The only exception is in the case of Luxembourg holding companies under Article 30 of the Luxembourg Treaty. That Treaty simply does not apply to those companies. As a practical matter this is now of little consequence because of the European Mutual Assistance Directive (77/799) which authorises exchange of information among Member States of the EU.

Article 16 of the U.S. Treaty (1975) contains an exclusion for certain U.S. and U.K. entities which are at least 25 per cent owned by third country residents who are not U.S. citizens. Treaty relief for dividends, interest or royalties are not available in the United Kingdom if the U.S. company receives more than 80 per cent of its income from outside the United States in circumstances governed by section 861(a)(1)(B) and (a)(2)(A) of the Internal Revenue Code. In the absence of this, third country residents might use such companies to obtain U.K. treaty benefits. The scope of the exclusion is narrowed by exceptions in Article 16(2). Most important from a treaty shopping perspective, if the U.S. company is at least 75 per cent owned by any non U.S. corporation which is not a close company for U.K. purposes, the U.S. company is not excluded from treaty benefits.

"Channel approach"

11-36   The "channel approach" involves a specific and straightforward identification of cases regarded as improper use of a treaty in the treaty itself. No U.K. treaties adopted this approach until the U.S. Treaty (2001). Article 11(7) (interest), Article 12(5) (royalties) and Article 22(4) (other income) of the U.S. Treaty (2001) disapply the benefits of those respective articles in relation to payments made "under or as part of a conduit arrangement". A conduit arrangement is defined in Article 3(1)(n) of the Treaty to mean "a transaction or series of transactions:

   (i)   which is structured in such a way that a resident of a Contracting State entitled to the benefits of this Convention receives an item of income arising in the other Contracting State but that resident pays, directly or indirectly, all or substantially all of that income (at any time or in any form) to another person who is not a resident of either Contracting State and who, if it received that item of income direct from the other Contracting State, would not be entitled under a convention for the avoidance of double taxation between the state in which that other person is resident and the Contracting State in which the income arises, or otherwise, to benefits with respect to that item of income which are equivalent to, or more favourable than, those available under this Convention to a resident of a Contracting State; and

  (ii) which has as its main purpose, or one of its main purposes, obtaining such increased benefits as are available under this Convention".

Unlike other anti-avoidance measures found in U.K. treaties, which are expressed in more general terms, this is specifically targeted at treaty shopping. In order to constitute a conduit arrangement, all or substantially all of the income must be paid to a person who is not a resident of either contracting state. The test does also retain features of other approaches, namely the look-through approach and a purpose test.

"Bona fide" provisions

11-37   The United Kingdom has made extensive use of bona fide provisions in treaties for a number of years. The precise wording of the clause has varied over the years. The Conduit Company Report recognised that configurations reflecting treaty shopping structures occur in many normal transactions of enterprises operating internationally. Therefore it recommended that provisions be included to ensure that treaty benefits are granted in bona fide cases. None of the bona fide articles found in U.K. treaties follow the suggested bona fide wording in the Conduit Company Report. They draw rather on domestic anti-avoidance legislative models.

The most common form of limitation of benefits articles reflecting the bona fide approach has generally read:

"The provisions of this article shall not apply if the [debt claim] in respect of which the [interest] is paid was created or assigned mainly for the purposes of taking advantage of this article and not for bona fide commercial reasons".

Clauses of this kind, started to appear in the late 1960s and are to be found in numerous interest and royalty articles.

11-38   These articles comprise two related tests. The first aim is to deny a treaty benefit where the debt claim, in the case of interest, or a right or property in the case of royalties, is created or assigned to take advantage of the treaty benefit. This wording is not dissimilar from that found in domestic anti-avoidance provisions, particularly Taxes Act 1988, section 787. In order to apply, the main purpose of the creation or assignment of the right must be the treaty benefit. This is similar to section 787 which applies only where the sole or main benefit is a reduction in tax liability by means of relief in respect of interest paid. The second test is that the creation or assignment of the rights in question must not be for bona fide commercial reasons. It will be necessary for a treaty claimant to satisfy both of the tests in order to qualify for the benefit.[23]

Clauses of this variety appear in some 20 treaties starting with Germany (1967) until Iceland (1991) despite minor differences in formulation of these provisions.

11-39   Although the courts have yet to consider these treaty provisions, similar concepts in domestic anti-avoidance rules do give some guidance as to how they might be viewed by the courts. It is far from clear precisely what a "bona fide commercial transaction" is. Most recently, in the Court of Appeal, Morritt L.J. noted in the context of the defence to Taxes Act 1988, section 739 under section 741(b) that the terms "bona fide commercial transactions" and "not designed" for the purpose of tax avoidance could give rise to considerable differences on construction, as had appeared from argument in that case. He declined to consider the issue as it was not necessary for the purpose of the case.[24]

Other cases involving bona fide commercial transactions under Taxes Act 1988, section 703 and its predecessors have similarly not sought to define the expression "bona fide commercial reason". In *CIR v. Brebner*,[25] it was held that determining whether the object of a transaction was a bona fide commercial one and that none of the main objects was to gain tax advantages were purely questions of fact. It was therefore for the Special Commissioners to decide upon a consideration of all the relevant evidence before them and the proper inferences to be drawn from that evidence. In the House of Lords, Lord Pearce noted that the object which must be considered is a subjective matter of intention. In the case of a company, this is determined by the directors who govern its policies or the shareholders who are concerned in and vote in favour of the resolution to follow a particular course of action. The purpose of the transaction is a subjective matter therefore determined from the intentions and acts of various members of the group. It may not be narrowed down to a company's objects. It had been argued in that case that a company, being indifferent as to how its assets were distributed, could not have a bona fide commercial reason or any reason other than a tax advantage.

11-40   A distinction was also drawn between the object of a transaction and ancillary result of that object. If the result was a tax advantage then section 703 would not apply. In that case the court considered that it was improper to isolate individual parts of interrelated transactions. It was nec-

---

[23] *Hasloch v. IRC* [1971] 47 T.C. 50, a case under Taxes Act 1988, s. 703.
[24] *IRC v. Willoughby* [1995] S.T.C. 143, CA at 184.
[25] [1966] 43 T.C. 705, HL.

essary to consider the main object or objects for which any of them was adopted rather than the effect of each or all of the interrelated transactions.

Most section 703 circumstances deal with more than one transaction. Treaty bona fide articles however focus on only a single transaction in each case. It is necessary to consider only whether the creation or assignment of the rights in question is effected for the purpose of taking advantage of the relevant treaty provision. Consequently, related transactions may only be viewed as part of the evidence in determining whether the relevant transaction has as its main purpose taking advantage of the relevant article.

11-41   Lord Upjohn also articulated one of the major difficulties in successfully applying anti-avoidance provisions. He observed[26] that in determining whether a genuine commercial transaction is carried out and there are two ways of doing so, one by paying the maximum amount of tax and the other by paying no or less tax, it is wrong as a necessary consequence to draw the inference that in choosing the tax favoured route that one of the main objects, for the purpose of the anti-avoidance provision, is the avoidance of tax. This has been cited frequently in avoidance cases. In the treaty shopping context this view will impose significant restrictions on successful application of the rules at least where taxpayers do have a choice. For example where a non U.K. multinational group has subsidiaries in several countries the fact that an investment into the United Kingdom is routed through one which has the most favourable treaty provision will not in and of itself necessarily infer that the purpose of the creation of the right in question was to gain treaty benefits. In other cases such as *IRC v. Godwin*,[27] the courts have similarly either found or not found bona fide commercial transactions without analysing the meaning of the words.

The treaty provision is silent as to whose intention is relevant in applying the test. In the *Brebner* case[28] it was clear that it was the intentions of the directors and shareholders of the company who were involved in the transaction that were relevant. In *Addy v. IRC*,[29] it was held, however, that the test must be applied to those in control of the company in question. Like the concept of beneficial ownership the courts seem to be able to spot a bona fide commercial reason when they see one although they have some difficulty in describing precisely what the concept embraces.

11-42   In *Clark v. IRC*,[30] one of the issues that arose was whether the transaction was carried out for "commercial reasons". It was not disputed that the transaction in question was "in every respect bona fide".[31] This seems to imply that there are two elements of the test, one that it be bona fide and additionally that it be for commercial reasons, rather than that the expression "bona fide" qualifies the nature of the commercial reasons. In that case the Special Commissioners had decided that the commercial reason had to be connected with the vendors' interests in the companies concerned in or affected by the transaction. However, on appeal Fox J. regarded this

---

[26] At 718.
[27] [1976] S.T.C. 28, HL.
[28] See above, n. 25.
[29] [1975] S.T.C. 610, Ch.D.
[30] [1978] S.T.C. 614.
[31] At 624.

too narrow an approach. In his view, section 703 does not contain such a qualification. It merely requires that the transaction be carried out for bona fide commercial reasons. That language is entirely at large and if the taxpayer can prove that the transaction was carried out for bona fide commercial reasons he satisfies the requirement of that section.

Carried out in this sense means carried out by the taxpayer. He went on to rule that the sole question is the nature of the reason for which the transaction was carried out. There is no requirement of nexus with particular parties affected by it or in some way concerned in the transaction.

11-43 Section 703 is distinguishable from most formulations of this treaty provision in that the section 703(1) escape clause includes both transactions carried out for bona fide commercial reasons or "in the ordinary course of making or managing investments". Only a few treaties contain this wording. They are those with Belgium, Italy Luxembourg, Norway and Switzerland, and then only in the context of dividends and repayment of the tax credit.

These treaties require the non U.K. resident shareholder claiming the repayment of a credit to show that the shareholding was acquired for bona fide commercial reasons. The alternative test, namely, that the share was acquired in the ordinary course of making or managing investments is not found in any other similar limitation of benefits provision. The non U.K. resident shareholder must also demonstrate that it was not the main object nor one of the main objects of the acquisition of shares to obtain entitlement to repayment of the credit. These provisions were first introduced into the Swiss Treaty by Protocol in 1982. Furthermore, It was the first time that the purpose test was extended to disqualify a payment if one or more of the objects of the transaction was the treaty benefit as compared to where the sole object of the transaction was the benefit (see below).

11-44 In *Clark v. IRC*, the court found that in the case of one taxpayer, the anti-avoidance provisions did not apply because looking at the transaction in the context of all of the circumstances, it was for bona fide commercial reasons. The overall purpose of the transaction was to purchase a farm adjoining the one that he already owned and there were good commercial reasons for doing so. The specific transaction which the Special Commissioners had concluded had no commercial reason were simply to finance that purchase. The court rejected the argument of the Crown that the commercial reasons must be intrinsic to the transaction. Instead the matter must be considered in the context of all the relevant facts and not merely a part of them.

In that case, another taxpayer was found not to have carried out the transaction for bona fide commercial reasons. No commercial reasons entered into his thinking. He was held, however, to have carried out the transactions in the ordinary course of managing investments since he believed that the value of his investment would be threatened and he accordingly joined in the transaction. The Commissioners ruled that although his transaction was not in the course of making investments it was in the ordinary course of managing investments. He adopted the most favourable way open to him to protect his investment. This, the Commissioners said, "is what any prudent investor would do in the ordinary course of managing investments".

11-45   Does the presence of the alternative defence of transactions carried out in the ordinary course of making or managing investments in these treaties mean that in other treaties where only the bona fide commercial transaction defence is found, treaty benefits may be denied because the purpose of the transaction is in the nature of "investment" rather than "commercial"? In the Italian and Norwegian treaties, both defences are found in the dividend articles. The Italian Treaty contains only a commercial reasons defence in relation to interest, while the Norwegian Treaty contains the commercial reasons defence only in relation to interest and royalties This issue is not addressed directly in the Conduit Company Report which refers generally to "bona fide transactions". The examples cited in the Report, however, refer to a commercial context in the sense of normal transactions of enterprises operating internationally.

In *IRC v. Willoughby*,[32] the Court of Appeal considered the nature of the defences to the application of the anti-avoidance provisions of Taxes Act 1988, section 739 contained in section 741(b). That clause only provides exemption for bona fide commercial transactions and makes no reference to the making or managing of investments. The Special Commissioner found that the transfers and associated operations were bona fide commercial transactions. Investment in an off-shore single premium personal portfolio bond in order to make provision for a pension by an individual was viewed as a commercial transaction. They were designed for the increase of Professor Willoughby's retirement funds taking advantage of a favourable tax regime.

In the Court of Appeal, the Crown argued in relation to section 741(b) that for a transaction to be commercial, it must be carried out as part of the trade or commerce of both parties. The taxpayer argued that the transfer and associated operations were bona fide commercial transactions because they were genuine, for value and at arm's length. Although the decision on section 741 rested on the application of section 741(a), (*i.e.*, the transactions were not for the purpose of avoiding tax) Morritt L.J. quoted in support of his conclusion, Lord Upjohn in the *Brebner* case: " No commercial man in his senses is going to carry out a commercial transaction except upon the footing of paying the smallest amount of tax that he can". This seems to suggest a close connection between the two defences. Thus, although the relationship between the two defences remains undefined, the dividing line if there is one, is likely to be very fine.

The same words can mean different things in different parts of the same treaty[33] and thus arguably, the same words may have different meanings in different treaties. A conclusion that both defences meant the same thing in these treaties would of course render the additional wording where it appears otiose. The position is far from clear.

11-46   In *Marwood Homes Limited v. IRC*,[34] a separation of the two consequences was agreed by the parties. They agreed that for the purposes of section 703(1), the transactions were not carried out in the ordinary course of making or managing investments. Consequently, the issue to be

---

[32] [1995] S.T.C. 143, CA.
[33] *IRC v. Exxon Corp* [1982] S.T.C. 356; *Memec plc v. IRC* [1998] S.T.C. 754, CA.
[34] [1997] S.T.C. (SCD) 37.

decided was whether the transactions were carried out for bona fide commercial reasons (and that none of the transactions had as their main object or one of their main objects to enable tax advantages to be obtained). The Special Commissioners concluded on the evidence that there was a bona fide commercial reason for the transaction. If the directors of the company in question were of the view that the transaction was important for the future prosperity of the business of the company and the group, it could be said that the transaction was carried out for bona fide commercial purposes, that to determine this, it is necessary to look at the overall position to see what was done for good commercial reasons.

11-47   If the Inland Revenue seek to maintain the distinction between the two types of defence in treaties as argued in the *Willoughby* case and are successful, the result may be that these clauses will impose significant limitations on the availability of benefits in the treaty articles which do not include the defence in relation to the making of investments. This is because to succeed a taxpayer will have to satisfy both limbs of the test. A non-resident who cannot show both that the source of income in question was not created or assigned mainly for the purpose of taking advantage of the article in question and the existence of bona fide commercial reasons will not be entitled to treaty benefits. This would restrict treaty claims only to those claimants engaged in trade or commerce. This would appear to go far beyond the suggestions of the OECD in the Conduit Company Report and on a purposive interpretation, contrary to the general objective of treaties in avoiding double taxation. It would impact particularly upon cross-border investment by individuals which is clearly contemplated at least in the OECD Model. For example the reference in the Commentary on interest and royalties to special relationships includes references to relationships by blood or marriage in the context of interest[35] and on royalties.[36]

11-48   Other interesting comments on the nature of bona fide commercial transactions were made in the *Willoughby* case.[37] In particular a letter from the Inland Revenue to Royal Life (the issuers of the off-shore bond) conceded that the personal portfolio bonds were bona fide commercial transactions. The Special Commissioners concluded that in the absence of any reason for impeaching the good faith of either party thereto it must be a bona fide commercial transaction for the purchaser as well. This conclusion was quoted by the Court of Appeal without comment.

If the bona fide clause is indeed similar to Taxes Act 1988, section 787 then the Inland Revenue may itself have doubts about its effectiveness. The clause is briefly referred to without comment by The Inland Revenue.[38] The *Handbook* also notes at paragraph 721 that it is common for parent companies to borrow to fund their subsidiaries and that in such cases it is difficult to distinguish between routing for tax and purely commercial purposes. At paragraph 1149 it states that the usefulness of section 787 is somewhat

---

[35] Commentary on Art.11, para. 34.
[36] Commentary on Art.12, para. 24.
[37] See above, n. 32.
[38] *International Tax Handbook*, para. 709.

circumscribed. It is not easily invoked and should only be used for out and out avoidance schemes and not "judiciously arranged borrowing".

11-49   As a rule, bona fide provisions have not been inserted in dividend articles in order to prevent treaty shopping in respect of the repayment of tax credits in relation to dividends paid by U.K. companies to shareholders in treaty countries. A number of treaties, however, have a limitation of benefits provision to prohibit tax credit stripping in relation to dividends earned out of profits by a U.K. company more than 12 months before a company resident in a treaty country became a 10 per cent owner in the paying U.K. company. These clauses are typically excluded if it can be shown that the shares were acquired not for the purpose of securing the benefit of the repayment and for bona fide commercial reasons. These clauses do not serve any wider anti-treaty shopping purpose.

In the case of Denmark, bona fide provisions originally found in the 1950 Treaty were dropped in favour of adopting a look-through approach in the 1991 Protocol.

"Purpose" provisions

11-50   There have been no cases on the bona fide provisions. The Inland Revenue, perhaps believing that it was not achieving what they had hoped, abandoned the bona fide wording for the first time in the 1991 Papua New Guinea Treaty.

A wholly new approach emerged in 1992 as reflected in the Guyana Treaty. The now standard provisions found in relation to dividends, interest, royalties and "other income" typically reads:

> "The provisions of this Article shall not apply if it was the main purpose, or one of the main purposes, of any person concerned with the creation or assignment of the rights in respect of which the income is paid to take advantage of this Article by means of that creation or assignment".

First, the bona fide test was dropped. This marked a significant departure from the OECD approach. It is also a departure from the wording normally found in domestic anti-avoidance provisions. Generally an exclusion is found for bona fide transactions[39] in such domestic rules.

11-51   Secondly, the purpose test was amended so that it would apply if "the main purpose or one of the main purposes" of the creation or assignment of the rights in question was to take advantage of the treaty benefits. This approach echoes wording used in most domestic anti-avoidance provisions which apply not only where the sole purpose is securing a tax advantage or tax avoidance, but where merely one of the main purposes is to secure such an advantage.

The third change is the identification of the person whose purpose it is to take advantage of the treaty benefits. The new rule applies if it was the purpose of "any person concerned with the creation or assignment" of the

---

[39] Taxes Act 1988, ss. 703, 739–741, 787; TCGA 1992, ss. 137, 140B, 140D.

rights in question. Several issues arise out of this new wording. First, by analogy to the section 703 cases, the courts have identified a number of persons whose intentions are relevant. If the intentions of the controlling shareholders of a company resident in a contracting state go to making up the purpose for which that company enters into a transaction, does this new wording usefully add anyone not already covered? Secondly, one of the important issues in the treaty shopping context is whether the intention of a person in a third country would be relevant for this purpose. The difficulty arises out of reading this provision in conjunction with Article 1 of the OECD Model. Article 1 states that "the convention applies to persons who are residents of one or both of the contracting states". The plain meaning of the words would seem to suggest that in applying the treaty, any *person* refers to a person who is a subject of the treaty rather than a resident of a third country. Article 24(1) of the OECD Model shows that express wording is required to apply the treaty to non-residents of both contracting states. On the other hand, the courts have departed from the plain meaning of words in a treaty and adopted different meanings for the same word in different parts of the treaty in *IRC v. Exxon*.[40] In that case, the court adopted a different construction of the meaning of resident in order that the purpose of the provision in question did not fail in effect. The use of the word "concerned" may be indicative of a broad intention to cover any person interested, involved or affected.[41]

11-52 A further unanswered question is how the drafters of these provisions intended to distinguish the new wording from the earlier form which did not explicitly seek to identify the person whose purpose was relevant in determining the application of the treaty. If the revised wording extends the object to persons unconnected with the taxpayer or residents of third countries, that may mean that under the earlier bona fide provisions the intentions of a narrower class of persons only are relevant.

Fourthly, advantage of the article must be taken "by means of the creation or assignment" of the rights in question.

At a meeting between representatives of certain professional bodies and the Inland Revenue in May 1994[42] the Inland Revenue confirmed that the form of anti-treaty shopping article contained in the Guyana Treaty represented the latest thinking on the form of such articles and would be the version which they sought to obtain in future negotiations. It has been used consistently since then.

11-53 A further significant change in treaty policy on limitation of benefits has also taken place at the same time. Until the mid-1990s these provisions have appeared particularly in interest and royalty articles in an unsystematic manner. There are some treaties where they do not appear at all and others where they may be restricted,usually to interest articles. Occasionally and more recently, these provisions are also found in clauses relating to management and technical and service fees, presumably at the instance of those governments seeking to follow the UN Model in distin-

---

[40] [1992] S.T.C. 366, Ch.D.
[41] *Shorter Oxford English Dictionary.*
[42] *ICAEW Technical Tax Release* (Tax 16/94).

guishing such fees from royalties. Presumably, the inclusion of these provisions in this manner reflected a policy of the Inland Revenue only to seek their inclusion specifically where they believed that a real risk of treaty abuse was in issue. All the most recent treaties now include this provision systematically in all interest and royalty articles without any particular indication as to whether there is perceived to be a real threat of treaty abuse or not. A further development in the most recent treaties, is to seek to include a clause along these lines in the "other income" article. This has now appeared for the first time in 1994 in Treaties with Kazakhstan and Mexico. This now appears to have become standard practice in later treaties. No reason for this has been given, although it may be as a result of the fact that derivative financial instruments which can replicate dividends and interests in particular, are normally governed by the "other income" article. Success in negotiating the inclusion of the provision is uneven. For example, in the recent Argentine Treaty, this rule is contained in the dividend, interest, royalty and other income articles. In the Singapore Treaty, it does not appear in the "other income" article.

Look-through rules

11-54   One solution suggested by the OECD is directed at disallowing treaty benefits to a company if it is not owned directly or indirectly by residents of the state in which the company itself is resident. It suggests that this approach may be adequate for treaties with countries which have no or very low taxation and where little substantive business activities would normally be carried on.

A variation of the look-through theory is to exclude companies resident in a contracting state from benefits under a treaty if the company is owned or controlled by residents of a third country who themselves would not qualify for similar treaty benefits.

The OECD acknowledges that the use of look-through provisions in the most radical solution to the problem of conduit companies. The United Kingdom has made very limited use of look-through rules. Only three treaties contain classic look-through rules. The first was Article 10(3)(d) of the Netherlands Treaty. The Netherlands was traditionally the major location for conduit companies in relation to reducing source country taxation on dividends. This treaty was one of the early treaties granting repayment of the tax credit under Article 10(3).

11-55   The other treaties which contain look-through provisions are the Danish Treaty, where look-through rules were introduced in the Protocol of July 1, 1991 relating to interest and royalties, and in the 1991 Icelandic Treaty in relation to dividends in Article 10(1)(d) and for interest in Article 11(7) to (9), as well as Article 12(6) to (8) in respect of royalties.

The basic structure of the U.K. look-through provisions is similar in all cases. In the case of companies, treaty benefits are denied unless the company concerned satisfies one of two tests:

(i)   its shares must be officially quoted on a stock exchange in the respective country of residence. In the case of Article 10 of the

Netherlands Treaty and Articles 11(7)(a) and 12(6)(a) of the Danish Treaty, the conditions for admission within those set out in Schedule A to EC Directive 79/279 dated March 5, 1979 must be met; in particular, the conditions governing the minimum value of shares to be listed, transferability and the dispersion of the share-holdings are mandatory; or

(ii) companies who shares are not so listed are required to show that they are not controlled by persons who themselves are not entitled to the treaty benefits.

11-56 In the case of Article 10 of the Netherlands Treaty and Article 10 of the Icelandic Treaty, this second requirement is met if the person or persons controlling the claimant company would not themselves have been entitled to a tax credit if those persons had been the beneficial owner of the dividends (paid by the U.K. company).

By determining entitlement to treaty benefits by reference to those other persons who would qualify for a tax credit, treaty benefits may apply where the relevant controlling persons are themselves U.K. residents (subject to the provisions of Article 10(3)(c) of the Netherlands Treaty and Article 10(3)(c) of the Iceland Treaty). It would also apply where the relevant beneficial owners are non-resident individuals entitled to claim for personal allow-ances and tax credits under Taxes Act 1988, section 278, as well as residents of other contracting states where the relevant treaty permits payment of the tax credit.

The analogous limitation provisions in the Danish and Icelandic Treaties relating to interest and royalties are far more severe. In relation to those items of income, treaty benefits are only available if the relevant beneficial owners are themselves able to take advantage of the treaty benefits relating to those items of income under the particular treaty in question. Therefore in effect, the elimination of U.K. tax on interest and royalty payments made to unquoted Danish and Icelandic companies will only apply where those companies are themselves controlled by residents of Denmark and Iceland respectively.

11-57 These clauses highlight the difficulties identified by the OECD in the Conduit Company Report relating to the use of look-through approach. The Report suggests that such provisions are incompatible with the princi-pal of the legal status of corporate bodies as recognised in the legal systems of all OECD member countries and except in the case of abuse in the OECD Model. The Report notes that machinery to apply the clause needs to be simple and secure and that this may require a shift in the burden of proof. In all of these clauses, the burden of demonstrating entitlement to treaty ben-efits is placed clearly on the claimant. Not only is the claimant required to demonstrate prima facie entitlement, but it is also required at the same time to demonstrate that the claim does not fall foul of the limitations imposed by the terms of the article.

The Conduit Company Report also notes that such provisions require extensive bona fide amplifications. None of these provisions in U.K. treaties contain exceptions in respect of bona fide commercial transactions. The severity of the rule is illustrated by the recent decision of the High Court in *Steele v. European Vinyls Corp (Holdings) BV*[43] (see further para 11-69 below).

11-58 All of these articles do, however, contain limited exceptions for minority shareholdings by individuals. In the case of the Netherlands Treaty, where an individual is treated as having control of a company by reason only of the fact that he holds ordinary shares in the company carrying full voting and dividend rights, the shares held by him may be left out of account in determining whether the company is controlled by qualifying persons, if that individual holds not more than 10 per cent of the total number of shares in the company. In addition, no more than 25 per cent of the total of such shares in the company may be excluded on this basis. The Icelandic Treaty contains the same rule in Articles 10, 11 and 12. In the case of Denmark, individual holdings of 20 per cent may be excluded for the purpose of applying the test provided that no more than 30 per cent of the total shares in the Danish company may be excluded in this way.

These exclusions from the limitation of benefits rules are narrow in scope. Furthermore, disqualification applies to a person or to two or more associated or connected persons together who or any of whom would not have been entitled to the treaty benefit in question if they controlled the Netherlands company. Control for this purpose means control for any purpose of U.K. tax law. One of the circumstances in which these provisions have significant impact is where there are a number of shareholders, one or more of whom is not entitled to treaty benefits as illustrated in the *Euro Vinyls* case. There, the very wide application of the meaning of control and of connection resulting from the provisions of a shareholders agreement excluded the Dutch company in question from treaty benefits as a result of a holding by an Italian company which itself was not entitled to a tax credit.

11-59 A further difficulty arises from the application of the domestic law meaning of "control" and "associated" or "connected" persons. Although the ultimate beneficial owners may qualify for the benefits in question, the interposition of a person who does not qualify for the benefits would cause the non-application of Article 10 of the Netherlands Treaty. Thus, for example, if a British citizen resident in South Africa owned all of the shares of a Netherlands company which in turn owned all of the shares of a U.K. company, the tax credit repayment would be allowed. If however that British subject interposed a Netherlands Antilles company between himself and the Netherlands company, the Netherlands company would not qualify for treaty benefits. The impact of these provisions may therefore permit a degree of treaty shopping in some cases.

In addition, repayment of the credit would appear to apply as long as the relevant beneficial owner is "entitled to a tax credit". It appears that the precise manner in which this entitlement operates need not necessarily be the same as under the Netherlands Treaty. Therefore in the case of a Netherlands company, owned by a Canadian company which is in turn owned by a Canadian individual, the provisions of Article 10 of the Netherlands Treaty will permit a repayment with the 5 per cent withholding tax for substantial

---

[43] [1995] S.T.C. 31, Ch.D.; [1996] S.T.C. 785, CA.

holdings even though a Canadian corporate shareholder investing directly in the United Kingdom would be subject to a 10 per cent tax if the holding in the U.K. company were held directly by the Canadian company.

11-60 In recommending the look-through approach, the Conduit Company Report regards such rules as relatively simple and straightforward. While the success in limiting treaty benefits for third country residents as illustrated in the *Euro Vinyls* case is possible, it clearly does not apply in all circumstances. In addition, it may still not entirely eliminate treaty shopping except by use of the most stringent tests such as found in the Danish Treaty. This would also have adverse effects in non-tax avoidance circumstances as well.

At a meeting in May 1996 between representatives of certain professional bodies and the Inland Revenue,[44] the Inland Revenue announced that discussions had taken place on the anti-abuse provisions in the interest and royalty articles in the Danish and Icelandic Treaties. The Inland Revenue confirmed at that meeting that the particular wording is not in any other treaty currently being negotiated. They also anticipated that a protocol may be signed with Denmark to amend the existing wording. A Protocol was signed on October 15, 1996. The look-through rule is abandoned for dividends (no repayment of the tax credit is allowed), interest and royalties and is replaced with the new standard purpose clause. It would have appeared that the look-through approach was likely to be consigned to the history books of U.K. treaty policy, until the signing of the U.S. Treaty (2001).

U.S. Treaty (2001)

11-61 The United States has gone to extraordinary lengths in drafting a "foolproof" look-through limitation of benefits provision contained in Article 26 of its Model Treaty. The United Kingdom agreed to the inclusion of a modified form of this clause in the 2001 Treaty signed on July 24, 2001. In addition to the adoption of a look-through approach, the treaty departs from existing U.K. treaty policy by applying to benefits under the treaty generally. Unlike other treaties, where limitations of benefits apply to specific articles only and are targeted at specific abuses, Article 23(1) of the U.S. Treaty only grants benefits to residents of a contracting state who are "qualified persons".

11-62 The article is lengthy and complex. The main categories of qualifying residents are[45]:

(1)   individuals;

(2)   certain governmental entities;

(3)   certain unit trusts;

(4)   certain companies:

    (a)   with shares listed on a recognised Stock Exchange;

---

[44]   *ICAEW Technical Tax Release* (Tax 14/96).
[45]   Article 23(2).

(b) which are direct or indirect subsidiaries owned through a chain of resident companies;

(c) which are principally owned by "equivalent beneficiaries" and less than half the company's gross income is deductible on payment to non-equivalent beneficiaries. Equivalent beneficiaries are essentially residents of the European Union, the European Economic Area or North American Free Trade Area, where there are broadly equivalent limitations of benefit rules and comparable treaty benefits under a treaty with the source state[46];

(5) pension plans principally for the benefit of resident individuals;

(6) certain trusts where the beneficiaries are qualifying residents or equivalent beneficiaries.

Treaty benefits may however be granted to a resident who is not otherwise entitled to benefits if the competent authority determines that the establishment, acquisition or maintenance of such resident and the conduct of its operations did not have as one of its principal purposes the obtaining of benefits under the treaty.[47]

Other approaches

11-63 Article 11(6) of the Japanese Treaty contains an unique limitation clause as far as U.K. treaties are concerned. It simply states that in the context of dividends, relief from tax of a contracting state is subject to the same limitations as are imposed in respect of relief or exemption from tax under the laws of the contracting state by any provision enacted in order to maintain the proper incidence of liability to tax and to prevent the obtaining of undue tax advantages. The article is particularly curious because the treaty applies a bona fide provision of the kind described above in the case of interest and royalties. The effect of Article 11(6) is to preserve domestic anti-avoidance enactments such as Taxes Act 1988, section 703.

Procedural methods

11-64 The United Kingdom has recently attempted to use procedural rules in order to combat avoidance. An Exchange of Notes in connection with the recent Protocol with Denmark contains an unusual arrangement whereby a contracting state seeking to invoke the anti-avoidance provisions relating to dividends, interest or royalties is to notify the other contracting state of that fact. This curious provision is also found in other more recent treaties such as that with Singapore. Article 11(10) of the Singapore Treaty, for example, reads as follows:

"In the event that a resident of a contracting state is denied relief from taxation in the other contracting state by reason of the provisions of

---

[46] Article 23(7)(d).
[47] Article 23(6).

paragraph (9) of this Article, the competent authority of that other
contracting state shall notify the competent authority of the first mentioned contracting state".

The treaties where this wording has appeared all contain exchange of
information provisions to cover this in any event. Why then is this wording
inserted into these treaties? No public explanation of it has been given by the
Inland Revenue to date. The reason is therefore a matter of speculation. It
may be simply viewed as a warning to those who might use the treaty in a
manner that one tax authority regards as impermissible, that this will not
remain a unilateral issue. The other contracting state will become involved
if treaty relief is denied as a result of these provisions.

JUDICIAL APPROACHES

11-65   This part examines the few judicial statements that might be
viewed as expressing opinions on treaty shopping as well as the potential
application of domestic law anti-avoidance doctrines to the question.

The high water mark of judicial tolerance towards treaty shopping is
perhaps the decision in *IRC v. Commerzbank*.[48] The court sanctioned benefits under the U.S. Treaty being conferred on residents of Brazil and Germany.
The basis on which this was allowed involved two simple propositions. The
first, which the Inland Revenue conceded in the High Court, is that there is
no legal reason why a treaty cannot deal with rights and obligations of
persons other than citizens, residents and corporations of the contracting
parties. The second was that the words of Article XV of the U.S. Treaty were
clear. Their natural and ordinary meaning was to exempt from U.K. tax,
interest which had been paid by U.S. corporations except for certain specified
U.K. recipients. The Treaty could not be construed as expanding the exception beyond the category of recipients described in the article.

11-66   Another case that may be viewed as judicial authorisation of
treaty shopping is *Padmore v. IRC*.[49] In that case a U.K. resident partner in
a partnership managed in Jersey claimed exemption on his share of the partnership profits by virtue of the Jersey Treaty on the basis that the partnership was a Jersey enterprise carrying on business in Jersey without a
permanent establishment in the United Kingdom.

The Inland Revenue argued that a business carried on in partnership for
example, between Jersey residents, U.K. residents and third country residents should be treated under the Treaty as a Jersey enterprise insofar as it
is carried on and its profits belong to the Jersey residents, a U.K. enterprise
insofar as it is carried on by and its profits belong to U.K. residents and
neither a Jersey enterprise nor a U.K. enterprise insofar as it is carried on by
and its profits belong to third country residents. This argument was dismissed on the basis that partnership income is assessed for U.K. and Jersey
purposes on an artificial basis in the name of the partnership on the partners

---

[48] [1990] S.T.C. 285.
[49] [1987] S.T.C. 36, Ch.D.

who are jointly liable for the whole of any tax which may be payable. Thereafter there is an apportionment of the income between the partners so as to arrive at each individual's liability.

11-67   The Crown, however, argued that this approach was not consistent with the general scheme of the Treaty. It was argued that the scope and purpose of paragraph 3(2) (the business profits provision) was to remove U.K. tax liability from the profits of a Jersey enterprise trading in the United Kingdom but not through a permanent establishment and that it was not directed at and did not apply to the U.K. tax liability of a partner receiving his share of the profits.

Again, Peter Gibson J. determined the matter on the basis of the plain meaning of the words of the Treaty. The effect of the Treaty was that all industrial or commercial profits of a Jersey enterprise are not subject to U.K. tax whether earned in Jersey, the United Kingdom or elsewhere, except to the extent that they are attributable to a permanent establishment in the United Kingdom. That left Jersey alone as between itself and the United Kingdom free to tax those profits. He concluded that in order to achieve the result the Crown argued for, extra wording was needed in the treaty such as that found in the Swiss Treaty. It provides that in the case of a partnership, the United Kingdom's right to tax U.K. resident partners on their share of partnership income is not restricted. The Crown's argument that the Treaty should not be read so as to produce an adventitious or anomalous benefit to the taxpayer was not accepted. There was no basis to imply any additional provisions into the clear wording of the Treaty.

11-68   In addition to the changes in U.K. domestic law in the Finance (No. 2) Act 1987, section 62 effectively overriding treaty provisions, the United Kingdom then adopted wording found in recent treaties, for example, Article 24 of the Ukraine Treaty, authorising the United Kingdom to tax U.K. resident partners of Ukrainian partnerships. That wording would not appear, however, to have ended the ability of partners resident in third countries to claim treaty benefits through the partnership where it is taxed as a separate entity. *Padmore* would appear to support the proposition that as long as a foreign partnership qualifies as an enterprise of another contracting state, partners not resident in that contracting state may be able to claim treaty benefits.

11-69   If the *Commerzbank* case represents the high water mark of judicial permissiveness toward treaty shopping, then *Steele v. European Vinyls Corp (Holdings) BV*[50] is the low water mark. In that case, a joint venture was established between Imperial Chemical Industries plc, a U.K. resident and EniChem SpA, an Italian resident. The joint venture vehicle was a Netherlands resident company effectively owned 50 per cent by the ICI Group and 50 per cent by EniChem. The Netherlands company claimed payment of tax credits pursuant to Article 10 of the Netherlands Treaty. Under Article 10(3)(d)(i), payment only applied if the Netherlands company could show that it was not controlled by a person, or two or more associated or connected persons together, who or any of whom, would not have been

---

[50] [1995] S.T.C. 31, Ch.D.; [1996] S.T.C. 785, CA.

entitled to a tax credit if he had been the beneficial owner of the dividends paid. EniChem would not have been entitled to a tax credit under the Italian Treaty at that time. It was accepted that the shareholders were not associated and the only question was whether they were connected persons.

11-70   Article 10(3)(d)(ii) required the question as to whether they were connected to be determined for this purpose by U.K. domestic law. Lightman J. held that under the relevant domestic law[51] they were connected with each other.

It was argued by the taxpayer in the Chancery Division that the mischief at which these provisions were aimed was the prevention of "treaty shopping". This would be sufficiently achieved if it applied only to persons who are genuinely connected. By that it was meant otherwise than through the mere coincidence of their exercising joint control of a company. It was argued that it would be arbitrary and unjust to deny tax credits to a company merely because its shareholders, otherwise unconnected, and acting together to exercise control over its affairs, should be denied the tax credit. It was therefore suggested that in the circumstances the "connection" contemplated in the Treaty should be restricted to "real and free standing connections". Connections should only therefore refer to subsections (2) to (6) of section 839 of Taxes Act 1988 and not the more extensive factors in subsection (7).

11-71   The court, however, rejected this argument on the basis that the reference to domestic law in Article 10(3)(d) referred to persons connected under the laws of the United Kingdom "for any purpose". These words required adoption of the full test rather than a more limited test argued for by the taxpayer.

On appeal to the Court of Appeal the taxpayer argued that unless and until section 839 is applied for some substantive tax purpose arising between the Inland Revenue and the taxpayer the definition in section 839(7) cannot come within Article 10(3)(d)(ii) of the Treaty. It argued that the analysis of Lightman J. was incorrect upon a "true construction of the convention which is in origin a treaty between the United Kingdom and the Kingdom of the Netherlands". It was argued that the principles expressed in the *Commerzbank* case should apply.

Morritt J. noted, however, that under the Treaty it was sufficient if the shareholders of the Netherlands company "could" be treated as connected under U.K. domestic law. Consequently, the essential issue was the true meaning and purpose of the additional words in the Treaty requiring connection "for any purpose". He ruled that the use of the word "could" in conjunction with "any purpose" excluded any requirement that there be some substantive issue between the Revenue and the taxpayer other than the availability of the tax credit for the purpose of which the connection arises or is relevant. If there was no other issue, then section 839 as a whole ought to apply and there is no basis for implying a condition that subsection (7) should be excluded.

11-72   The second argument was that the provisions of section 839 generally could not have been intended to apply in a case where there was no

---

[51] Taxes Act 1988, ss. 839(7) and 416.

suggestion that the intermediate company had been set up for the purpose of obtaining a tax credit to which its members were not entitled and the application of the article would remove the entitlement to the tax credit from all the members not merely from that member who by an historical accident was not entitled to it.

This argument was similarly rejected by the Court of Appeal. It was held that the requirement was that the persons in question could be treated as connected for any purpose, not for all purposes. Any purpose would include a limited purpose such as that contemplated by subsection (7) by the words "in relation to the company" as well as the unlimited purposes contemplated by subsection (1).

Morritt L.J. said that these conclusions did not arise from an unduly literal construction of the Treaty. He said that the provision in question is an anti-avoidance measure designed to prevent the artificial creation of entitlement to tax credits under the law of the United Kingdom. That law had several provisions dealing with control, connection and association. He said it was fanciful to suppose that the draftsman of the Treaty intended to restrict the application of those provisions to cases where they already applied or to limit it to those which did not apply.

11-73 The court accepted that the shareholders' agreement and the interposition of EVC between its shareholders and its U.K. subsidiary were not parts of a scheme designed for the purpose of creating an entitlement to a tax credit where none would otherwise exist. The absence of such a purpose did not render the anti-avoidance provision inapplicable.

The taxpayer argued that even if the definition in section 839(7) would apply, the limitation in it that members were to be treated as connected "in relation to that company" took it out of the scope of Article 10(3)(d) of the Treaty. The requirement in that provision of the Treaty, it was argued, was that the persons in question could be treated as connected for any purpose not for all purposes. It was, however, held that any purpose would include a limited purpose such as that stipulated in subsection 839(7).

It was also argued by the taxpayer that the treaty provision should be construed as an anti-avoidance provision and that it should therefore not apply on the basis that the shareholders agreement and the interposition of the Netherlands company between the members of the joint venture and the U.K. subsidiary were not part of a scheme designed for the purpose of creating an entitlement to tax credit when none would otherwise exist. The Court of Appeal concluded that Article 10(3)(d) was of general application and could not be limited to cases of "avoidance" only. Such a construction would confine the general application of the provision to an area smaller than that which the draftsman must have had in mind. This statement in particular confirms that limitation of benefit provisions merely form part of the text of the treaty and are integral conditions to be fulfilled in order to qualify for treaty benefits. No special rules of construction apply by virtue of the fact that they are "anti-avoidance" provisions.

11-74 The common feature of these cases is that no general anti-treaty shopping doctrine appears to exist under U.K. law. A number of theories about the application of treaties in this area have been argued both by the Revenue and taxpayers in these cases. The courts have, however, relied largely on the plain meaning of words in coming to their conclusions whether they favoured allowing treaty benefits or not. In the *Euro Vinyls* case the Courts were concerned with construing a limitation of benefits provision. In the *Commerzbank* case, they were concerned with construing a treaty provision which was not limited to residents of contracting states. A further feature in common is that the courts relied on the natural and ordinary meaning of the words. The application of a more purposive approach, as adopted in *IRC v. Exxon Corporation*[52] for example, may well have produced different results.

The *Ramsay* doctrine

11-75   Is there a relationship between domestic jurisprudence relating to tax avoidance and treaty shopping in the United Kingdom? The question of treaty shopping in the context of domestic anti-avoidance doctrine has not come directly before the courts. The precise scope of the doctrine annunciated in *Ramsay v. IRC*[53] and *Furniss v. Dawson*[54] and the following line of cases and its application to limit access to treaty benefits is frequently asked but as yet unanswered. The line of cases has given rise to sufficient difficulties as to its precise scope and application under domestic law which make a full analysis of the line of cases beyond the scope of this work. The Inland Revenue have given some indication that they will seek to apply these rules to treaty shopping.[55] A number of comments are however pertinent to any discussion on this subject.

It is clear that as a rule, treaties override domestic enactments.[56] However, since the characterisation of the *Dawson* principles as merely a rule of construction as stated by the House of Lords on several occasions in *Craven v. White*,[57] the question arises as to whether these rules of construction may be applied to treaties in the same manner as they are applied to construe domestic enactments. More recently, Lord Steyn in *IRC v. McGuckian*[58] described the principle as one "developed as a matter of statutory construction". He said: "it was founded on a broad purposive interpretation giving effect to the intention of Parliament". Lord Hoffman said in *Macniven v. Westmoreland Investments Ltd*[59]: "Everyone agrees that *Ramsay* is a principle of construction". He continued[60]:

> "There is ultimately only one principle of construction, namely to ascertain what Parliament meant by using the language of the statute. All other 'principles of construction' can be no more than guides to which past judges have put forward, some more helpful and insightful than others, to assist in the task of interpretation".

---

[52] See above, n. 33.
[53] [1981] S.T.C. 174.
[54] [1984] S.T.C. 153.
[55] See Inland Revenue, *International Tax Handbook*, para. 708.
[56] Taxes Act 1988, s. 788(3); *General Reinsurance Co. Limited v. Tomlinson* (1970) 48 T.C. 81; *Ostime v. Australian Mutual Provident Society* (1960) 38 T.C. 492.
[57] [1988] S.T.C. 476, HL.
[58] [1997] S.T.C. 908, HL at 916.
[59] [2001] S.T.C. 237, HL, at para. 28.
[60] At para. 29.

11-76   Is there a difference in principle in the application of the rules on the construction of treaties sufficiently different from those applied to domestic taxing statutes to suggest that this should not be the case?[61] The fact that the *Ramsay* doctrine is a rule of construction does not itself automatically import the approach into treaty interpretation, although a purposive approach is consistent with the rules to treaty interpretation. The *Ramsay* doctrine is by its nature a developing one and particularly in the light of *Westmoreland* its application difficult to predict.

A number of fact patterns in the *Ramsay* line of cases bear a striking similarity to the classic treaty shopping structure. In the *Dawson* case,[62] a non-resident company was interposed between U.K. resident shareholders and U.K. resident operating companies immediately prior to the sale of the operating companies. The intended tax consequence was deferral of gain on the sale of the shares until the sale of the shares of the non-resident company by the shareholders. The facts in *Craven v. White*[63] were very similar.

11-77   Likewise in *Piggott v. Staines Investments Ltd*,[64] a company was interposed between the parent and an operating subsidiary. Dividends were paid by the operating company to the intermediate company under a group income election.

It is not difficult to imagine transactions in an international context where the relief sought from U.K. tax is a treaty benefit rather than one under domestic law. If the speech of Lord Oliver in *Craven v. White*[65] is adopted as the essential elements of the rule where a series of transactions containing an intermediate transaction is designed to avoid tax:

(1)   the series of transactions must at the time when the intermediate transaction was entered into have been preordained in order to produce a given result;

(2)   the intermediate transaction has no other purposes than tax mitigation;

(3)   there was no practical likelihood at that time that the pre-planned events would not take place in the order ordained, so that the intermediate transaction was not even contemplated practically as having an independent life; and

(4)   the preordained events did in fact take place.

11-78   In such circumstances, he said that the court can be justified in linking the beginning with the end so as to make a single composite whole to which the physical results of the single composite whole are to be applied. It would therefore appear that the archetypal treaty shopping operation which involves the interposition of a company in a particular contracting

---

[61] Commentary on Art.1 para. 7 OECD Model Treaty might support the inclusion of the doctrine.
[62] See above, n. 54.
[63] See above, n. 57.
[64] [1995] S.T.C. 114, Ch.D.
[65] [1988] S.T.C. 507, HL.

state by residents of a third state for no purpose other than to secure the treaty benefit may be a candidate for attack under this line of cases. Here the issue would be whether a company which is able to demonstrate that it otherwise qualifies for treaty benefits as a resident, ought nonetheless to be denied those benefits under the *Ramsay* doctrine. As a counter to this approach, where specific benefits are given by treaty to residents of a contracting state, the Inland Revenue cannot complain that a fiscal advantage has been secured where the taxpayer has complied with all of the requirements of the treaty. This is by analogy to the statements of Lord Templeman in *Reed v. Nova Securities Ltd*[66] and Lord Nolan in *IRC v. Willoughby*.[67] Thus where a treaty benefit has been intentionally conferred on a resident of a contracting state the benefit should not be denied. The rejection of the Crown's formulation of the *Ramsay* approach in *Westmoreland*[68] and its reformulation based on a distinction between commercial and legal concepts in the legislation may however fit more appropriately within current approaches to treaty interpretation.

11-79   There are circumstances when an intermediate company is inserted for reasons other than tax. In the treaty shopping context one of the additional points that will need to be established is not only that an intermediary company was used but that the intermediary was specifically established in the particular country in order to take advantage of the treaty in question. In the *Euro Vinyls* case,[69] it is noteworthy that the joint venture vehicle was a Netherlands company. Its shareholders were Italian, German, Swiss and U.K. companies. There was no other obvious connection with the Netherlands. Indeed its co-ordination centre/administrative headquarters were in Brussels. Clearly some attention was paid to the tax planning aspects.

In that case, the Court of Appeal noted that there was no suggestion that the intermediate company EVC had been set up for the purpose of obtaining a tax credit to which its members were not entitled. The point was not argued and Morritt L. J. assumed that the shareholders' agreement and the interposition of the Netherlands company were not parts of a scheme designed for the purpose of creating an entitlement to tax credit where none would otherwise exist. In that case the Revenue were content to rest their case on the wording of the Treaty. However, the fact that there was no suggestion that the company was interposed for "no commercial (business) purpose apart from the avoidance of liability to tax" indicates that perhaps in some cases the selection of a suitable treaty jurisdiction alone will not render the structure liable to attack under this doctrine.

11-80   As stated, in the *Euro Vinyls* case, the Inland Revenue were content to rest their argument on the wording of the treaty. Where specific limitation of benefits provisions have been included, is it open to the Inland Revenue to argue the *Dawson* approach? In the exchange of correspondence between the ICAEW and the Inland Revenue of September 25, 1985, the

---

[66] [1985] S.T.C. 124 at 131.
[67] See above, n. 32.
[68] See above, n. 59, at paras 28, 29.
[69] See above, n. 50.

Revenue expressed the view that both approaches are available to them. In *Bird v. IRC*,[70] it was suggested that the Revenue could not rely both on the statutory anti-avoidance provision and the *Dawson* approach in respect of the same transaction. In *McGuckian*, the application of statutory anti-avoidance provisions was upheld under *Ramsay* principles. Most treaties today contain some limitation of benefit provisions, although they only apply to specific articles and therefore there may be circumstances where this argument will be applicable.

AVOIDANCE AND EUROPEAN COMMUNITY LAW

11-81 In the context of treaty shopping, questions arise as to whether Community law may invalidate anti-treaty shopping provisions contained in the national law of Member States or treaties. The most important question is whether provisions inserted in treaties designed to limit the entitlement of residents of a contracting state which is an EU Member State can be upheld.

The Ruding Committee report in its consideration of treaty aspects of european tax harmonisation gave particular attention to benefit limitation provisions. It noted that such provisions, though designed to minimise treaty shopping, can discriminate against enterprises of other Member States. It also observed that despite this, Member States continued to conclude treaties with such provisions. Similar views have been expressed by the Commission on several occasions. In the Commission's communication to the Council and to the European Parliament of June 26, 1992, reporting its conclusions on the Ruding Committee,[71] the Commission undertook to ensure that treaties which Member States conclude between each other and with non member countries are strictly in accordance with the principle of non-discrimination. In an Information Release at the time, the Commission said that treaties concluded with non member countries must be strictly in accordance with EC law and the Commission is to ensure that this position is observed.[72] Speaking at the time, the Taxation Commissioner Mrs Scrivener said that the Commission is studying treaties to consider if they disadvantaged companies in other Member States.

11-82 In reply to a parliamentary question, the Commission indicated that Community law did not require a Member State to grant automatically the withholding tax rate of its most favoured bilateral agreement to taxpayers of another Member State which was not covered by that agreement.[73] On this basis, taxpayers of Member States are limited to claiming the treaties concluded by the Member State in which they are resident only. Thus, while they may be able to access treaties indirectly through the establishment of companies in other Member States, they have no entitlement to the application of more beneficial treaties concluded by the Member States directly.

In *EC Commission v. France*,[74] the ECJ considered whether France was in

---

[70] [1985] S.T.C. 584, Ch.D.
[71] (SECTION 92)/118 Final.
[72] Commission Information Release dated June 24, 1992.
[73] [1993] OJ C40/93.
[74] Case 270/83 [1986] E.C.R. 273.

breach of its obligations under the EC Treaty, in particular Article 43 (ex 52), by not granting the benefit of shareholders' tax credits to branches and agencies in France of insurance companies established in other Member States. The ECJ ruled that by virtue of Article 43 (ex 52), freedom of establishment for nationals of one Member State on the territory of another includes the right to take up and pursue activities and to set up and manage undertakings under the conditions laid down for its own nationals.

11-83   The French Government argued that difference in treatment arose by virtue of differences between the tax systems of Member States and the existence of tax treaties. Different measures are necessary in each case, it argued, in order to take account of the differences between taxation systems which ought to be justified under Article 43 (ex 52). The tax rules in question were governed by double taxation treaties between the relevant Member States whose existence is expressly recognised in Article 293 (ex 220) of the EC Treaty. Furthermore, the rules which were contested were necessary in particular to prevent tax avoidance.

On the role of tax treaties, the ECJ held that rights conferred by Article 43 (ex 52) are unconditional and a Member State cannot make them subject to the contents of an agreement concluded with another Member State. This clear statement has been reaffirmed in subsequent cases.[75] In particular Article 43 (ex 52) does not permit those rights to be made subject to a condition of reciprocity imposed for the purposes of obtaining corresponding advantages in other Member States. Consequently provisions in treaties between Member States that do not comply with Community law cannot stand. The court also rejected the risk of tax avoidance as justification in this context. It held that Article 43 (ex 52) does not permit any derogation from the fundamental principle of freedom of establishment on such a ground.

11-84   Tax avoidance as a justification for limiting fundamental rights under the EC Treaty was also rejected by the ECJ in *ICI v. Colmer*.[76] This was put beyond doubt in *Metallgesellschaft Ltd and others v. CIR and Hoechst AG and another v. CIR*, when it was said[77]: "it is settled case law that diminution of tax revenue cannot be regarded as a matter of overriding general interest which may be relied upon in order to justify a measure which is, in principle, contrary to a fundamental freedom". If this statement correctly reflects European law, then no limitation of benefit provisions which interfere with rights under the EC Treaty and in particular Article 43 (ex 52) will be valid. Secondary European legislation does, however, authorise anti-avoidance provisions. Examples in relation to direct taxation are found in the Mutual Assistance Directive,[78] the Mergers Directive,[79] Article 11, and the Parent-Subsidiary Directive,[80] Article 1(2). One possible way to view these enactments is that in the light of the deci-

---

[75] For example, Case C-330/91 *R. v. IRC, ex parte Commerzbank AG* [1993] S.T.C. 605, Advocate General's opinion.
[76] Case C-264/96 [1998] S.T.C. 874.
[77] Joined Cases C-397/98 and C-410/98 [2001] S.T.C. 452, at para. 59.
[78] Directive 77/799, 19 December 1977 [1977] O.J. L336/15.
[79] Directive 90/434, 19 December 1977 [1990] O.J. L225/1.
[80] Directive 90/435, 23 July 1990 [1990] O.J. L225/6.

sions in *EC Commission v. France*[81] and *ICI v. Colmer*,[82] such provisions require legislative authority.

In two cases, Advocates General have argued the contrary position. In *Bachmann v. Belgium*, the Advocate General argued[83] that the approach taken by the ECJ in the *France* case should not be upheld. In the *Bachmann* case, he noted that the issue concerned a rule applying without distinction to nationals and non-nationals. This, he said, is lawful if it is objectively justified despite the fact that it is principally non-nationals who are disadvantaged by it. He noted that it is possible to devise machinery which obviates the risk of evasion [avoidance?].[84] In that case, an absolute bar to the deduction of contributions made to insurance companies went beyond what was objectively necessary to achieve the intended aim. On this argument, provisions which are solely limited to preventing evasion [avoidance?] would appear to be justifiable. In its judgment, the ECJ did not address this issue.

11-85 In commenting on this question in *Finanzamt Köln-Altstadt v. Schumacker*,[85] the Advocate General noted again at paragraph 45 that the test for permitting a discriminatory tax law to be upheld is if it is an objective in the public interest such as upholding the coherence of the national tax system and is strictly necessary in order to achieve that aim. In that case, the Danish Government had submitted, in support of the German position, that the discrimination in question was justifiable because there was a risk of "fiscal forum shopping" where taxpayers would chose to establish in the state where taxation is most favourable. The Advocate General concluded that on the issues in that case, treating non-residents and residents alike because of their similarity of circumstances would in fact render the choice of residence neutral from the tax point of view. Again, the ECJ did not comment specifically on these issues, other than to say that the distinction argued for was not justifiable by the need to ensure the cohesion of the tax system.

11-86 In *Wielockx v. Inspecteur der Directe Belastingen*,[86] the ECJ ruled that although a Member State is entitled to rely on the principle of fiscal cohesion in such circumstances, it may also waive that right. Treaties following Article 18 of the OECD Model including the Belgium–Netherlands Treaty provide that pensions and similar remuneration in consideration of past employment are only taxable in the state of residence. This article constitutes such a waiver. Thus, fiscal cohesion is not established in relation to that taxpayer in respect of a correlation between deductibility of contributions and the taxation of pensions. This occurs where such a treaty provision is present and the Member State has waived the right to tax pensions received abroad (*i.e.* by non-residents) even if they are derived from deductible contributions paid in the territory of a Member State. The treaty therefore establishes fiscal cohesion at another level, namely, that of the

---

[81] See above, n. 74.
[82] See above, n. 76.
[83] [1994] S.T.C. 855 at 873, para. 26.
[84] The word "evasion" appears in the English version. "Avoidance" is referred to in the *France* case.
[85] Case C-279/93 [1995] S.T.C. 306.
[86] Case C-80/94 [1995] S.T.C. 876.

reciprocity of the rules applied in the contracting states. Where fiscal cohesion is secured in respect of reciprocity of rules in a treaty with another Member State, domestic fiscal cohesion may not be relied upon to justify the refusal of a deduction as in this case.

11-87   The *Wielockx* case seems to stand for the proposition that once a Member State has waived fiscal cohesion in respect of its domestic tax system the issue of fiscal cohesion can only be considered in relation to reciprocal treatment given by the contracting states to each other in the treaty. One way of viewing limitation of benefits rules is that their effect is to grant reciprocal treatment conditional on the limitation criteria being met. Thus domestic cohesion is not fully waived. Even if the limitation provisions themselves are reciprocal and viewed as establishing cohesion at the treaty level, the same tests would seem to be applicable if discriminatory provisions are to be justified. In the context of treaty shopping, the issue is whether limitation provisions that prevent residents of one Member State claiming treaty benefits in relation to another Member State are valid if the effect of those provisions is to limit the rights of residents of a third Member State under the EC Treaty.

In the *Wielockx* case, the Advocate General while noting that establishing a coherent tax system is a legitimate objective in the sense that it may justify restrictions on fundamental rights, observed that it does not determine which particular forms of limitation are acceptable. He viewed the test as one of proportionality as set out in *Bachmann v. Belgium*,[87] namely are the measures essential to protect the cohesion of the system. Since preventing tax avoidance has not been accepted as a legitimate objective in justifying otherwise illegal discrimination, even this limited defence is of little significance.

Limitation of benefit provisions susceptible to invalidation

11-88   No cases have come before the European Court of Justice on the validity of provisions of a treaty, which might limit entitlement to claim benefits by residents of contracting states, nor on similar provisions under domestic law. Therefore, any views on their likely validity or otherwise must be tentative. There are several provisions of the EC Treaty that may potentially impact on limitation of benefit provisions generally. In this chapter, the focus is on Article 43 (ex 52) because it is normally the participation by non-residents of the country where the intermediate company is found in the ownership or control of that company that gives rise to the controversy.

Look-through rules

11-89   Look-through provisions appear to be the most easily impugned under European law. A similar concept was examined by the ECJ in *R. v. Secretary of State for Transport, ex parte Factortame Ltd.*[88] The case involved "quota hopping" a concept that might be regarded as analogous to treaty shopping. This involved the formation of companies in the United Kingdom by Spanish nationals. The directors and shareholders of the com-

---

[87] See above, n. 83.
[88] [1991] 3 All E.R. 769.

panies were mostly Spanish nationals. Fishing vessels which had previously been registered in Spain were re-registered as British vessels under the Merchant Shipping Act 1894. The purpose of this was to enable Spanish fishermen to access British fishing quotas.

According to the U.K. Government, these companies lacked any genuine link to the United Kingdom. As a result new legislation was introduced in 1988 limiting eligibility for registration on a new register of British fishing vessels. Fishing vessels were only eligible to be re-registered if the vessel was British owned, managed and its operations were directed and controlled from within the United Kingdom. Similarly any charterer or manager or operator of the vessel had to be a qualified person or company. Both legal and beneficial ownership in the vessel had to vest with a qualified person or companies.

11-90 A qualified company was one incorporated in the United Kingdom with its principal place of business there and with a minimum of 75 per cent legal and beneficial ownership by qualified persons. At least 75 per cent of the directors also had to be qualified persons.

A qualified person was a British citizen, resident and domiciled in the United Kingdom or a U.K. local authority. Administrative discretion was granted to dispense with nationality in the case of long term residents who had lengthy involvement in the U.K. fishing industry.

The ECJ held that it was contrary to Community law and Article 52 of the EC Treaty in particular to impose conditions requiring the legal and beneficial owners, charterers, managers and operators to be U.K. resident and domiciled nationals. In the case of a company the requirements that shareholders and directors be resident and domiciled was unjustifiable discrimination on grounds of nationality.

11-91 The court, however, ruled that it is not contrary to Community law for Member States to require as a condition for registration that the vessel must be managed and its operations directed and controlled from within that Member State. The court pointed out that this requirement in relation to the Member State of registration essentially coincides with the concept of establishment within the meaning of Article 52. The right of establishment must be exercised in order for the benefits of Article 52 to be claimed. Therefore the concept of freedom of establishment cannot be interpreted as precluding such a requirement. The ECJ noted that this requirement would breach Community law if it was interpreted as precluding registration where a secondary establishment or centre for directing the operations of the vessel in the Member State acted on instructions from a decision-taking centre located in the Member State of the principal establishment.

All the rules relating to the U.K. look-through provisions are defined by reference to shareholding. The look-through provisions in the Danish Treaty appear most likely to be vulnerable to attack. This is because no unlisted Danish company controlled by anyone other than Danish residents, themselves entitled to treaty benefits, will qualify for relief from U.K. tax on interest or royalties. Thus a Danish company controlled by residents of any other Member State will not qualify for relief under any circumstances.

11-92 Other aspects of the look-through rules are also vulnerable to attack. In listed company test contained in both the Danish and Netherlands

Treaties, qualifying companies must be quoted on the Stock Exchange in their country of residence. Quotation on another European Stock Exchange is insufficient.

In the Netherlands Treaty, a number of complex issues arise. For example, a Netherlands company controlled by EAA nationals would appear to qualify for benefits under Article 10 by virtue of Taxes Act 1988, section 278(2)(a). This would not be so in all cases where it is controlled by companies resident in the Member States that do not themselves qualify for repayment of tax credits. Similarly, a Netherlands company controlled by company in a Member State where it did qualify for the tax credit would also be disqualified if it in turn is controlled by another company in or outside the EU which did not qualify. The application of the associated or connected persons test might also be vulnerable to attack where its effect is to deprive EU nationals of benefits by virtue of their association or connection with non-qualifying persons. The Protocol to the Danish Treaty signed on October 16, 1996 is, no doubt, a response to these concerns.

11-93   The Ruding Committee report expressed the view that Article 16 of the 1981 U.S. Model Treaty, a look-through provision, could be discriminatory under European principles. At the time, the Commission said that treaties concluded with non member countries must be strictly in accordance with EC law and the Commission is to ensure that this position is observed.[89] Speaking at the time, the Taxation Commissioner Mrs Scrivener said that the Commission was studying treaties to consider if they disadvantaged companies in other Member States. Mrs Scrivener indicated that she preferred a "softly-softly approach" and would not act precipitously.[90] No specific comments have been made public on this to date. A question on this subject by Gijs de Vries MEP in 1990 remains unanswered by the Commission.[91] The main proponent of the look-through approach is the United States and the Commission is perhaps unwilling to raise the political stakes on the issue.

Excluded entities

11-94   The analysis in respect of the look-through rules emphasise that rules which disadvantage ownership of companies by residents of other Member States are open to attack. The rules relating to excluded entities are often inserted in treaties, because of the combination of tax favoured status and the fact that those entities may only be owned by non-residents of the contracting state. The only ineligible entity within the EU referred to in U.K. treaties is the Luxembourg holding company (Luxembourg, Article 30).[92] Would such a company owned by other Member State residents or nationals be entitled to treaty benefits? Such rules may be distinguished from the look-through rules. In particular, the look-through rules are of general application to all companies in a Member State while the excluded entity rule only applies to a single tax favoured form of entity. There is a stronger argument that excluding such specific tax favoured entities from treaty benefits are

---

[89] Commission Information Release dated June 24, 1992.
[90] *Financial Times World Tax Report* (July 1992), p.122.
[91] Written question, September 5, 1990, No. 2046/90, [1991] OJ C-79/28.
[92] Luxembourg Treaty, Art.30.

strictly necessary to maintain the cohesion of the tax system at the treaty level and that in respect of such entities, there has been no waiver of cohesion.

"Subject to tax" basis

11-95   Other approaches to limitation of benefits which do not rely on identifying the ownership of a treaty claimant are less likely to be found to contravene European law. Limitations on a "subject to tax" basis as found in the Portugal Treaty[93] ought generally to be compatible with European principles where no double taxation occurs. This might limit a treaty claim by a Madeira-based company regardless of ownership which was not subject to tax, for example.

"Bona fide" and "purpose" provisions

11-96   Bona fide and purpose provisions do not prima facie discriminate on the basis of ownership. Most important in the context of treaty shopping is the question whether either bona fide provisions or purpose provisions will be permitted under European law in circumstances where a resident of a third Member State has sought to avail itself of treaty benefits by establishing a company in another Member State where the treaty benefits are more attractive.

Since European law on these topics is at an early stage of development, views in this area are somewhat speculative. A number of possibilities arise, however. For example, treaties with bona fide provisions that refer only to "commercial transactions" and not additionally to transactions made in the ordinary course of making or managing investments, may allow benefits in only limited circumstances. Does Article 43 (ex 52) of the EC Treaty read with Article 48 (ex 58) require that the bona fide test apply to investment transactions as well as commercial transactions? Similarly, do the more recent purpose-based provisions which do not contain a separate bona fide defence, contravene the doctrine of proportionality?

11-97   In the context of Article 1(2) of the Parent-Subsidiary Directive, the European Court of Justice held in the *Denkavit* and related cases[94] that the article is aimed in particular at counteracting abuse where holdings are taken in the capital of companies for the sole purpose of benefiting from the tax advantages available and which are not intended to be lasting. The case is not a detailed consideration of the concept of abuse or avoidance under European law. It is perhaps indicative of the fact that a sole or main purpose test reflects European principles.

Where bona fide or purpose clauses are applied in such a way that they effectively discriminate against companies owned or controlled by residents of another Member State, they may well be liable to attack. In *Sotgiu v. Deutsche Bundespost*,[95] the ECJ held that the rules regarding equality of

---

[93] See Art.10(2) "Dividends", Art.11(2) "Interest", Art.12(2) "Royalties" and Art.20 "Other income".

[94] Joined Cases C-283/94, C-291/94 and C-292/94 *Denkavit International BV, VITIC Amsterdam BV and Vormeer BV v. Bundesampt Für Finanzen* [1996] S.T.C. 1445.

[95] Case 152/73 [1974] E.C.R. 153.

treatment forbid not only overt discrimination by reason of nationality, but also all covert forms of discrimination which by the application of other criteria of differentiation lead in fact to this same result.

The doctrine of covert discrimination in the context of corporate taxpayers was first relied on by the ECJ in *R. v. IRC, ex parte Commerzbank AG.*[96] Similarly, unacceptable covert discrimination was found in *Halliburton Services BV v. Staatssecretaris van Financiën.*[97] There, a Dutch company was excluded from benefiting from a tax exemption because the transferor of land was a German company. The discrimination in these two cases was intrinsic to the rules in question. Arguably however, even if bona fide and purpose provisions are not *per se* discriminatory, their application to certain fact patterns may well be. In particular, if the facts that are alleged to give rise to the tax avoidance purpose are no more than ownership or control by nationals or residents of another Member State, impermissible discrimination may arise.

Burden of proof

11-98 Incompatibility with European law may arise in more indirect or subtle ways. For example, the current view of the Inland Revenue is that the burden of proving entitlement to treaty benefits rests with the claimant. This burden of proof includes satisfying the limitation of benefit provisions which are of general application. If this approach amounts to a presumption of abuse, it could well be contrary to European law. For example in the *Denkavit* and related cases,[98] Advocate General Jacobs noted that a presumption of abuse until the contrary is proved is incompatible with European law on the basis of proportionality. This argument was made by the Commission in that case. The ECJ in its judgment did not deal expressly with this point, but simply ruled that there was no fraud or abuse inherent in the payment of a dividend prior to expiry of the 12 month holding period, where in fact the shares are subsequently held for at least that time. The ECJ considered the application of the presumption of tax avoidance or evasion where a transaction is not carried out for valid commercial reasons in the context of the Mergers Directive in *Leur-Bloem v. Inspecteur der Belastingdienst.*[99] It held that in the absence of more detailed Community provisions, it is for Member States to determine what is needed for the purpose of applying this provision, subject to Member States observing the principle of proportionality. In applying this principle to the right of free movement of capital under Article 56 (ex 73b) of the EC Treaty, the ECJ held in *EC Commission v. Belgium*[1] that a general presumption of tax avoidance cannot justify a general fiscal measure inconsistent with the exercise of a fundamental freedom. Thus, although Article 58 (ex 73d) permits measures to prevent tax avoidance, a presumption of avoidance did not meet the requirement of proportionality.

---

[96] Case C-330/91 [1993] S.T.C. 605.
[97] Case C-1/93 [1994] S.T.C. 655.
[98] See above, n. 94.
[99] Case C-28/95 [1997] S.T.C. 1205.
[1] Case C-478/98 [2000] S.T.C. 830.

Directive shopping

11-99 The Parent-Subsidiary Directive 90/435 and the Mergers Directive 90/434 which entered into force on January 1, 1992 created the potential for a new form of international tax planning activity which might be called "directive shopping". The Parent-Subsidiary Directive is of particular interest, both because it occupies the same area covered by Articles 10 and 23 of the OECD Model and because treaty shopping in respect of dividend arrangements is not uncommon. The interpretation and application of the Directive may also be helpful in relation to analogous treaty issues. It is worth noting that the Parent-Subsidiary Directive has not adopted the requirement of "beneficial ownership" as found in the OECD Model. Other aspects of the OECD Model are also missing such as a reference to dividends (it covers "distributions of profits").

The basic principle of the Directive is that there should be no withholding or other tax on distributions of profits made by a subsidiary in one Member State to a parent company in another. The jurisdiction of the parent company receiving such distributions must eliminate double taxation on profits either by exempting the distributions received from tax or granting to the parent company a full credit for any underlying corporate tax. These arrangements are enacted in order to harmonise corporate taxes and to ensure fiscal neutrality in corporate structures within the European Union.

Two issues arise in relation to directive shopping. The first is the extent to which a corporate entity established within the European Union may be used as an intermediary to take advantage of a more favourable manner in which it has been implemented by a particular Member State, either unilaterally or by treaty. The second is the extent to which taxpayers established outside the Community can utilise the Directive. In this case, the fiscal motivation would be to benefit from the combination of the application of the Directive and favourable treaty arrangements between particular Member States which would not be available if investment from outside the Community were made directly to the Member State or States concerned.

11-100 The Parent-Subsidiary Directive contains its own limitation provisions.[2] In order to qualify for the benefits of the Directive, a company must be one of the forms specified in the Directive established under the laws of a Member State. Secondly, it must be treated as a resident of a Member State for the tax purposes of that state. Thirdly, it must not be treated as a resident of a non EU country by virtue of a treaty concluded with a third state. Fourthly, it must be subject to corporation tax without the possibility of an option or have been exempt. Whilst these rules clearly prohibit non EU incorporated or resident company from benefiting from the Directive, there is no express prohibition on non EU owned companies benefiting from the Directive.

The principal anti-avoidance of provision[3] simply states that the Directive does not preclude the application of domestic or agreement-based provisions required for the prevention of fraud or abuse. The

---

[2] Article 2.
[3] Article 1(2).

wording of this article is somewhat unclear. For example, it is unclear whether the provisions are intended to apply specifically to fraud or abuse of the Directive, or more generally to fraud or abuse of the tax laws of the Member State in question, or indeed of the tax laws of another Member State.

11-101 The Directive does not explain what is meant by the terms "fraud" or "abuse". The then European Commissioner responsible for taxation, Mrs Christiane Scrivener, has stated that the Community has no intention of adopting a common definition of tax evasion at least for the purposes of the Mutual Assistance Directive,[4] and that this is a matter to be left entirely to the Member State concerned. The first views on this expressed by the European Court of Justice in the *Denkavit* case would suggest that the court will not simply leave this issue for Member States.

In the *Denkavit* case,[5] the ECJ rejected an argument of the German Government that its requirement that a shareholding be held for a minimum of 12 months before a dividend qualified for the withholding tax exemption could be justified on the basis of Article 1(2). It does not regard this rule as one required for the prevention of fraud or abuse. In coming to this conclusion, the court held that Article 1(2) is aimed in particular at counteracting abuse whereby holdings are taken in the capital of companies for the sole purpose of benefiting from the tax advantages available and which are not intended to be lasting.

11-102 The United Kingdom has not enacted any anti-avoidance provisions prohibiting non-EU companies from directive shopping, neither for inward nor outward-bound distributions.

The Mergers Directive[6] adopts the same requirements for companies to qualify as that adopted in the Parent-Subsidiary Directive. It adopts a far more specific limitation of benefits provision which is not dissimilar from a number of U.K. anti-avoidance provisions. Article 11(1)(a) permits the exclusion of benefits of the Directive for a transaction which has "as its principal objective or as one of its principal objectives tax evasion or tax avoidance".

It also adopts a form of "bona fide" test. It prescribes that if the transaction in question is not carried out for valid commercial reasons, this may constitute a presumption that the transaction has tax evasion or avoidance as its principal objective or as one of its principal objectives. This wording has been translated into U.K. enacting legislation as "bona fide commercial reasons which do not form part of a scheme or arrangements of which the main purpose or one of the main purposes is avoidance of liability to income tax, corporation tax or capital gains tax".[7] This wording follows the existing expressions relating to corporate reorganisations in TCGA 1992, section 137(1). While similar expressions have been considered by U.K. courts, their application will in future be a matter for the ECJ. The fact that the transactions are not carried out for

---

[4] 77/799/EC of December 19, 1977.
[5] See above, n. 94.
[6] Article 3.
[7] See, for example, TCGA 1992, ss. 140B and 140D.

valid commercial reasons may constitute a presumption that the transaction has tax evasion or avoidance as its principal objective or as one of its principal objectives.

11-103   The ECJ has interpreted the provisions of Article 11(1)(a) of the Mergers Directive in the context of a share for share exchange in *Leur-Bloem v. Inspecteur der Belastingdienst.*[8] The taxpayer, an individual resident in the Netherlands, was the sole shareholder and director of two Dutch private companies. She planned to contribute the shares in the two companies to a holding company in exchange for the issue of shares in that company. The taxpayer requested a clearance from the Tax Inspector that the proposed transactions should be treated as a "merger by exchange of shares" within the meaning of the legislation which would have allowed her to exclude from tax gains arising on the transfer of shares in the two companies to the third company and the possibility of setting off losses within the corporate group thus created.

The Inspector took the view that there was no such merger by exchange of shares and that the purpose of the transaction was not to permanently combine the undertaking of the companies in a large single entity from an economic and financial point of view as required by Netherlands law. Such an entity, he argued, already existed from a financial and economic perspective since both companies already had the same director and shareholder.

11-104   Pursuant to Article 2(d) of the Merger Directive, an exchange of shares is an operation whereby a company acquires a holding in the capital of another company such that it obtains a majority of voting rights in that company in exchange for the issue of securities representing the capital of the acquiring company.

Article 11(1)(a) authorises Member States to refuse to apply the benefits of the Directive where there is tax avoidance. This is the case where the transaction has as its principal objective, or as one of its principal objectives, tax evasion or avoidance.

The ECJ noted that the requirement that the companies concerned merge their business permanently into a single unit from a financial and economic point of view was inserted into the Netherlands Rule pursuant to Article 11 of the Mergers Directive. The court noted that Article 2(d) of the Directive laid down clearly that the tax advantages conferred by the Directive must apply without distinction to all mergers, divisions, transfers of assets or exchanges of shares, irrespective of the reasons whether they be financial, economic or simply fiscal.

11-105   As far as the anti-avoidance provisions of Article 11(1)(a) of the Directive is concerned, the court held that it was clear that Member States must grant the tax advantages provided for by the Directive in respect of exchanges of shares referred to in Article 2(d), unless those transactions have, as their principal objective or as one of their principal objectives, tax evasion or avoidance. In order to determine whether the proposed transaction has such an objective the tax authorities cannot confine themselves to

---

[8] Case C-28/95 [1997] S.T.C. 1205.

apply predetermined general criteria but must subject each particular case to a general examination.

In framing its questions to the ECJ, the Dutch court asked whether certain specific criteria could limit the scope of application of exchange of share provisions where:

(1) the acquiring company itself was not carrying on a business;

(2) the same person is the sole shareholder and director of the acquired company and prior to the exchange the director and sole shareholder in the acquiring company of the exchange;

(3) the only effect of the exchange is to merge the business of the acquiring company and that of another permanently in a single unit from a financial and economic point of view;

(4) the only effect of the exchange is to merge the businesses of two or more acquired companies permanently in a single unit from a financial and economic point of view;

(5) the exchange is carried out in order to bring about a horizontal set-off of tax losses between participant undertakings within a fiscal unity contemplated by Dutch law.

11-106   The ECJ noted that the general examination may include all of the first four factors. None of them may be decisive on its own. Thus a merger or restructuring carried out in the form of an exchange of shares involving a newly created holding company which does not have any business may be regarded as having been carried out for valid commercial reasons. Similarly such reasons may render necessary the legal restructuring of companies which already have a form of unity from an economic and financial viewpoint. Even if this does constitute evidence of tax evasion or avoidance it is nevertheless possible that a merger by exchange of shares with the aim of creating a specific structure for a limited period of time and not permanently may have valid commercial reasons.

Laying down a general rule which automatically excludes certain categories of transaction from the tax advantage such as those mentioned by the Netherlands court, whether or not there is actually tax evasion or avoidance, goes further than is necessary in preventing such tax evasion or avoidance and would therefore undermine the aim pursued by the Directive. This would also be the case if a rule of this kind were to be made subject to the mere possibility of the grant of a derogation at the discretion of the administrative authority. The ECJ noted that the general examination of such transactions must be open to judicial review.

11-107   The court ruled that this interpretation is consistent with the aims of both the Directive as a whole and Article 11. According to the preamble, the aim of the Directive is to introduce tax rules which are neutral from the point of view of competition, to allow enterprises to adapt themselves to the requirements of a common market, to increase their productivity and to improve their competitive strengths internationally. Transactions contemplated by the Directive ought not to be hampered by restrictions, disadvantages or distortions arising in particular from the tax provisions of Member States. It is only when a proposed transaction has tax evasion or avoidance as its objective that Member States may refuse to apply the Directive.

The court, however, noted that the concept of "valid commercial reasons" in Article 11 is one which involves more than the attainment of a purely fiscal advantage. Consequently a merger which only has as its aim the horizontal set-off of losses between group companies cannot therefore have a valid commercial reason within Article 11.

CHAPTER 12
Practical Application

12-01   Taxpayers seeking to benefit from the application of treaties are faced with a range of procedures which vary according to the nature of the income or gain, the benefit sought and in some cases the treaty in question.

CLAIM OR SELF-ASSESSMENT OF TREATY BENEFITS

12-02   The precise manner in which treaties have effect varies depending upon the particular income or gain in question. Where the treaty provides for relief from income tax or from corporation tax in respect of income or chargeable gains, a claim for relief must be made to the Board of Inland Revenue.[1]

However, pursuant to Taxes Act 1988, section 788(3), treaties may also provide:

(1)   for charging U.K. income or chargeable gains of non-residents; or

(2)   for determining the income or chargeable gains to be attributed to:

    (a)   non-residents and their agencies, branches or establishments in the United Kingdom; or

    (b)   residents who have special relationships with non-residents; or

(3)   for conferring on non-residents the right to a tax credit in respect of qualifying distributions made to them by U.K. resident companies.

12-03   The legal effect of treaties in domestic law arising out of this obscure legislation is considered in Chapter 1 above. This chapter examines the practical implications as to how treaty benefits may be relied on by taxpayers in dealing with their tax affairs. The first practical question is to decide whether a "claim" needs to be made in order to benefit from a treaty. Although, as has been seen, treaties are generally relieving in nature, the implementing legislation clearly contemplates a distinction between a relief provided by treaty and benefits pursuant to a treaty which it may confer on a taxpayer. The problems with the expression "relief" are illustrated in *Sheppard and another (Trustees of the Woodlands Trust) v. IRC (No. 2)*,[2] and *IRC v. Universities Superannuation Scheme Ltd.*[3] How precisely does the administration of the tax system give effect to this?

---

[1] Taxes Act 1988, ss. 788(3)(a) and 788(6).
[2] [1993] S.T.C. 240 at 254.
[3] [1997] S.T.C. 1 at 17–18.

This answer is significantly altered by the fundamental reform that the administration of direct taxes in the United Kingdom has undergone. These changes are central to the 10 year Change Programme of modernisation and streamlining of the Inland Revenue's administration of the tax system. The Finance Act 1994 introduced self-assessment for individual taxpayers generally with effect from the year of assessment from April 6, 1996. In the case of companies, full self-assessment commenced as respects accounting periods on or after July 1, 1999. Self-assessment requires a tax return to be filed by a fixed date and payment of all income and capital gains tax or profits in the case of companies for the year by fixed dates. More importantly, self-assessment requires taxpayers to form their own conclusions about their liability to tax and to report those conclusions in the form of reported income and gains on the tax return. Compliance is monitored by enquiries into returns and taxpayers will have to retain records and information in order to support the basis on which income and gains are returned. Under the previous system, taxpayers generally provided factual information to the Inland Revenue who then assessed them on the basis of information gathered.

12-04   The precise impact of these reforms on the application of both domestic and treaty law is evolving. Prior to self-assessment, the Revenue gave effect to clams submitted by taxpayers. Under self-assessment, the taxpayer normally gives effect to a claim in a self-assessment return in computing liability.

The full implication of self-assessment of tax liability taken to its logical conclusion is particularly noticeable in relation to non-residents who, but for the provisions of a treaty, would be liable to tax under domestic law and where no tax is deducted at source on payments to them. Where the relevant provisions of a treaty can be said to provide for the "charging of non-residents" and exclude all liability to U.K. tax, then no obligation to notify chargeability should arise. The most important and acute illustration of this arises in relation to the question as to whether a non-resident trading in the United Kingdom, but who by virtue of a treaty does not have a permanent establishment, is required to notify chargeability to tax and to file a tax return. One approach is to say that if the non-resident had no permanent establishment, then notwithstanding the other provisions of the domestic legislation, it is not within the charge to income tax or corporation tax on this account. On this basis, it need not notify chargeability and need not file a return. On the other, if such a person is chargeable pursuant to the domestic provisions and is required to assert that it relies on the benefit of a treaty, is it sufficient simply to assert that fact in the return or is it required to compute its income under domestic law on the return and to assert that it does not have to pay tax on the amounts computed by virtue of the effect of an applicable treaty?

12-05   Much of the difficulty is as a result of the use of a handful of expressions that are used in more than one sense and whose meaning may have changed over time. The argument for saying that the existence or non-existence of a permanent establishment is a provision for "charging United Kingdom income" of non-residents under section 788(3)(b) and that the non-existence of a permanent establishment negates chargeability to tax is compelling. The Inland Revenue *International Tax Handbook* may provide some implicit support for this. It explains that the expressions "charged" and "chargeable" are used in two ways in the Taxes Acts. The first is in the sense of "liable" or "within the charge" to tax as in tax charged on income under Schedule D. The second is in the sense of "assessable" as when tax under Schedule D is charged on the person receiving or entitled to the income. Since, for example, in the permanent establishment context, treaty provisions typically do not impact on the assessment machinery, the existence or non-existence of a permanent establishment does appear to go to the meaning of chargeable in the first sense referred to by the Inland Revenue.[4] The Inland Revenue Handbook also refers to the existence of permanent establishments as "the treaty charge".[5] This is equivalent to the "subject to tax" expression in current OECD Model Treaty parlance.

Where the treaty benefit relied on falls short of a complete exclusion from U.K. tax, the distinction between a claim and any other assertion of an applicable tax rule becomes less significant as the claim is given effect to in a taxpayer's return.

CLAIMS

12-06   Where a claim is to be made it must be in accordance with the procedure for claims generally contained in Taxes Management Act (TMA) 1970, section 42 and Finance Act 1998, Schedule 18, paragraphs 9 and 10 and Part VII for corporation tax. Generally, a claim for a relief or repayment of tax must be for an amount which is quantified at the time when the claim is made.[6] A separate code of rules is provided for claims which are not included in returns.[7]

Time limits

12-07   Time limits for making claims are prescribed generally by TMA 1970, section 43. In the case of income tax, a claim must be made within five years from January 31 next following the year of assessment to which it relates. In the case of corporation tax, a claim must be made within six years from the end of the accounting period to which it relates.[8] Similar time limits are imposed specifically in relation to claims for foreign tax credits provided by treaties under Taxes Act 1988, section 806(1). For claims made after March 21, 2000, claims for credit for foreign tax in respect of income or chargeable gain which falls to be charged for a year of assessment must be made before the fifth anniversary of January 31 next following that year of assessment or, if later, January 31 next following the year of assessment in which the foreign tax is paid. In the case of corporation tax, the claim must be made not more than six years after the end of the accounting period or if

---

[4] *International Tax Handbook*, para. 902.
[5] *ibid.*, para. 849.
[6] TMA 1970, s. 42(1A) and Finance Act 1998, Sched. 18, para. 54 for corporation tax.
[7] TMA 1970, s. 42(11), Sched. 1.
[8] Finance Act 1998, Sched. 18, para. 55.

later one year after the end of the accounting period in which the foreign tax is paid. These changes were made as a result of representations dealing with unusual circumstances in which the foreign tax may be paid too late for credit relief to be claimed within the normal six-year limit. For example, where interest is received on a loan, the loan agreement may specify that interest is paid eight years after the loan is made. It is only then that the foreign tax is paid by means of withholding from the interest payment. Tax may have been charged in the United Kingdom on the interest on an accruals basis from the start of the loan. When the foreign tax is ultimately paid in year eight, a claim for credit relief in relation to that part of the interest in the earliest years would have been outside the normal six-year limit.[9]

12-08 One of the features of self-assessment is that where a taxpayer is required to file a return, a claim may not be made otherwise than being included in the return if it could be made by being so included. Although the full impact of this is as yet unclear, it may mean that non-resident taxpayers required to file a return will not be permitted to make claims for relief earlier than when a return is filed. Consequently, claims for refunds of tax paid in excess of the levels authorised by a treaty may well be delayed until the end of the year of assessment in which the payment is made.

12-09 The amendment of the scope of claims under TMA 1970, section 42[10] may have far-reaching implications in relation to treaty practice. In accordance with section 42(1A), a claim for a relief, allowance or repayment must be for an amount which is quantified at the time when the claim is made. Such claims which are unquantified when they are made are thus excluded. Consequently, an application for relief at source in relation to future payments may no longer be a claim properly so called where the amount is not quantified. This may be the case in relation to interest where the amount is not determined in advance or royalties which may vary according to the terms of the licence agreement.

Documentation

12-10 There are no non-tax procedures, such as registration with other authorities, as a pre-condition to entitlement to treaty relief. Generally, excessive documentation or evidence is not required to support a claim. However, unlike the approach to self-assessment in relation to domestic law, supporting evidence is required in some cases.

Published Inland Revenue materials indicate the documentation required for normal claims in relation to dividends, interest and royalties. Wide power to call for documents for the purpose of enquiries exists.[11] Where a claim is made which is not included in a return in respect of residence, ordinary residence or domicile, evidence may be required on affidavit.[12]

Where the Inland Revenue question the validity of the claim, further

[9] The effect of the wording of s. 806(1) before Finance Act 2000 was considered by the Court of Appeal in *Commercial Union Assurance Co. v. Shore* [1999] S.T.C. 109 at 117.
[10] By Finance Act 1995, s. 107(1).
[11] TMA 1970, s. 19A in relation to returns and Sched. 1A, para. 6 in relation to claims not included in returns.
[12] TMA 1970, Sched. 1A, para. 2(6).

evidence may be required to demonstrate the claimant's fulfilment of the treaty requirements. If the matter is disputed on appeal to the Special Commissioners, the rules of evidence may apply.[13] In *Forth Investments Ltd v. IRC*,[14] the Inland Revenue rejected a claim under the Barbados Treaty for repayment of the dividend tax credit on the basis that they were not satisfied that the claimant company was a resident of Barbados. When the matter came before the Special Commissioners, the claimant sought to rely on statements made by the secretary of the company as to the residence of the company and a certificate of residence signed by the Deputy Commissioner for Inland Revenue in Barbados. The Special Commissioners held that both documents were hearsay and thus inadmissible as evidence of the residence of the company. They further declined to exercise their discretion under the rules of court[15] to admit them in evidence because of the company's long delay in prosecuting its appeal and failure to comply with procedural rules which permitted the admission of hearsay evidence on a discretionary basis. The High Court upheld the Commissioners' decision and ruled that the exercise of discretion not to admit the documents under the rules of court was not unreasonable in the circumstances.

12-11   The Special Commissioners, in their decision, noted with surprise the argument of the Inland Revenue that a certificate of residence provided by the tax administration of a contracting state, the form of which the Inland Revenue themselves prescribed, should be excluded as hearsay. They found it incongruous that such a certificate should be available as evidence to the Inland Revenue, but denied to the appellate body whose function it was to review the Inland Revenue decisions. Nonetheless they concluded that the certificate was hearsay under existing law. The rule against hearsay was abolished by the Civil Evidence Act 1995, although the Act continues to impose procedural requirements in respect of such evidence. The rules of evidence before the Special Commissioners are less formal and the Revenue will find it more difficult to exclude such evidence. Other challenges on the basis of the weight of foreign official certification may also be difficult.

Problems can occasionally arise when original documents may be required for other purposes. Some cases, notably dividends and payments made under deduction of tax at source, including interest and royalties, require original vouchers according to forms and guidance notes. In the context of individual self-assessment tax returns, the treaty claim form attached to Inland Revenue Helpsheet IR304 now contains a box to tick if original documents are to be returned. Other older claim forms do not offer this.

Where documents may be subject to U.K. stamp duty if they are brought into the United Kingdom,[16] liability to stamp duty would arise in circumstances where the original document is required by the Inland Revenue. Copies are stated to be sufficient for this purpose in relation to intercompany royalty and interest payments.[17] Recently, the Inland Revenue have

---

[13] Special Commissioners (Jurisdiction and Procedure) Regulations 1994 (S.I. 1994 No. 1811), reg. 17(4), (17).
[14] [1976] S.T.C. 399 Ch.D.
[15] Rules of the Supreme Court (S.I. 1965 No. 1776) Ord. 38, r.29.
[16] Stamp Act 1891, s. 14.
[17] Inland Revenue pamphlet FD/CW.

announced that if documents are to be relied upon by a person in support of any claim to relief, or otherwise used in evidence in relation to any liability to tax, or the amount thereof, the Revenue cannot be compelled to accept in support of such claim or as evidence unstamped originals or conformed unstamped copies of documents.[18]

DEDUCTION AT SOURCE

12-12   The withholding of tax by a payer on payments to non-residents is found in a variety of different circumstances under domestic law. The obligation to deduct tax imposed on a payer is a separate issue from the liability of the payee to tax thereon. Consequently, in U.K. practice, the treaty benefit in relation to a non-resident payee is that of the payee only and not that of the payer. Qualifying non-residents are able to benefit from treaties in two ways:

(1)   where tax is deducted at source giving rise to a tax liability on the part of the payee in excess of that authorised by treaty, a claim may be made by the payee for repayment of the excess as described above;

(2)   a variety of rules and arrangements permit payees either to make payments without deduction of tax or at rates authorised by treaty. These rules vary according to the source of income.

The procedure for obtaining treaty benefits is generally the same in relation to deduction at source, the difference being simply whether the relief is given at the time of payment or by subsequent refund. The Board of Inland Revenue are authorised to make regulations generally for carrying out the provisions of Taxes Act 1988, section 788 and treaties.[19] Specific authority is given to provide in regulations for securing that relief from taxation does not enure for the benefit of persons not entitled to such relief. Regulations may also be made to address circumstances where tax deductible from any payment has not been deducted in order purportedly to comply with any treaty and it is discovered that the treaty did not apply to that payment. The recovery of tax by assessment on the person entitled to the payment or by deduction from subsequent payments may be authorised by regulation.

12-13   General regulations made pursuant to this power deal with exemption from or reduction in the rate at which tax is deducted at source on certain income.[20] The Regulations apply to treaty residents who are entitled to exemption or partial relief from U.K. income tax deducted at source. This does not include distributions chargeable under Schedule F. It only applies in respect of persons who are beneficially entitled to the income.

---

[18]   *Inland Revenue Tax Bulletin* (Issue 30, August 1997), p.459.
[19]   Taxes Act 1988 s. 791.
[20]   Double Taxation Relief (Taxes on Income) (General) Regulations 1970 (S.I. 1970 No. 488).

NOTICE TO PAY AT TREATY RATES

12-14 The payer of such income may be directed by notice in writing given by the Board that he shall:

    (a)   not deduct tax, or

    (b)   not deduct tax at a higher rate than is specified in the notice, or

    (c)   deduct tax at a rate specified in the notice instead of at the lower or basic rate otherwise appropriate.

Where notice is given, any income paid after the date of the notice for a year for which the treaty has effect, must be paid as directed in the notice. The effect of such a notice is to substitute the treaty rate for the domestic law rate of deduction for all domestic law purposes in relation to the payer as well as the non-resident.

A notice may be expressed to become ineffective if certain specified events happen. If to the knowledge of the payer, any of the specified events happens, any payment made to the non-resident after the happening of that event becomes known to the payer must be subject to deduction of tax at domestic rates in accordance with domestic law. Any notice may be cancelled by notice by or on behalf of the Revenue. After the receipt of a cancellation notice, deduction of tax must be at domestic rates in accordance with domestic law.

12-15 If after a notice has been given it is discovered that the non-resident is not entitled to the treaty benefit referred to in the notice, any tax which, but for the notice, would have been deductible from any payment made to the non-resident by the payer but in compliance with the notice has not been so deducted may be assessed on the non-resident under Case VI of Schedule D by an Inspector. Alternatively, on the direction of the Revenue, tax may be deducted by the payer out of so much of the first payment made to the non-resident after the date of the direction as remains after the deduction of any tax deductible in the absence of the treaty. Any balance which cannot be deducted out of the first payment must be deducted, subject to the same limitation, out of subsequent payments until the whole of the tax has been deducted.

MANUFACTURED OVERSEAS DIVIDENDS

12-16 Specific regulations[21] authorise the making of arrangements with payers of manufactured overseas dividends to enable the payment to be made without deduction of U.K. tax. This applies to recipients who are resident in a treaty country where the treaty contains an "other income" article which exempts such payments from tax. These arrangements made pursuant to the Regulations are not fully published, although information on them

---

[21] Double Taxation Relief (Taxes on Income) (General) (Manufactured Overseas Dividends) Regulations 1993 (S.I. 1993 No. 1957).

is available from the Inland Revenue and specific arrangements may be tailored to meet the needs of particular taxpayers or classes of taxpayers, particularly in relation to financial institutions. As an important international financial centre, the United Kingdom has developed a variety of arrangements involving claims and payments made through intermediaries or custodians. For example, arrangements have been made with a number of U.K. banks who act as global custodians for large numbers of non-residents and managed U.K. investment portfolios. These aim at streamlining the handling of claims using agreed and defined criteria. Such banks send blocks of claims at a time to a dedicated section at the CNR. In return, they receive single aggregate payments for each such block.

COLLECTION OF CANADIAN AND U.S. WITHHOLDING TAX

12-17   An unusual feature of U.K. treaty arrangements, also relevant to its position as an international financial centre, has been the specific regulations dealing respectively with Canadian tax on dividends and interest and U.S. tax on dividends received from each of those contracting states by U.K. collection agents until the repeal of the withholding obligations of U.K. collecting agents in the Finance Act 2000.[22] Dividends and interest paid by Canadian payers to addresses in the United Kingdom are subject to withholding in Canada at the rates provided in the Canadian Treaty. Where such dividends or interest were collected by a U.K. collecting agent for a person not resident in the United Kingdom, the collecting agent would deduct additional Canadian withholding tax and account for it to the Inland Revenue, who then accounted for it to Revenue Canada. The additional Canadian withholding tax was deducted at whatever rate is appropriate depending upon whether the beneficial owner of the dividends or interest was resident in a third country which had a treaty with Canada at the rate appropriate to that treaty. A similar arrangement existed in respect of the United States on dividend payments received by U.K. collecting agents. The regulations authorising deduction of Canadian and U.S. taxes were revoked in December 2000.[23]

FORMS

12-18   The same forms are used to seek authorisation to pay at the treaty rate as are used for repayment and the same evidence of entitlement must be submitted in support of the application. In most cases a standard form[24] may be used, although there are also forms tailored to specific treaties and specific forms of income. Forms are generally available in English, although many are also available in the language of the other contracting state and

---

[22] Canada: Dividend and Interest Regulations 1990 (S.I. 1990 No. 780) and U.S.A: Dividend Regulations 1946 (S.I. 1946 No. 1331).
[23] Double Taxation Relief (Taxes on Income) (Dividends, etc.) (Revocations) Regulations 2000 (S.I. 2000 No. 3330).
[24] Form X.

from the tax authorities of such state. Questions on the form are designed to determine eligibility for treaty benefits and follow generally the criteria set out in the relevant treaty provision. These include questions relating to the residence of the claimant, the presence of a permanent establishment in the United Kingdom and beneficial ownership. Other conditions, such as whether the recipient is subject to tax where the treaty so requires, are usually included.

BENEFICIAL OWNERSHIP

12-19   Claims for benefits in relation to dividend, interest or royalty payments must be made by the beneficial owner of the dividend and all forms require a declaration of beneficial ownership by the claimant. Consequently, if shares are registered in the name of any person who is not the beneficial owner, it is the beneficial owner and not the registered owner who is entitled to claim. Additional information may be required where the registered owner as appearing on dividend vouchers is not the same as the declared beneficial owner. Where beneficial ownership of dividends is questioned and the relevant treaty contains a beneficial ownership provision, then the claimant will have to prove this element to receive the payment. Several forms of limitation of benefit provisions appear in the relevant articles of U.K. treaties. Most claim forms do not solicit specific information relating to all these provisions. There are certain exceptions. For example, in relation to the U.S. Treaty (1975), questions are designed to consider the application of Article 16 (limitation of benefits).

PROCEDURE

12-20   The claim must be certified by the tax authority of the claimant's state of residence. Certification must include the residence of the claimant and in certain cases that the claimant is subject to tax on the income in question. In some cases the taxpayer identification number (TIN) must also be certified by the foreign tax authority. Some forms may demand information that is beyond that required by the treaty in question. The U.S. Treaty form US7/Credit, for example, requires that the U.S. tax authorities certify that a corporate claimant has filed a U.S. tax return for the year. In the case of dividends, original tax vouchers indicating the tax credit and dividend paid must be attached.

The procedure for filing claims varies. All require submission to the foreign tax authorities for certification. Thereafter, some are filed in the United Kingdom (*e.g.* Canada), while in others the claim is simply submitted through the foreign tax authority (*e.g.* Switzerland). In some cases a distinction is drawn between the first claim and subsequent claims. Thus, in a number of cases a first claim must be submitted to the tax authorities in the other contracting state with subsequent claims being submitted to the U.K. authorities[25] (*e.g.* Japan).

---

[25] The Centre for Non-Residents.

The treaty claim forms included in the self-assessment tax return are more general and depart from the claim forms in relation to specific treaties in that they do not solicit information corresponding to treaty provisions. In the case of form IR302, the taxpayer simply claims the benefit by reference to the type of income, the relevant treaty article and the domestic and treaty rates of tax. In the case of form IR304, a similar approach is taken although a space is provided for "other information". The more general obligation on claimants to produce evidence of their entitlement to the treaty benefit may mean that the provisions of the dividend article in question must be more comprehensively supported than under the older treaty specific forms. There is no official guidance as to whether a non-resident who is required to complete a self-assessment return is compelled to use these new forms or whether the older forms may be included with the return.

DIVIDENDS

12-21 The United Kingdom does not generally impose a withholding tax on dividends. Certain treaties provide that for so long as the United Kingdom grants a tax credit to a U.K. resident individual, partial repayment of the tax credit is permitted to qualified treaty residents, subject to an income tax withholding. The Regulations[26] which authorised the Inland Revenue to make arrangements with U.K. companies for payment of the tax credit in accordance with treaty provisions were revoked with effect from July 21, 1999. These Regulations authorised arrangements for companies to pay the additional amount determined under the treaty in addition to making a repayment claim. The variety of arrangements available under those Regulations to permit U.K. dividend paying companies to pay non-resident shareholders an additional amount equal to the net tax credit repaid after deducting tax at the appropriate rate were terminated. A claim for payment of the tax credit must now be made by or on behalf of the beneficial owners.[27]

INTEREST AND ROYALTIES

12-22 In the absence of notice from the Inland Revenue, tax must be deducted by the U.K. payer at source at the domestic rate and not the treaty rate. Under domestic law, the taxpayer will not obtain tax relief for the payment unless tax is deducted at source. The Inland Revenue position is that the obligation on the part of U.K. payers to deduct tax is separate from the non-resident's entitlement to treaty benefits. Where tax is not deducted or is deducted at the treaty rate in the absence of Inland Revenue authorisation, interest on unpaid tax will be due on the difference between the full domestic rate and the tax actually deducted from the time of payment of the

---

[26] Double Taxation Relief (Taxes on Income) (General) (Dividend) Regulations (S.I. 1973 No. 317).

[27] *Inland Revenue Tax Bulletin* (Issue 39, February 1999), p.626.

interest or royalty concerned, even if the beneficial owner subsequently claims relief.

Directions are not made to payments in respect of coupons for any interest, but, under arrangements approved by the Revenue, any such payments may be made without deduction of tax or with tax deducted at treaty rates, if the non-resident or any person acting on his behalf makes a claim to the payer in prescribed form. In that case payments may be made at treaty rates generally on the same basis as if a notice were given.

12-23   Qualifying non-residents may claim repayment of tax deducted at source. The Inland Revenue require underlying documentation in addition to the claim forms. Thus, a copy of the text of any agreement or exchange of correspondence regulating the terms on which interest is paid is required for a claim relating to interest. In the case of royalties, a copy of the licence agreement or contract must be submitted in support of the claim. Certificates of tax deducted are also required. Application may also be made for relief at source. The Inland Revenue have adopted specific rules to deal with agreements between the parties relating to interest, royalties and other annual payments which provide for a specified sum after deduction of tax at the basic rate[28] and for agreements that provide for such amounts to be paid "free of tax" or without deduction of U.K. tax.[29] Retrospective relief on claims to pay gross or at reduced rates may be given, but only back to the date the claim was received by the Inland Revenue.[30]

12-24   Although the Inland Revenue is understood not to be unwilling to move to an entirely self-certification system, they have experimented with a more relaxed approach to authorising deduction of tax at source in low risk cases in relation to interest. Their first steps in this direction are set out in the Provisional Treaty Relief Scheme.[31] This voluntary scheme applies to two types of loans where there is only a "negligible risk" that an application for treaty relief would fail. They are:

(1)   "one to one" company loans where there is no shareholding relationship or common ownership between the parties involved, for example, where the lender is an overseas lending institution;

(2)   syndicated loans where there is a syndicate manager.

In view of the time taken for the process from start to finish of the submission of a treaty claim to a foreign tax authority for certification of residence and final issue of a notice, the Inland Revenue have offered a complimentary arrangement. The risk of an unsuccessful treaty claim rests with the payer of the interest. Thus, although provisional authorisation will be given for transactions falling within those described in the *Tax Bulletin*, the risk is effectively with the payer who will be liable for both tax and other consequences if a successful treaty claim is not made.

---

[28] Inland Revenue *Double Taxation Relief Manual*, para. 1835.
[29] *ibid.*, paras 1836–1839.
[30] *Tax Bulletin* (August 1994), p.153.
[31] See *Tax Bulletin* (June 1999), p.670.

CAPITAL PAYMENTS

12-25 As a general rule, the United Kingdom does not tax capital gains of non-residents other than in respect of gains relating to assets for the purposes of a trade carried on in the United Kingdom through a branch or agency.[32] Exceptions to this rule include the sale of U.K. patent rights,[33] gains on the disposal of unquoted shares deriving their value from exploration or exploitation assets in the United Kingdom[34] and gains of a capital nature from the disposal of land or any property deriving its value from land, where the land is acquired with the object of realising a gain or is held as trading stock or is developed in certain circumstances covered by anti-avoidance provisions.[35]

Where U.K. patent rights are sold by a non-resident, the proceeds are generally subject to income tax which is deducted at source by application of the rules relating to annual payments under Taxes Act 1988, section 349. In the case of disposal subject to the anti-avoidance provisions of Taxes Act 1988, section 776, the Inland Revenue may direct that tax be deducted at source if it appears that any person entitled to consideration taxable under those provisions is not resident in the United Kingdom. Again, the rules relating to annual payments under Taxes Act 1988, section 349(1) will apply. The same procedures for applications for relief at source or repayment claims where a treaty eliminates tax for qualified treaty residents would apply.

BUSINESS PROFITS

12-26 Business profits under U.K. domestic law is either taxed under Schedule D Case I as income from a trade, which corresponds to Article 7 (business profits) of the OECD Model, or as professional income under Schedule D Case II, which corresponds broadly to Article 14 (independent personal services) of the OECD Model. The current law is set out in the Finance Act 1995. The mechanism adopted is to impose all compliance obligations jointly on the U.K. representative of a non-resident and the non-resident. The U.K. representative is defined as the branch or agency through which the non-resident carries on any trade, profession or vocation. The U.K. representative is jointly responsible with the non-resident for all tax obligations and liabilities in relation to the trade, profession or vocation carried on through the branch or agency. This extends to all matters relating to self-assessment of tax and to the collection and recovery of tax and covers notification of chargeability, the obligation to make a return and self-assessment, liability to make interim and final payments of tax and liability to surcharges, interest and penalties in connection with these obligations and liabilities.[36] The United Kingdom does not generally require deduction of tax

---

[32] TCGA 1992, s. 10(1).
[33] Taxes Act 1988, s. 524.
[34] TCGA 1992, s. 276.
[35] Taxes Act 1988, s. 776.
[36] Finance Act 1995, s. 126, Sched. 23.

at source on payments to non-residents under this heading.[37] Unlike persons making payments under deduction of tax, the U.K. representative is able to make a treaty claim in that capacity on behalf of the non-resident it represents.

None of the Inland Revenue publications dealing with self-assessment in the context of non-residents address the application of treaties to business income. No view is expressed whether a claim need be made or whether non-residents and their representatives are entitled to self-assess the application of permanent establishment issues. The Inland Revenue self-assessment technical guide[38] merely indicates that the question of non-residents' liability is complex and that they should seek professional help if they are in any doubt as to how the new rules will apply to them. The Inland Revenue Internal Manuals take a similar approach to permanent establishments under treaties.

12-27   The *International Tax Handbook* notes, for example, that agency permanent establishment is a difficult area and advice should be sought by Inspectors from International Division.[39]

Arguably, non-residents and their agents are entitled to self-assess the existence of a permanent establishment. Such a view would be based on the proposition that permanent establishment provisions of treaties provide for charging U.K. source income or gains of non-residents pursuant to the Taxes Act 1988, section 788(3)(b). By so doing, they define taxing jurisdiction and do not provide for "relief" from income tax or corporation tax under section 788(3)(a) for which a claim is required.

The stringent interest and penalty regimes applicable to self-assessment and pay and file (in the case of companies) create considerable incentive for non-residents and U.K. representatives to make accurate assessments in this respect. This is particularly so in the case of U.K. representatives who, as a practical matter, will be within the jurisdiction of the U.K. courts. Consequently, where a non-resident forms the view that its activities constitute trading in the United Kingdom through a branch or agency for domestic law purposes, but fall short of those constituting a permanent establishment for treaty purposes, there is a premium on coming to the correct conclusion. Where the Inland Revenue interpretation is sought on this, a positive answer will put the matter at an end. A negative reply with which the non-resident disagrees may mean that the matter would ultimately need to be resolved through formal dispute resolution mechanisms.

EMPLOYMENT INCOME

12-28   Most employment income is taxed by deduction at source under the PAYE rules. In the case of individuals, who are not resident or not ordinarily resident in the United Kingdom, their liability to U.K. tax under

---

[37] Payments to entertainers or sportsmen are an important exception: Taxes Act 1988, s. 555.
[38] SAT 2 (1995).
[39] *International Tax Handbook*, para. 853; *Double Taxation Relief Manual*, paras 1714 and 1715.

Schedule E case II is limited to emoluments in respect of duties performed in the United Kingdom. Where the employee also performs duties outside the United Kingdom a direction may be sought for PAYE to be operated only in relation to the proportion taxable in the United Kingdom. Application for such a direction must provide "such information as is available and is relevant to the giving of the direction". Where a treaty (typically following Article 15 of the OECD Model) precludes U.K. taxation, this route may be used to restrict PAYE to income taxable in accordance with the treaty. Other reporting obligations are not limited by treaty such as returns of persons treated as employees under Finance Act 1974, section 24 which continue to apply.

ENTERTAINERS AND SPORTSMEN

12-29 Where non-resident entertainers or sportsmen perform in the United Kingdom, deduction of tax at source may be required (Taxes Act 1988, section 555(2)). It is possible under Regulations to apply for a reduction in the withholding payments.[40] The Regulations make no reference to treaties. The Inland Revenue approach is that the tax must be withheld, even if the income is not subject to U.K. tax as a result of the application of a treaty.[41] The Inland Revenue view is that the withholding is merely on account of the final tax liability, and that whether or not a particular treaty is applicable cannot be considered fully at the withholding stage. Thus, non-residents subject to withholding under these rules can only make a claim for repayment of the tax withheld on submission of a claim with a return.

RESIDENCE

Individual residence

12-30 An assertion of the appropriate residence is an essential element for the application of treaty benefits. An individual arriving in the United Kingdom, if he or she is chargeable to income tax or capital gains tax, must notify the Inland Revenue of chargeability.[42] Until self-assessment, such individuals could complete or could have been required to complete an arrival form P86. The form is designed to solicit information about the residence status of the individual both from the time of arrival and relating to previous periods. U.K. domestic law distinguishes between residence, ordinary residence and domicile in relation to individuals. Questions are designed to enable a determination to be made of these issues. In certain cases, additional information with respect to domicile may be requested.[43] In the past, the Inland Revenue would commonly advise on whether it viewed the individual as a resident, ordinarily resident or domiciled in the United Kingdom. The procedures made no specific reference to residence for treaty purposes.

---

[40] Income Tax (Entertainers, etc.) Regulations 1987 (S.I. 1987 No. 530), reg.5.
[41] FEUSO, para. 8A.
[42] TMA 1970, s. 7.
[43] Form DOM1.

The form P86 would not normally provide sufficient information to address the tie-breaker provisions of the OECD Model Article.

In the context of self-assessment, individuals are now required to self-assess their status and certify this on their tax returns. The Inland Revenue have indicated that they will now not rule on residence in most cases. They will, however, continue to certify residence to enable individuals to obtain relief from foreign tax under a treaty, for example by certifying a foreign claim form.[44]

12-31   The self-assessment tax return specifically raises the question of dual residence. The current individual self-assessment tax return requires individuals who are resident in a country other than the United Kingdom under a treaty and at the same time resident in the United Kingdom to indicate that fact on the return (non-residents etc. to indicate the country in which dual residence is claimed).

Individuals who are non-resident or are resident in another country for the purpose of a treaty and are claiming relief under a treaty are required to indicate the amount of relief that they are claiming. Moreover, material published by the Inland Revenue to assist with individual tax return preparation now deals with the question of dual residence and the application of treaty tie-breaker provisions.[45] It contains a summary of the tie-breaker rules under the OECD Model. Also included is specific information in relation to the U.S. Treaty. This comprises an explanation of the main U.S. domestic rules on residence as well as the treaty fiscal residence provisions. A separate form to accompany the self-assessment return is also provided to claim treaty benefits where the tie-breaker is not in issue.[46]

12-32   A certificate of residence from the tax administration of the other contracting state is required under both forms. This is modified in the case of the United States. U.S. citizens are required to self-certify the application of the U.S. "substantial presence" test. U.S. resident aliens must produce either a copy of their Green Card or, if they are not Green Card holders, a certificate of residence from the IRS. Thus, although taxpayers are generally required to self-assess or self-certify the facts relevant to their tax position, this is not the case in relation to assertions of residence of a contracting state where treaty benefits are claimed. In this case, a certificate of residence is required to be submitted with the return. The certificate of residence is an annual requirement. In addition, where the treaty so requires, the certificate must confirm that the individual is subject to tax in whole or part in the country of residence. Where only part of the income is taxed in the country of residence, that part must be shown in the certificate.

Other conditions

12-33   The new self-assessment forms require non-residents to satisfy themselves that all of the conditions of the relevant treaty are met in making

---

[44] *Inland Revenue Tax Bulletin* (Issue 29, June 1997), p.425.
[45] Helpsheet IR302.
[46] Helpsheet IR304. More detailed explanations are found in *Double Taxation Relief Manual*, paras 301–320.

a treaty claim.[47] Sufficient evidence to support the claim must be obtained and submitted with the return. This, again, is an exception to the self-certification principle of self-assessment.

If any general conclusion can be drawn from the new tax return guidelines about the Inland Revenue attitude towards self-assessment, it is that although domestic tax questions, including residence, are dealt with by self-assessment and self-certification without the need to submit factual information in support of the return, in the case of treaty benefits, supporting evidence is still required.

12-34   Individuals departing from the United Kingdom may file a form P85 which is designed to solicit information to enable the Inland Revenue to determine whether the individual has ceased to be resident or ordinarily resident in the United Kingdom. Again, until self-assessment, a determination was issued only on a provisional basis and subject to re-consideration if, for example, the individual returned to the United Kingdom under the pre-self-assessment rules. Under self-assessment, individuals must make their own determination of status.[48] The Inland Revenue now state that information on departure in the P86 may still be used for specific purposes. These include making in year repayments of tax to individuals leaving part way through the year or giving appropriate PAYE deduction codes for deduction of tax at source on employment income. These are not regarded as decisions about residence which may form part of an enquiry if appropriate. Thus, certainty will only be possible once a tax return has been filed in which non-residence is asserted and the time limit for enquiry into the return has expired or the return has been examined and the status asserted has been confirmed. Notwithstanding this, the Inland Revenue may consider the residence of an individual after receipt of a form P85, but before a tax return is filed. Where residence status has been agreed, it would not normally be taken up again after the return has been filed.

U.K. domestic law does not contemplate persons being resident in the United Kingdom for part of a year only. By a concession individuals may be resident for part of the year only,[49] application of the extra-statutory concession being subject to the discretion of the Inland Revenue.[50] Inland Revenue practice also distinguishes between persons who leave the United Kingdom to work full-time abroad and those leaving permanently for other reasons.[51]

Company residence

12-35   A company may be resident in the United Kingdom under domestic law either because it is incorporated in the United Kingdom[52] or because

---

[47] Helpsheet IR304.
[48] *Inland Revenue Tax Bulletin* (Issue 29, June 1997), p.426.
[49] ESCA11, IR40, ESCD2, ESCA78.
[50] Booklet IR1 states that "in a particular case there may be special circumstances which will require to be taken into account in considering the application of a concession. A concession will not be given in any case where an attempt is made to use it for tax avoidance".
[51] Inland Revenue booklet IR20, ch.2.
[52] Finance Act 1988, s. 66.

its central management and control is exercised in the United Kingdom.[53] If it is also resident in a country under the domestic law of that country, an applicable treaty with a tie-breaker may resolve dual residence.

A company chargeable to corporation tax is required to give notice of chargeability.[54] If it is considered that the company is U.K. resident pursuant to the tie-breaker, no special steps would be required in the United Kingdom unless mutual agreement procedure is invoked under the relevant treaty in respect of the application of a tie-breaker in the other contracting state.

Under domestic law,[55] a company which is resident outside the United Kingdom by virtue of the application of a treaty is treated for all U.K. domestic tax purposes as non-resident. A company is deemed to have made a claim for relief under the treaty in question when it is necessary to resolve the residence of the company for treaty purposes.[56] It may therefore be necessary to demonstrate in the United Kingdom that the application of the tie-breaker results in the U.K. company being treated as U.K. resident for treaty purposes. There is no specific procedure.

Where it is sought to demonstrate that the effect of the tie-breaker is to make a dual resident company resident outside the United Kingdom, an assertion will need to be made to this effect, even though a claim is deemed made. No formal procedure is provided. In the context of a company ceasing to be resident in the United Kingdom , the pre-migration notification procedure required in Finance Act 1988, section 130[57] is also required.

MINIMISING FOREIGN TAX

12-36   U.K. treaty provisions normally permit a credit against U.K. tax, tax payable under the laws of the other contracting state and in accordance with the treaty in question.[58] Inland Revenue practice will permit credit to be given only for foreign tax which is payable in accordance with the treaty. Consequently, the claimant must take all necessary steps to reduce foreign liability to the level required by the treaty.

This general limitation of credit to that payable under the treaty has been elevated to an obligation to minimise foreign tax in the Finance Act 2000. Paragraph 6 of Schedule 30[59] restricts credit for foreign tax under any treaty to the tax which would be allowed:

"had all reasonable steps been taken:

(a)   under the law of the territory concerned; and

(b)   under any arrangements made with the government of that territory to minimise the amount of tax payable in that territory".

---

[53]   See generally SP1/90.
[54]   TMA 1970, s. 10(1).
[55]   Finance Act 1994, s. 249.
[56]   *ibid.*, s. 249(2).
[57]   See also Statement of Practice SP2/90.
[58]   See, for example, Netherlands Treaty, Art.22(1).
[59]   Taxes Act 1988, s. 795A(1).

Not only is there a general obligation to minimise the amount of tax payable in the other contracting state, but specific steps which are required to be taken include claiming or otherwise securing the benefit of reliefs, deductions or allowances, and making elections for tax purposes. For this purpose, any question as to whether it would have been reasonable for a person to take these steps is determined on the basis of "what might reasonably be expected to have been done in the absence of double taxation relief". The application of such a rule in practice can give rise to considerable difficulties. The Inland Revenue is to publish guidance on when it will accept that a taxpayer has taken all reasonable steps in this context. Examples given by the Inland Revenue in *Outcome of Consultation on Double Taxation Relief* include acceptance of an estimated tax assessment in the other country which is likely to be excessive, not claiming an allowance or relief (for example expenses, capital allowances or losses) that is generally known to be available; and where the other country's domestic law or the relevant treaty provides for alternative bases of taxation, not choosing the basis which would produce the lowest tax bill.

12-37   Examples where, in the view of the Inland Revenue, the provision would not apply are not claiming a relief, the availability of which is uncertain, and where disproportionate expenditure would have to be incurred in researching the other country's law and pursuing the claim; claiming that a loss incurred in the other country should be carried forward rather than backwards or vice versa; and the case of underlying tax paid by a subsidiary company where the U.K. company which claims relief for that tax is not in the position to influence the amount of tax paid.

It is immediately noticeable that the provision is drafted in the passive. In other words, the obligation is not only on the U.K. resident taxpayer. It extends to the actions of both related and unrelated parties and its implications will need to be considered in all dealings with those jurisdictions. The only limitation is reasonableness. These provisions apply in relation to claims for credit made on or after March 21, 2000. There is clearly an element of retrospectivity for claims made in relation to past years. In *Outcome of Consultation on Double Taxation Relief*, the amendments are expressed as "clarification". The Inland Revenue interpretation of the rule described in the *Double Taxation Relief Manual*, paragraph 550(e) reads:

> "(e)   minimum tax rule—credit is to be allowed only for the 'minimum' amount of foreign tax chargeable under the laws of the foreign country and the provisions of any relevant double taxation agreement".

12-38   Paragraph 675 refers to foreign tax "which is a proper charge under the foreign country's law and, where there is an agreement, for foreign tax which is payable in accordance with that agreement". It continues that: "The claimant must take all necessary steps to have his foreign tax liability reduced to that minimum for example, by claiming all the allowances and reliefs (for example foreign personal allowances) due to him under the provisions of an agreement". The simple example given in the *Double Taxation Relief Manual* refers to the fact that no credit would be due for Netherlands tax payable on Netherlands royalties arising to a resident in the United Kingdom not engaged in a trade or business in the Netherlands since such royalties are exempt under Article 12 of the Netherlands Treaty. (The example is a poor one since the Netherlands does not apparently impose tax under domestic law in these circumstances anyway). More appropriately, the Manual states that if full Netherlands withholding tax of 25 per cent is suffered on a dividend, credit is given only at the treaty rate since the U.K. resident taxpayer can claim a reduction of this rate under Article 10 of the Netherlands Treaty. At least in cases relating to claims in respect of tax prior to the announcement of the current rule, the standard should be no higher than that set out in the *Double Taxation Relief Manual*, paragraph 675 as it stood at that time. The paragraph also notes that cases should be referred to International Division where a claim for foreign tax credit is brought, but the claim is refused for procedural reasons such as a failure to observe time limits, or the foreign tax authority does not respond to or act upon the claim or circumstances where the foreign country imposes tax on income which does not arise in that country.

The Manual also notes that the foreign tax which is allowable for credit is the tax which represents the final liability and not tax paid on account. Similarly, interest or penalties which may be paid in the other country are excluded.

ADMINISTRATION OF TREATIES

12-39   Claims for treaty relief are administered by the Centre for Non-Residents (CNR). It administers the tax affairs of non-resident individuals, trusts and intermediaries in the financial sector and is responsible for deduction and relief at source schemes.[60] Certain issues involving the application of treaties are dealt with by the Inland Revenue International Division.

In common with the rest of the Inland Revenue, the CNR, which handles non-resident claims, aims to process claims generally within 28 days of receipt. Their performance target is to pay 100 per cent of non-resident claims within 28 days of receipt of the claim in the case of those qualifying for the "limited examination procedure". For example, their provisional performance indicators show that this target was met for the financial year 1996/97. They aim to pay 80 per cent of other claims within 28 days of receipt of the claim.[61] The Inland Revenue claim that in the "other applications" category, the overwhelming majority of claims are paid within a further 28 days.

12-40   Limited examination procedures refer to the most easily identifiable payment claims that are suitable for accelerated checking. Such arrangements are subject to review and details are not publicised. The Inland Revenue view is that the effectiveness of such measures might be prejudiced by making these types of guidelines widely available where relaxation or

---

[60] Inland Revenue Press Releases dated January 24, 1994 and April 19, 1994; Inland Revenue Plan 1997/98, p.25.
[61] Inland Revenue Plan 1997/98, p.25.

acceleration of work procedures may give rise to a greater risk of abuse. There is no indication as to what percentage of all claims fall within the limited examination regime.

Delays will typically occur in more complex cases, which may involve more than one part of CNR or another Inland Revenue office. This arises, for example, from the fact that CNR will not necessarily hold all relevant information. Thus, district offices may be in a position to know whether a special relationship exists between a U.K. payer and an overseas recipient.[62] In addition, consultation with other branches, such as Inland Revenue International or Inland Revenue Solicitor, may be involved.

Other reasons for delay may arise where new issues develop. For example, recently, in relation to the entitlement of U.S. limited liability companies to seek relief under the U.S. Treaty, a monitoring exercise was conducted and CNR was requested to bring claims or applications to the attention of the International Division and to defer taking action that might prejudice their position.[63]

12-41   Claims for treaty relief in the context of interest payments within a multinational group may require additional processing time and documentation where thin capitalisation under domestic law or treaty limitation of benefit provisions is relevant. Thin capitalisation may be examined in several circumstances. One of these is when a treaty claim for relief on interest payments is made.[64]

Although the Inland Revenue have published some information in the context of procedures for the application of treaties, it is incomplete and sporadic at the present time. The extent to which the Inland Revenue are bound by published guidance is an evolving area of administrative law. Most official publications contain caveats indicating typically that the information is "guidance only". The courts have indicated that a statement formally published by the Revenue to the world might safely be regarded as binding, subject to its terms in any case falling clearly within them.[65]

There is no general advance ruling procedure. The Inland Revenue will advise on their interpretation of the law in relation to a specific transaction, including where the application of treaties is in issue, in accordance with Inland Revenue Code of Practice No. 10. Taxpayers are entitled to rely on such guidance only in accordance with administrative law principles.[66]

CONCLUSION

12-42   The United Kingdom has traditionally relied to some extent on certification of claims by the competent authorities of other contracting states in order to assist with compliance. A move away from this may be detected to some extent where certification by foreign competent authorities is limited to residence.

---

[62] *Double Taxation Relief Manual,* para. 1910.
[63] *R v. IRC, ex parte Opman International U.K.* [1986] S.T.C. 18, QBD is an example, albeit rather old, of delay as a result of bureaucratic bungling.
[64] *Inland Revenue Tax Bulletin* (Issue 17, June 1995), p.218.
[65] *R v. IRC, ex parte MFK Underwriting Agencies Ltd* [1989] S.T.C. 1873, QBD at 892.
[66] See particularly *R v. IRC, ex parte Matrix Securities Ltd* [1994] S.T.C. 272, HL.

The move to self-assessment is the most important administrative reform to the U.K. tax system in decades and its impact on treaty administration is as yet uncertain. Immediate positive benefits have been publication of Inland Revenue guidance and procedures which were previously difficult to access. In the financial services sector particularly, a number of arrangements are dealt with by agreement between the Inland Revenue and the parties involved under broad enabling regulations. This informal ad hoc approach has facilitated considerable flexibility in tailoring arrangements to meet specific purposes and changing circumstances. It remains to be seen whether this flexibility can be retained in the context of published and possibly less flexible administrative arrangements.

CHAPTER 13

Disputes and Mutual Agreement Procedure

SUBSTANTIVE DISPUTES

13-01   Generally, disputes with the Inland Revenue at a substantive level are dealt with by way of appeal. All appeals in respect of double taxation relief are dealt with before the Special Commissioners.[1] Specific provision for appeal to the Special Commissioners in relation to questions of domicile or ordinary residence are provided in the Taxes Act 1988, section 207 for income tax and Taxation of Chargeable Gains Act (TCGA) 1992, section 9(2). Further appeals from determinations of the Special Commissioners may be made to the High Court on a point of law.[2] Such appeals are heard in the Chancery Division of the High Court. An appeal from the Special Commissioners may be made direct to the Court of Appeal, if all the parties so consent, if the Special Commissioners certify that the decision involves a point of law relating wholly or mainly to the construction of legislation which has been fully argued before them and fully considered by them and if the leave of the Court of Appeal has been obtained.[3]

JUDICIAL REVIEW

13-02   Additional remedies may be available as a matter of administrative law in certain circumstances. Where there is no statutory right of appeal, judicial review may be obtained of the manner in which the Inland Revenue or, in certain circumstances the Special Commissioners, made the decision complained of.

Judicial review is generally available where the decision complained of was such that no authority properly directing itself on the relevant law and acting reasonably could have reached it, a failure to comply with the rules of natural justice, a want or excess of jurisdiction or error of law on the face of the record. Recent cases of judicial review in the tax field have focused particularly on the extent to which the Inland Revenue may depart from a guidance they have given on the tax consequences of particular transactions.

13-03   Few reported applications for judicial review have involved treaty

---

[1] Tax tribunal of first instance. Taxes Management Act (TMA) 1970, s. 46C(3).
[2] *ibid.*, s. 56A(1).
[3] *ibid.*, s. 56A(2).

issues. Those that have illustrate difficulties that have arisen in the applications of treaties. In *R v. IRC, ex parte Commerzbank AG*,[4] the taxpayer Commerzbank AG was incorporated and resident in Germany. After protracted litigation,[5] the taxpayer succeeded in recovering tax paid in respect of interest under Article 15 of the U.S. Treaty. The taxpayer then sought to obtain the repayment supplement (interest) in respect of the tax overpaid. This was refused by the Inland Revenue on the basis that under domestic law the repayment supplement was only payable to U.K. residents. The taxpayer applied to the High Court for judicial review. One of its arguments was that the residence requirement was inconsistent with the non-discrimination provisions of Article 20 of the German Treaty since it resulted in treatment in connection with taxation that was more burdensome than that imposed on U.K. nationals. The claim under the treaty was not upheld by the court, although similar arguments on non-discrimination under the EC Treaty were ultimately upheld by the European Court of Justice.[6]

In *R v. IRC, ex parte Opman International U.K.*,[7] a company applied for a determination that they were not liable to tax on certain royalties paid to them in the United Kingdom pursuant to the Netherlands Treaty. Internal difficulties at the Inland Revenue over a long period of time caused the applicant's accountant to believe that the application would be refused. Without informing the Inland Revenue, the applicant applied for leave to seek judicial review which was granted. Within a month, the Inland Revenue determined the matter in the applicant's favour. The applicant then sought to discontinue the judicial review proceedings and claim payment of their costs. No order for costs was made on the grounds that the applicant did not inform the Inland Revenue of their intention to seek judicial review. If an indication of that sort had been given, the court believed that the matter would have been dealt with at a higher level and would likely have been more promptly resolved.

13-04 Woolf J. (as he then was) also noted that although an appeal procedure was available on the substance of the dispute, this did not exclude the possibility of judicial review, which even though a procedure of last resort, may be appropriate where the alternative procedure does not achieve a just resolution of the applicant's claim.[8]

In *R v. IRC, ex parte Howmet Corp.*,[9] the applicant sought leave to apply for judicial review of a decision of the Inland Revenue to revoke a ruling that the U.K. subsidiary of a U.S. parent company should be regarded as U.K. resident for tax purposes.

The ruling arose out of a proposed restructuring of the U.K. subsidiary which would involve payment of a dividend to the U.S. parent which would qualify for a half credit under Article 10 of the U.S. Treaty. The applicants claimed that they had made clear that the ruling was required in connection with the restructuring of the company and that they were not seeking clear-

---

[4] [1991] S.T.C. 271, QBD.
[5] *IRC v. Commerzbank* [1990] S.T.C. 285.
[6] Case C-1330/91 [1993] S.T.C. 605.
[7] [1986] S.T.C. 18, QBD.
[8] See however *O'Neil and Others v. C.I.R.* [2001] UKPC 17; S.T.C. 742 PC where is was held that judicial review would only be granted in exceptional cases where appeals could be made by the statutory procedure.
[9] [1994] S.T.C. 413, QBD.

ance for the overall effect of the reconstruction, but only the residence of the company. The applicant argued that details of the capitalisation and the declaration and payment of the dividends were not relevant to the test of residency. The Crown argued that the utmost candour was required and that all the facts were not disclosed including the intention to make a claim under Article 10 of the Treaty. The court held that there was an arguable case and that consequently leave to seek judicial review was granted.

13-05   In *R v. IRC, ex parte Camacq Corporation*,[10] an application for judicial review was sought of a decision by the Inland Revenue to revoke a direction given to a U.K. company to pay a dividend gross. A U.S. escrow agent held shares for the benefit of the U.S. Treasury as part of a civil penalty levied against Mr Ivan Boesky. In the course of attempting to sell the shares of the company, it was proposed to pay a dividend on the shares and consent was sought for the tax credit to be repaid on the basis that the beneficial owner was the U.S. Government and entitled to repayment of the credit by virtue of sovereign immunity. Without repayment of the tax credit, the transaction would not have gone ahead, because the sale price would not have been acceptable to the seller.

As soon as authorisation to repay the tax credit was given, the Inspector of Foreign Dividends (now the Centre for Non-Residents (CNR)) reported the authorisation to the International Division. The latter had doubts about whether, in the particular circumstances, it was appropriate to pay the tax credit. Consequently, the authorisation to pay gross was revoked. The Inland Revenue view was that the dividend seemed to have been artificially arranged in order to take advantage of the U.K. tax rules in circumstances in which it would appear that under Taxes Act 1988, section 235 and Article 10 of the U.S. Treaty, the tax credit would not be available to other shareholders.

13-06   Although the case did not deal specifically with the application of the Treaty, it was analogous to a claim for a reduction of tax at source. In the course of his judgment, Lloyd L.J. indicated, *obiter*, that although the Double Taxation Relief Regulations[11] permitted the making of arrangements in relation to dividends, there is no obligation on the Inland Revenue to enter into any such arrangement. If the Tax Inspector had never given his original authorisation, he could not have been compelled to do so by way of a judicial review. He concluded that the actions of the Inspector were not unreasonable in the circumstances and that the original direction to pay gross did not produce a legitimate expectation that the credit would be paid. The case is indicative of the fact that although the court has jurisdiction to review the accuracy in law of the Revenue's reason for revoking a decision to pay dividends gross, in appropriate circumstances such decisions will be justified.

COMPLAINTS

13-07   The Inland Revenue have established procedures for dealing with complaints. Where taxpayers believe that the Inland Revenue Code of

---

[10] [1989] S.T.C. 785, QBD, [1989] S.T.C. 796, CA.
[11] S.I. 1973 No. 317.

Practice has not been followed or that their rights have been denied or that they have been badly treated, they may ask for the case to be reviewed by the person in charge of the office in which the matter arose. The name of the Controller of the CNR appears on its letterhead *inter alia* for this purpose.

If the Controller does not settle the complaint to the taxpayer's satisfaction, the matter may be referred to the Revenue Adjudicator to consider the matter and recommend appropriate action. The Adjudicator is an impartial referee whose recommendations are independent.

Complaints dealt with by the Adjudicator are limited to the way in which the Inland Revenue has handled a taxpayer's affairs, such as mistakes, delays, behaviour of staff, departmental procedures or the use of discretion in making an individual decision.

13-08 The Adjudicator's mandate does not cover ministerial decisions or appeals on substantive matters that are handled by the General or Special Commissioners of the Inland Revenue. It does not cover complaints already investigated by the Parliamentary Ombudsman or those on which a court has already ruled or which are already subject to court proceedings.

In certain circumstances complaints may be made to the Parliamentary Ombudsman where administrative failure has led to injustice. All complaints must be referred to the Ombudsman by a Member of Parliament. No investigation may be made into any action for which the person aggrieved has entitlement to apply to a tribunal or to a remedy in a court of law, although investigations may be made if, in the circumstances, it is not reasonable to expect the person aggrieved to resort to such a right or remedy.[12]

By way of example, delay in refunding tax to a Canadian company and delay in adjusting the PAYE code number of a research fellow at a Swiss University resulted in financial loss to these taxpayers because of an official currency devaluation in 1967. The Ombudsman considered that the only adequate remedy in these cases would be an *ex gratia* payment of compensation equal to the financial loss suffered as a result of the maladministration. This approach was agreed by the Inland Revenue.[13]

MUTUAL AGREEMENT PROCEDURE

13-09 Mutual agreement procedure is provided for in most U.K. treaties other than those following the colonial model. A modern example is found in the Czech Treaty. Article 24 reads as follows:

> "24(1) Where a resident of a Contracting State considers that the actions of one or both of the Contracting States result or will result for him in taxation not in accordance with this Convention, he may, notwithstanding the remedies provided by the national laws of those States, present his case to the competent authority of the Contracting State of which he is a resident.

---

[12] Parliamentary Commissioner Act 1967, s. 6(4).
[13] Second Report of the Parliamentary Commissioner for Administration. Annual Report for 1968 Cases C230/68 and C258/68.

24(2) The competent authority shall endeavour, if the objection appears to it to be justified and if it is not itself able to arrive at an appropriate solution, to resolve the case by mutual agreement with the competent authority of the other Contracting State, with a view to the avoidance of taxation not in accordance with the Convention.

24(3) The competent authorities of the Contracting States shall endeavour to resolve by mutual agreement any difficulties or doubts arising as to the interpretation or application of the Convention.

24(4) The competent authorities of the Contracting States may communicate with each other directly for the purpose of reaching an agreement in the sense of the preceding paragraphs".

13-10 Where double taxation occurs in the context of differing views between contracting states on the application of a treaty, most treaties that follow the OECD Model allow taxpayers to submit the issue for discussion between the competent authorities to see if they can agree a resolution. The precise terms on which the mutual agreement procedure operates needs to be considered by reference to individual treaties. Although the vast majority follow the OECD Model, they are not all identical. Since the mutual agreement procedure exists by virtue of treaties only, the starting point must be the relevant treaty.

Mutual agreement procedure was operated entirely by administrative practice until it was put on a statutory basis in Finance Act 2000. Section 815AA provides a mechanism for giving effect to a case presented either to the Board of Inland Revenue or the competent authority of the other contracting state that he is taxed otherwise than in accordance with the treaty.

In the United Kingdom, there is no set form of claim to initiate the mutual agreement process. Applications should be made in writing specifying the years concerned, the nature of the action giving rise to taxation not in accordance with the treaty, as well as the names and addresses of the parties to which the procedure relates, including U.K. taxpayers' tax district and reference numbers.[14] Mutual agreement procedure is dealt with by the International Division, except in the case of the petroleum industry which is dealt with by the Oil Taxation Office.

13-11 The legislation clarifies that invoking the mutual agreement procedure under a treaty does not constitute a claim for relief and is accordingly not subject to section 42 of TMA 1970 or other enactments relating to the making of claims.

Recourse to the mutual agreement procedure is most commonly found in relation to transfer pricing, both between associated enterprises and in determining the attribution of profits to permanent establishments. Typical mutual agreement articles provide both for the invoking of the procedure to resolve individual cases of the application of a treaty and authority for the

---

[14] *Inland Revenue Tax Bulletin* (Issue 25, October 1996), p.346. *Double Taxation Relief Manual*, para. 232 specifies that the position of the foreign revenue authorities together with copies of correspondence with those authorities should be provided.

contracting states to "resolve by mutual agreement any difficulties or doubts arising as to the interpretation or application of the Convention". This second authority does not require to be invoked by taxpayers. It may facilitate practical issues, such as the operation of procedures for relief at source or the application of the treaty to changed domestic circumstances. There are also specific issues that are to be resolved by mutual agreement. The most common is the resolution of dual residence under Article 4(2)(d) of the OECD Model where other tie-breaker tests have failed to produce a result. In the U.S. Treaty (2001), a list of items suitable for agreement on the interpretation or application of the treaty are identified. The competent authorities may agree:

"a) to the same attribution of income, deductions, credits, or allowances of an enterprise of a Contracting State to its permanent establishment situated in the other Contracting State;

b) to the same allocation of income, deductions, credits, or allowances between persons;

c) to the same characterization of particular items of income, including the same characterization of income that is assimilated to income from shares by the taxation law of one of the Contracting States and that is treated as a different class of income in the other Contracting State;

d) to the same characterization of persons;

e) to the same application of source rules with respect to particular items of income;

f) to a common meaning of a term;

g) that the conditions for the application of the second sentence of paragraph 5 of Article 7 (Business Profits), paragraph 9 of Article 10 (Dividends), paragraph 7 of Article 11 (Interest), paragraph 5 of Article 12 (Royalties), or paragraph 4 of Article 22 (Other Income) of this Convention are met; and

h) to the application of the provisions of domestic law regarding penalties, fines, and interest in a manner consistent with the purposes of this Convention".[15]

13-12   In the Exchange of Notes of July 24, 2001 to the U.S. Treaty (2001), the competent authorities agree to publish any principle of general application established by agreement between them.

Mutual agreement procedure is an imperfect remedy in that contracting states are only required to "endeavour" to resolve difficulty, rather than actually to solve them. U.K. experience would indicate that most problems are ultimately resolved, although in many cases, this can take a considerable amount of time.

---

[15] U.S. Treaty, Art. 26(3).

In relation to the U.S. Treaty, the competent authorities have agreed to endeavour to deliver a position paper to the other party within 120 days of receipt of the presentation of a case. The objective of the two competent authorities is generally to resolve cases by concluding a mutual agreement within 18 months from transmittal of the position paper by one contracting state to the other. In the context of transfer pricing and advanced pricing agreements, they will endeavour to agree a joint timetable for dealing with the various stages of the application with the aim of securing mutual agreements within a similar time-frame taking into account the complexities of the particular cases involved. There are no other published statements involving other contracting states. In some cases, delays may be extended, for example because of language difficulties where both underlying documentation and the position papers of each contracting state are required to be translated. In relation to the United States, where negotiations continue beyond a time-frame agreed upon, senior officials will undertake a review of the case to ensure that all appropriate action is taken to facilitate a resolution of the matter. In addition, the United Kingdom and United States have undertaken not to withdraw from mutual agreement proceedings without meeting face to face to discuss specifically the problems or concerns that give rise to the consideration of withdrawal.

13-13   Mutual agreement procedure is a government to government activity and taxpayers have no legal entitlement to participate in or observe the negotiations. As a practical matter, the United Kingdom recognises the interest of the taxpayer and does endeavour to keep taxpayers informed about progress and will invite taxpayers to make further submissions as may be helpful in reaching a resolution. The extent to which the taxpayer is invited to participate informally is at the discretion of the competent authorities.

The treaty article normally authorises the competent authorities to "communicate with each other". Although the precise scope of this authority is undefined, mutual agreement procedure articles are always found in conjunction with exchange of information provisions. This supports the mutual agreement process which necessarily involves the sharing of information.

Time Limits

13-14   Care should be exercised particularly in relation to time limits for presenting a case. The time limits in relation to treaties must be considered in the context of domestic limitations in each country and in the treaty.

Finance Act 2000, section 815AA(6) requires any case for the mutual agreement procedure to be presented within six years of the end of the chargeable period to which the case relates, or such longer period as may be specified by treaty. The presentation of a case under the new legislation does not constitute a claim for relief and accordingly TMA 1970, section 43 and other statutes relating to time limits are inapplicable. It also resolves the problem which exists under other self-assessment legislation relating to claims, namely that the claim should be quantified at the time that it is made. These rules only apply in relation to cases presented from July 28, 2000 and therefore earlier cases will continue to be governed by the old rules.

In addition, careful attention will need to be paid to time limits in other contracting states. The new legislation imposes a further time limit for claiming relief. Where a case is resolved through this procedure, a claim for relief under any provision of the Taxes Acts may be made pursuant to the resolution at any time within 12 months after notification of the resolution to the person affected. This applies notwithstanding any other time limits for making claims.[16]

Methods of Giving Relief

13-15   The new legislation contemplates two ways in which a case may be resolved where a person is taxed in the United Kingdom or the other contracting state other than in accordance with the relevant treaty. Section 815AA(1)(b) permits the Revenue either to arrive at a solution to the case or to make a mutual agreement with the competent authorities of the other contracting state. Where this is done, the Revenue must give effect to the solution or mutual agreement "notwithstanding anything in any enactment"—this gives huge powers to the Board of Inland Revenue to adapt the tax rules to give effect to a treaty, either unilaterally or by mutual agreement. Any adjustment as is appropriate in consequence may be made whether by way of discharge or repayment of tax, the allowance of credit against tax payable in the United Kingdom, the making of an assessment or otherwise.[17]

Under the earlier informal procedures, following agreement between the competent authorities, the U.K. company will normally be invited to submit revised tax computations reflecting the agreed relief. This will now need to be implemented in the form of a claim as contemplated by section 815AA(3).

13-16   The Inland Revenue does not accept that a taxpayer may make unilateral adjustments through its accounts in order to obtain corresponding relief for an adjustment imposed by another jurisdiction. The only avenue, it argues, is to claim relief under the mutual agreement procedure. This statement may now be in conflict with the general self-assessment rules, at least if adjustments are made within permitted time limits. As a practical matter, in most cases the time taken for the other contracting state to make adjustments will put the matter outside normal time limits.

In the context of transfer pricing, the U.K. competent authorities recognise that investigations may take many years to resolve and will therefore accept protective claims.

Appeal versus Mutual Agreement Procedure

13-17   Mutual agreement procedure is an administrative process. It is in essence a request to the United Kingdom and its treaty partner to act reasonably in resolving a dispute. As a result, from a practical point of view, launching an appeal is unlikely to encourage a sympathetic attitude from either administrations. Where an enquiry is not completed, the opportunity for

---

[16] Finance Act 2000, s. 815AA(3).
[17] *ibid.*, s. 815AA(2).

bringing an appeal does not arise. The question is less straightforward where an appeal has been brought and subsequently competent authority proceedings are invoked. Where an adjustment is made in relation to an issue raised in the United Kingdom and settled either by determination of an appeal under TMA 1970, section 54 or by the courts, the United Kingdom would take the matter up under the mutual agreement procedure with the treaty partner to obtain that country's agreement to a corresponding adjustment. The precise implications of this approach have given rise to some controversy. TMA 1970, section 54 provides for the settling of appeals by agreement. The effect of the section is that a settlement by agreement is deemed to be a determination by the Special Commissioners. The effect of this would be to limit mutual agreement procedures to seeking corresponding relief in the other contracting state, where the dispute has been settled by agreement between the Inland Revenue and the taxpayer. As a result of discussions between the Inland Revenue and professional bodies, the Inland Revenue have indicated that they may be willing to discuss the scope for entering into competent authority discussions before an assessment is settled. They also welcome early notification of disputes with overseas authorities. A claim for corresponding adjustment in respect of action by an overseas authority must be made within six years and a claim may be made within six years even if an appeal has been settled by agreement under section 54 or earlier.[18]

MUTUAL AGREEMENT PROCEDURE AND GATS DISPUTE RESOLUTION

13-18   The OECD has identified problems that have arisen out of the application of the General Agreement of Trade in Services (GATS) which entered into force on January 1, 1995 and to which the United Kingdom is a party.

Articles XXII(3) of GATS provides that a dispute on the application of Article XVII of the agreement in national treatment rule may not be dealt with under the dispute resolution mechanisms of Articles XXII and XXIII if the disputed measure falls within the scope of an international agreement relating to double taxation. Where there is a dispute as to whether the measure is within the scope of a tax treaty, either state may refer the matter to the Council on Trade in Services which must refer the matter for binding arbitration.

Difficult legal interpretations have arisen in relation to this. A footnote states that if the dispute relates to a treaty which exists at the time of entry into force of GATS, then the matter may only be brought to the Council on Trade in Services if both states agree. There is some debate about the legal status of a footnote.

13-19   The implication of this footnote is that tax treaties would be treated differently depending on whether they were concluded before or after

---

[18]   Chartered Institute of Taxation, Notes of Meeting between the Inland Revenue International Division and representatives of professional bodies held on December 10, 1996, and published on April 10, 1997.

the entry into force of GATS. The OECD considers this inappropriate, particularly where a treaty in force on January 1, 1995 is subsequently re-negotiated or where a protocol is included after that time.

The OECD regards the expression "falls within the scope" as inherently ambiguous. This is demonstrated by the inclusion of both an arbitration clause and a clause exempting pre-existing conventions from its application in order to deal with disagreements related to its meaning. In the view of the OECD, a country could not argue in good faith that a measure relating to tax to which no provision of a tax treaty applied fell with the scope of that convention. They argue that it is unclear whether the phrase covers all measures that relate to taxes covered by all or only some of the provisions of the tax treaty.

13-20   In order to avoid these difficulties, the OECD suggests a clause for inclusion in the treaty which state that, for the purpose of Article XXII (3)3 of GATS, any dispute as to the application of the tax treaty in question will only be brought before the Council for Trade in Services with the consent of both contracting parties. They recommend that the interpretation of the paragraph should be resolved by mutual agreement procedure in the event of any doubt or any other procedure that the contracting states may adopt. The first treaty to address this issue is the U.S. Treaty (2001). Article 1(2) specifies that the Treaty does not restrict in any manner any benefit presently or in the future accorded by any other agreement between the contracting states. Furthermore, the application of Article XVII of GATS is specifically disapplied and any question arising as to the interpretation or application of the Treaty and, in particular, whether a tax measure is within its scope, is to be determined exclusively in accordance with the mutual agreement procedure.[19] For this purpose, a "measure" is a law, regulation, rule, procedure, decision, administrative action or any similar provision or action.[20] In the Exchange of Notes, the United Kingdom and the United States identified the (non-tax) treaties between them that may impose national treatment or most favoured nation obligations. They have undertaken to ensure the proper interpretation of the tax treaty and other agreements with respect to tax measures, if further treaties come into force creating such obligations.

---

[19] U.S. Treaty, Art.1(3).
[20] Article 1(3)(b).

CHAPTER 14

Transfer Pricing Arbitration Convention

14-01   European Community Member States executed a unique multilateral treaty on the elimination of double taxation in connection with the adjustment of profits of associated enterprises on July 23, 1990. Austria, Finland and Sweden acceded to the Convention when they joined the European Community in 1994. It is based on a draft Directive first presented by the European Commission to the Council on November 25, 1976 and adopts some elements of the arbitration system originally proposed in the draft Directive. The Convention is drawn up in a single original in the Danish, Dutch, English, French, German, Greek, Italian, Irish, Portuguese and Spanish languages—all 10 texts being equally authentic. Although a treaty rather than other European Community instruments, the approach of the European Court of Justice in reconciling different language versions is likely to be followed.[1]

The Convention was initially concluded for a period of five years. Six months before expiry of that period, the contracting states were required to meet to decide on the extension of the Convention and any other relevant measures.[2] However, on May 19, 1998, EU finance ministers agreed to extend the Convention for a further five years to January 1, 2005, with automatic five-year extensions beyond that unless contracting states decide otherwise.

The Convention represents a remarkable development in dealing with double taxation within the European Union; first, because it is a multilateral treaty on the subject, and secondly, because it proposes to adopt a form of arbitration between tax authorities in settling transfer pricing issues. It is the first U.K. treaty to deal with dispute resolution between competent authorities by arbitration. It offers an alternative to bilateral treaties in some cases, although both may be invoked at the same time.

PERSONAL SCOPE

14-02   Article 1(1) of the Convention specifies that the Convention applies to "an enterprise of a contracting state". No further explanation of the term is provided, although Article 3(2) specifies that any term not defined in the Convention is to have the meaning it has under the applicable treaty between the Member States concerned, unless the context requires otherwise. Article 3(1)(b) of the OECD Model Convention defines the term to mean "an

---

[1]   See, for example, Case C-420/98 *W.N. v. Staatssecretaris van Financiën* [2001] S.T.C. 974.
[2]   Article 20.

enterprise carried on by a resident of a contracting state". The Commentary on the OECD Model in turn indicates that this has always been interpreted according to the provisions of domestic law and that no definition properly speaking of the term "enterprise" is attempted. Presumably, this will mean that the application will be somewhat uneven depending on the countries concerned, particularly in relation to partnerships and joint ventures. The position is particularly uncertain where more than two countries are involved or where there is no treaty between the countries concerned.

Article 1(2) states that a permanent establishment of an enterprise of a contracting state situated in another contracting state is deemed to be an enterprise of the state in which it is situated. The definition thus excludes the application of the Convention to residents of third states. Permanent establishments of non EC enterprises in two or more EC countries would not be able to rely on the provisions of the Convention, although obviously subsidiaries of U.S. corporations established within the Community would be able to.

TAXES COVERED

14-03   The Convention applies generally to taxes on income. It covers in particular direct tax on individuals and companies that are imposed by Member States (income tax and corporation tax in the United Kingdom) and where adjustments are made to profits of an enterprise in a contracting state, either under its domestic law or under the transfer pricing principles established in the Convention. The Convention is applicable only to taxes on income as specifically set out and any identical or similar taxes that may be imposed by member states. Thus, the controlled foreign company charge[3] is included notwithstanding the decision in *Bricom Holdings Ltd v. IRC.*[4] Thus, transfer pricing disputes involving controlled foreign companies will be within the Convention.

The taxes covered in the Convention do not always correspond precisely with the taxes referred to in bilateral treaties between Member States. For example, in the case of Germany, it excludes the capital tax (*Vermogensteuer*) covered in the German–U.K. Treaty. The trade tax (*Gewerbesteuer*) is covered only in the Convention insofar as it is based on trading profits. By comparison, the trade tax in the German–U.K. Treaty is covered in relation to the tax as it applies both to income and to capital. There is also some inconsistency between the various Member States. The Danish church tax is covered by the Convention, but the German church tax is not.

ARM'S LENGTH STANDARD

14-04   The arm's length standard set out in Article 4 of the Convention adopts precisely the wording developed in Article 9(1) of the OECD Model in connection with related party dealings. It also reproduces Article 7(2) of

---

[3] Taxes Act 1988, s. 747.
[4] [1997] S.T.C. 1179, CA.

the OECD Model, which requires the profits of a permanent establishment to be determined on a separate enterprise basis. By adopting these well-established standards, the contracting parties avoid any new controversy on the subject. No explicit reference is made to the OECD Transfer Pricing Guidelines. Adoption of OECD language means that interpretation is facilitated by reference to the OECD Commentary on these articles and the various OECD studies on transfer pricing are implicitly recognised.

PARTICIPATION IN MANAGEMENT, CONTROL OR CAPITAL

14-05   The Convention applies the OECD Model test as to when profits of associated enterprises are subject to adjustment. It thus applies where an enterprise of a contracting state participates directly or indirectly in the management, control or capital of an enterprise in another contracting state. Alternatively, it applies where the same persons participate directly or indirectly in the management, control or capital of an enterprise in two different contracting states. The Convention does not address the application of bilateral treaties to interest and royalties where amounts are affected by "a special relationship between the payer and the beneficial owner of the interest or the royalties, or between both of them and some other person". The effect of the application of the royalty or interest articles on double taxation will however need to take this into account in any event.

ELIMINATION OF DOUBLE TAXATION

14-06   The Convention establishes its own standard as to when double taxation is deemed to be eliminated. Double taxation of profits is treated as having been eliminated if either the profits are included in the computation of taxable profits in one state only, or the tax chargeable on those profits in one state is reduced by the tax chargeable on them in another. Relief from double taxation in the form of corresponding adjustments where profit that has been taxed in one state is increased in another specified in Article 9(2) of the OECD Model Convention is not included. This is not surprising given the reservations of Belgium, Germany, Italy and the United Kingdom, as well as Portugal, on Article 9(2) of the OECD Model. No provision is made either for so-called secondary adjustments to restore the overall relationship of the parties after adjustments have been made.

TIME LIMITS

14-07   The EC Arbitration Convention adopts the three-year limitation rule found in the OECD Model. The time limits in relation to other treaties must still be viewed in the context of domestic limitations. Where the mutual agreement is sought with competent authorities in an EU Member State, there will be a choice as to whether the mutual agreement provisions of a bilateral treaty are invoked or whether the equivalent provisions under Article 6 of the Arbitration Convention are used. In many cases, it will make no difference. In the case of Greece, there is no mutual agreement provision in the bilateral treaty and therefore the Arbitration Convention offers the only basis for competent authority proceedings. In other cases, where there are problems of foreign time limits, invoking the Arbitration Convention may permit an otherwise out of time election. In the United Kingdom, where the general time limit for invoking mutual agreement procedure is six years, if the Convention is not evoked within the three-year limit, arbitration will not be possible.

The three-year time limit starts to run upon the first notification of the action which results or is likely to result in double taxation. The meaning of this expression is unsettled. The Inland Revenue interpret the first notification of the action as the finalising of a transfer pricing enquiry, which gives rise to double taxation.[5] This stage will be marked by the determination of the quantum of the additional profits arising from the transfer pricing adjustment to be taken into account in a tax assessment, loss determination or other official demand for tax. The issuing of a direction under the previous transfer pricing legislation in connection with an estimated assessment is not regarded as first notification. This interpretation places the notification earlier than, for example a closure notice or other step under Finance Act 1988, section 10(1), which, in the context of transfer pricing, requires sanction of the Inland Revenue. More helpfully, the Revenue indicate that where they consider a case is being presented prematurely in respect of U.K. initiated transfer pricing adjustments, they will nonetheless contact the other contracting state or states to explain why the presentation is considered to be premature and seek agreement of the other state as to what the first notification would be in that case.[6]

ADJUSTMENT PROCEDURE

14-08   Details of the mutual agreement and arbitration procedures comprise the bulk of the Convention and constitute its most innovative features. Unlike most bilateral treaties, the procedures for seeking mutual agreement are set out at length. Transfer pricing adjustments are commenced by notification by a contracting state to the taxpayer of its intention to make adjustments. Sufficient time must be given to the taxpayer to notify relevant related parties and the other contracting state. If the other state and the taxpayer agree to the adjustment, no arbitration takes place.

A taxpayer who claims the arm's length principles of the Convention have not been properly applied may submit a case to the appropriate competent authorities pursuant to the Convention, irrespective of any other remedy provided under domestic law. If the competent authorities jointly fail to resolve the matter by agreement that eliminates double taxation, they must establish an advisory commission in accordance with the Convention's procedures. If agreement is reached, the competent authorities must implement it even if time limits under domestic laws have expired. This is given effect

---

[5] *Inland Revenue Tax Bulletin* (October 1997), p.465.
[6] *ibid.*, p.466.

to in the United Kingdom by section 815B(1)(a) of Taxes Act 1988 and section 815B(3) in relation to the extension of time limits.

14-09 The competent authorities are not required to initiate arbitration proceedings if domestic, legal or administrative proceedings against the taxpayer have resulted in a final ruling that one of the enterprises is liable for a serious penalty by virtue of an action giving rise to an adjustment or transfer of profits. A schedule to the Convention details what each Member State regards as a serious penalty. Typically, these relate to fraudulent or criminal conduct. In the United Kingdom, "serious penalty" means criminal and administrative sanctions in respect of the fraudulent or negligent delivery of incorrect accounts, claims or returns for tax purposes. A mere allegation that serious penalty proceedings will commence will not eliminate competent authority proceedings which may be stayed until the judicial or administrative proceedings have been concluded.

ADVISORY COMMISSION

14-10 The term "arbitration" does not appear in the Convention. The Advisory Commission is the panel established on an ad hoc basis to hear disputes under the Convention. It consists of a chairman plus two representatives of each competent authority and an even number of independent persons of standing to be appointed by agreement or by the drawing of lots by the competent authorities concerned. A list of independent persons of standing is maintained by the Secretary General of the Council of the European Communities with five persons nominated from each Member State. It specifies in detail the qualifications for nomination. The chairman must be either qualified to hold the highest judicial office in his or her country or a jurisconsult of recognised competence. The taxpayer has no participation in the selection of the panel. The competent authorities may object to independent panel members if they work for the tax administration concerned, or if they are owners, employers, or advisers of one of the parties, or where adequate objectivity is not assured.

The arbitration process is between the contracting states concerned and not between the taxpayer and the authorities. This is also one of its disadvantages—in principle, the taxpayer is not involved in the process. However, Article 10(2) of the Arbitration Convention permits the associated enterprises in question to appear or be represented before the Advisory Commission on request. The enterprises concerned must appear before the Commission if requested by the Commission to do so.

Information

14-11 The taxpayers concerned may provide any information, evidence or documents that they consider likely to be of use to the Commission. Taxpayers and the competent authorities must give effect to any request for information from the Commission, although contracting states are not required to carry out administrative measures at variance with their domestic law or normal administrative practice, or to supply information not obtainable under domestic law or normal administrative practice. Similarly, competent authorities are not obliged to supply information that would disclose any trade secret or be contrary to public policy. Disclosure of information by the Inland Revenue to the Commission is authorised by Taxes Act 1988, section 816(2A). The Commission itself is also subject to security obligations. The United Kingdom enforces this with criminal sanctions under Finance Act 1989, section 182A.

Costs

14-12   The taxpayer is entitled to representation and must bear its own costs in connection with the proceedings. The other costs of the procedure are borne equally by the contracting states concerned. Participation by the enterprise, whether at its request or at the request of the Commission, will be at its own cost. Article 11(3) of the Convention provides that the costs of the arbitration procedure are to be borne by the contracting states concerned equally, other than those of the associated enterprises. The Convention is silent on the taxpayers' costs and therefore it would appear that no award of costs is possible in that regard.

Opinion of Advisory Commission

14-13   The opinion of the Advisory Commission is to be adopted by simple majority and must be delivered not more than six months from the date on which the matter was referred to it. A decision that will eliminate double taxation must be taken within six months of the date on which the Advisory Commission delivers its opinion. The competent authorities may take a decision that deviates from the Advisory Commission's opinion, but if they fail to reach agreement, they are required to act in accordance with that opinion. In the United Kingdom, opinions of the Advisory Commission are to be given effect to pursuant to section 815B(1)(b) of the Taxes Act 1988.

Where transfer pricing disputes arise in the context of other EU Member States, there are advantages in invoking the Arbitration Convention rather than simply the bilateral treaty, beyond the question of time limits. The availability of arbitration does provide an incentive for the tax authorities to resolve the question. Arbitration may be requested by a taxpayer, if double taxation has not been eliminated by agreement between the competent authorities within two years of the date on which the case was first submitted to one of them.

CHOICE OF FORUM

14-14   The Arbitration Convention permits the arbitration procedures to operate, even where the matter is before the courts of a Member State. In this setting, taxpayers are not precluded from appealing transfer pricing assessments while proceeding with competent authority proceedings. In such a case, the two-year limitation period will only start to run when the judgment of the final court of appeal is given. The establishment of the Advisory Commission charged with addressing the double taxation question need only be established either when the time for appeal has expired or any appeal has been withdrawn before a decision is delivered.

The Inland Revenue position is that before the arbitration stage can commence, the time for appeal must have expired without an appeal having been made or the taxpayer must have withdrawn the appeal or settled it by agreement.[7] This is as a result of the unilateral declaration by the United Kingdom that Article 7(3) of the Convention will apply. Article 7(3) deals with circumstances where the domestic law of a contracting state does not permit the competent authorities of that state to derogate from the decisions of their judicial bodies. As a result, U.K. taxpayers are put to the choice in effect of choosing arbitration or the domestic appeals process. Since the Convention only applies to transfer pricing, appeals may relate to issues of double taxation not addressed by the Convention. In this context, the Inland Revenue will agree that taxpayers will not be denied access to arbitration, purely because of the outstanding appeal or appeal rights, as long as suitable undertakings are given by the taxpayer acknowledging that the appeal's process will not extend to the transfer pricing issue which is the subject of arbitration.[8]

The Convention applies strictly to transfer pricing disputes and not to any other matters that may be the subject of mutual agreement proceedings. Presentation of a case under the Convention involves the same procedure in the United Kingdom as under bilateral treaties. The remedy for a failure to carry out the provisions of the Convention would be by way of judicial review.

CONCLUSION

14-15 The Convention is a significant step forward in solving increasingly difficult transfer pricing issues. Since the Convention entered into force on January 1, 1995, it is understood that there is only one case of arbitration that is actually proceeding. This has led some to conclude that the Convention is of little practical significance. A number of practitioners, both in the private sector and in tax authorities have, however, commented that even if there were not to be a single arbitration, the Convention has a helpful role to play by encouraging revenue authorities to take a reasonable approach to transfer pricing within the EU, rather than risk the arbitration procedure. The success of the Convention is therefore in the absence of cases, rather than in their presence. The Convention provides that the rulings of the Commission may be published subject to the consent of the taxpayer concerned. It would undoubtedly be an important contribution to learning on the subject if they are, particularly if detailed reasons for decisions are provided.

The original draft Directive proposed that existing treaty arrangements with respect to transfer pricing would remain intact. The Convention is silent on this point. A single standard and a single procedural approach for

---

[7] *Inland Revenue Tax Bulletin* (October 1997), p.467.
[8] *ibid.*

all transfer pricing issues within the Community are clearly desirable. However, more generous time limits under U.K. domestic law do continue to offer relief from double taxation arising from transfer pricing adjustments where Convention time limits have expired.

14-16   Rules for ensuring procedural safeguards and due process in the proceedings of the Advisory Commission are not addressed. The Convention does not specify any judicial authority for supervision of the Advisory Commission, nor are any standards of fairness set out. The result is that a taxpayer who claims a lack of fairness will have to resort to domestic law remedies within the jurisdiction in which the proceedings might take place. It would have been preferable for the Convention to deal with this both by stating a set of guidelines on procedural fairness, such as the 1977 Resolution of the Council of Europe on the "Protection of the Individual in Relation to Acts of Administrative Authorities", and by providing an appeal process, preferably to the European Court of Justice as recommended by the European Commission.

CHAPTER 15

Exchange of Information

INTRODUCTION

15-01 Historically, sovereign states did not cooperate with each other in the administration of taxation. An important exception to this is in the area of exchange of information. This has been viewed as the single route whereby contracting states gave effect to the purpose stated in the heading of model treaties in relation to the prevention of tax evasion.

DUTY OF CONFIDENTIALITY

15-02 At common law, there appears to have been no duty of confidentiality, although there is apparently a convention that the Inland Revenue does not supply the Treasury or other government departments with confidential information relating to individual taxpayers. Direct taxation is under the care and management of the Board of Inland Revenue.

Under domestic law, every person who is appointed as an Inspector or collector, or who is appointed by the Revenue to serve in any other capacity is required to make a declaration of confidentiality.[1] In addition, a person who discloses information which he holds or has held in the exercise of tax functions is guilty of an offence.[2] These provisions replace section 2 of the Official Secrets Act 1911. Article 8 of the European Convention of Human Rights may have the effect of imposing a duty of confidentiality.

15-03 Under U.K. domestic law, the Inland Revenue may disclose personal information to other government departments under a variety of statutes. These include:

(a) Land Registration Act 1925, section 129;

(b) Parliamentary Commissioner Act 1967, section 8;

(c) Finance Act 1972, section 127;

(d) Social Security Pensions Act 1975, section 59K(6)[3];

(e) Finance Act 1978, section 77;

(f) Tenant's Rights etc. (Scotland) Act 1980, section 1;

(g) Social Security and Housing Benefit Act 1982, section 25;

---

[1] Taxes Management Act (TMA) 1970, s. 6, Sched. 1.
[2] Finance Act 1989, s. 182.
[3] From July 18, 1990 by virtue of S.I. 1990 No. 1446.

(h) National Audit Act 1983, section 8;

(i) Data Protection Act 1984, section 17;

(j) Housing Associations Act 1985, section 62;

(k) Social Security Act 1986, section 59;

(l) Taxes Act 1988, section 375(9), (10), 816;

(m) Social Security Administration Act 1992, section 122;

(n) Charities Act 1993, section 10(2).

The Inland Revenue may also disclose personal information to the police under:

(o) Drug Trafficking Offences Act 1986, section 30;

(p) Prevention of Terrorism (Temporary Provisions) Act 1989, section 17, Schedule 17.

AUTHORITY FOR EXCHANGE OF INFORMATION IN TAX TREATIES

15-04 The legislation authorising income tax treaties makes provision for exchange of information by treaty. Taxes Act 1988, section 788(2) specifies that treaties may include provisions with respect to the exchange of information necessary for carrying out the domestic laws of the United Kingdom and the territory to which the treaty relates concerning taxes covered by the treaty, including in particular provisions about prevention of fiscal evasion with respect to those taxes. This authority is expressed to be without prejudice of the generality of the treaty-making authority. It also requires that where a treaty includes an exchange of information, the Order in Council enacting the treaty into domestic law must contain a declaration to that effect.

Authority to include exchange of information provisions does not itself relieve the obligations of confidentiality. Specific authority is provided. Accordingly, the secrecy obligations imposed by any enactment do not prevent the Inland Revenue or any authorised officer of the Revenue from disclosing to any authorised officer of the government of a contracting state such information as is required to be disclosed under the relevant treaty.[4] Exoneration from the obligation of secrecy is similarly given in relation to information required to be disclosed under the Arbitration Convention in pursuance of a request made by an Advisory Commission set up under that Convention.[5]

15-05 A narrower exception to the secrecy obligation is also made in relation to shipping and air transportation agreements. This permits disclosure of "such facts as may be necessary to enable relief to be duly given in accordance with the arrangements specified".[6]

---

[4] Taxes Act 1988, s. 816(2).
[5] *ibid.*, s. 816(2A).
[6] *ibid.*, s. 816(4).

Authority for disclosure under section 816 is extended to capital gains tax by Taxation of Chargeable Gains Act (TCGA) 1992, section 277(4). Authority to conclude inheritance tax treaties includes authority to conclude exchange of information provisions, along the lines similar to those applicable to income tax.[7] Authority for disclosure is also provided.[8]

EXCHANGE OF INFORMATION AGREEMENTS

15-06 Until 2000, exchange of information with treaty partners was only possible within the framework of a tax treaty generally. However, as part of the United Kingdom's participation in the OECD Programme against Harmful Tax Practices, Taxes Act 1988, section 815C was inserted by the Finance Act 2000, section 146(1). It contemplates the conclusion of agreements between the United Kingdom and governments of any territory:

"with a view to the exchange of information necessary for carrying out:

(a) the domestic laws of the United Kingdom concerning income tax, capital gains tax and corporation tax in respect of income and chargeable gains; and

(b) the laws of the territory to which the arrangements relate concerning any taxes of a similar character to those imposed by the laws of that territory".

Section 815C(1) is similar in structure to section 788 from a constitutional perspective. It permits treaties which have been made to be enacted into domestic law by Order in Council. Similar arrangements are made for revoking previous Orders and for transitional provisions. The usual constitutional norm of requiring a draft Order to be laid before and approved by a Resolution of the House of Commons continues. Similar provisions are inserted by Finance Act 2000, section 147 into the Inheritance Tax Act 1984.

The scope of the authorisation is similar to that in section 788(2), but it simply disconnects the exchange of information element from any other aspects aimed at relieving double taxation. The purpose of such agreements is not so much to exchange information, but to obtain information from tax haven jurisdictions, although the legislation contemplates the supply of information to the other contracting state.

TREATY PROVISIONS

15-07 Every treaty that the United Kingdom has entered into contains an article dealing with exchange of information. U.K. practice follows the OECD Model which is reflected, for example, in the current Korean Treaty. Article 27 reads as follows:

---

[7] Inheritance Tax Act 1984, s. 158(1A).
[8] *ibid.*, s. 158(5).

"*Exchange of Information*

27(1) The competent authorities of the Contracting States shall exchange such information as is necessary for carrying out the provisions of this Convention or of the domestic laws of the Contracting States concerning taxes covered by the Convention insofar as the taxation thereunder is not contrary to the Convention. The exchange of information is not restricted by Article 1. Any information received by a Contracting State shall be treated as secret in the same manner as information obtained under the domestic laws of that State and shall be disclosed only to persons or authorities (including courts and administrative bodies) concerned with the assessment or collection of, the enforcement or prosecution in respect of, or the determination of appeals in relation to, the taxes covered by the Convention. Such persons or authorities shall use the information only for such purposes. They may disclose the information in public court proceedings or in judicial decisions".

15-08   Treaties in this form provide for information exchanged to a very wide extent. Information falls within this article if:

(1)   it is necessary for carrying out the provisions of the Treaty; or

(2)   it is necessary for carrying out the provisions of the domestic law of either contracting states concerning taxes covered by the Treaty insofar as taxation thereunder is not contrary to the Treaty.

This gives broad authority to exchange information. Although information is limited to the taxes that form the subject matter of the treaty, it is not restricted to persons who are within the scope of the treaty. Thus, information may be exchanged about persons who are not residents of either contracting state.

Earlier treaties do not authorise such extensive exchange. A number of treaties limit the exchange to information necessary for carrying out the provisions of the treaty, or for the provision of fraud, or the administration of statutory provisions against legal avoidance in relation to taxes which are the subject of the agreement. Examples of this are to be found in the Guernsey Treaty, Article 10, and the South African Treaty, Article 25. In these treaties, where the application of the treaty itself, tax evasion or statutory anti-avoidance provisions are not in issue, no exchange of information is authorised. Since residents of third countries will not generally be able to benefit from such treaties, information relating to them can only be exchanged in cases involving tax fraud or the application of statutory anti-avoidance provisions in one of the contracting states.

15-09   The scope of authority to supply information is further limited. Article 27(2) of the Korean Treaty for example reads:

"*Limits on obligation to provide information*

27(2) In no case shall the provisions of paragraph 1 be construed so as to impose on a Contracting State the obligation:

(a) to carry out administrative measures at variance with the laws and administrative practice of that or of the other Contracting State;

(b) to supply information which is not obtainable under the laws or in the normal course of the administration of that or of the other Contracting State;

(c) to supply information which would disclose any trade, business, industrial, commercial or professional secret or trade process, or information, the disclosure of which would be contrary to public policy (*ordre public*)".

In modern treaties, a contracting state is not under an obligation to supply information which is not obtainable under the laws or in the normal course of the administration of that or the other contracting state. It may be noted that the article uses the word "shall", implying that the exchange of information is mandatory, rather than discretionary. Some limits on the obligation are contained in the article. The wording of the current model is important. It relieves a contracting state from the obligation. The fact that there is no discretion to provide information has the effect of a prohibition on providing information that falls within this article, on the basis that the tax authorities are under a general duty of confidentiality.

15-10 Secondly, there is no obligation to supply information which would disclose any trade, business, industrial, commercial or professional secret, or trade process, or information, the disclosure of which would be contrary to public policy. Some treaties such as that with South Africa and Germany do not contain the public policy exclusion.

The narrowest exchange of information provision is contained in the Swiss Treaty. Article 25(1) limits exchange of information to that which is necessary for carrying out the provisions of the Treaty in relation to the taxes which are the subject of the Treaty. Article 25(2) of the Swiss Treaty contains further restrictions on exchange of information which would be subject to the "sovereignty security or public policy" of a contracting state.

Other treaty provisions involving exchange of information

15-11 Certain procedures under treaties implicitly involve exchange of information. Treaties that include Article 9(2) of the OECD Model in relation to transfer pricing adjustments require the competent authorities to consult each other if necessary in determining adjustments. Similarly, resort to the mutual agreement procedure in Article 25(1) requires communication with each other. It would, however, appear that in these cases, information on taxpayers still needs to be handled in accordance with the exchange of information articles of the relevant treaty.

Article 10(1) of the Arbitration Convention also contains information provisions. Apart from enabling the affected enterprises to submit information, the Convention requires the competent authorities of contracting states to effect any requests made by the Advisory Commission for information, evidence or documents. This is subject to the limitations commonly found in double tax treaties that they are not under any obligation:

(a) to carry out administrative measures at variance with domestic law or normal administrative practice;

(b) to supply information which is not obtainable under domestic law or normal administrative practice; or

(c) to supply information which would disclose any trade, business, industrial or professional secret, or trade process or information, the disclosure of which would be contrary to public policy.

15-12   An Exchange of Notes of December 15, 1996 in connection with the 1996 Protocol to the Treaty with Denmark contains an unusual specific obligation to exchange information in relation to the application of limitation of benefit provisions connected with dividend, interest and royalty payments. The Exchange of Notes requires the competent authority of each contracting state to notify the other where the limitation of benefit provisions of the Treaty as amended by the Protocol in relation to dividends, interest and royalties are applied to deny relief from taxation. This is a somewhat curious item. The reason for it is far from clear. It does not appear to impose any particular additional obligation on the contracting states beyond the existing exchange of information provisions contained in both the Treaty and in the EC Mutual Assistance Directive 77/799/EEC. Similar wording appears in the text of the Treaty itself in Article 11(10) of the Singapore Treaty.

In particular, Article 4(1) of the EC Mutual Assistance Directive, which provides for spontaneous exchange of information in a number of circumstances particularly where tax avoidance may be suspected, should cover the circumstances referred to in the Exchange of Notes completely. One may speculate that the contracting states have concerns that the limitation of benefits provision may give rise to difficulties under European law, particularly if they are applied in a discriminatory manner, and they would wish to be seen to be collaborating with each other in order to avoid this. Both contracting states might be defendants in an action attacking the provision even if it was applied only by one of them.

EC MUTUAL ASSISTANCE DIRECTIVE

15-13   Bilateral treaties between EC Member States invariably provide for exchanges of information. In addition, the question of exchange of information is also dealt with by Community law. The first Exchange of Information Directive in 1976 did not deal with direct taxation. It only covered customs duties, agricultural levies and certain claims under the common agricultural policy, with VAT added in 1979. It differs from other Directives in that it provides for mutual assistance for the recovery of claims in respect of certain indirect taxes.

Council Directive 77/799/EEC[9] covers mutual assistance by competent authorities in the field of direct taxation and VAT. It is considerably more

---

[9] December 19, 1977.

detailed than the provisions of Article 26 of the OECD Model. It specifies all of the taxes to which it applies in each Member State and the competent authorities. It provides for specific authorisation of exchanges on request, automatic exchanges of information and spontaneous exchanges of information.

15-14 In relation to exchanges on request, the competent authority of the requested state need not comply with the request if it appears that the requesting authority has not exhausted its own usual sources of information which it could have utilised according to the circumstances without running the risk of endangering the attainment of the sought-after result. The requested Member State must arrange for the conduct of appropriate enquiries necessary to obtain such information. This does change what was sometimes thought to be the position in at least some Member States under bilateral treaties. It is believed that in some cases, Member States' tax authorities would exchange information that they held, but would not use their information-gathering powers on behalf of a requesting authority.

In relation to automatic exchanges of information, once the competent authorities of Member States have agreed under the Consultation Procedure on the categories of information to be exchanged, it must be exchanged without prior request. There is no option of refusing to supply the information.

15-15 Spontaneous exchanges of information may be made in the following circumstances[10]:

(a) the competent authority of one Member State has grounds for supposing that there may be a loss of tax in another Member State;

(b) a person liable to tax obtains a reduction in or an exemption from tax in the one Member State which would give rise to an increase in tax or to liability to tax in the other Member State;

(c) business dealings between a person liable to tax in a Member State and a person liable in another are conducted through one or more countries in such a way that a saving in tax may result in one or the other Member State or both;

(d) the competent authority of a Member State has grounds for supposing that a saving of tax may result from artificial transfers of profits within groups of enterprises;

(e) information forwarded to the one Member State by the competent authority of another has enabled information to be obtained, which may be relevant in assessing liability to tax in the latter Member State.

The application of Article 4(1) in relation to spontaneous obligations to provide information has been considered by the European Court of Justice in *W.N. v. Staatssecretaris van Financiën*.[11] In that case, a taxpayer resident

---

[10] Mutual Assistance Directive, Art.4(1).
[11] Case C-420/98 [2001] S.T.C. 974.

in the Netherlands deducted maintenance payments which he made to his estranged wife in computing his taxable income in the Netherlands. His wife lived in Spain. The Netherlands tax authorities took the view that the payments might affect the levying of tax in Spain. They proposed to send information on the payments to the Spanish authorities. The taxpayer objected that they were not entitled to under Article 4(1)(a) of the Mutual Assistance Directive. He complained that it was not established that the payments would give rise to taxation in Spain.

15-16 The court, however, held that for the purposes of this article in the Directive, it was sufficient for the tax lost to be supposed by the informer state. It was not necessary to have to be proved or to be referred to in an express measure by the recipient state. That interpretation was in accordance with both the literal terms of the provision and the purpose of the Directive which was to enable the correct assessment of income and capital taxes in various states and to combat evasion.

In the context of the Directive's purpose, the information would only be of any use to the recipient's state tax authorities if it arrived before the relevant assessment to tax was made. It was not to be expected that the informer state had extensive knowledge of the legal and factual framework in the other state which would have to be implied by a requirement that an assessment to tax had already to have been made. The article meant that a state was to forward information to another where the former had grounds for supposing that without that information, an unjustified saving in tax might be going to arise in the latter state. It is implicit in the judgment that a payment of any kind to a recipient of another Member State may have tax consequences in that state and that this alone justifies the provision of the information.

15-17 Provision is made for collaboration by state officials in accordance with procedures as may be laid down.

The Directive provides for consultations to be held if necessary in order to deal with exchange of information issues both under the Directive and pursuant to any bilateral arrangement. Authorisation is given for designated authorities to communicate directly with each other in specified cases or in certain categories of cases.

Member States are not required to take any steps which are at variance with their own law or administrative practice and may refuse disclosure of commercial, industrial or professional secrets, or of a commercial process or where disclosure would be contrary to public policy. Where for practical or legal reasons the information cannot be provided, this is also a limit to disclosure.

The secrecy provision requires information to be made available only to persons directly involved in the assessment of tax or in administrative control of the assessment, as well as in connection with judicial proceedings. The information may not be used other than for tax purposes. Where a Member State has information requirements narrower than those of the Directive, they may refuse information if the recipient state does not undertake to respect those narrower limits. If the informing state could, however, use the information for other purposes, then it may be sent to other states for similar purposes. Provision is also made for information to be passed on to third Member States if this is considered appropriate.

U.K. DOMESTIC LAW ON THE PROVISION OF INFORMATION

15-18   Most treaties also specifically exclude contracting states from the obligation to carry out administrative measures at variance with the laws and administrative practice domestically. In this respect, the United Kingdom entered an observation on the Commentary to Article 26 of the OECD Model setting out its view that the article imposes no obligation on it to carry out enquiries on behalf of a contracting state in cases where no liability to U.K. tax is at issue, since to carry out such enquiries would be contrary to its administrative laws and practice. As will be seen, this limitation is no longer applicable.

Article 26(1) also places limitations on the use to which information exchanged may be put and the persons to which it may be disclosed. Several observations may be made in this respect. Although these are obligations of international law, their application within contracting states following the U.K. constitutional model is determined entirely by domestic law. The lack of domestic law implementation of these provisions may render them meaningless in relation to individuals. For example, in *R. v. IRC, ex parte Commerzbank AG*,[12] the court noted that the non-discrimination provisions of the U.S. Treaty were not given effect to in U.K. domestic law and could therefore not be relied upon by a taxpayer. Thus, taxpayers in other contracting states applying a similar constitutional doctrine may be faced with the situation where the treaty gives them no rights as such and they are thrown on local law in this respect.

15-19   The only limitation imposed under domestic statute in this respect is that the Inland Revenue may not disclose information pursuant to a treaty, unless they are satisfied that:

> "the government with which the arrangements are made is bound by or has undertaken to observe rules of confidentiality with respect to the information which are not less strict than those applying to it in the United Kingdom".[13]

It would not be unfair to note that in a few of the United Kingdom's treaty partners, respect for domestic law by those in power is weak. This may be accompanied by a disregard of international legal obligations and legal rights may be more theoretical than practical. If information is used for improper means, particularly in a covert manner, local legal remedies are unlikely to be of much use.

Furthermore, as already noted a number of exceptions to the general rule apply to confidentiality in the domestic context which serve to permit the supply of potentially sensitive information to foreign administrations. In the context of international exchanges of information, authority under the Prevention of Terrorism (Temporary Provisions) Act 1989 is perhaps the

---

[12] [1991] S.T.C. 271, QBD.
[13] See, for example, Taxes Act 1988, s. 816(2ZA) in relation to exchange of information agreements.

most troublesome. The legitimacy of the label of "terrorist" varies enormously depending on political perspective. Furthermore, anti-terrorist legislation is notoriously used by undemocratic regimes in order to suppress opposition that falls far short of the notion in democratic societies.

15-20   The Inland Revenue have been granted increasing authority to provide information to other tax administrations, where relief for U.K. income tax or corporation tax is provided by the law of another country. The secrecy obligations imposed on Inland Revenue officials does not prevent the disclosure of information to authorised officers of the relevant foreign government of "such facts as may be necessary to enable the proper relief to be given under that law".[14] This rule does not appear to be restricted to countries where there are treaties.

In giving effect to the EC Mutual Assistance Directive, Finance Act 1978, section 77 authorises disclosure of information to tax authorities in other Member States, subject to the same exceptions found in the case of treaty exchanges of information, namely that the Inland Revenue are satisfied that the competent authorities of the other state are bound by or have undertaken to observe rules of confidentiality which are no less strict than those applying in the United Kingdom. Secondly, they may not authorise the use of information disclosed under the Directive other than for the purpose of taxation or to facilitate legal proceedings for the failure to observe the tax laws of the receiving state.

15-21   Finance Act 1990, section 125 extended the information-gathering powers of the Inland Revenue under section 20 of the Taxes Management Act (TMA) 1970 to include exercising powers on behalf of other Member States in relation to their taxes on income and capital. As a result, the Inland Revenue may exercise the powers under section 20 to obtain documents and information, both of a taxpayer and third parties. As an exception, the section does not authorise the issue of notices pursuant to section 20(8A), which permits documents and information to be demanded without the naming of the taxpayer to whom the notice relates, subject to approval of a Special Commissioner. Similar powers pursuant to section 219 of the Inheritance Tax Act 1984 are given to require information for the purpose of inheritance tax or other taxes chargeable by reference to death or gifts *inter vivos* in other Member States which are referred to in the Mutual Assistance Directive.[15]

Finance Act 2000, section 146(3) extends these powers to the Inland Revenue in relation to the tax of territories beyond the European Union, where there is either a double taxation treaty authorised under Taxes Act 1988, section 788 or an exchange of information agreement under section 815C and containing provisions with respect to the obtaining and disclosure of information. Consequently, the Inland Revenue has power to call for documents and information in relation to taxpayers of the relevant foreign countries in circumstances where the United Kingdom has no interest of its own in the information demanded, but where it may be relevant to a tax liability in the requesting country only.

---

[14] Taxes Act 1988, s. 816(1).
[15] Finance Act 1990, s. 125(2).

15-22   A number of provisions enhance the ability of the Inland Revenue to provide information to tax authorities in other contracting states by requiring this information to be available. For example, special powers to obtain information as to income from securities, particularly from intermediaries, under TMA 1970, section 24. Subparagraph 24(3) excludes banks from the obligation to disclose any particulars relating to income from securities in cases where the person beneficially entitled to the income is not resident in the United Kingdom. However, where the beneficial owner of the income from such securities is resident in a country where a double taxation treaty under section 788 is in effect, this exemption is inapplicable. Thus, banks are required to provide information where the beneficial owners are resident in treaty countries.

Parliament has given further significant powers to the Inland Revenue to assist foreign countries in carrying out the tax laws of those foreign countries. As a result of Finance Act 2000, information returns made by financial institutions under TMA 1970, section 17 have to include amounts paid or credited to individuals and the estates of persons who are not ordinarily resident in the United Kingdom and to trustees of discretionary and accumulation trusts where the trustees and beneficiaries are not U.K. resident. Provision is made for regulations to specify the form of return together with additional information to be furnished, including in prescribed cases the name and address of persons beneficially entitled to interest paid or credited. Although the audit power under Taxes Act 1988, section 482 is abolished, the regulations may provide for a similar audit power.

The information powers contained in TMA 1970, section 18 relating to returns of interest paid or received are amended to apply to paying and collecting agents, as well as banks. This is to replace the paying and collecting agent schemes which are abolished. The effect of these rules is to put the Inland Revenue in a position to provide information on savings income to authorities of other countries by way of treaty.

PROCEDURE

15-23   The Board of Inland Revenue have delegated responsibility for exchanges of information to a Central Information Unit within the London Special Compliance Office. The Inland Revenue Internal Manuals give some indication of procedures and suitable cases for exchange of information.

Although the mechanisms for exchange of information are set out as a matter of law, the process is conducted entirely in secret. No provision is made for notification or consultation with taxpayers. The Inland Revenue *Double Taxation Relief Manual*[16] does refer to "matters of a potentially sensitive nature (for example, a 'trade secret')", which should be brought to the attention of the liaison group responsible for exchanges of information. Indication to the Revenue that there is information which should not be exchanged is a delicate matter. There are obvious problems related with the lack of transparency in the process. In this context, the rules relating to

---

[16] At para. 351.

sharing information with other government departments in the United Kingdom are varied and may require interpretation. Giving effect to the limitations contained in section 816(2ZA), for example, may be a legally complex issue requiring detailed knowledge of the legal system of the other contracting state. This places a heavy burden on those responsible for administering the exchange of information. Officials who are beyond reproach, hardworking and diligent will find proper compliance with the existing rules extremely demanding. The secrecy of the process undermines confidence in it when viewed from the outside in the same way that tax administrators view taxpayer secrecy as undermining confidence in compliance with tax rules.

15-24   The Keith Committee[17] recommended that procedures should be introduced to enable taxpayers to be informed of requests for commercially sensitive information and that an opportunity to challenge exchanges of information before an independent tribunal should be established. The Inland Revenue resisted this.[18] Such a right is likely to exist now under the Human Rights Act 1998 and a failure on the part of Inland Revenue officials to respect it may give rise to a claim for damages.[19]

---

[17] *Report of the Committee on Enforcement Powers of Revenue Departments* (Cmnd 8822), paras 23, 4.1–3.
[18] *Inland Revenue and the Taxpayer* (December 1986), para. 6.5.5.
[19] Human Rights Act 1998, s. 8.

APPENDIX

Tax Treaties in Effect as at November 1, 2001

COMPREHENSIVE DOUBLE TAXATION TREATIES

Country	Statutory instrument	Country	Statutory instrument
Antigua and Barbuda	S.I. 1947 No. 2865	Iceland	S.I. 1991 No. 2879
		India	S.I. 1993 No. 1801
Argentina	S.I. 1997 No. 1777	Indonesia	S.I. 1994 No. 769
Australia	S.I. 1968 No. 305	Ireland (Republic	S.I. 1976 No. 2151
Austria	S.I. 1970 No. 1947	of)	
Azerbaijan	S.I. 1995 No. 762	Isle of Man	S.I. 1955 No. 1205
Bangladesh	S.I. 1980 No. 708	Israel	S.I. 1963 No. 616
Barbados	S.I. 1970 No. 952	Italy	S.I. 1990 No. 2590
Belarus[(1)(3)]	S.I. 1986 No. 224	Ivory Coast (Côte	S.I. 1987 No. 169
Belgium	S.I. 1987 No. 2053	d'Ivoire)	
Belize	S.I. 1947 No. 2866	Jamaica	S.I. 1973 No. 1329
Bolivia	S.I. 1995 No. 2707	Japan	S.I. 1970 No. 1948
Botswana	S.I. 1978 No. 183	Jersey	S.I. 1952 No. 1216
Brunei	S.I. 1950 No. 1977	Kazakhstan	S.I. 1994 No. 3211
Bulgaria	S.I. 1987 No. 2054	Kenya	S.I. 1977 No. 1299
Canada	S.I. 1980 No. 709	Kiribati	S.I. 1950 No. 750
China	S.I. 1984 No. 1826	Korea (Republic of)	S.I. 1996 No. 3168
Croatia[(2)]	S.I. 1981 No. 1815	Kuwait	S.I. 1999 No. 2036
Cyprus	S.I. 1975 No. 425	Latvia	S.I. 1996 No. 3167
Czech Republic	S.I. 1991 No. 2876	Lesotho	S.I. 1997 No. 2986
Denmark	S.I. 1980 No. 1960	Luxembourg	S.I. 1968 No. 1100
Egypt	S.I. 1980 No. 1091	Macedonia[(2)]	S.I. 1981 No. 1815
Estonia	S.I. 1994 No. 3207	Malawi	S.I. 1956 No. 619
Falkland Islands	S.I. 1997 No. 2985	Malaysia	S.I. 1997 No. 2987
Fiji	S.I. 1976 No. 1342	Malta	S.I. 1995 No. 763
Finland	S.I. 1970 No. 153	Mauritius	S.I. 1981 No. 1121
France	S.I. 1968 No. 1869	Mexico	S.I. 1994 No. 3212
Gambia	S.I. 1980 No. 1963	Mongolia	S.I. 1996 No. 2598
Germany	S.I. 1967 No. 25	Montserrat	S.I. 1947 No. 2869
Ghana	S.I. 1993 No. 1800	Morocco	S.I. 1991 No. 2881
Greece	S.I. 1954 No. 142	Myanmar (Burma)	S.I. 1952 No. 751
Grenada	S.I. 1949 No. 361	Namibia	S.I. 1962 No. 2352
Guernsey	S.I. 1952 No. 1215	Netherlands	S.I. 1980 No. 1961
Guyana	S.I. 1992 No. 3207	New Zealand	S.I. 1984 No. 365
Hungary	S.I. 1978 No. 1056	Nigeria	S.I. 1987 No. 2057

Country	Statutory instrument	Country	Statutory instrument
Norway	S.I. 2000 No. 3247	Swaziland	S.I. 1969 No. 380
Oman	S.I. 1998 No. 2568	Sweden	S.I. 1984 No. 366
Pakistan	S.I. 1987 No. 2058	Switzerland	S.I. 1978 No. 1408
Papua New Guinea	S.I. 1991 No. 2882	Thailand	S.I. 1981 No. 1546
Philippines	S.I. 1978 No. 184	Trinidad and	S.I. 1983 No. 1903
Poland	S.I. 1978 No. 282	Tobago	
Portugal	S.I. 1969 No. 599	Tunisia	S.I. 1984 No. 133
Romania	S.I. 1977 No. 57	Turkey	S.I. 1988 No. 932
Russian Federation	S.I. 1994 No. 3213	Tuvalu	S.I. 1950 No. 750
St Kitts and Nevis	S.I. 1947 No. 2872	Uganda	S.I. 1993 No. 1802
Sierra Leone	S.I. 1947 No. 2873	Ukraine	S.I. 1993 No. 1803
Singapore	S.I. 1997 No. 2988	United States of	S.I. 1980 No. 568
Slovak Republic (Slovakia)	S.I. 1991 No. 2876	America	
Slovenia [2]	S.I. 1981 No. 1815	Uzbekistan	S.I. 1994 No. 770
Solomon Islands	S.I. 1950 No. 748	Venezuela	S.I. 1996 No. 2599
South Africa	S.I. 1969 No. 864	Vietnam	S.I. 1994 No. 3216
Spain	S.I. 1976 No. 1919	Yugoslavia (Federal Republic)[2]	S.I. 1981 No. 1815
Sri Lanka	S.I. 1980 No. 713	Zambia	S.I. 1972 No. 1721
Sudan	S.I. 1977 No. 1719	Zimbabwe	S.I. 1982 No. 1842

Notes

Many of the above Treaties have been amended by Protocols, which are published separately with a new S.I. number. Any Protocol should be read in conjunction with the original Treaty.

[1] The 1986 Treaty with the Soviet Union (S.I. 1986 No. 224) is currently to be regarded as in force between the United Kingdom and the former Soviet Republics marked. The position with regard to former Soviet Republics not listed is less clear, but the United Kingdom will in all cases apply the provisions of the Treaty on the basis that it is still in force (until such time as new Treaties take effect with particular countries).

[2] The 1981 Treaty with Yugoslavia (S.I. 1981 No. 1815) is to be regarded as in force between the United Kingdom and the former Yugoslav states marked. The position with regard to the remainder of what was Yugoslavia is undetermined.

[3] The 1995 Treaty with Belarus (S.I. 1995 No. 2706) has not yet entered into force.

TREATIES COVERING TAXES ON INCOME FROM INTERNATIONAL TRANSPORT

Country	Subject matter	Country	Subject matter
Algeria	(Air transport)	Jordan	(Shipping and air transport)
Belarus	(Air transport) [1]		
Brazil	(Shipping and air transport)	Kuwait	(Air transport)
		Lebanon	(Shipping and air transport)
Cameroon	(Air transport)		
China	(Air transport) [1]	Saudi Arabia	(Air transport)
Ethiopia	(Air transport)	Zaire	(Shipping and air transport)
Hong Kong	(Air transport)		
Iran	(Air transport)		

Notes

[1] Indicates air transport agreements which were not terminated by later comprehensive agreements and remain in force alongside them.

TREATIES COVERING ESTATES, INHERITANCES AND GIFTS

Agreements signed prior to 1975 in respect of estate duty:

Country	Statutory instrument	Country	Statutory instrument
India	S.I. 1956 No. 998	France	S.I. 1957 No. 1522
Pakistan	S.I. 1957 No. 1522	Italy	S.I. 1968 No. 304

Agreements signed after the introduction of capital transfer tax in 1975:

Country	Statutory instrument	Country	Statutory instrument
Republic of Ireland	S.I. 1978 No. 1107	Sweden	S.I. 1981 No. 840
South Africa	S.I. 1979 No. 576	(amending	S.I. 1989 No. 986
United States	S.I. 1979 No. 1454	Protocol)	
Netherlands	S.I. 1980 No. 706	Switzerland	S.I. 1994 No. 3214
(amending	S.I. 1996 No. 730		
Protocol)			

Index